THE POLITICS OF COMPASSION

This book provides a critical overview of the role of the emotions in politics. Compassion is a politically charged virtue, and yet we know surprisingly little about the uses (and abuses) of compassion in political environments.

Covering sociology, political theory and psychology, and with contributions from Martha Nussbaum and Andrew Linklater amongst others, the book gives a succinct overview of the main theories of political compassion and the emotions in politics. It covers key concepts such as humanitarianism, political emotion and agency in relation to compassion as a political virtue.

The Politics of Compassion is a fascinating resource for students and scholars of political theory, international relations, political sociology and psychology.

Michael Ure is a Lecturer in Politics at Monash University, Australia.

Mervyn Frost is Professor of International Relations, and former Head of the Department of War Studies, King's College London, UK.

THE POLITICS OF COMPASSION

Edited by Michael Ure and Mervyn Frost

LONDON AND NEW YORK

First published 2014
by Routledge
2 Park Square, Milton Park, Abingdon, Oxon OX14 4RN

Simultaneously published in the USA and Canada
by Routledge
711 Third Avenue, New York, NY 10017

Routledge is an imprint of the Taylor & Francis Group, an informa business

British Library Cataloguing in Publication Data
A catalogue record for this book is available from the British Library

Library of Congress Cataloging in Publication Data
A catalog record for this book has been requested

ISBN: 978-0-415-67158-3 (hbk)
ISBN: 978-0-415-67159-0 (pbk)
ISBN: 978-1-315-85138-9 (ebk)

Typeset in Bembo
by Sunrise Setting Ltd, Paignton, UK

Printed and bound in Great Britain by
TJ International Ltd, Padstow, Cornwall

CONTENTS

INTRODUCTION

Michael Ure and Mervyn Frost

This book is about the politics of compassion. Its goal is critically to examine the current rehabilitation of compassion as a political virtue. The book's aim is twofold: to make a significant contribution to the nascent study of the politics of the emotions; and to do so by examining in depth one of the most politically charged emotions: compassion, and cognate terms such as pity, sympathy and clemency.

In the past decade we have witnessed an explosion of humanities and social science research on the emotions. As moving forces of political change and transformation, it is natural to expect that the emotions should also be an important topic of political research. Yet, as Susan James observes, a great deal of mainstream work continues to ignore or marginalise the emotions (James 2003: 221). Indeed until recently modern political and legal thought, especially liberal and liberal democratic theory, paid little attention to the role that the passions can and ought to play in the political arena (see Hall 2005; Nussbaum 2006; Kingston & Ferry 2009). By contrast, early modern thinkers like Hume, Smith and Rousseau made the human passions a central topic of political philosophy. They understood the investigation of how the emotions shape and are shaped by political agents, practices and institutions as one of its central concerns. They assumed that the passions bear directly on the art of politics. The passions, in their view, set the limits on political possibilities and transformations (James 2003: 224).

It is only in recent years that political scholars have once again begun to focus on the interdependence between the passions and politics. The politics of the emotions is now beginning to emerge as a new and important research agenda. Drawing inspiration from recent developments in evolutionary biology and ethology (De Waal 2009), social psychology (Goetz *et al.* 2010), social neuroscience (Decety 2009; Iacoboni 2009) and the cognitive account of the emotions (Nussbaum 2001), a new wave of political theorists has begun to revive the notion of politics as an art of the emotions. Importantly, this emergent political paradigm rejects the hitherto common-sense view of emotions exclusively as political obstacles, distractions, seductions or hazards, and investigates their positive contribution to good politics. As Charles Taylor asserts, we can no longer 'factor emotions ... out of what makes for democratic politics, in which people can be brought together' (Taylor 2008: viii). This collection integrates and builds on this new turn in political thought.

The collection focuses specifically on compassion and its cognates because they are widely recognised as among the most controversial and politically significant emotions. Compassion has been hailed as both the key democratic virtue and condemned as politically toxic. Yet despite the controversy over the politics of compassion, we are still lacking a wide-ranging investigation of its significance for democratic politics, global civil society and cosmopolitanism and political reconciliation and repair. Indeed, we know surprisingly little about the political uses and abuses of compassion. The aim of this collection is to provide scholars in political theory, international relations, political sociology and social psychology with a first exposition and assessment of the politics of compassion.

Main themes and objectives

This book addresses one of the most significant and fiercely contested contemporary political issues: the rehabilitation of compassion as a political virtue. In the eighteenth century Adam Smith and Jean-Jacques Rousseau both made novel claims for the political and moral importance of sympathy or pity. Smith claimed that sympathy is the foundation of political harmony. In *The Theory of Moral Sentiments,* Smith identified sympathy, properly cultivated, as the basis of co-operative communities. Sympathy, he suggested, enables citizens emotionally to attune themselves to one another so that they 'have such a correspondence ... as is sufficient for the harmony of society' (Smith 2002 [1790]: 27). Smith, as De Waal observes, saw sympathy as a second invisible hand that might combat the divisive, centrifugal effects of the invisible hand of the market (De Waal 2009: 222). Rousseau famously argued that pity should be the first and most important emotion cultivated in future citizens, on the grounds that only shared suffering creates bonds of affection and with them the sense of common humanity required to support the ideals of liberty, equality and fraternity (Rousseau 1974 [1762]). Compassion, he claimed, was the democratic emotion *par excellence.* In the mid to late nineteenth century many European thinkers made the epoch's dominant positivistic outlook the foundation of a new 'religion of humanity'. These attempts to wed naturalism and morality formed an important strand of the nineteenth century: the invention of altruism (Dixon 2008). Auguste Comte captured this new ethical mood in his moral formula *'vivre pour autrui'.* Inspired by Adam Smith's theory of moral sentiments, Charles Darwin's evolutionary explanation of sympathy sparked a still-raging controversy within evolutionary biology about its moral and political significance (van der Weele 2011):

> In however complex a manner [sympathy or reciprocal altruism] may have originated, as it is one of high importance to all those animals which aid and defend one another, it will have been increased through natural selection; for those communities, which included the greatest number of the most sympathetic members, would flourish best and rear the greatest number of offspring.
>
> (Darwin 1981: 82)

For Darwin, the evolutionary success of political units turns on the selection of sympathetic and altruistic members and traits.

In the past decade, we have witnessed a renewed defence of the moral and political pertinence of compassion, sympathy and altruism for maintaining, consolidating and expanding democratic values and practices. With the recent rediscovery of the political importance of the passions, political theorists have revisited the idea that democratic institutions cannot remain stable unless citizens' emotional narratives support democratic norms and relationships (Nussbaum 2001, 2008; Mihai 2010).

According to its contemporary defenders, compassion is an essential democratic and cosmopolitan emotion. They believe that the security of democratic institutions and practices depends on compassion as a moral and motivational foundation. Martha Nussbaum, its most influential contemporary advocate, claims that compassion is *the* basic social emotion and that the task of generalising compassion is one of the greatest moral problems of our time (Nussbaum 1996, 2008). In her remarkable psychological studies of rescuers of Jews in Nazi Germany, Kristen Monroe suggests that political theory has failed to take into account the political and moral significance of altruism and compassion as precious sources of a fragile sense of common humanity (Monroe 1998, 2006). 'The hand of compassion', as one of these rescuers put it, '(is) faster than the calculus of reason' (Monroe 2006). Compassion, on this view, motivates citizens to respond to others' suffering more quickly and reliably than rational choice, even to the point of risking themselves for the sake of protecting others from harm and injustice. In his sociology of global morals, Andrew Linklater argues that compassion underpins democratic citizenship and the evolution of a just world community (Linklater 2007a, 2007b). Properly cultivated, its defenders claim, compassion can significantly contribute to addressing key problems of democratic order, global justice and political reconciliation. It is a political emotion that promises to help sustain stable democratic communities, expand the scope of moral and political responsibility and motivate reparations for the violence that haunts post-conflict and post-colonial societies. For this reason, its advocates warn, the failure to cultivate compassion will severely limit the capacity of states and citizens to address these fundamental contemporary political issues.

For the critics of compassion, however, this sentiment does not deliver on these political promises. Compassion, they observe, promises to enlarge the moral and political boundaries of communities, to motivate the politics of justice and reparations and to engender and sustain equal respect across lines of time, place and nation. Yet in practice, they argue, compassion fails to deliver: it is far too partial, fickle and unreliable to rely on as a social motive (Crisp 2008); it motivates actions and policies that unwittingly entrench victimhood and resentment rather than create agency (Brown 1995; Torpey 2006); expresses itself as a shaming pity that diminishes its recipients and fails to redress the injustices it identifies (Nietzsche 1997 [1881]; Boyd 2004; Acorn 2005; Ure 2006); exhausts empathetic identification and generates indifference and fatigue (Boltanksi 1999; Moeller 1999; Tester 2001) and worse still, is profoundly connected to other morally questionable emotions like anger, revenge and cruelty (Hunt 2006). On this view, compassion belongs in the private sphere and has no place in the democratic public realm because it is a sentiment that compels its agents to use any power at their disposal to remedy suffering. If compassion 'sets out to change worldly conditions in order to ease human suffering', Arendt warns: ...

> ... it will shun the drawn-out wearisome processes of persuasion, negotiation and compromise, which are the processes of law and politics, and lend its voice to the suffering itself, which must claim for swift and direct action, that is, for action with the means of violence.

> (Arendt 1973: 86–7)

In light of the Reign of Terror, Arendt feels justified in warning that 'pity taken as the spring of virtue, has proved to possess a greater capacity for cruelty than cruelty itself' (Arendt 1973: 88). Politicised pity, she maintains, runs at cross-purposes to the liberal values of respect and tolerance and the democratic values of persuasion and debate.

Both defenders and critics agree that we are playing for very high political stakes in coming to terms with the politics of compassion. This collection attempts to illuminate, clarify and evaluate the competing positions in this debate.

The essays in Part 1 engage in the hotly contested debate in modern and contemporary political theory about whether compassion is a political virtue or vice. They examine whether it is an emotional disposition that democracies should foster in their citizens and embody in their institutions. Do its contemporary defenders answer the charge that compassion is too unreliable, partial, polarising or dangerous as a political motive? Can compassion avoid the danger of demeaning, insulting or harming its recipients? The essays in Part 2 address the sociology of compassion. They examine the social conditions that have made it possible for the motive of compassion to take root within states, the system of states and global civil society and that may enable it to become one of the motivational bases of a cosmopolitan ethos. The essays in the final part take a sceptical view of compassion and sympathy's political credentials, identifying how and why it goes politically awry, but also how we might develop a *critical* compassion that is not partial, demeaning or excessive in its demands. If compassion is to realise its political potential as a sentiment that can inspire citizens to take responsibility to protect others from undeserved suffering and injustice, then we must identify ways and means of ensuring it does not confine itself to those nearest at the exclusion of the distant, or motivate paternalistic, intrusive political institutions that strip others of their dignity and agency.

Part I: Compassion as a political virtue

As we have seen, Arendt launched a scathing attack on the politicisation of pity as a motive that fundamentally undermines basic democratic principles and practices. If like the French Revolutionaries our political actions are motivated by the sufferings of the poor, she argues, we will necessarily cast aside or trample on democratic norms of tolerance and freedom. In *On Revolution* she argues the American Revolution succeeded in establishing a stable constitutional democracy because its founding fathers focused on building institutions designed to protect political or civic freedom rather than attempting to remedy the suffering of the poor and obscure. On the other hand, Arendt sees the French Revolution as a political disaster that necessarily led to the Reign of Terror precisely because the revolutionaries were motivated by pity for the masses. According to Arendt, if political agents make pity their motive, and overcoming suffering their goal, they will necessarily resort to untrammelled violence. She conceives the so-called 'pre-political' or biological needs that pity seeks to satisfy as blind and limitless. In taking these as their motive, therefore, political actors also acknowledge no political limits on their actions. '[G]oodness', she claims, '... shares with elemental evil the elementary violence inherent in all strength and is detrimental to all forms of political organization' (Arendt 1973: 87). Arendt maintains that the guillotine is the logical outcome of politicising pity. Notoriously, Arendt argued that for the sake of democracy we must not allow pity to corrupt the political sphere by making need and suffering matters of public concern. Democracies should address social needs as administrative issues rather than as matters of public concern and debate.

In various ways the essays in the opening part challenge Arendt's equation between pity and violence. Against Arendt, Maureen Whitebrook aims to elucidate compassion as a specifically *political* virtue. She argues that compassion becomes properly political when it identifies the systemic or institutional causes of collective suffering and addresses itself to remedying these causes rather than focusing on the intensity of feeling that it can generate in individual sufferers. While political compassion requires spectators to feel distress for and on behalf of suffering individuals, and hence retains a crucial element of compassion, it is not sufficient for this virtue: it also requires that they ascertain the objective or systemic sources of this suffering. Political compassion, in short, does not merely assuage suffering; it identifies and acts against the causes of suffering.

We can illustrate Whitebrook's notion of political compassion by contrasting it with the Good Samaritan model of compassion (Luke 10:25-38).[1] The limits of the Good Samaritan ethic can serve to highlight this alternative concept of political compassion. In the parable, we might recall, a man – a Jew – travels from Jerusalem to Jericho, and on the way he is attacked, robbed, wounded and left half-dead on the roadside. By chance a certain priest comes down that way, and then a Levite. Both are fellow Jews with religious standing, and both pass by on the other side. Then comes the Samaritan who belongs to a nation hostile to Israel – as the verse tells us – and he takes care of the wounded man. Now, many commentators focus our attention on the central idea here that the concept of 'neighbour' is powerful enough to cross tribal, religious and ethnic boundaries; and that it is so when it is tied to compassion (Margalit 2002).

Yet, we should also observe that the Good Samaritan pays no heed to the legal, criminal or political context of the event. The Samaritan responds exclusively to the fact of the victim's suffering. The Samaritan's compassionate response begins with his dressing of the victim's wound and ends with his payment to a third party to nurse the man back to health. While the victim remains mute and passive in the parable, the one salient fact we do learn about him beyond his religious affiliation is that he has been the innocent victim of a violent crime. At no point, however, does the parable indicate that the Samaritan's compassion might entail that he address the victim's legal or political circumstances. The Samaritan remedies the immediate harm inflicted on the victim, but he shows no concern about the causes of his suffering or interest in remedying these causes. We might say that the Good Samaritan addresses the other person's individual suffering, but not the causes of his suffering. By contrast, political compassion, as Whitebrook defines it, requires not simply assuaging others' immediate suffering, but tracking and addressing systemic causes of suffering.

The Good Samaritan ethic depoliticises compassion insofar as it occludes the political dimensions of suffering that victims can express through resentment towards those responsible. Richard Sennett suggests one reason why Christianity truncates compassion in this manner. Christian *caritas*, he argues, is necessarily limited in its response to others because it conceives the act of giving or helping as an occasion for self-transformation. Christians transform their relationship to God through giving. As we have seen from the Good Samaritan parable, compassionate Christians do not necessarily seek to repair the victims' standing in relation to perpetrators or the broader community. Rather they seek to establish their own good standing with God by giving to those who suffer. *Caritas*, Sennett claims, 'means becoming a good person through making gifts; the act of giving combats one's own disposition to sinfulness. The value of the gift is irrelevant and even, in some versions, whether the gift does others good is irrelevant' (Sennett 2004: 134). Drawing on Arendt's analysis of St. Augustine, he argues that Christian compassion is intrinsically impersonal insofar as Christians conceive the neighbour simply as an occasion for the exercise of virtues that bring them closer to God's love. 'The Christian', as Arendt explains:

... can love all people because each one is only an occasion ... the enemy and even the sinner ... mere occasions for love. It is not really the neighbour who is loved in this love of neighbour – it is love itself.

(Arendt 1996: 97)

On this view, Christian *caritas* entails a form of what we might call self-serving compassion: it aims at feeling good through giving, not doing good.

Whitebrook's notion of political compassion exposes the political limits of the Good Samaritan ethic: the Samaritan appears to experience no anger or indignation about the victims' underserved suffering. The Samaritan focuses on the others' suffering, not those responsible; and at stake in his response is his own standing before God, not the victims' legal or political standing. By looking beyond others' distress to its causes, political compassion establishes the conditions necessary for anger or indignation. Anger motivated by political compassion, Whitebrook maintains, has an important cognitive and political function: it alerts states and citizens to sources of harm and suffering that require political redress and focuses our compassion on its systemic causes. Against Arendt, she argues that there is no necessary or compelling reason to believe that such compassion-fuelled anger or indignation necessarily leads to violent excess, nor is the risk that it might sufficient to disbar it from politics any more than we think fear should be disbarred from politics because it might generate cowardice or impotence. The task at hand is not to dismiss compassionate anger, but to regulate and discipline it so that it can fulfil its important political function: identifying and protesting against systemic injustice.

In her chapter, Gudrun von Tevenar turns the tables on Arendt and demonstrates how political communities that fail to acknowledge compassion as a political virtue and guide to action necessarily perpetuate significant social injustice. Compassion, she argues, is a politically important cognitive and normative resource that enables us to identify hidden or unacknowledged forms of social and material suffering. Compassion addresses the problem of the political invisibility of the poor, marginalised and excluded: it makes us aware of this suffering and it compels us to remedy it. 'Only when seen with sympathetic eyes', as she explains, 'can social problems become visible and suitable for the political stage'. Since only compassion can make social suffering visible, and Arendt bans it from public life, her politics necessarily perpetuate political injustice. Tevenar acknowledges that pity and compassion can be fickle and partial. Yet, as she plausibly observes, this alone is not sufficient to rule it out of political life, any more than we consider banning other emotions because of their unreliability or riskiness. 'The positive aspect of opening our eyes and minds to the conditions and needs of others', she maintains, 'is far greater than, say, their possible lack of proportionality and measure'. Rather than following Arendt (and others) in rejecting compassion on these spurious grounds, Tevenar argues we need to redeem compassion's cognitive and normative potential by educating and disciplining it. Compassion, like any other emotion, poses risks when it becomes the basis of political judgement and action, but the issue is how to manage these risks so that we can yield the benefits of this emotional intelligence. Like Whitebrook, she concludes that the important political task is not to banish compassion, but to educate and discipline it so that we realise its cognitive and normative potential to identify and address systemic social and political injustice.

One of the potential political benefits of compassion is that it can motivate citizens to care about and take responsibility for the underserved suffering of 'distant' others. Its political significance lies in extending the horizon of citizens' concerns beyond lines of time, place and nation. Yet compassion's elasticity also carries significant political risks. Lola Frost argues that politically and ethically the risk of compassion is well worth taking. She draws on idealist aesthetic categories to illuminate this risk. The experience of compassion, she suggests, can be analogous to the experience of the sublime: it can overwhelm rational, self-contained, self-interested agents, compelling them to experience their common vulnerability and their openness to others' suffering. In destroying the sharply demarcated boundaries of rational agents, compassion can motivate them to act on the basis of an ethics of generosity – the ethics of giving without thought of return – rather than an ethics of exchange and reciprocity. Sublime compassion explodes the moral and political limits of legal and market-based relations.

Frost argues that modern citizens and members of global civil society need ongoing recourse to aesthetic and political practices that engender such sublime experiences. They do so because through such experiences they can transcend the political, historical and cultural boundaries and distinctions – friend/enemy, insider/outsider, citizen/stranger – that divide them from one another and that prevent them from responding to one another first and foremost as mortal, needy suffering creatures rather than exclusively as agents whose relations are largely regulated by pre-existing legal, economic, cultural and historical dynamics. Frost uses South Africa's *Truth and Reconciliation Commission* as an example of a political practice that affords citizens the possibility of exercising compassion across deeply entrenched political divisions. In such cases citizens can exercise unconditional compassion: they bracket the question of whether those who receive their compassion warrant or deserve their assistance, and focus exclusively on assuaging others' suffering. As David Konstan reminds us in his chapter, the danger of such 'sublime' compassion is that it becomes unhinged from questions of desert. Based on such compassion citizens can, for example, forgive former enemies who bear legal and moral responsibilities for harmful actions. Frost suggests that we should maintain the possibility of such risky, unhinged compassion in liberal democracies and in global civil society because it can help citizens overcome entrenched political divisions and hostilities. Frost suggests that the ordinary liberal imaginary and legal measures are not always sufficient to overcome the traumas and divisions that flow from historic injustices or violent conflict. Unconditional compassion, she implies, can act as a catalyst to break the deadlock where normal legal and political remedies prove incapable of restoring or creating good human relations. Political communities and global civil society, she concludes, should risk political practices and institutions that use compassion to break the spell of the past and inspire in citizens an ethics of generosity. If, as Whitebrook and Tevenar show, compassion has an important role to play in identifying and motivating responses to 'ordinary', yet often invisible injustices, Frost makes a plea for an excessive, unhinged sublime compassion as a response to the 'extraordinary' injustices that often defy conventional legal and political remedies.

Part II: Sociology of compassion

The chapters in Part 2 investigate the sociology and social psychology of compassion in domestic and global politics. As we have seen, in his broader research program Andrew Linklater maintains that the evolution of a cosmopolitan world community partly hinges on the cultivation and extension of compassion across the lines of place and nation (Linklater 2007a, 2007b). In this chapter he investigates the social conditions that facilitate or impede the extension of compassion within and between nation states. The fundamental issue Linklater confronts is that the scope of compassion is strongly tied to circuits of reciprocity and dependence. Compassion, it seems, requires forms of reciprocity that exist when people's lives are closely woven together in relations of mutual dependence. If compassion is tied to reciprocity, as he observes, it is likely to be absent where it is most needed: i.e. in cases of the poor, marginalised or excluded who cannot reciprocate. On the other hand, compassion has very little chance where states and citizens are locked in zero-sum competitions.

Linklater suggests, then, that for compassion to take root and become the basis of cosmopolitan concern we need to find ways to make our moral and cultural self-image as 'compassionate' relatively independent of our 'enlightened' self-interests so that we can help those who have nothing to give in return and conditions of rough equity so that we do not see the world strictly in terms of the insider/outsider, friend/enemy dualisms. Linklater notes that in the eighteenth century, theorists of moral sentiments were already investigating whether and how compassion might become a political virtue that citizens could exercise more evenly and universally, even towards those from whom they stood to gain nothing. Adam Smith, for example, developed and recommended neo-Stoic exercises or therapies that might serve to limit citizens' 'over-valuation' of their own immediate concerns, and novel exercises in sympathy aimed at enhancing their understanding and estimation of others' emotions and interests (Muller 1995; Forman-Barzilai 2011; Ure 2013). Smith, in other words, sought to elaborate a range of practices or exercises that might make compassion an emotional habitus that enables citizens to have regard for others' sufferings independently of their own pragmatic or strategic self-interest. Linklater's chapter leaves us with the challenge of investigating the social conditions and practices of the self that might make it possible to establish compassion as a motive that operates with some degree of independence from strategic, self-interested concerns so that it can extend to the distant, vulnerable and powerless.

Terry MacDonald's chapter reinforces Linklater's claim that moral motivations such as compassion are crucial to the evolution of cosmopolitan political institutions. She argues that harnessing support from *moral* motivations (not just coercion or self-interest) is critical to the political prospects for cosmopolitan institutions. They are critical because unlike other types of motivation, moral motivations remain operative even with shifts of power and interest – i.e. with such motivations we can remain committed to cosmopolitan justice even when we are not subject to external coercion or driven by self-interest. Macdonald argues that compassion promises to be an especially effective moral motive because it is capable of supporting the development of new institutions that realise cosmopolitan ideals. If the institutional status quo does not effectively alleviate suffering then compassion motivates citizens to create and support new institutions that achieve this end. However, MacDonald also acknowledges that compassion is limited by its partiality. She argues that compassion's partiality is a contingent rather than necessary condition. Cosmopolitans, she argues, can address this partiality not only by working to expand their own and others' imaginative understanding of distant others, but also by working with and developing current social relations in which members of global civil society engage with one another co-operatively. In other words, MacDonald argues that the lack of cosmopolitan compassion is not a permanent human flaw, but a sociologically generated problem that is amenable to change via institutional design and advocacy.

Iain Wilkinson argues that we can deepen our understanding of the sociological conditions of compassion by examining the history of modern humanitarian social movements. He suggests that we can learn valuable lessons from these movements about how to educate our moral sentiments in pro-social directions and how to develop our visual 'literacy' so that it motivates cosmopolitan compassion. What we need to investigate is how in mobilising compassionate responses to the mass dissemination of images of suffering these movements developed a new cosmopolitan political agenda and also new methods of conducting social research. By examining the social and cultural history of modern humanitarianism, Wilkinson challenges the widespread and pessimistic view that our expanded field of vision must necessarily generate a sense of political powerlessness, moral indifference or sheer compassion fatigue (Boltanski 1999).

Nicholas Faulkner's chapter suggests that compassionate anger is one of the key mechanisms for counteracting political impotence or compassion fatigue in the face of the scale of human suffering. Drawing on social psychology findings, he suggests that anger is more effective than guilt in motivating individuals and groups to engage in compassionate action to help those suffering; and to confront or challenge those responsible for this suffering and/or the policies and practices that sustain it. Empirically confirming Whitebrook's supposition, he argues that anger about others' suffering effectively focuses our compassionate responses on the political sources of harm. Anger is politically galvanising. Faulkner also maintains that compassionate anger is politically valuable because it has a much wider compass than guilt: our anger can be triggered by injustices suffered by *any* individual or group, whereas our guilt is triggered only when we feel personally or collectively responsible for this injustice.

In his chapter Mervyn Frost acknowledges that compassion has indeed become one of the emotional registers in our two major political practices: the state system and global civil society. Frost is confident that the scope of our compassion is already global. The key issue for him is not how to educate members of these practices to expand the boundaries of their moral concern; for all intents and purposes, he claims, they are already cosmopolitans. Rather the key concern for these members is how they are to assess who most merits compassion. Granted that compassion for all underserved suffering is already a requirement for participants in these two global practices, they still need to determine how they ought to distribute their concern.

However, he suggests that even if we extend the scope of compassion as the sentimental basis of a cosmopolitan community, feeling compassion is not sufficient to answer the ethical or political questions about *how* to alleviate suffering. Compassion, he observes, may indeed require that agents do what is ethically appropriate to alleviate others' suffering, but it is not sufficient to indicate *what* ought to be done or by *whom* in order to realise this end. The mere having of compassion, as he explains, does supply the answer to these ethical or political questions. This is not to say that compassion cannot inform a theory of ethical value or the good. Nussbaum argues, for example, that compassion entails judgements of seriousness and desert. It contains a theory of what counts as integral to a good human life that determines what losses and misfortunes we believe are sufficiently serious to merit our concern. She argues that occasions for pity represented in Greek tragedy give us a defensible basis for developing a universal theory of value. Compassion also entails judgements of desert that shapes our sense of *who* merits our concern: we have compassion for those who we believe suffer undeservedly, but not for those who deserve their suffering. It is on this basis of the insights of compassion that she develops her capabilities approach to development, which identifies practical prescriptions about what states and global civil society ought to provide citizens so that they have all they require to achieve human flourishing. Frost's point is that even if compassion can inform a defensible theory of value, it alone cannot answer political questions about, for example, what institutional arrangements and policies best realise this goal or how to balance tensions between universalist accounts of capabilities and those accounts which stress cultural and religious diversity.

Part III: Critical compassion

The chapters in Part 3 focus more sharply on the political pitfalls and dangers of compassion. While these chapters do not reject the idea of compassion as a political virtue, they do warn that it can go dangerously awry in ways that jeopardise an impartial application of principles of justice. Calling upon citizens' compassion to bolster their motivational support for democratic principles of fairness and equity carries the serious risk of backfiring. If we are to justify politicising compassion then we need carefully to consider how to institutionalise and inculcate a critical form of compassion: one that enables citizens to identify how and when their sentiments become misplaced or inappropriate. In essence, the chapters in this part demonstrate that the scope of compassion can easily become too broad or too narrow, with disastrous political consequences, and that even well-intentioned compassion can unwittingly motivate political actions that encroach on its recipients' autonomy or undermine their flourishing. Collectively these chapters suggest that the generation of critical compassion depends on its interactions with a range of other emotions, including shame, disgust, envy and honour (Nussbaum 2010).

In his chapter, the classicist David Konstan draws upon classical ideas that are broadly within the semantic neighbourhood of compassion to suggest some distinctions among a range of concepts that may be useful in evaluating the role of compassion in politics. Konstan shows that the classical notion of pity (*eleos*) carries an ethical judgement that arguably is absent from modern notions of sympathy. His primary aim is to suggest that in contemporary political contexts, we should think long and hard before abandoning the classical wisdom of making pity dependent upon an ethical judgement of desert. Following Aristotle, Konstan defines classical pity as a decidedly moral emotion that entails several judgements, including whether those who suffer misfortune deserve their fate or not. In cases where we have good reason for believing they deserve their misfortune we rightly feel no pity. By contrast, Konstan claims, the modern Enlightenment notion of sympathy entails an identification with another, and in doing so abandons the crucial moral element: the judgement of desert. Konstan sees this uncritical notion of sympathy at work in the current politicisation of forgiveness (Janover 2005; Ure 2007; Konstan 2010). In contemporary pleas to forgive political offenders, he maintains, we are asked to have compassion for them independently of the question of desert. Konstan worries that such sympathy is in danger of exonerating the wrongdoer and condoning the crime. It broadens the scope of sympathy to the point that it is fundamentally at odds with basic principles of justice. It was a worry such as this, he observes, that led ancient thinkers to insist that pity not be eviscerated of its ethical or judgemental content, and so be casually extended even to those who deserve their suffering.

Focusing on Sophocles' tragedy *Philoctetes*, Paul Muldoon also examines how compassion can distort our political judgement, but in the other direction: he suggests that it can narrow and concentrate our concern to the point that we fail to balance our compassion against the broader needs of our political community. Compassion, he suggests, carries the danger that those moved by this sentiment are liable to allow their concern for a particular suffering individual to trump broader political concerns and responsibilities. Compassion can distort our political judgement by compelling us to console damaged, suffering individuals and assuage their grief and resentment at *any* cost, including sacrificing the needs and interests of our political community. Rather than showing us the political value of compassion, Muldoon argues, *Philoctetes* highlights the tragic tension between the ethical demands of community and the ethical demands of humanity, between law and love.

However, Muldoon also shows when citizens exercise this kind of 'excessive' or 'unconditional' compassion it can pave the way for re-establishing the social trust of injured parties. He suggests that this may prove particularly valuable in post-conflict societies struggling to find ways to address the legacy of state-sanctioned violence and injustice: entrenched hatred and resentment. By fully and unreservedly acknowledging the legitimacy of the injured parties' resentment and offering to accede to their often 'excessive' demands, unconditional compassion can contribute to restoring the political trust and faith of those traumatised by past injustices. By restoring social trust, it prevents legitimate political resentment (Muldoon 2008) sliding into deeper, intractable forms of ontological *ressentiment* (Ure, forthcoming). Paradoxically then, Muldoon suggests that in some circumstances unconditional compassion can serve the political – it can reintegrate traumatised, aggrieved individuals – but only by putting it (the political) at risk.

However, we also need to investigate why compassion expands and contracts in such politically fraught ways. Joanne Faulkner's chapter casts a sceptical, critical eye on the grand claims about the political value of compassion first made by eighteenth-century moral sentiment theorists and now echoed by those we might call advocates of 'sentimental' democracy. In doing so she aims to reveal some of the dangers and pitfalls of uncritically relying on compassion to address or resolve significant political conflicts and divisions. Drawing on the example of the fraught political relations between indigenous and non-indigenous Australians, she argues that spectators' sympathetic identification can lead them to misrecognise or obscure the conditions, motives, demands and goals of victims of political injustice. Through sympathetic identification, she claims, spectators can paper over the differences between themselves and the victims of injustice, especially where would-be sympathisers are beneficiaries of this injustice. She argues that sympathetic agents not only risk obscuring politically salient differences between themselves and recipients, they can also infantilise the latter and dismiss their claims to political agency and self-determination. Compassion, Faulkner shows, can all too easily lend itself to political paternalism. As many examples of paternalistic measures to repair past injustices show, it is a very short step from conceiving victims as needy and suffering to treating them as helpless children who require authoritarian governance and social discipline. Faulkner presses us to address the hard question of whether and how we can formulate and institutionalise a type of compassion that fully acknowledges, recognises and addresses the political agency of victims/sufferers. She shows how the formation of critical compassion is likely to prove most difficult where there are historical and political grounds for significant discord or disagreement between compassionate agents and those they attempt to assist. In post-colonial societies it has proven difficult, if not impossible, for compassionate citizens to acknowledge indigenous peoples' political agency and claims because these often cut against not just their material interests, but also their identity or pride. In other words, in these important political cases the formation of critical compassion relies on citizens overcoming shame about themselves or their collective past. Arguably, citizens ashamed of their political community's past injustices will displace their shame onto those whose grievances trigger this painful feeling. The displacement of shame, as Nussbaum argues, can underpin paternalism and violence towards those onto whom we project our frailties and weaknesses (Nussbaum 2004, 2010). Shame is one of the key sentiments that regulate the expansion and contraction of political compassion.

Martha Nussbaum, one of the most influential proponents of a sentimental model of democracy, argues that compassion is the sentimental basis of democratic political community: without it we lack the motive to respect others, protect them from harm and respond to their undeserved sufferings. She argues that respect for others' rights or dignity is not sufficient to motivate the kind of care and responsibility integral to democracy. Yet she too recognises we need to *educate* compassion so that it can facilitate and support democratic political institutions, practices and norms. We need to educate compassion, she observes, because our compassion has a tendency to be narrow and polarising: I only care for my own and I care about them to the exclusion of others' interests or concerns. Nussbaum, however, believes we can develop a *critical compassion* that overcomes this emotion's 'degeneration' into partiality and partisanship. We can address these two problems, she suggests, by following the example of Athenian democracy and using tragic narratives to educate citizens to recognise their common human vulnerability; and by not overvaluing those external goods (money, honour, status and fame) that divide us from others or motivate us to treat them with contempt. Instead she argues that democracies should encourage citizens to pursue less problematic external goods (love of family, friends and work, perhaps even nation). According to Nussbaum, a culture that overvalues honour or esteem establishes the conditions necessary for toxic shame, and with it serious distortions of our capacity for political compassion.

In her chapter, Dorothy Noyes also examines the educative role of theatre and narrative. She conducts a novel exploration of a subcategory of compassion, that of clemency. She explores it through a fine-grained consideration of three pieces of theatre that present different ways in which an act of clemency can play out in a polity. What distinguishes clemency from the more general idea of compassion is that it is exercised by an actor who has power over another, but who, prompted by compassion, decides not to wield it. Where clemency is exercised by political authorities we find power-holders doing precisely the opposite of what those who adopt a standard reading of compassion recommend. On the common understanding, compassion belongs within the realm of intimate relationships – this is the realm within which emotions are properly at home, whereas compassion ought to be eschewed in larger collectives such as the state because it can undermine its foundations of law and justice. On this view, what are required in larger institutions are stable systems of rational rule, rather than bonds that rest on unstable emotions. What makes clemency so interesting is that when it is exercised we can see an intimate relationship unfolding between a sovereign and a subject within the context of the polity as a whole. In such acts, the personal and the political come together in a particularly intriguing way. In the three works explored in this chapter (Mozart's *La Clemenza di Tito*, Schiller's *Don Carlos* and a play by Victor Hugo, *Hernani, ou l'Honneur castillan*),

Dorothy Noyes explores how the drama involved in acts of clemency brings to light the insurmountable tensions between the compassion a ruler might feel for a subject and the requirement of distant authority required to rule a large collective of individuals. Her chapter ends with an intriguing insight, derived from a consideration of clemency, for the modern phenomenon of 'compassion fatigue'.

In his chapter, Michael Ure picks up the thread of Nussbaum's analysis of the attitudes and judgements that impede or skew compassion. He does so by investigating Adam Smith's account of the extra or non-moral motives that shape the scope and quality of our sympathy and compassion. On Smith's analysis, 'extra-moral' vanity constrains compassion. The chapter argues that Smith's attempt to address the problem of this partial, skewed sympathy reproduces the problem in a new guise. Smith identifies two versions of this partiality problem: our propensity to give our sympathy to those who exercise self-command and withhold it from those who do not; and our vain tendency to live vicariously through the sentiments of great or exalted individuals. He proposes that we resolve the first problem by exercising a neo-Stoic therapy which would aim to lower the pitch of our passions to make it easier to receive sympathy despite others' reluctance to go along with our passions. Ure argues that this neo-Stoic therapy actually reproduces the second version of the partiality problem: our partiality for sovereignty and contempt for vulnerability. The chapter then suggests that Smith proposes a more generalised Stoic attitude as a response to human vanity. Ure argues that Smith's Stoic solution to the problem of vanity does not prime us to act compassionately and take others' goals and feelings into account, but to treat our own and others' passions as matters of indifference. Stoicism does not enable us to counteract our partial sympathies, but to flee from our own and others' passions. Smith eventually acknowledges the moral limits of Stoicism, but he offers no alternative solution to the problem of partiality. Ure suggests that if our capacity for sympathy is to become a moral compass, it must be informed by a perspective that acknowledges rather than despises human vulnerability.

Overall then, the editors of this volume hope that it has demonstrated just how rich and subtle a discussion of compassion in the political context can be. Their ambition is that this analysis of compassion will lead to similar considerations of other emotions that are key to the political domain, both domestic and international. Such further work might focus on anger, fear, security and insecurity. Also important are emotions pertaining to forgiveness, generosity and fraternity.

Note

1 Witnessing another's suffering, the Samaritan 'had compassion on him [or he was moved to pity]'. It is worth noting that in the Greek version of the Bible, the parable uses the rare Greek term *splagchnizomai* (σπλαγχνίζομαι) in the middle voice modality: *eis-plagchnizomai*. This term and its usage indicate that the Samaritan shares the wounded man's suffering in a powerfully visceral way, which is obscured by the translation of *splagchnizomai* simply as pity or compassion. *Splagchnizomai* indicates a sensation in one's entrails; it literally means to be moved to one's bowels.

References

Acorn, A. (2005) *Compulsory Compassion*. Washington: University of Washington Press.

Arendt, H. (1973) *On Revolution*. Harmondsworth: Penguin.

Arendt, H. (1996) *Love and St. Augustine*. Chicago: University of Chicago Press.

Boltanksi, L. (1999) *Distant Suffering: Morality, Media and Politics*. Cambridge: Cambridge University Press.

Boyd, R. (2004) 'Pity's Pathologies Portrayed: Rousseau and the Limits of Democratic Compassion', *Political Theory* 32(4): 519–46.

Brown, W. (1995) *States of Injury: Power and Freedom in Late Modernity*. Princeton, NJ: Princeton University Press.

Crisp, R. (2008). 'Compassion and Beyond', *Ethical Theory and Moral Practice* 11: 233–46.

Darwin, C. (1981) *The Descent of Man and Selection in Relation to Sex*. Princeton, NJ: Princeton University Press.

Decety, J. (ed.) (2009) *The Social Neuroscience of Empathy*. Massachusetts: MIT Press.

De Waal, F. (2009) *Primates and Philosophers: How Morality Evolved*. Princeton, NJ: Princeton University Press.

Dixon, T. (2008) *The Invention of Altruism: Making Moral Meanings in Victorian Britain*. Oxford: Oxford University Press.

Forman-Barzilai, F. (2011) *Adam Smith and the Circles of Sympathy: Cosmopolitanism and Moral Theory*. Cambridge: Cambridge University Press.

Goetz, J., Keltner, D. and Simon-Thomas, E. (2010) 'Compassion: An Evolutionary Analysis and Empirical Review', *Psychological Bulletin* 136(3): 351–74.

Hall, C. (2005) *The Trouble With Passion: Political Theory Beyond the Reign of Reason*. New York: Routledge.

Hunt, L. (2006) 'Martha Nussbaum on the Emotions', *Ethics* 116: 552–77.

Iacoboni, M. (2009) *Mirroring People: The Science of Empathy and How We Connect with Others*. New York: Picador.

James, S. (2003) 'Passion and Politics', *Royal Institute of Philosophy Supplement* 52: 221–34.

Janover, M. (2005) 'The Limits of Forgiveness and the End of Politics', *Journal of Intercultural Studies* 26(3): 221–35.

Kingston, R. and Ferry, L. (eds) (2009) *Bringing the Passions Back In: The Emotions in Political Philosophy*. Vancouver: UBC Press.

Konstan, D. (2010) *Before Forgiveness: The Origins of a Moral Idea*. Cambridge: Cambridge University Press.

Linklater, A. (2007a) 'Distant Suffering and Cosmopolitan Obligations', *International Politics* 44: 19–36.

Linklater, A. (2007b) 'Towards a Sociology of Global Morals with an "Emancipatory Intent"', *Review of International Studies* 33: 135–50.

Margalit, A. (2002) *The Ethics of Memory*. Cambridge: Harvard University Press.

Mihai, M. (2010) 'Transitional Justice and the Quest for Democracy: A Contribution to a Political Theory of Democratic Transformations', *Ratio Juris* 23(2): 183–204.

Moeller, S. (1999) *Compassion Fatigue: How the Media Sells Disease, Famine, War and Death*. New York: Routledge.

Monroe, K. (1998) *The Heart of Altruism*. New Jersey: Princeton University Press.

Monroe, K. (2006) *The Hand of Compassion: Portraits of Moral Choice during the Holocaust*. Princeton, NJ: Princeton University Press.

Muldoon, P. (2008) 'The Moral Legitimacy of Anger', *European Journal of Social Theory* 11(3): 299–314.

Muller, J. (1995) *Adam Smith In His Time and Ours*. Princeton, NJ: Princeton University Press.

Nietzsche, F. (1997 [1881]) *Daybreak: Thoughts on the Prejudices of Morality* (R. J. Hollingdale Trans.). Cambridge: Cambridge University Press.

Nussbaum, M. (1996) 'Compassion: The Basic Social Emotion', *Social Philosophy and Policy* 13(1): 27–58.

Nussbaum, M. (2001) *Upheavals of Thought: the Intelligence of the Emotions*. Cambridge: Cambridge University Press.

Nussbaum, M. (2004) *Hiding from Humanity: Shame, Disgust and the Law*. Princeton, NJ: Princeton University Press.

Nussbaum, M. (2006) *Hiding from Humanity: Disgust, Shame and the Law*. Princeton, NJ: Princeton University Press.

Nussbaum, M. (2008) 'The "Morality of Pity: Sophocles' *Philoctetes*"' in Rita Felski (ed.) *Rethinking Tragedy*. Baltimore: John Hopkins University Press, 148–69.

Nussbaum, M (2010) 'Compassion: Human and Animal' in N. Ann Davis, Richard Keshan and Jeffrey McMahan (eds) *Ethics and Humanity: Themes from the Philosophy of Jonathan Glover*. New York: Oxford University Press, pp. 202–26.

Rousseau, J.-J. (1974 [1762]) *Émile* (B. Foxley Trans.). London: Dent.

Sennett, R. (2004) *Respect in a World of Inequality*. New York: W.W. Norton & Co.

Smith, A. (2002 [1790]) *The Theory of Moral Sentiments*. Cambridge: Cambridge University Press.

Taylor, C. (2008) 'Foreword: Politics and Passion' in R. Kingston and L. Ferry (eds) *Bringing the Passions Back In: The Emotions in Political Philosophy*. Vancouver: UBC Press, pp. vii–viii.

Tester, K. (2001) *Compassion, Morality and the Media*. Milton Keynes: Open University Press.

Torpey, J. (2006) *Making Whole What Has Been Smashed: On Reparations Politics*. Cambridge: Harvard University Press.

Ure, M. (2006) 'The Irony of Pity: Nietzsche *contra* Rousseau and Schopenhauer', *Journal of Nietzsche Studies* 32: 68–91.

Ure, M. (2007) 'The Politics of Mercy, Forgiveness and Love: A Nietzschean Appraisal', *South African Journal of Philosophy* 26(1): 56–69.

Ure, M. (2013) 'Nietzsche's Political Therapy' in Keith Ansell-Pearson (ed.) *Nietzsche and Political Thought*. London: Bloomsbury Press.

Ure, M. (forthcoming). 'Resentment/*Ressentiment*', *Constellations: An International Journal of Critical and Democratic Theory*.

van der Weele, C. (2011) 'Empathy's purity, sympathy's complexities; De Waal, Darwin and Adam Smith', *Biological Philosophy* 26: 583–93.

PART I

COMPASSION AS A POLITICAL VIRTUE

1

LOVE AND ANGER AS POLITICAL VIRTUES

Maureen Whitebrook

Introduction: *political* compassion

To develop a model of compassion appropriate to the political sphere would require *either* some modification of the understanding of the virtue as it stands (that is, as it is understood in practice in personal, private or social life, and in theory as its genealogy has been established and its characteristics stipulated) *or*, alternatively, a different set of principles that would go beyond the personal exercise of the virtue to act as the basis of a practice that could operate as an integral part of the political process. That is, rather than trying to translate the characteristics of what has generally been understood as primarily a type of relationship between individual persons into an acceptable form for extra-individual activities, systems and processes, the concept itself needs to be looked at from a specifically political perspective.

Taking that latter approach, working from the political point of view as it were, I want to establish a clear contrast between political compassion and other accounts of the virtue, retaining the basic and essential feature of compassion, the concern for suffering, but examining what form the virtue would take as and when that concern is extended beyond purely one-to-one relationships in the private sphere into areas where group suffering becomes an issue, where a response to that suffering needs to be expressed in political terms and/or is necessarily contained within the political sphere.

Argument

Basic considerations

A serious consideration of compassion as an appropriate virtue for politics depends on moving away from familiar accounts of its characteristics, moving away from the intensity of one-to-one relationships, and strong association with 'feelings' conventionally understood to characterise the virtue, and away from any association with patronage, charity, benevolence and the like. Compassion has to operate beyond personal relationships, in public (as a precondition of politics), translate feeling into action, and avoid charges of sentimentality or irrationality as inappropriate for politics by way of the exercise of judgement in the course of the move from feeling to action.

I work with a basic understanding of compassion that distinguishes it from pity, whereby 'pity' denotes the *feeling* (towards suffering) whereas 'compassion' refers to *feeling together with action*.[1] Compassion is a matter of acting on the basis of feelings of pity rather than simply feeling an emotion. Where feeling does lead to action, the transition depends on judgement, reasoned consideration of the need to deal with suffering in some way. Compassion is linked to the first awareness of suffering or need, but results as a practice from the move from feeling pity to compassionate action generated by reflective judgement ('understanding'), consideration of the best way to respond to the perceived need – including those occasions when compassion will be judged an inappropriate response to the suffering. Sight of the suffering other invokes feeling (pity), and possibly then action where judgement indicates that it is considered appropriate – and thence a form of compassion particularly relevant to politics (Whitebrook 2002; Nussbaum 1996: 28 and *passim*).

Love, compassion and politics

The predominance in theoretical work on compassion of reference to 'the Greeks' is questionable, particularly in its reliance on Greek tragedy (as for instance in the influential work of Martha Nussbaum). Drawing conclusions from references to those dramas can be misleading: how appropriate is it to draw on that tradition to define and discuss compassion in 'a world with no gods' and where the plight of the tragic hero has little or no relevance for the individual in a democratic age where 'there are no heroes now' – certainly not in the ancient sense? The Judaeo-Christian tradition offers an alternative, politically relevant, source: for example, an academic theologian, Marcus Borg, has paid specific attention to the contemporary implications of biblical understandings of compassion – including its connections to justice. His work suggests a way into the development of a viable formulation for political compassion, and thence an argument for the inclusion of compassionate agency in modern politics.

Borg's interpretation of biblical teaching and practice – as, for instance, in the Old Testament prophets and the life and teaching of Jesus – offers a politically relevant reading of the contemporary implications of compassion which corresponds, in his usage, to love, or *agape*. Love has been held to be a politically inappropriate emotion because of its restricted focus on intense one-to-one relationships, its association with feelings, with a tendency to irrational, unreasonable thinking – thus for example Arendt's major objection to love having any place in politics is that there is no space between people, for the 'in-between', the space in which politics takes place (Arendt 1958: 51–3).[2] However, what is commonly being judged as apolitical or anti-political is *eros* – erotic, or romantic, sexual or familial love – rather than *agape*. *Agape* is not solely focused on strong feelings between two people, not dependent on the qualities of the other, and not bound up with need for the other but with the other's neediness. This is love for others 'without judging them, asking anything of them, or thinking of one's own needs' (Tinder 1991: 21), with no power relationship between agent and recipient of compassion, concern for the welfare of all, and for justice (Greenholm 1973: 68–9, 72, 80–1). It thus takes the individual beyond the immediacy of one-to-one relationships into the public world, allowing for recognition of the unknown other and hence a certain detachment from the self appropriate to the need for political compassion to exercise reasoned judgement.

Borg's discussion of compassion based on *agape* moves beyond attention to individual suffering towards recognition of the *causes* of suffering, injustice and inequality, and thence to action to redress the effects of those causes. He initially characterised compassion simply as being associated with feeling the suffering of someone else and being moved by that suffering 'to do something' (Borg 1994: 47). Subsequently, he has moved on towards the development of a specific and politically relevant argument that such motivation entails attention to the cause(s) of suffering beyond concern for the single case, the individual. Attention to the needs of the sufferer alone is not sufficient: compassion should cause the 'onlooker' to ask 'What caused the suffering?', and then seek to remedy not just the plight of a particular victim but also the systemic fault involved. 'Compassion without justice can mean caring for the victims while quietly acquiescing to a system that creates ever more victims. Justice means asking why there are so many victims and then doing something about it' (Borg 2001: 301). This is the crux of Borg's argument for a 'politics of compassion' and what can be developed from it.

This view of compassion meets the requirement referred to above that for a political relevance it must extend beyond individual relationships; and it expands my fundamental contention that sight of the suffering other invokes feeling (pity), and then action (compassion) may follow, including, where appropriate and necessary, *political* action. Paying attention to the causes of suffering entails that compassion is accompanied by judgement: response to suffering tied to awareness of the culpability of the prevailing socio-political system constitutes an impetus to change the system where it is perceived as and judged to be unjust.

Borg's argument rests on the premise that 'Justice is the social or systemic form of compassion', as against 'what is commonly called "systemic injustice" – sources of unnecessary human misery created by unjust political, economic and social systems' (Borg and Wright 1999: 245; Borg 2003: 129). He links compassion to *social* justice, 'substantive or systemic justice, concerned with the structures of society and their results', including but not confined to procedural or restorative justice. Because social justice is results oriented, it discerns whether the structures of society – in other words, the social system as a whole – are just in their effects. 'The test of the justice of systems is their impact on human lives. To what extent do they lead to human flourishing and to what extent to human suffering?' (Borg 2003: 129) As Borg puts it most strongly, 'compassion that does not see that much of the world's misery flows from systemic injustice is a compassion that is still partially blind. We are called upon to become politically aware as well as loving' (Borg and Wright 1999: 245; see also Campbell 1986: 101–3).

Development: compassion and anger

Working from these initial considerations – the basic stipulation that a political form of compassion would be a matter of considered public action on the basis of feelings, together with Borg's insistence that compassion should extend beyond action focused on the individual and be concerned with acting against the *causes* of suffering, including the adverse effects of socio-political processes and systems – I suggest that there is a potential foundation here for the development of a viable conceptualisation of political compassion.

Anger as motivation of and basis for political action

> As a political paradigm, what might compassion lead us to see? ... It leads us to see the impact of social structures on people's lives. It leads to seeing that the economic suffering of the poor is not primarily to do with individual failure. It leads to seeing that the categories of 'marginal', 'inferior' and 'out-cast' are human impositions. It leads to *anger* towards the sources of human suffering, whether individual or systemic.
>
> (Borg 1997: 150, my italics)

While a connection to social justice does not necessarily give compassion any explicit political role, beyond a general obligation to attend to suffering and its causes, a more specific contribution of Borg's work to thinking about political compassion is to suggest the possibility that anger can be a justified element in the political as impetus to and sustaining force for political agency and action.

In arguing that compassion requires more than mere charity, Borg allows for bringing understanding of the virtue into the sphere of the political: compassion-ate action has a specific political focus where suffering is perceived to be a result of systemic injustice.[3] As Borg has it, compassionate action will challenge existing political arrangements where the causes of suffering are systemic failures of social justice rooted in a given socio-political order ('the dominant system'). Recognising the *causes* of suffering should make the compassionate agent angry; and anger might then be acceptable as strengthening political compassion inasmuch as it interacts with the process of judgement whereby feeling is transformed into action and then sustains that action thereafter.

Compassion understood as a form of *agape*/love generates defensible anger on the part of those who recognise suffering and injustice, make judgements as to its cause and decisions about appropriate action. Attempting a formulation of 'political compassion' then involves the complex inter-relationship of perceptions of injustice, feelings of compassionate anger and reasoned judgement as to the appropriate response in motivating and sustaining political action to bring about change. The distinction I draw for a political compassion between compassion as a *feeling*, tied to notions of sentimentality and closely linked to pity, and compassion as *action* following from the first sight (perception) of suffering is pivotal here. The movement from feeling to action entails understanding and assessment of the situation and consideration of the appropriate response, a process of judgement, taking the anger into account in deciding on suitable action.

This is anger which is not merely expressive, 'emotional' or impulsive, but purposeful, 'controlled' anger issuing in a reasoned response to a situation. Compassion may induce anger, but 'however much compassion might appear to originate from, or rely on, spontaneous and impulsive reactions, it is based on thought and evaluation' (Nussbaum 1996: 28). It is directed at the causes of suffering, and informed by knowledge of situation and context, and in that sense is objective and rational.[4] Similarly, Amartya Sen remarks:

> Resistance to injustice typically draws on both indignation and argument. Frustration and ire can help to motivate us, and yet ultimately we have to rely, for both assessment and effectiveness, on reasoned scrutiny to obtain a plausible and sustainable understanding of the basis of those complaints (if any) and what can be done to address the underlying problems.

And he goes on to say:

> The role and reach of reason are not undermined by the indignation that leads us to an investigation of the ideas underlying the nature and basis of the persistent inequities which characterize … the world in which we live today.
>
> (Sen 2009: 390, 392)

Leah Bradshaw's discussion of the passion/reason distinction includes the comment that 'pity' (used as synonymous with compassion in her discussion) 'is rooted in the emotions, while indignation is a compound of emotion and judgement', and 'Even if we feel pity for someone, there is nothing virtuous about *feeling* bad about their situation. For compassion to have any substance politically, it has to be converted to virtue, which is measured by reasoned actions' (Bradshaw 2008: 180, 182).[5]

Although political agency can take various forms, and resulting political action might have various outcomes, in this case agency – 'compassionate political agency' – is exercised specifically in respect of the causes of suffering and vulnerability, thus distinguishing between the political agent active within the political system and the victim of systemic injustice effectively excluded from the exercise of political agency by their socio-political conditions. When vulnerable individuals or groups are prevented from joining in political dialogue by reason of incapacity result-ing from the systemic causes of their vulnerable state, they lack the capacity for agency, in this case to communicate effectively within the prevailing conventions of political dialogue. That is, 'political agency' in this context refers to the capacity for political activity exercised by those within the political system who observe and decide on action with respect to causes of suffering consequent upon the workings of the prevailing political system, standing in contrast to the incapacity for politi-cal agency on the part of those affected by systemic injustice. Victims of systemic injustice may express and may also act upon feelings of anger about their indi-vidual situation: but such anger – 'victim anger' – is self-interested and specific to a particular situation (and thence liable to objections to anger as having any part in the political process), whereas 'compassionate anger', as I characterise it here, is not self-interested but impartial, and is directed at change to remedy injustice.[6]

To recapitulate: the political version of compassion argued for here is exercised in respect of the recognition of systemic injustices where the focus is not on indi-vidual sufferers under the prevailing political system but on the system itself where it produces considerable suffering evident beyond the single case. Anger as a compo-nent element of the exercise of political compassion does not centre on individual relationships. It is felt and acted on by compassionate political agents driven to act in situations where suffering or vulnerability entails that the conditions for self-agency are lacking for victims of social injustice. It is anger *about* structures and their effects rather than *at* persons, and is largely detached from personal considerations, distinct from the intense relationships indicated by *eros*. Compassionate anger extends the reach of compassion from (individual) feeling or action for the needy other to action aimed not at the amelioration of suffering experienced by certain individuals but action with and on behalf of those subject to systemic injustice, where some sec-tions of society are effectively denied access to the regular methods of protest and/or effecting change, where the conditions of suffering exclude them from the possibil-ity of communicating within the political system effectively, if at all. A formulation of political compassion is thus extended, by way of an anger-fuelled imperative to act, away from the purely theoretical into the sphere of political practice.

Compassionate anger: theory and practice

A clear instance of such practice is provided in a study of the role of values in the working lives of public service professionals where 'Anger at the state of the world and of public service was a constant theme'. For the majority of the respondents in a series of case studies:

> [T]he motivational basis for their work commitment was manifest in a desire to repair some of the damage that they felt had been done to others. This was

a solidaristic motivation typically based upon an identification with the needs of a particular group, which harnessed compassion with anger.

(Hoggett, Mayo & Miller 2006: 764)

Their personal life experiences and the values they held impacted on their work. For several of the interviewees, their commitment to social justice 'was simply part of what they grew up with': experiences of class and race become linked to 'an experienced abusiveness of authority', and personal experience is then joined to the struggles of the people they are working with. The researchers conclude:

> [I]t is not only care or compassion which has an affective basis, but justice also… what seems to emerge from our interviews is the way in which *a complex mix of compassion and anger* fuels a reparative desire to undo the damage and suffering experienced by particular groups or communities.
>
> (Hoggett, Mayo & Miller 2006: 763, 766, my italics)

The way in which justifiable anger can function as an impetus to compassionate agency in the political sphere is recognisable in instances of the inextricability of the relationship in practice such as the social workers' experiences referred to here, and in other similar (relatively low-level) examples of reaction to what is perceived to be unacceptable, or judged to be harmful in public life (Goodwin, Jasper & Pollitt 2001). The headline claim that 'What makes you angry makes you motivated' is made by a Minnesota state senator who is also a doctor, trying to provoke his professional colleagues into political involvement.

> Ten physicians calling a legislator to tell how a measure would hurt patients is a powerful incentive to vote no … How do we get the physicians motivated? Will it take the pain caused by bad laws and bad policies to get them motivated?
>
> (Schaaf 2007: 8)

His appeal rests on the assumption that his colleagues, members of a caring profession, should be angry enough about legislative curtailment of the provision of medical care to be stimulated into exercising the political influence available to them as professionals. This effectively responds to Wilkinson's examination of the problem of 'bringing the lived reality of social suffering to public attention'. It might be possible to 'evoke greater outpourings of compassion towards the pain of others … to bring the standpoint of those "in" suffering to bear directly upon the hearts and minds of policy makers, politicians and publics'; and where people can be made to *feel* more sympathy and responsibility for the suffering of others, 'then they shall be motivated to act against the political decision and social conditions that damage and ruin human life' (Wilkinson 2006: 114).

An extensive theoretical examination of the place of anger in politics, 'The domestication of anger: the use and abuse of anger in politics' also offers relevant support for the place of compassionate anger in politics: 'When anger is taken seriously as a communication, rather than as psychological disorder or uncivil behaviour, a spirited but ultimately constructive public dialogue about the justice of the dominant political order is possible' (Lyman 2004: 133). In similar language to Borg's, Lyman argues that compassion that is silent, restricted to single and separate acts of charity, colludes with the system: the absence of angry speech is 'an important political text when that absence of speech about injustice is a characteristic response to situations that are unjust. Silence suggests acceptance of the injuries of domination, by denying the existence of an injury'. In contrast, 'If anger were to become a voice in politics, every kind of subordination – and by extension, domination itself – would become a legitimate political topic' (Lyman 2004: 138, 139).[7]

Both practice and theory support the link between compassion and anger derived from Borg: that the sight of suffering should lead to anger towards the sources of human suffering. What is under discussion here is a particular form of compassion – *political* compassion: compassion admissible as a political virtue, as an active element in political life. And that correspondingly affects the form of anger which is integral to the argument here. It is directed at those systemic effects which cause suffering, impelling engagement with the political process to achieve reform.

Anger can function positively for political systems: the expression of anger should alert governments to problems within the political system, indicating a need for attention. If, within a functioning political system, that system is failing certain groups, then compassionate anger can be critical in drawing attention to the underlying causes of dissatisfaction or disorder:

> If, following Nussbaum, we accept that the foundation of liberal democratic societies lies in a shared sense of human vulnerability, then an effect like anger that 'tracks harm' will need to be granted its place among our most important moral sentiments.
>
> (Muldoon 2008: 310; Nussbaum 2004: 345)

Within the remit of political compassion as premised here, anger expressed by those acting as political agents speaking in the cause of those who lack a voice in the political system can alert the state to 'harm' that needs attention. There is then a specific function for compassion and, thence, anger, as a check on liberal democracies, where the working political system may momentarily, occasionally or even habitually, fail to pay attention, and thus effectively disallow full participation in the political conversation.

Anger need not be considered problematic in the context of politics if the anger is that of compassionate agents working within and for the good of the political system *and* when the function of 'tracking harm' is recognised as an integral and valuable part of the political system. Problems may occur when that function is not recognised. The need for political compassion, compassionate anger, arises in conditions where suffering is perceived to be caused by the operations of the political process itself, where a government or its agencies are *not* listening, or are hearing but *not* responding. What then happens when 'harm' – suffering or injustice – is identified, when compassion fulfils its function in this respect but the state ignores what is brought to its attention? It can be supposed that such inattention is likely to be met by continuing, or increased, anger on the part of compassionate agents particularly concerned for the those unable to participate in the political process.

At this point, there is a particular dilemma for a theorisation of political compassion which involves anger. Despite the constraints intrinsic to political compassionate anger which contribute to the avoidance of its escalation, a formulation of political compassion which involves anger will still be subjected to the suspicion of an inherent link between anger and violence, 'the general charge that "anger inevitably leads to violent excess"' (Muldoon 2008: 309). However, Muldoon's comment is made in the context of a focus on the specific situation of post-apartheid South Africa and the work of the Truth and Reconciliation Committees; and he himself also says that 'anger can be recovered as a critical emotion in liberal societies once it is differentiated from associated effects such as resentment and revenge' (Muldoon 2008: 300; see also Arendt 1958; Nussbaum 2001: 339–45). And in general the link between anger and violence in a political context tends to be made in respect of victim anger and is not then applicable to the type of anger under discussion here.

The distinction of compassionate agent anger from more personal forms of the emotion, including 'victim anger', allows for an adequate response to the issue of the connection between anger and violence. The specific characteristics of compassionate anger acting as constraints lessen the likelihood that anger will lead to violence, distancing compassion from an association with irrational or violent behaviour considered prima facie inappropriate for political purposes.[8] Thus it might be argued that the element of care inherent in compassion would have a constraining effect in terms of versions of the instruction to 'love thy neighbour' present in understandings of compassion in many religions, together with a more general, and widespread, notion of 'the Golden Rule'. Concern for the other would tend towards an ingrained peaceful disposition, or a commitment to non-violence (as for instance with the Occupy movement, which has established non-violence as a working principle and has largely maintained it in practice, for example in response to police and bailiff action against Occupy camps).

Because this is anger arrived at by way of reasoned judgement between feeling and action and directed at improving the system for the benefit of those suffering from its malfunctioning, the likelihood that it will be associated with violence is low. Compassionate agents angered by their perception of injustices arising from the workings of the political system are more likely to want results *within* that system, to be achieved by modification and adaptation rather than risk its complete breakdown, by unpicking the causes of suffering and replacing them with better systems and procedures rather than turning to violent action. Anger is then less likely to lead to violence when there is an awareness that it would be a hindrance to getting results. There is no affective/emotional or rational reason for agent anger to turn to violence because to do so would be potentially disruptive, getting in the way of avoiding harm by achieving reform.

Compassionate political anger will not generally lead to violence, and the risk that it might is not of itself sufficient to disbar it from politics altogether: that risk should not place a limitation *per se* on recognising the viability of a working idea of political compassion in which anger plays a part.

Further considerations

The primary purpose here has been to establish the viability of bringing compassion into play in the political sphere, suggesting how compassion might operate beyond the personal one-to-one expression of the emotion, and focusing in this case on how concern for suffering might be directed at systemic causes of suffering or deprivation through the expression of compassionate anger. The first section of this chapter set out in general terms a case for a distinctively *political* form of compassion; on that basis, a formulation of political compassion linking compassion and anger has been developed in the second section. It remains to draw attention to some of the implications of this theorisation – interactions, issues and questions capable of further development beyond the scope of this chapter – if the concept of a distinctively political compassion is to be recognised and utilised.

The most immediate reaction may well be to the anger–compassion connection itself: anger is an unfamiliar emotion for consideration as a virtue in political terms, and a surprising proposed element of political compassion. The terms under which compassionate anger can form a positive part of political compassion have already been covered in the second section of this chapter. Any further development, as for instance an assessment of the extent to which the characteristics of political compassion such as the compassion–love synonymity or the requirement of reasoned judgement limit the escalation of anger, has to avoid becoming trapped in an examination of anger in the most general or conventional terms. The focus here is on compassionate anger where the emphasis remains on *compassion*.

As I have already indicated, the inclusion of anger in this formulation becomes contentious if a strong link is made between anger and violence, as in classic objections to anger in politics; that issue is defused to a large extent by the specific nature of the anger in question here, particularly in its distinction from the anger felt and expressed by victims of suffering or oppression resulting from state duress. However, the questions already raised in the relatively brief treatment of anger in this chapter around the state's reaction to expressions of compassionate anger, together with the risk that anger might turn to violence, suggest that although, as I have indicated, the risk of escalation is low, the residual possibility that anger might turn to violence – the 'what if …' question – persists.

In response, there are a number of factors which should be taken into account if development of the argument here does need to deal with this concern. Are the characteristics of political compassion sufficient restraints on future action when that anger is still justified but the state does not move on its failure to deal with the systemic causes of injustice? If the state does not listen, then violence may follow as a last resort: debatably, political violence might be recognised as 'a public political strategy, carried out by groups and individuals ... who claim responsibility for acts of violence and justify them as a necessary means to achieve a political end', so that violence might be regarded not as 'an irrational expression or outburst of pathological individuals', but 'intended as a conscious and focused strategy to achieve political ends which, it is claimed, are not achievable by non-violent means' (Schwarzmantel 2010: 2).[9] It is also quite possible that the problem of violence is two-sided – that state violence as well as agent violence should be brought into the argument. References to violence in the political context are more inclined to focus on violent behaviour in the course of opposition, dissidence, protest and the like than to include attention to violence on the part of the authorities dealing with that action. But if the state's response to expression of compassionate anger is to suppress it by forceful methods, would it follow that the onus for avoiding violence then passes from compassionate agents' activity in the political system to the state's response to having harm brought to its attention? What is at issue here is the extent of the state's deployment of the resources and methods at its disposal, including force, to control, contain or suppress expressions of anger which *might* turn to violence.[10]

Questions about the possible escalation of anger towards violence are undoubtedly of importance in respect to this formulation of political compassion. However, attention to violence as such should not be allowed to distract from a more significant matter to be emphasised in respect to political compassion as presented here: simply put, what happens if the state fails to respond positively to compassionate agency and anger? Compassionate anger is prompted in the first place by the malfunctioning of policies and processes in the political system, the failure to recognise the 'tracking function' of political compassion. So, to reiterate, violence is unlikely to follow from the activity of compassionate political agents unless radical, enforced, change appears to be the only answer where all lawful (non-violent) methods of effecting change have been tried and failed. When the state is dysfunctional in respect of causing suffering (albeit unintentionally or inadvertently) and then fails to rectify the situation when it is brought to its attention, might violent action come to seem the only solution?

That the state can be characterised as 'dysfunctional' and that violence might then be justifiable does not sit easily with arguments for compassion as an appropriate virtue with a useful function in the political process. References to 'bringing the virtues back in' – arguments for including 'emotions' or 'virtues' in thinking about politics – are generally made in the context of the practices, policies and processes of liberal democracies, as for instance in treatments of compassion in politics such as Nussbaum's cited above. The assumption is that compassion would operate best – or, indeed, only – in liberal democratic states, where the practices of the dominant political regimes are in line with the basic values of liberal theory. But when the failure to address systemic injustice results in inability to communicate on one hand and failure to listen on the other, the liberal democratic ideal has clearly broken down.

Opening up this examination of a formulation of political compassion linked with anger draws attention to the evident disjunction between theory and practice in the actual operation of modern states claiming to be and/or generally taken to be liberal democracies. Anger stemming from and exercised in compassion demands that the root causes of suffering should be addressed: where liberal democracies fail to listen and respond, compassionate anger challenges and may oppose the political system. Opposition to the dominant regime may then go as far as change involving violence. This is an unusual and probably unsettling conjecture, not least because mainstream liberal theory is being asked to face the strong possibility that a 'virtue', compassion, brought into politics might have outcomes that effectively undermine rather than support the practice of liberal democratic politics.

The 'tracking function' of the *theorising* of political compassion as delineated here is that of drawing attention in a particularly trenchant way to a long-standing but still relevant problem for political theory, that of how to deal with the gap between liberal democratic theory and practice. When the political system is dysfunctional, not functioning in line with its own principles, failing in respect of social justice, it appears that the liberal democratic model does not work in practice – thus resulting in what Connolly refers to as 'the bifurcation of liberalism', whereby 'the commitment to liberal principles is increasingly matched by the disengagement from practical issues'. It is pertinent to the argument here that Connolly adds:

> The principles themselves tend to become more abstract, more difficult to articulate specifically or to link to particular issues', to the extent that 'it is not an unjust infringement of freedom to do what is necessary to promote rational ends.
>
> (Connolly 1987: 83–7)

Liberal theory needs attention in respect of those increasingly frequent instances of the apparent incapacity of liberal democratic states to incorporate all of their citizens – to respond to the suffering caused by their own policies and processes, accepting 'the challenge of developing itself so as to make possible the realisation of ideas of rational dialogue among equals in conditions that make such an aim more difficult' (Schwarzmantel 2010: 15, 20).[11]

There is a feasible case to be made for a distinctive concept of compassion in political terms; and if a fully realised formulation of political compassion were to be developed on the basis of this initial formulation, it would require extension beyond the obvious questions surrounding the anger–violence tension and the focus on the liberal democratic state. For instance, the assumption that liberal democracies are the proper location for political compassion is open to challenge. Are liberal democracies the only ('natural') place for political compassion – do political compassion and political anger depend on the liberal context? Could they transfer to other (non-liberal democratic) political systems, where the basis in liberal theory would hardly apply? Do any modern states adequately recognise liberal moral ideals in practice; and in any case, is political compassion's function of 'tracking harm' possible in other types of political system?[12] (An incidental outcome of attention to such questions could well be that arguments for a formulation of a distinctively political form of compassion would also be strengthened, in that political compassion would stand as a political possibility independent of being tied to a particular form of state.) Overall, the issues that have arisen, and the questions upon questions that have resulted from this attempt, would seem to indicate that the basic formulation has some validity, and that this initial attempt to bring compassion into the sphere of politics with a specific function within the political process, is capable of generating further constructive work within political theory.

Final comments

Whatever the reactions to this initial attempt to establish the validity of a distinctive *political* compassion and thence a distinctive form of anger, and whatever development from the argument presented here becomes possible, the basic considerations – the requirement that politics involves actions done in public, together with compassion understood as requiring attention to systemic injustices – remain essential. Compassion directing attention to the systemic causes of suffering prompts the compassionate political agent to attend to the effects of unjust political practice and seek to remedy that situation. Working on that basis, I have attempted to establish a clear distinction between *political* compassion and other understandings of the virtue, retaining the basic and essential feature of compassion, the concern for suffering, but examining what form it would take as and when that concern is extended beyond purely one-to-one relationships in the private sphere into areas where group suffering becomes an issue, where a response to that suffering needs to be expressed in political terms.

Of itself the formulation examined in this chapter offers a way of thinking from the political perspective about what compassion has to offer politics – most basically, how would the introduction of this understanding of compassion benefit the political system? The answer, surprisingly enough, is by challenging it. Interesting questions then occur for both political theory and political practice as to the nature and effects of such a challenge. However, whatever the outcome of any such enquiry, it does seem clear that compassion in its political form is not a 'soft' virtue but will in effect require the dominant political system to both recognize and realize certain principles and values, including a fundamental basis in social justice.

Notes

1 Compared to pity, 'compassion involves far greater commitment to substantial help. Compassion involves a willingness to become personally involved, while pity usually does not. Pity is more spectator-like than compassion; we can pity people while maintaining a safe emotional distance from them. While pity involves the belief in the inferiority of the object, compassion assumes equality in common humanity' (Ben-Ze'Ev 2000: 328; see also Nussbaum 2001: 301–4).

2 But see also Shin Chiba's trenchant refutation of Arendt's views and objections (Chiba 1995; see also Nussbaum 2001: Part III 'Ascents of Love').

3 'Suffering' calls for some clarification in political terms: suffering may be physical – the effects of bad housing, discriminatory health care, poverty resulting from fiscal and economic policy; or it may be the more general matter of incapacity to take a full part in political life, or restricted rights or citizenship; 'vulnerability' indicating potential suffering, the possibility that the system *may* do harm, awareness that agent anger may be directed at the effects or *potential* effects of political policies and processes, is also an applicable term in this context.

4 Compare the comment that contemporary ways of thinking 'in an imaginative and calculative way through all aspects of a given issue and connecting that thinking to broader uses of rationality' then involves 'insisting on explanations, addressing the problems we face in an objective calculative fashion, and taking into account the consequences for all parties, not just ourselves' (Waldron 2012: 38).

5 Sen and Bradshaw's use of the term 'indignation' here is entirely consonant with my use of 'anger'. Lexically the two words are interchangeable, so that to claim that indignation is the better term to indicate 'a sustainable disposition in alignment with rational judgement' may be appropriate to a particular philosophical disposition but is not relevant to this argument. My preference here is for anger, not least because it is the term of choice in Borg's work used here as a key source for the understanding of compassionate anger. (In respect of preference for one term over another, see Nussbaum's acute comments on choice of terms where she concludes that 'In short, the most sensible way to proceed is to give clear account of each term one uses and to be consistent' (Nussbaum 2001: 301–4). 'Anger' can have negative associations with resentment, retribution and revenge – as indeed can 'indignation', 'wrath' or 'rage'. But such feelings are associated with victim anger, and thus applicable, if at all, to those suffering within the political system from systemic injustice, and thereby denied the capacity for full political agency. Accordingly, *anger* remains the appropriate term here in respect of compassionate political agents capable of acting against the effects of the causes of suffering.

6 Compare *conscious* anger – 'being consciously aware of feeling angry and of being physically motivated by anger' in sharp contrast to the Nietzschian characterisation of anger which 'manifests itself as a self-righteous world-view that seeks to resolve conflict by assigning blame and exacting revenge'; and he comments that 'the problem with this critique is that it is often used to blame the victim by ignoring the social relationships – perhaps the injustices – that caused an angry response' (Lyman 2004).

7 Lyman here refers to 'the anger of the powerless', and his general focus is on those who are disadvantaged, made powerless, by the political system, but his remarks are also applicable, in the overall context of his study, to the anger of those speaking on behalf of those 'lacking the willingness or even ability to speak'.

8 The meaning of 'violence' is not always clarified in arguing about it in the political context: are various forms of violence – physical, verbal violence against persons as distinct from violence against property – equally unacceptable; to what extent is non-physical violence – verbal violence, for example – acceptable within the political system; what is the place of the *threat* of violence in the political process; where 'acts of violence' and 'obstruction' are concerned, what is the nature and extent of the 'violence' in question – including state violence in the course of dealing with protest (Waldron 2012)?

9 Schwarzmantel's references to political violence are made in the context of his discussion of 'the ways in which political violence challenges some of the basic assumptions and foundations of liberal political philosophy' (Schwarzmantel 2010: 1); I am grateful for Schwarzmantel's presentation of this paper, and subsequent communication with him in the course of constructing my argument here; see also his subsequent book, *Democracy and Political Violence* (Schwarzmantel 2011).

10 Compare Lyman's comments on the 'domestication' of anger, sublimating anger into 'its socially useful forms' in the context of an overall understanding that in liberal societies, anger is utilised as 'a resource for the dominant': the conscious anger which is a

motivating force is constrained by 'social norms ... that define who has the right to speak angrily to whom, and in what circumstances'; and one way in which control is exercised over the expression of anger is that 'the procedural approach to justice of liberal regimes devalues the substantive protest of angry speech by interpreting it as a loss of emotional control and as a potential prelude to violence' (Lyman 2004: 133–6).

11 Compare work in realist political theory which recognises and addresses the gap between political theory, especially that characterised as 'liberal moralism' and political practice. Political philosophy must be concerned 'in the first instance ... with the way the social, economic, political etc., institutions actually operate in some society at some given time, and what really does move human beings to act in given circumstances' (Geuss 2008; see also Williams 2005; Frazer 2010).

12 Compare 'the assumption that democracy belongs exclusively to the West' with 'the history of people's participation and public reasoning in different parts of the world, and the pervasive and omnipresent idea of justice, which inspires discussion and agitation right across the world' (Sen 2009: 322, 327 and Chapter 15 'Democracy as public reason' *passim*).

References

Arendt, H. (1958) *The human condition*. Chicago: The University of Chicago Press.

Ben-Ze'Ev, A. (2000) *The subtlety of emotions*. Cambridge, MA & London: MIT Press.

Borg, M. J. (1994) *Meeting Jesus again for the first time: the historical Jesus and the heart of contemporary faith*. San Francisco: HarperCollins.

Borg, M. J. (1997) *The god we never knew: beyond dogmatic religion to a more authentic contemporary faith*. San Francisco: HarperCollins.

Borg, M. J. (2001) *Reading the Bible again for the first time: taking the Bible seriously but not literally*. San Francisco: HarperCollins.

Borg, M. J. (2003) *The heart of Christianity*. San Francisco: HarperCollins.

Borg, M. J. & Wright, N. T. (1999) *The meaning of Jesus: two visions*. London: SPCK.

Bradshaw, L. (2008) Emotions, reasons and judgements. In R. Kingston & L. Ferry, *Bringing the passions back in: the emotions in political philosophy*. Vancouver: UBC Press.

Campbell, A. V. (1986) *The gospel of anger*. London: SPCK.

Chiba, S. (1995) Hannah Arendt on love and the political: love, friendship and citizenship. *The review of politics, 57*(3), 505–35.

Connolly, W. E. (1987) *Politics and ambiguity*. Madison, Wisconsin & London: University of Wisconsin Press.

Frazer, E. (2010) Review essay: What's real in political philosophy? *Contemporary political philosophy, Vol. 9*, 490–507.

Geuss, R. (2008) *Philosophy and real politics*. Princeton & Oxford: Princeton University Press.

Goodwin, J., Jasper, J. M. & Pollitt, Francesca (eds) (2001) *Passionate politics: emotions and social movements*. Chicago & London: University of Chicago Press.

Greenholm, C. H. (1973) *Christian social ethics in a revolutionary age. An analysis of the social ethics of John C. Bennett, Heinz-Dietrich Wendland and Richard Shaull* (Sally-Ann Gotegard, trans., in the series *Uppsala studies in social ethics*). Uppsala: Tofters Tryckeri.

Hoggett, P., Mayo, M. & Miller, C. (2006) Private passions, the public good and public service reform. *Social policy and administration, 40*(7), 758–73.

Lyman, P. (2004) The domestication of anger: the use and abuse of anger in politics. *European journal of social theory, 7*(2), 133–47.

Muldoon, P. (2008) The moral legitimacy of anger. *European journal of social theory, 11*(3), 299–314.

Nussbaum, M. (1996) Compassion: the basic social emotion. *Social philosophy and policy, 13*(1), 27–58.

Nussbaum, M. (2001) *Upheavals of thought: the intelligence of emotions.* Cambridge: Cambridge University Press.

Nussbaum, M. (2004) *Hiding from humanity: disgust, shame and the law.* Princeton & Oxford: Princeton University Press.

Schaaf, R. (2007) What makes you angry makes you motivated. *Missouri medicine, 104*(1), 7–8.

Schwarzmantel, J. (2010) Political violence and its challenge to liberalism [Conference presentation, July 5–7, 2010]. White Rose Association for Political Philosophy conference on 'The Future of Political Philosophy'. Sheffield.

Schwarzmantel, J. (2011) *Democracy and political violence.* Edinburgh: Edinburgh University Press.

Sen, A. (2009) *The idea of justice.* London: Allen Lane, Penguin.

Tinder, G. (1991) *The political meaning of Christianity: the prophetic stance: an interpretation.* San Francisco: HarperCollins.

Waldron, J. (2012) A cheerful view of mass violence. *The New York review of books, LIX*(1), 36–9.

Whitebrook, M. (2002) Compassion as a political virtue. *Political studies, 50*(3), 529–44.

Wilkinson, I. (2006) The problem of suffering as a problem for sociology. *Medical sociology online, 1,* 45–47.

Williams, B. (2005) *In the beginning was the deed: realism and moralism in political argument.* Princeton, NJ: Princeton University Press.

2

INVISIBILITY IN ARENDT'S PUBLIC SPACE

Gudrun von Tevenar

Arendt's political theory, with its strict divide between the public/political sphere and the private/social sphere, famously bans pity and compassion as well as goodness and love from the public/political sphere (Kateb 1984; Birmingham 1995). Arendt argues that compassion is politically corrosive because, straying outside its legitimate private and social domain, compassion champions the incursion of social and moral concerns into the political sphere, where, according to Arendt, they are strictly off limits. This position is highly controversial and heated debates about it are ongoing. While one should acknowledge that Arendt's position can be defended, particularly from a Kantian perspective, my argument in this chapter claims that any such defence remains deeply unsatisfactory so long as the problem of invisibility, exposed by Arendt's position, is ignored or inadequately addressed.

This chapter first rehearses Arendt's arguments against pity and compassion and the way their presence or absence impinges on the question of invisibility of the poor and disenfranchised. This is followed by an examination of Arendt's proposed alternatives such as administration, solidarity and the Kantian notion of 'enlarged mentality'. I conclude by arguing that these alternatives do not adequately address the problem of invisibility and, further, that the absence of a constructive role of pity and compassion robs us of an important cognitive and normative resource in the political domain.

Pity vs compassion

Regarding terminology: the term 'invisibility' is taken from Arendt's use of it in her book *On Revolution* (Arendt 1973) and in her essay *Bertolt Brecht* (see Arendt 1968) when describing the obscurity of the poor and otherwise marginalised. Regarding the terms 'pity' and 'compassion': while these are often used as if they refer to identical emotional states, Arendt makes a clear and, to my mind, very perceptive distinction between them. She claims that compassion is a passion, is to be stricken in the flesh by the suffering of another, while pity is a sentiment able to keep its distance and thus suitable to enter 'the marketplace'(Arendt 1963: 81ff.). Because compassion as genuine co-suffering can only be truly felt for singular others, it belongs, according to Arendt, by its very nature to the private sphere, while pity as a mere sentiment can enter the marketplace. The marketplace is, of course, not an economic space but, like the agora of the Greek *polis*, a political one.

So Ardent's distinction between compassion and pity follows the lines of her private/social and public/political one by assigning to each its distinctive sphere. Yet Arendt goes even further by raising doubt over the basic similarity of pity and compassion. She claims:

> For compassion, to be stricken with the suffering of someone else as though it were contagious, and pity, to be sorry without being touched in the flesh, are not only not the same, they may not even be related.
>
> (Arendt 1963: 85)

This strong claim explains, at least in part, Arendt's view that the essentially personal nature of compassion as a passion limits its applicability to the private sphere, while the sentiment of pity can go public and must there compete publicly, that is, in the marketplace, with other and maybe hostile attitudes via rhetoric, persuasion, manipulation and other political means. Yet, surprisingly, given her strict distinction between pity and compassion, Arendt tends to use these terms almost interchangeably, due, perhaps, to the fact that there is just one term for them in German, namely *Mitleid*.[1]

Moreover, despite her claim that pity can enter the marketplace, Arendt dismisses pity in the public sphere as a disastrous failure. Her most outspoken critiques are found in her book *On Revolution* and in her essay *Bertolt Brecht*.

The corruption of politics through pity: Robespierre and Brecht

In *On Revolution* Arendt compares the American and French Revolutions of the late eighteenth century and finds the French one wanting. While the American Revolution resulted in a politically sound constitution, much praised by Arendt though with some reservations, the French Revolution, in contrast, resulted in failure despite promising beginnings. This was largely because, unlike the Founding Fathers of the American Revolution, who did not permit 'pity to lead them astray from reason'(Arendt 1963: 95), Robespierre allowed himself to be deflected from the establishment of a political realm of freedom by giving in to his pity for the poor and making relief of poverty *the* revolutionary priority. Arendt states that Robespierre, strongly influenced by Rousseau, raised pity to the ultimate political virtue. She also claims that such was the scale of suffering and misery of the multitude at that time that in order to cope with and contain the seemingly limitless demands of their needs, ever more extreme and repressive measures had to be adopted, so that, in the end, 'pity proved to possess a greater capacity for cruelty than cruelty itself'. And the phrase 'For the sake of pity, for love of humanity, we must be inhumane' (both Arendt 1963: 89) became one of the most powerful slogans of the revolution.

Part of Arendt's explanation of this deplorable outcome is the ready, but mostly hidden link of pity with sentimentality as well as lust for power and cruelty. These fed Robespierre's rhetoric and the slide into terror. Whilst these alleged links are indeed frequently voiced by critics of pity, it is not usually the case that pity has to support such a weighty explanatory burden as here. However, Arendt's greatest objection to pity in the public sphere is not the terror it can allegedly lead to, but the fact that it allowed the social problem of poverty to usurp the revolution's legitimate political goals.

Turning now to Arendt's essay on Brecht (Arendt 1968: 207–49), one must first enquire why a poet should figure in an examination of compassion in the public sphere. There are two reasons: first, Arendt claims an elevated position for poets. Poets, she argues, have unique access and responsibility to truth: they must speak when everybody is silent and be silent when everybody speaks. Poets can discharge their guardianship of truth only if they stay truthful within themselves. Should they start to live in bad faith or lie, should they, in other words, betray their essential tie with truth, they will inevitably forfeit their poetic gift. Second, by Arendt's criteria, Brecht was a public figure not only as a poet but also due to his outspoken commitment to the ideology and values of the Communist Party. Arendt suggests that Brecht's motivation to do so lay in his deep and overwhelming compassion for the miserable and dispossessed. She also claims that Brecht's initial commitment to communism and the Party was still within the compass of his truth, the lived truth of an authentic poet. His subsequent loss of authenticity – his lie – she locates in the fact that he seemed to remain committed to the Party even when the Party's horrendous abuses and crimes, perpetrated within the sphere of its political influence and power, had already become all too obvious. Arendt therefore charges Brecht with the sin of remaining silent when he should have spoken and thus with failure in the exacting task specific to poets – their responsibility to truth. She supports this charge with the claim that an analysis of Brecht's late works does indeed show that his lack of truth, his lie, resulted in the loss of his poetic gifts.

Arendt's essay, with its sensitive and insightful comments on Brecht's works and their genesis in, and reflection of, the harshness of his time, argues that it was most likely the passion of his compassion that made him blind to, if not indeed condone, the Party's many failures and crimes. Nonetheless, Arendt is unwilling to accept this as an excuse for Brecht's failure of not speaking when he should have done; hence her forthright condemnation of his pity-induced corruption of the public sphere.

In both cases, Arendt emphasises negative results often alleged of pity and compassion, such as, in the case of Brecht, lack of judgement, lack of justice and lack of courage, and in the case of Robespierre, in addition to these, lust for power and cruelty as well as overwhelming sentimentality. However, what makes Arendt's analysis particularly remarkable is the urgency, indeed, the vehemence of her exposure of these alleged pernicious effects. Perhaps this urgency explains what appear as grave distortions in her account of Robespierre's and Brecht's supposed predilection to succumb so readily to the 'vices' of pity, since her account seems rather extreme and somewhat biased. I suggest therefore that, unless verified by competent historians or literary critics, we treat her disturbing re-description of the French Revolution's infamous Reign of Terror as a 'Reign of Pity' with due caution, and do so also regarding her conclusion that Brecht failed as a poet at the end. However, despite the gravity of these doubts and misgivings, they do not threaten our examination of the problem of invisibility.

The problem of invisibility

In order to examine the problem of invisibility, we must first grasp what 'being visible' amounts to in Arendt's public space. Being visible in Arendt's public space requires more than merely being perceivable by visual means. Visibility is the entrance (Arendt's favourite term is 'to appear') in the public domain in order to be seen and heard there by others and thus to take part as an equal in political discourse and action.

Arendt describes two ways one can fail to be visible in the public domain. One can retreat into invisibility by withdrawing from political engagement because the public domain is such as to hinder this, as was the case, for instance, with Jews in the early days of Nazi Germany. Yet this kind of invisibility can also be entirely self-imposed and quite independent of outside pressure, when it is the outcome of indifference, boredom or distaste with political performance as such. When withdrawing from the public sphere out of protest or as protection against prevailing political conditions, withdrawal can become what is sometimes described, reputedly by Jaspers, as 'inner emigration'. In all these cases, the withdrawn have obviously not disappeared or vanished: they simply are no longer visible in Arendt's politically relevant sense, since they no longer 'appear' in public to be seen and heard there by others.

It is interesting that Arendt describes withdrawal into the private sphere as an opportunity for gifted individuals to develop great personal and cultural enrichment (Arendt 2007: 275ff.). Here, withdrawal encourages intense emphasis on the personal qualities of individuals and promotes their channelling away from outer expression to inner articulation, thus enabling not only great cultural achievements but also a richer personal life through friendship, love and mutual reliance on inter-human support and warmth. Arendt considers Jews, because of their almost continuous exclusion from active participation in the political life of their host nations, to be a paradigm example of this inner personal and cultural flourishing. However, she most certainly does not approve of this condition, which she calls the existence of a 'Pariah' (Arendt 1968: 13). She states:

> [...] it is true that in 'dark times' the warmth which is the pariahs' substitute for light exerts a great fascination upon all those who are so ashamed of

the world as it is that they would like to take refuge in invisibility. And in invisibility, in that obscurity in which a man who is himself hidden needs no longer see the visible world either [...].

(Arendt 1968: 16)

So withdrawal, whether for safety or solace, into the seclusion of the private realm amounts to abandonment of the shared public world because one no longer wants to be part of it. Withdrawal is hence a kind of refusal of the world as it is. The world referred to here is not, of course, the given or natural world, which must, according to Arendt, be transcended in any case for a worthwhile human life to be possible. Rather, it is the public world built and structured in the space *between* active participants. In other words, the worthwhile world is the common, the political world, made and shared with others. Refusing and hence losing this shared public world has very serious consequences since it results in the kind of worldlessness Arendt denigrates and deplores as 'a form of barbarism' (Arendt 1968: 13).

This stunningly harsh verdict can only yield sense, though not necessarily agreement, by considering, first, that Arendt modelled the features of her public realm on those of the classic Greek *polis*, which did indeed regard anyone living outside a *polis* as barbaric. And second, in line with her exclusive validation of the public sphere, Arendt was extremely suspicious of an individual's ambition to self-realisation and autonomy (Kateb 1990). She mistrusted individual efforts at inner and hence essentially apolitical self-development and self-expression. Her utterly uncompromising partiality for active political life made her deprecate anything which might deflect from it, such as a predominance of private and social interests. This is not to say that Arendt did not value contributions to one's flourishing in the private sphere. Indeed, she holds that 'the qualities of the heart need darkness and protection against the light of the public to grow and remain what they are meant to be, innermost qualities which are not for public display' (Arendt 1963: 96).[2] Nonetheless, she utterly rejects the cultivation of the private *to the exclusion* of the public sphere, which always has preference. With this in mind, we can conclude that for Arendt, withdrawal into the private sphere, whether voluntarily or under duress, results in the loss of the shared public world by making oneself invisible to it.

There is a second form of invisibility, which I call the 'radical invisibility' of utter obscurity that is almost a defining feature of the poor and suffering everywhere. This invisibility is mentioned and acknowledged by Arendt as a fact, perhaps even as a problematic fact, yet she nonetheless never seriously discusses it in all its wide-ranging moral, cultural and political implications.

We find acknowledgement of the problem of invisibility in Arendt's account of the American Revolution (Arendt 1963: Chapter 2), where it features as the last of three distinctive reactions to the problem of poverty.

First, when contrasting the American and French Revolutions, Arendt locates the success of the American in the adherence to principles of reason and the absence of pity and compassion in the deliberations of the Founding Fathers. Arendt cites the statement of John Adams: 'The envy and rancour of the multitude against the rich is universal and restrained only by fear and necessity. A beggar can never comprehend the reason why another should ride in a coach while he has no bread' in support of her claim that 'the passion of compassion was singularly absent from the minds and hearts' (both Arendt 1963: 84) of the American revolutionaries.

Second, Arendt quotes Jefferson's comment on his visit to France: 'of twenty millions of people [...] there are nineteen millions more wretched, more accursed in every circumstance of human existence than the most conspicuously wretched individuals in the United States' and Franklin's proud recollection that back home in New England 'every man is a freeholder, has a vote in public affairs, lives in a tidy warm house, has plenty of good food and fuel' (both Arendt 1963: 67).

Third, Arendt points out that the so-called 'absence of misery' in America was quite deceptive, and she asks whether the relative comfort of the poor whites did not depend to a considerable degree upon black labour and black misery. She estimates that there were approximately 400,000 blacks in a population of approximately 1,850,000 whites. Yet, even when present in such large numbers, blacks were simply invisible – in the literal and metaphorical sense. 'The institution of slavery', writes Arendt, 'carries an obscurity even blacker than the obscurity of poverty; the slave, not the poor man, was "wholly overlooked"'(Arendt 1963: 71).

When comparing these three distinctive reactions to misery, we can see that the first is a common reaction of contempt and indifference, and Arendt comments that 'no one familiar with misery can fail to be shocked by the peculiar coldness and indifferent "objectivity" of his [John Adam's] judgement' (Arendt 1963: 84). Regarding the second reaction, the position is less clear: describing the pervasiveness in Europe of utter wretchedness and depravity in comparison with conditions in New England could be an expression of pity, or of contempt, or simply an observation of facts, similar to noting that the weather was bad or the roads unsafe, while the sun shone in New England. But Arendt's statements regarding the extent and penetration of invisibility of black slaves are unambiguous. Black slaves are totally covered by 'radical invisibility', by an obscurity even greater than the obscurity of the ordinary poor as described by John Adams in the following passage, cited by Arendt:

> He feels himself out of the sight of others, groping in the dark. Mankind takes no notice of him. He rambles and wanders unheeded. In the midst of a crowd, at church, in the market ... he is in as much obscurity as he would be in a garret or a cellar. He is not disapproved, censured, or reproached, *he is only not seen* [Arendt's italics].
>
> (Arendt 1963: 69)

Notice how Adams's description, too, is without disapproval, censure or reproach, but it is also, to my mind, without sympathy or concern. As such it connects to Arendt's suggestion that the invisibility of black slaves was not due to lack of either sympathy or solidarity with fellow men, but 'must be blamed on slavery rather than on any perversion of the heart or upon the dominance of self-interest'(Arendt 1963: 71). Is Arendt suggesting that there is something inherent in slavery as such, in its very essence, which makes slavery susceptible, of itself so to speak, to invisibility? She does not discuss this problem but simply observes that the institution of slavery did not even have the status of a social question at that time, so that:

> [...] the social question, whether genuinely absent or only hidden in darkness, was non-existent for all practical purposes, and with it the most powerful and perhaps the most devastating passion motivating revolutionaries, the passion of compassion.
>
> (Arendt 1963: 72)

Here we are confronted with an inconsistency in Arendt's thought, surfacing in places throughout her work: she states unequivocally *both* that it was not lack of pity and compassion that made the slaves invisible, and also that absence of compassion prevented slavery's visibility as a social question. The latter claim is indeed in agreement with the topic of this chapter, i.e. my claim that only pity and compassion, sympathetic emotions in general, can bring about visibility. Yet Arendt derides the influence of the sympathetic emotions in the public sphere, while acknowledging at the same time that lack of these very emotions prevents moral and social problems from surfacing to visibility – of this more later.

Compassion and the problem of invisibility

The problem of invisibility is also discussed by Arendt in her essay on Brecht. Among the many poems quoted by her are the following haunting lines:

> For some are in darkness / And others are in light. / And one sees those in light / But those in darkness are not seen.
> [my translation of
> *Denn die einen sind im Dunklen / Und die andren sind im Licht. / Und man siehet die im Lichte / Die im Dunklen sieht man nicht.*]
>
> (quoted in Arendt 1968: 237)

This moving statement of invisibility, of utter obscurity, is typical of Brecht's intense yet unsentimental style. By citing it, Arendt gives due credit to Brecht for exposing the problem of invisibility. Also noteworthy is the fact that Brecht was never tempted to romanticise misery and poverty as the French revolutionaries allegedly did, according to Arendt. In Brecht we find crime sitting close, very close, to poverty. Indeed, it is precisely this closeness which makes the poor 'wretched and accursed', to use Jefferson's words. Brecht allows just one solution, forcefully expressed in his pungent line: *Erst kommt das Fressen, dann kommt die Moral* (First grub, then morality).[3]

In her discussion of some of Brecht's plays,[4] Arendt points out how his work deepens our awareness and understanding of the difficulties goodness encounters when trying to manifest itself in the world. Perhaps Arendt wanted to secure Brecht's allegiance for her own rejection of this very possibility? Yet, this cannot be the case. While Brecht brutally exposes the usually hidden fact that in depraved environments goodness is a luxury the wretched can generally ill afford, he does not deny goodness as such. Indeed, in his plays and poems he highlights, with tenderness, the goodness behind the dirt, the subterfuge, and the various grim obstacles which makes the emergence of goodness so awkward, stunted or inconsequential. Perhaps Arendt cannot recognise goodness in this turgid mess, at least not officially, but then, not many recognise goodness in her elevated account of it![5] The presence of compassion makes all the difference here. Brecht has compassion as well as penetrating vision – thus he can see what is hidden to others. With great humility he pleads for *forbearance* on behalf of the 'wretched and accursed' and also on behalf of the compassionate with their many failures and weaknesses. The following lines are cited by Arendt:

> You who will emerge from the flood in which we drowned remember when you speak of our weaknesses the dark time from which you escaped.
> [...] Alas, we who wanted to prepare the ground for kindness could not be kind.
> [...] Remember us with forbearance.
>
> (Arendt 1968: 224)
>
> *Ihr, die ihr auftauchen werdet aus der Flut / In der wir untergegangen sind / Gedenkt / Wenn ihr von unseren Schwächen sprecht / Auch der finsteren Zeit / Der ihr entronnen seid. / ... Gedenkt unsrer / Mit Nachsicht.*[6]

Yet, despite Arendt's appreciation of Brecht's work and her recognition that Brecht's compassion greatly contributed to the visibility of the disenfranchised, this did not redeem him in her eyes for the failures of his pity and the consequent contamination of the political sphere.

It is clear from the above that Arendt was aware that political visibility of the poor and dispossessed depended mainly, as with Robespierre and Brecht, on the presence of pity or compassion. Only when seen with sympathetic eyes can social problems become visible and thus suitable for the political stage. But this is precisely the point: Arendt does not want social problems on the political stage – problems like poverty are not to be addressed politically!

The few pages of *On Revolution* on which much of my analysis is based are a passionate *tour de force* through a world of misery. Yet the passion is not the passion of compassion but a passionate exaltation of the political sphere. It is Arendt's passion for political performance and action that underlies her fierce attack on anything which in her eyes might threaten or sully it, such as pity and compassion. These she condemns because of her belief that sympathetic concern for the miserable and wretched with their ignorance, their basic lacks, their intruding and never-ending demands for life's necessities, is ultimately corrupting politically; as was the case, for instance, with the French Revolution's attempt to redress these problems through terror. That these necessities are indeed necessary Arendt does not deny, yet she allocates them to the private and social spheres where they are to remain 'hidden'. Under no circumstances must they come out into the open and under the scrutiny of the political sphere. It is precisely this harsh and unyielding position which makes her theory so controversial, if not indeed repugnant.

Should one judge Arendt a callous person just because she so vehemently rejects and deplores what to her eyes is a disastrous intrusion of social concerns onto the political stage? This is a difficult question, and despite all my misgivings I am inclined to say No. However, I feel strongly that Arendt's verdict on Adams quoted above, namely, that 'no one familiar with misery can fail to be shocked by the peculiar coldness and indifferent "objectivity" of his judgement' applies to her as well. Yes, she does know and comments with horror and grief on the countless atrocities of her time, and tries hard to comprehend and explain their vastness and incomprehensibility. Yet it seems to me that there is nonetheless a pervasive sense of distance, of a 'peculiar coldness and indifference' in her highly 'objective' account of suffering, of victims, of the seemingly hopeless predicament of the vast majority of humankind. We can find regret and sorrow in her descriptions, but not compassion.

Alternatives to pity in the political sphere

Now we must ask, if politics does not concern itself with these problems, where are we to find their solution? As an alternative to politics, Arendt advocates that problems of poverty be solved by economic and administrative means. This claim, namely, that economic and administrative programmes can be independent of the political, is regarded by most commentators as extremely dubious, indeed, as outrageous. Their misgivings are generally not assuaged by the promise that such arrangements could possibly protect relief of poverty from the vagaries and turbulence of political decision-making. Even if such a promise could be made to hold, it would only work if administrators received correct guidelines reflecting both actual states of affairs and the professed values of citizens. And now the problem of invisibility arises again: if the poor are not visible in the relevant sense, then, obviously, their needs cannot possibly find any resonance and accommodation in the normative sensibilities of citizens, and thus cannot become incorporated in economic and administrative programmes. Consider here that an administrative programme for black slaves during the American Revolution could not possibly be formulated since their radical invisibility made the slaves non-existent as it were. Hence again the necessity for sympathy and compassion to make the needy visible. Only when visible can the needy figure in appropriate political decisions and economic and administrative programmes.

Let us also consider solidarity as an alternative to pity and compassion which might avoid their alleged excesses. Arendt is a champion of solidarity in the political sphere where, she claims, it fosters a sense of equality amongst persons engaged in shared projects. Yet note that this solidarity is temporary and fluid and attaches itself readily to other persons if other projects are pursued. For instance, we can feel solidarity, simultaneously or consecutively, with ship workers in Gdansk, or with members of a particular religious movement, or with sufferers of a specific illness, or with members of criminal gangs, and so on. A necessary feature of such solidarity is the requirement that participants consider themselves equals at least within their particular current common context, a fact Arendt emphasises repeatedly. Accordingly, she considers solidarity amongst political or social *non-equals*, as is the case in a more global solidarity with all (suffering) humankind, politically irrelevant. So political solidarity with the 'invisibles' seen by Robespierre and Brecht is ruled out, precisely because as 'invisibles' they are unable to enter the political stage in order to be seen and heard there as equals. It follows that solidarity too, like economic and administrative projects, does not solve the invisibility problem.

Another alternative is found in Arendt's reflections, gleaned from Kant's *Critique of Judgement*, on a form of judgement that can lead to an 'enlarged mentality'.[7] A detailed account of Kant's theory cannot be given here, so I will briefly summarise Arendt's version of it.

There are four key features of judging shared in varying degree and with varying emphasis by both Kant and Arendt. These are: imagination, reflection, enlarged mentality and consensus. It is claimed that we can develop an enlarged mentality by imaginatively gathering in our mind various possible perspectives and opinions and reflecting disinterestedly upon them. The relevant imagination and reflection is made possible through our *sensus communis* – 'community or public sense' which Kant contrasts with 'private sense'. Arendt uses the evocative phrase of 'the mind going visiting' to describe this imaginative process. Such 'visiting' is supposed to facilitate consensus not only amongst present equal and active participants in a given discourse, but also with those not actually there, thus enabling a wide and inclusive plurality.

No doubt, the enlarged mentality thus described can be a most valuable resource for our coming to the kind of judgements and decisions most likely to benefit all or many others. Nonetheless, I maintain, first, that even this enlarged mentality cannot solve the invisibility problem in the absence of sympathy. Indeed, my claim is that enlarged mentality is only possible when *based* on sympathy. I suggest that only sympathy will awaken our imagination in such a way as to make us sufficiently receptive toward the kind of reflections able to develop and expand into the requisite enlarged dimension. Only with rational sympathy, that is, compassion, imagination and reason appropriately combined, can the demands of others be justly considered. Second, the process described by Arendt can lead to plurality-preserving-consensus only amongst those already established as equals. Since invisibles are not equals, it follows that the plurality Arendt is so keen to promote through enlarged mentality turns out to be very limited indeed. In fact, plurality here is as limited as it was in the classic Athenian *polis* on which so much of Arendt's political theory is based. In the Athenian *polis*, citizens did indeed meet and discuss matters publicly in order to reach consensus. Yet we know that political meetings in Athens excluded women, minors, merchants, tradesmen, foreign residents and slaves. Obviously, consensus based on small elites cannot possibly result in wide and inclusive plurality, since its results are generally too meagre to exhibit the kind of multiplicity of perspectives Arendt is so keen to promote. Yet, surprisingly, Arendt did not mind this particular lack of plurality and its possible translation into modern political discourse.

Arendt's evaluation of sympathetic affects and emotions in the public sphere

Let us probe more deeply into Arendt's evaluation of compassion to deepen our understanding of her position. She writes:

> Modern times and antiquity agree on one point: both regard compassion as something totally natural, as inescapable to man as, say, fear. It is therefore all the more striking that antiquity took a position wholly at odds with the great esteem for compassion of modern times. Because they so clearly recognised the affective nature of compassion, which can overcome us like fear without our being able to fend it off, the ancients regarded the most compassionate person as no more entitled to be called the best than the most fearful. Both emotions, because they are purely passive, make action impossible.
>
> (Arendt 1968: 14)

This requires careful unpacking. The claim that compassion (like fear) is 'something totally natural', was also held by Rousseau, who described pity as a natural disposition present in all humans. Arendt was no admirer of Rousseau. Not just because she regarded his influence on Robespierre and modern sentiment generally as disastrous, but also because his political theory of a unified general will runs counter to her advocacy of plurality. Yet the claim that compassion is as natural as fear should itself be queried, since lamentable lack or easy exhaustion of compassion is an often observed fact.

Another claim alleges that we are 'overcome' by compassion and fear and are unable to 'fend them off'. We do indeed tend to be overcome by compassion and fear simply because both are instant, instinctive, reactions to whatever is out there. But this does not entail being unable to fend them off. To suggest this of fear is extremely odd because Arendt, an ardent admirer of ancient Greek culture, was obviously familiar with the fact that their paradigm virtue, courage, is precisely the fending off of natural fear. It is also odd to suggest that compassion and fear are 'purely passive' and 'make action impossible', since both emotions typically issue in instant action: in flight, defence or attack with fear, and in unrestricted impulsive giving with compassion. So, fear and compassion are certainly not passive. However, Arendt disallows naturally occurring impulsive action to qualify as true action – more of this later.

While accepting that compassion and fear are affective states, we need not accept that this implies pure passivity or lack of control. Affects, as Nietzsche has shown convincingly, are highly active and open to influence not only by other affects, instincts and drives, but also by values, whether consciously or subconsciously held. As such they can be ruled and guided. Hence pity and compassion, like other emotional affects, need not be mere unreliable or arbitrary episodes over which we can exercise no control as Arendt describes them. On the contrary, sympathy, just like fear, can be influenced and disciplined and so can contribute to stable dispositions and sound judgements. This idea is, of course, not new – just think of Hume's moral philosophy.

Of great importance to our enquiry is also the subtle, quasi-Kantian, devaluation of the natural in Arendt's statement above and indeed in most of her work. Arendt was an admiring, though critical and selective, disciple of Kant, and her political theory reflects the Kantian opposition of nature's necessity with freedom. The claim that freedom excludes necessity is axiomatic to both. Accordingly, Kant's statement that nature is determined by necessity leads logically to the obligation to set aside our natural inclinations in order for us to be free and thus worthy of the dignity of the moral law. Similarly, Arendt argues that the necessities imposed on us by our biological and social natures, such as food, shelter and procreation, must be kept apart, must be hidden, in order for us to share in the glory of true action which is only possible in the political realm of freedom. The terminology is different, of course, as Arendt was neither a transcendental idealist nor rationalist. Yet she shares with Kant a certain, clearly discernible impatience and disdain for the insistent, often unwelcome and often embarrassing demands of our natural constitution. Thus both claim that the natural, including natural compassion and fear, obstructs freedom and hence true action or genuine morality. We can see, then, that fundamental to both Kant's and Arendt's theory is the disciplined transcendence of natural features and dispositions before a truly worthy human life can begin.

Concluding remarks

Clearly, pity and compassion can get things wrong. We all know from personal and public experience that pity can be helpful and beneficial as well as fickle, unreliable and lacking in impartiality. However, this instability is not specific to the sympathetic emotions. On the contrary, instability is a feature common to most emotions and affects. Yet, we would not consider banning fear because it can be unwarranted, or banning love because it can be misplaced, since the positive qualities of fear and love far outweigh their negative ones. The case is similar with pity and compassion. Their positive aspect of opening our eyes and minds to the condition and needs of others is far greater than, say, their possible lack of proportionality and measure.

It is an everyday fact that emotions and affects have to be managed. We usually do this with the aid of reason and, probably more frequently, with the help of other affects. Nietzsche, that shrewd observer of the competitive and agonistic interaction in our affective lives, issued the following advice: not repression or rejection of affects, instincts or drives, but to govern them into an ordered, hierarchical structure. Such structure, Nietzsche argued, results in a rich emergence of perspectives and responses to challenging situations, along with an enhanced capacity of individuals to find and fulfil their potential.

Naturally one cannot guarantee stable and well-balanced emotional dispositions to develop with certainty, since the development of, say, compassion is in natural competition with other and often opposing affects and thus will vary with persons and circumstances. But this is only to be expected and puts pity and compassion in line with other emotional dispositions operable in the political sphere, such as vanity, fear, desire for security or justice, or ambition for power and fame. These dispositions too have to be open to continuous checks and scrutiny by oneself and others in order to avoid dangerous imbalances – a process that is in any case very much part of healthy political discourse and thus supportive of Arendt's claim that agonistic engagement fosters dynamic plurality.

Arendt admits herself that the poor and marginalised will be invisible if pity and compassion do not bring them to view and thus to attention. But she dismisses this contribution of the sympathetic emotions without providing a viable alternative to replace their cognitive function – hence the 'invisibles' will remain invisible politically. There is, moreover, as we have seen, next to the cognitive function a uniquely strong and, so I suggest, non-replaceable normative function attached to compassion, since compassion's distinctive seeing is naturally linked to an almost irresistible impulse to attend and help. Obviously, compassion's initial and almost irresistible impulse to attend and help usually requires the addition of substantive practical and rational skills to provide and sustain help, particularly in the public domain. Nonetheless, we must not lose sight of the fact that only the sympathetic emotions generate and maintain that all-important and irreplaceable initial normative impulse.

If we follow Arendt's directive and ban pity and compassion from the political sphere, we will be bereft of these valuable cognitive and normative resources.[8]

Notes

1 Like Arendt, I too use 'pity' and 'compassion' interchangeably in this chapter. I also use sympathy for its wider application. While pity and compassion focus on severe and obvious suffering, sympathy can also 'see' anger, resentment, joy etc. – all of potential political relevance.

2 I am indebted to Michael Janover for this point.

3 *Dreigroschenoper*, Act II.

4 Such as *Die Heilige Johanna der Schlachthöfe* and *Der gute Mensch von Sezuan*.

5 For instance in *The Human Condition*, Section 10:

> [...] it is manifest that the moment a good work becomes known and public, it loses its specific character of goodness, of being done for nothing but goodness' sake. When goodness appears openly, it is no longer goodness, though it may still be useful as organised charity or an act of solidarity [...]. Goodness can exist only when it is not perceived, not even by its author; whoever sees himself performing a good work is no longer good [...]. Good works, because they must be forgotten instantly, can never become part of the world.

6 Arendt omits a line of the poem in the German edition of her essay: Piper Verlag, München, 1971, (one of many differences between those editions).

7 I am grateful to Christine Lopes for pointing this out.
8 I thank Michael Ure for helpful comments and am particularly indebted to Ken Gemes for valuable discussions.

Bibliography

Arendt, Hannah. (1958) *The Human Condition*. Chicago: University of Chicago Press.

Arendt, Hannah. (1963) *On Revolution*. London: Penguin Books.

Arendt, Hannah. (1968) *Men in Dark Times*. San Diego, London: Harcourt Brace & Company.

Arendt, Hannah. (1978) *The Life of the Mind*. San Diego, London: Haurcourt Brace & Company.

Arendt, Hannah. (2000) *The Portable Arendt*. Peter Baehr (ed.), New York: Penguin Books.

Arendt, Hannah. (2007) *The Jewish Writings*. Jerome Kohn & Ron H. Feldman (eds), New York: Schocken Books.

Bernauer, J. (ed.). (1987) *Amor Mundi. Explorations in the Faith and Thought of Hannah Arendt*. Dordrecht: Martinus Nijhoff.

Bernstein, R. (1996) *Hannah Arendt and the Jewish Question*. Cambridge: Polity.

Birmingham, Peg. (1995) *Hannah Arendt's Dismissal of the Ethical*, in 'Dissensus Communis, Between Ethics and Politics'. Ph. van Haute and P. Birmingham (eds), Kampen, The Netherlands: Kok Pharos.

Brunkhorst, Hauke. (2000) Equality and Elitism in Arendt, in Dana Villa (ed.), *The Cambridge Companion to Hannah Arendt*, Cambridge: Cambridge University Press.

Dish, Lisa Jane. (1994) *Hannah Arendt and the Limits of Philosophy*. Ithaca: Cornell University Press.

Kateb, G. (1984) *Hannah Arendt: Politics, Conscience, Evil*. New Jersey: Rowman & Allanheld.

Kateb, G. (1990) Arendt and Representative Democracy, in Reuben Garner (ed.) *The Realm of Humanitas, Responses to the Writings of Hannah Arendt*. New York: Peter Lang.

Villa, Dana. (1996) *Arendt and Heidegger. The Fate of the Political*. Princeton: Princeton University Press.

Villa, Dana (ed.). (2000) *The Cambridge Companion to Hannah Arendt*. Cambridge: Cambridge University Press.

Young-Bruehl, E. (1982) *Hannah Arendt. For Love of the World*. London: Yale University Press.

3

COMPASSION AS RISK

Lola Frost

If compassion involves a kind of 'co-suffering' with those who suffer, it follows that compassion can only be experienced singularly and 'in the flesh' (Arendt 1973: 85). In feeling the passion of compassion, not unlike feeling the passion of love, there is little distance between the sufferer and the co-sufferer and consequently, in the case of compassion, its risky, contagious, enfleshed proximity cannot operate politically in the 'real' world. Yet what I will explore in this chapter is how we might understand how compassion is exemplary of a risky set of practices associated with an agonistic and affective social imaginary and which operates in an indirect political and ethical way. This affective social imaginary is contained in, but not synonymous with nor antagonistic to, a rights-respecting liberal cosmopolitan imaginary. In this regard, we might understand that a cosmopolitan liberal imaginary is itself agonistically composed of ethicalities, which on the one hand rely on the distancing techniques of practical and purposive reason and on the other on those which are risky and performatively affective. This chapter is a consideration of this *agon*.

Both risky, agonistic and affective practices and risk-shy deliberative practices are part of what Ulrich Beck calls 'world risk society' in which settled and traditional norms have been overturned by the advent of globalisation and individualisation, in short by modernity (Beck 1999). This world risk society informs all participants in the new global world order and is a response to the unintended and risky consequences of modernisation. At one end of the spectrum world risk society is characterised as the risk-averse and purposive mapping and control of all risks (medical, social, political and financial) and is as such connected to technical decision-making processes and also to discourses which critique these technologies of control.[1] Furthermore, world risk society is also articulated through a cosmopolitan liberal imaginary whose risk-shy ethics and politics are informed by commitments to freedom, tolerance, diversity and human rights as a response to the risks posed by global modernity. And by extension, world risk society is also articulated through a culturally unspecific affective and agonistic imaginary, also at work in the liberal cosmopolitan order, and whose risky practices are both aesthetic and ethical.

Through a consideration of the nature of, and of various philosophical engagements with, compassion, this chapter explores some of the tensions in a liberal cosmopolitan imaginary whose ethicalities both entail risk-shy, rights respecting practices and risky, agonistic and affective practices. My argument starts with a brief consideration of the risks posed in aesthetic practices. Scott Lash's account of Risk Culture makes recourse to Kant's idea of reflexive or indeterminate judgement as the possibility of a certain kind of sublime risk, but one which makes possible a new kind of community based on 'chronic uncertainty, a continual questioning, an openness to innovation' (Lash 2000: 60). Suspicion about such affective, risky and agonistic indeterminacy and of the riskiness of passions in general lies at the heart of certain hegemonic values of the liberal and cosmopolitan project. I briefly explore this risk-shy suspicion of affects and emotions through a consideration of some of Immanuel Kant's, Hannah Arendt's and Mervyn Frost's engagements with the passions, whose riskiness poses a threat to liberal, rights-based values and norms.

In mobilising a defence of the ethical value of risky, agonistic and affective practices in a liberal and cosmopolitan order, this chapter engages Rosalyn Diprose's account of the risky ethics of Corporeal Generosity. Such a non-instrumental ethics and politics of embodied and affective inter-subjectivity informs the writings of Merleau-Ponty, Derrida and Levinas, whose ethics enable the framing of a general field of affective and agonistic practices available to an indirect and reflexive politics (Diprose 2002, *passim*). By way of conclusion I consider the tensions between purposive political projects and the indirect politics and ethics of agonistic affect through a discussion of charity and aid agencies, and of compassion and its role in the Truth and Reconciliation Commission in South Africa.

To begin, if we understand compassion as the ability to feel with the suffering or misfortune of others, we might also note that compassion differs from the feeling of sympathy, because unlike the operations of sympathy in which we sustain our understanding of the implications of such suffering and thereby sustain a balanced distance from those who suffer, when we give over to the feelings of compassion we not only feel for the suffering of others and understand its implications, we also feel overwhelmed by the risk that such feeling and understanding poses for us. Seen in this way, I suggest that compassion demands that we oscillate agonistically between an act of feeling for the suffering of others and an awareness of the emotional cost and ethical implications such solidarity poses to ourselves. It is through such an emotionally heightened and risky practice that we become ethically implicated in the suffering of others even as we struggle to overcome, resolve or even back off from this relation. Compassion thus conceived is a practice whose rules constitute us as both the beneficiaries of an act of solidarity and as co-sufferers or victims of the pain of feeling for the suffering of others. By extension then, compassion constructs us as participants in a non-instrumental inter-subjective, agonistic and affective practice whose riskiness is not unlike the risks posed by feelings of the sublime.

In his essay titled *Risk Culture* Scott Lash makes a case for a reflexive, disorienting and indeterminate discourse of aesthetic risk that is at odds with the hegemonic norms of a liberal and cosmopolitan order in which politics belongs to the world of rational action, purposive deliberation, the management of risk and the suppression of affect and indeterminacy (Lash 2000). In building his argument Lash explores the distinctions between Kant's notion of determinate judgements and indeterminate or aesthetic judgements, explored in the *The Critique of Judgement*. Lash argues that the aesthetic, indeterminate and reflexive experience of the sublime involves a type of agonistic risk that puts the unity of the subject under pressure. And following from this the sublime is not only an agonistic and affective practice that disperses and disorganises the relation between self and otherness, but also constitutes a new kind of community, one based on sects and cultural practices which 'deal with risk, with identity risks, with ecological risks, not so much through rational calculation or normative subsumption, but through symbolic practices and especially through symbolic innovation' (Lash 2000: 60). Following from this we might understand the sublime to be especially through the paradigmatic practice of aesthetic negativity insofar as its performative effects are not available to the positivity of reason or understanding, even as such aesthetic negativity is indirectly political, in part because it constitutes a community through disruptive practice, but also because it interrupts and destabilises any positivising notions of the self.

Such aesthetic and symbolic-based practices of risk, like compassion, which are predicated on a heightened, risky and agonistic affectivity, are seemingly at odds with the preservation of the rights-respecting and tolerant values of a liberal and cosmopolitan order, whose risk-shy ethicalities are often figured through the distancing protocols of practical reason. And by practical reason I refer to a discourse largely indebted to the ideas of Immanuel Kant in which:

> [...] practical reason is an *autonomous* source of normative principles, capable of motivating behaviour independently of ordinary desire and aversion. On this view it is the passions that lack intrinsic moral import, and the function of practical reason is to limit their motivational role by formulating normative principles binding all rational agents and founded in the operation of practical reason itself.
>
> (Audi 1995: 728)

Such practical reason clearly informs the principles of a liberal and cosmopolitan order committed to the rule of law, the delivery of justice, the preservation of human rights, and a respect for and tolerance of differences, but it also informs those theorists who are committed to a certain version of a cosmopolitan liberal order in which there is a general suspicion about the role of emotions in managing risk, the general disorderliness and possible instrumentalisation of the emotions, and which has at times an anxious, if respectful, appreciation for the disruptions of aesthetic negativity.

In line with this general suspicion of the passions and affects, a liberal and cosmopolitan imaginary remains indebted to Kant's understanding of compassion, which is conceived of as a contagious event which 'spreads naturally among human beings living near one another' (Kant 1996: 575) and through which the suffering of another overwhelms us to such an extent that our understanding and capacity to reason may be impaired or distorted. Compassion, seen in this way, renders us *unfree*. Sympathy, for Kant, by contrast does make us 'free' because it constitutes us as members of a community in which we 'share in others' feelings' (Kant 1996: 575) by understanding them. Seen from this perspective of practical reason, compassion may enable us to register the suffering of others, but effects no justice nor addresses the causes of such suffering because we are unable to sustain our capacity to understand and act reasonably insofar as we are overwhelmed or infected by the suffering of others. Indeed for Kant there is no benefit from feeling compassion, for its contagiousness only increases suffering in this world. For Kant then there is no direct duty to feel compassion even if there is 'an indirect duty to cultivate the compassionate natural (aesthetic) feelings in us, and to make use of them as so many means to sympathy based on moral principles' (Kant 1996: 575).

Hannah Arendt's extended meditation on compassion in her chapter 'The Social Question' in her book *On Revolution* is more sympathetic to the riskiness of compassion, but also proceeds from the assumption that the passions constitute a risk for the successful functioning of a political and liberal order. For Arendt, compassion understood as 'co-suffering' is a non-instrumental and unspeakable practice which 'is a sign of goodness' (Arendt 1973: 83), opposed to the loquacity and purposiveness of pity, which lacks intrinsic moral value. Yet for Arendt the difficulty of compassion is not because it is unworldly and cannot establish 'lasting institutions' (Arendt 1973: 86) but because it might be used instrumentally and perversely, which she argues was the case when both Robespierre and Rousseau mobilised an idea of compassion in the service of the construction of 'national will' and by extension contributed to 'the reign of terror' all of which contributed to the failure of the liberal project in the French Revolution. Arendt's ambivalence about compassion is that it might be used maliciously and in the service of a totalitarian politics in spite of its foundationally good, interpersonal and affective moral value.

That risk certainly exists, and emotions and passions have been instrumentally and perversely mobilised throughout history with disastrous results. With this in mind, Mervyn Frost's Constitutive Theory is a practice-based theory which takes agonistic affect seriously. For example, in *Tragedy and International Relations*, Frost outlines an agonistics in which individuals who are participants of different ethical practices are constituted by those practices, and are therefore in the impossible position of having to negotiate the opposing ethical demands of competing practices. 'At the heart of all tragedy is an ethical *agon* (the metaphor refers to duel or competition)' (Frost 2012: 26), famously exemplified in Sophocles' play *Antigone* in which the heroine of the same name is tragically caught between the ethical demands of both state and family. Similar tragic consequences may apply to any number of conflicting ethical situations, for example when the UN set up structures to provide humanitarian aid in Bosnia, these safe havens trapped people in locations which could be easily targeted by Serbian forces. Thus the ethical ambitions of the UN backfired tragically in unintended ways. Such tragic agonistic ethics for Frost 'reveals to us how we are constructed as actors in a whole range of different social practices, each with its own ethic' (Frost 2012: 33), an insight that reveals how agonistic ethical practices are central to our social existence.

Constitutive Theory approaches the negotiation of the challenges and risks posed by modernity in terms of two great global and anarchic practices which are ethically foundational for all members of world risk society. Frost identifies these two practices as global civil society (GCS) and the society of sovereign states (SOSS). The former is a social practice within which people 'hold status as civilians, the possessors of a set of fundamental first-generation human rights; in the latter they are constituted as citizens in sovereign states' (Frost 2009: 96). The foundational nature of these practices then presumes that as members of these anarchic practices we understand their ethical underpinnings, which commit us to the values of freedom, tolerance and diversity, even as such ethical practices are also the product of an *agon* in which we understand the necessity of delaying, repressing or deferring our individual needs, emotions and desires by recognising the interests and desires of others. We might of course ignore such an ethical agonistics, but in so doing, we would be undercutting our own ethical standing. These values are also central to the liberal cosmopolitan imaginary sketched above, an imaginary which is sceptical of all passions and of affects insofar as the irrationality, affectivity and misappropriation of emotion threaten the values of freedom, tolerance and diversity.

But do they? What if we understand that there are *certain* ethical passions, like compassion, which can be understood as an authoritative but non-purposive practice which not only 'confer(s) on us valued standing and create(s) for us values which can only be had through our participation' (Frost 2002: 46) but also 'constitutes us as actors with that standing we take to be foundational to who we think we are as human beings' (Frost 2002: 47)? Compassion is an ethical practice precisely because we are enjoined to not only consider the interests of the suffering other, but to share in their suffering.

Shifting the frame slightly, we might understand that good works and charity are also authoritative practices, but because they are deliberative or purposive practices[2] they are not caught up in the mobilisation of affective and non-instrumental agonistics. For example, charitable practices are oriented toward relieving the suffering of the poor, the derelict or wounded. Like compassion, which may be maliciously instrumentalised, good works and charity also suffer the risk of unintended consequences insofar as such practices might be caught in ethical, tragic and unforeseeable predicaments like the UN in Bosnia. However, the ethical values of both compassion and charity are not at odds with the ethics of what Frost identifies as the practice of global civil society in which we value and preserve one another's human rights. All of these ethical practices engage a constitutive and generous relation between ourselves and others. Yet I would suggest that goods works and charity, with their emotional distance, rather than the heightened agonistics of compassion, are more commonly associated with the liberal and cosmopolitan values of freedom, tolerance and diversity. And this association has a long history, one which I have briefly traced through Kant's fear of the contagiousness of compassion and endorsement of practical reason, a view re-articulated by Arendt, insofar as passions, like compassion, are understood to be politically risky because they are available to malicious misappropriation. To some extent the values of emotional detachment are re-iterated in Constitutive Theory, which sustains a hierarchy in which the dispassionate values of tolerance, contained in the GCS and SOSS, trump (but do not preclude) ethicalities predicated on affects and passions.

Philosophers like Merleau-Ponty, Levinas and Derrida have engaged an ethics of embodiment and affect, otherness, gifting and undecidability as a critique of the ethical values of a liberal and cosmopolitan imaginary which privilege the distancing and regulating techniques of the autonomous self, instrumental reason and purposive politics. From a different perspective, Rancière's engagement with what he calls the aesthetic regime, a regime in which artworks 'make thought strange to itself' (Rancière 2004), is informed by a Kantian aesthetics predicated on reflexive and indeterminate judgements. Following Rancière we might understand that such aesthetic performativity also operates politically as a critique of the discourse of reason and that art is one of the key fields in which an agonistic and affective imaginary is in play. As already noted, Scott Lash's essay *Risk Culture* is a critique of the liberal cosmopolitan presumptions of Ulrich Beck's view of world risk society, and theorises how non-rational and reflexive affects are made possible by sublime art. Extending this discussion beyond aesthetic practices and approaching compassion via the contours of an embodied, agonistic and affective social imaginary, I briefly turn to Rosalyn Diprose's engagement with Merleau-Ponty's inter-subjective corporeality; Derrida's (im)possibility of the gift and Levinas' 'interruption of autonomy and the imperialism it implies' (Diprose 2002: 141).

Diprose is concerned to understand social justice through corporeal affects and her discussion of Merleau-Ponty's idea of chiasmic exchanges, corporeal enfleshings and of the ambiguity of subject–object distinction are an opportunity to explore erotic generosity and its limits. If eroticism is figured as the 'body at risk' (Diprose 2002: 86), this is a body that is open to the other. Such corporeal openness and generosity for Merleau-Ponty operates at 'the heart of existence itself' (Diprose 2002: 89). Yet for Diprose, bodily encounters are also marked by both generosity and parsimony, norms which infect sensibility below conscious or purposive intention. Similarly, we might understand that the agonistic, corporeal inter-subjectivity of compassion also provokes norms which operate beyond cognition. Risky compassion makes equal demands on our generosity and parsimony, values which are socially embedded in us from childhood, and marked not only by our dispositions, but also by our experiences. Yet compassion is also marked out as social practice in which we are encouraged to veer toward the values of generosity rather than of parsimony. But such encouragement can never be formalised, for compassion, like eroticism, operates on the boundaries of an economy of 'the gift'. As such, compassion, eroticism and generosity are not calculable; they are not exchangeable commodities, nor can they be mobilised instrumentally or dutifully. They engage foundational human practices grounded in an ethics of openness to others.

In order to give some shape to the incalculable, non-instrumental, non-purposive, inter-subjective values of generosity that are central to an economy of 'the gift', Diprose considers Derrida's idea of the (im)possibility of the gift and of Levinas' commitments to alterity. According to Derrida:

> The gift is only possible if it goes unrecognized, if it is not commodified, if it is forgotten by the donor and donee so that the presence (the gift as (a) present and the presence of both the donor and the donee) is deferred.
>
> (Diprose 2002: 6)

Diprose expands on this insight by claiming that 'like difference, generosity describes the operation that both constitutes identity and difference and resists the full presence of meaning' so that as 'one's identity and social value are produced through the differentiation between the self and the other then the identity of the self is dispersed into the other' (Diprose 2002: 7). If such dissemination figures the ethical value of generosity, compassion both invites dispersal into the other, but also marks the riskiness that such un-bounding provokes.

A Levinasian ethics (like a Merleau-Pontian or Derridaen ethics) entails a 'sociality that would be open to the difference of the other without thought of return' (Diprose 2002: 127), namely a set of social norms not predicated on purposive or instrumental values and practices. Diprose considers how Levinas' ideas challenge the presuppositions of Western philosophy which privilege the rational, autonomous and individualised subject. For the Levinasian project puts alterity at the heart of thinking and scrambles the usual self/other, mind/body (sense) distinctions so that there is no possibility of rational thinking without sense and affect, nor can the autonomous and individualised self constitute himself without the other. In Levinasian terms, 'The other's otherness is what makes me feel and makes me think what I feel' (Diprose 2002: 137).

Following from these insights, we can understand that practices of compassion stage an agonistic, risky and affective crisis that is neither purposive nor instrumentally dutiful, and which engages/troubles the boundary between self and the other and also between corporeal generosity and parsimony. Understood in this way, compassion has no direct political role. Yet not only does it belong to a field of ethical, agonistic and affective practices that put pressure on the rational values of the individualised and autonomous subject privileged by a liberal and cosmopolitan imaginary, but it may also enable social and personal transformation.

For example, when Archbishop Tutu called upon the victims of apartheid to forgive their oppressors and torturers through the processes of the Truth and Reconciliation Commission, he was also calling upon both the perpetrators and victims of that violence, and indeed those South Africans witnessing this public event, to mobilise their compassion. The victims of apartheid were invited to confront those who they feared most, and to overcome this fear by stretching their tolerance, by listening to confessions of guilt and recounting tales of abuse and having this process recorded and endorsed in public. Arguably this agonistic, political, emotional and irrational process not only assisted the processes of national and racial transformation in the new South Africa, but also offered each of those victims a new form of agency, one in which they lost their status as victim and gained one of having the strength to forgive. The perpetrators of the violence of apartheid were obliged to come face to face with those they had brutalised; they had to face the truth of what had happened, possibly risk themselves sufficiently to feel compassion for those whom they had degraded and tortured. Such interpersonal transfers required the perpetrators to ask for forgiveness and for the victims to forgo an economy of resentment and take up the economy of the gift, a request that then extended to all South Africans to position themselves within an ethical crisis, namely to have compassion for those who suffered under apartheid, and in so doing defer or displace other more politically dangerous feelings like hate, revenge or disavowal. Such non-instrumental emotional feeling and identification might not be a permanent solution to the racial hatreds and inequalities that persist in South Africa today, but they do mark a certain political achievement. This achievement does not pertain to the purposive delivery of justice, but to the mobilisation of an inter-subjective, agonistic and affective ethicality.[3]

Conversely, aid agencies which send letters through the post asking us to send aid to victims of natural disasters (drought-stricken, at-risk communities in Africa for example) usually mobilise our feelings of sympathy, and perhaps pity. If we are able to overcome our parsimony, our generous responses usually result in unambiguous action: we do good works or dispense charity insofar as we send cheques, clothing and food, expect our governments to send doctors and emergency equipment to victims of disasters, demand human rights for those denied it, attempt to reduce our carbon footprint, develop aid programmes, refugee camps and educational links etc. In short, our feelings of sympathy for those who suffer are displaced into purposive thought and action. As individuals and groups of actors who produce and disseminate such good works we remain at a distance from the suffering we hope to alleviate. Such distance and displacement mark the successful functioning of the liberal and cosmopolitan world order, one with clear political and ethical benefits. In this scenario we are not troubled by the risky ethicality of compassion, and the relation between us and those who suffer is purposive, programmatic and interpersonally sterile.

What we have under discussion, then, are two ethical systems with contradictory commitments to risk. In the example of the aid agencies, our liberal, cosmopolitan and sympathetic and ethical responses are guided by the values of tolerance, justice, liberty and equality. This anarchic and ethical system requires the displacement, or deferral, of our individual and risky emotions into action, and in so doing, might address both the causes of, and solutions to, the suffering of others. Such political action is undoubtedly of inestimable value. But, arguably, the distancing techniques through which such ethicality is produced not only puts pressure on our ability to sustain an agonistic, affective and interpersonal ethical relation to one another, but might also produce a fiction in which we might misrecognise ourselves as autonomous, disembodied, rational and individualised. Whereas the mobilisation of a different ethical register, in which compassion and forgiveness remain intense and where affective, risky and agonistic practices have not been displaced into the smooth functioning of a liberal and cosmopolitan order but sustain, as in the Truth and Reconciliation Commission, a transformative power predicated on emotional risk, invite a different and inter-subjective ethical order. And following from this, one of the risks of compassion is that we might be changed by it. We might learn the values of generosity and the pitfalls of parsimony. We might learn to forgive those we have hated. Emotionally charged practices like these do not deliver quantifiable or immediate results, but they might render us ethically 'alive', accountable to and responsible for, one another.

Such a transformative and agonistic ethics has been traditionally associated with religion, and even if compassion is a core value of all the great world religions, it is of course available to all participants of world risk society, including participants in a liberal and cosmopolitan imaginary. The success of the Truth and Reconciliation Commission in South Africa is in no small measure attributable to the overarching influence of Christianity in the lives of many South Africans, for whom compassion and forgiveness are meaningful terms continuously re-circulated in daily religious practice.

The *agon* under consideration in this chapter has been whether we simply acknowledge a divide between on the one hand, a discourse of human rights committed to tolerance, freedom and diversity and its emotionally flat and regulatory stance toward the passions and on the other, an agonistic and affective imaginary whose ethical practices instantiate a non-purposive, non-instrumental and generous encounter between self and other, or is there some way of rethinking this impasse? This divide is sometimes rehearsed as the liberal cosmopolitan order predicated on norms and practices which privilege the rational, individualised, detached, male and western subject versus the embodied, often female, performative, affective inter-subjectivity of the other, putatively not contaminated by the norms and practices of the liberal cosmopolitan order. This division is present in this chapter, but not in the service of either the fiction that these two positions exist respectively inside and outside a liberal and cosmopolitan imaginary, for they both clearly operate within it, nor is this chapter written in the service of a binarist subaltern politics.

Furthermore, affective and agonistic ethical practices do not necessarily diminish the success of practical reason, and there is no absolute contradiction in being both a practitioner of the ethics of practical reason and a practitioner of ethicalities predicated on agonistic affect, as is compassion. Indeed many civilised people would sign up to both ethicalities. So why do ethical passions like compassion remain suspect and why is its contagiousness so feared in a cosmopolitan liberal order? Is compassion too 'difficult', or are we out of practice, lacking the skill, time and opportunity to practice agonistic inter-subjective risk? Is the current reappraisal of the value of emotions, like compassion, in International Relations Theory an acknowledgement that the emotional legacy of practical reason has resulted in something of an ethical void where we are only able to purposively encounter one another as reasonable rights holders? Against such an impasse, this chapter invites a reconsideration of the hierarchy which privileges hegemonic liberal cosmopolitan practices and norms predicated on the autonomous, purposive, rational and individualised subject, so that the agonistic, affective, risky and inter-subjective affects of certain ethically constitutive passions and affective practices, and certainly not all passions, practices or emotions, are included as core features of a liberal cosmopolitan ethics.

Such an inclusion would not mean the loss of our reason, rights and tolerance of differences. But, in the case of compassion, it would imply that we would need to do the difficult emotional work of trying to sustain our sense of ourselves against the risks entailed in feeling with the suffering of others. It would also require an understanding of the ethical and political benefits produced by this form of inter-subjective engagement. The difficulties of achieving such ethical benefits are perhaps detailed in all world religions including Christianity, but these difficult and non-instrumental benefits have also been articulated through a variety of secular theories, from psychoanalytic theories[4] to Continental philosophy, where, as previously detailed, Maurice Merleau-Ponty, Jacques Derrida and Immanuel Levinas have challenged the hegemony of the rational autonomous subject whose ethicality is constituted as a tolerant rights holder. Instead, such theorists consider the possibility of a non-purposive ethical inter-subjectivity, open to and responsible for the otherness of the other.

The agonistic ethics of inter-subjectivity are of course not only the preserve of theorists, but are embedded in all sorts of practices like faith, kindness, love, eroticism and democracy. Furthermore, the pervasive success of purposive practices and instrumental values in the Western world might mean that many people have no idea how to be compassionate or how to engage agonistic practices of aesthetic negativity, kindness or dialogue.[5] Where everyday agonistic, ethical and inter-subjective practices have been degraded, we are perhaps only able to approach the suffering of others through technologies of risk management where, for example, aid agencies take care of the suffering of others. As Claudia Aradau has argued, a similar ethical dereliction applies where governments, in regulating the risks of immigration, perversely put trafficked women and migrants at risk (Aradau 2004).

In conclusion, then, I hope to have made a case that in sustaining an experiential crisis that compassion demands of us, we give ourselves over to an agonistic and affective set of ethical values that invite our inter-subjective care and generosity. In privileging a discourse of inter-subjective, agonistic and affective ethicality I have taken the opportunity to challenge dispassionate and risk-shy values contained within a liberal cosmopolitan imaginary, values which foster suspicion of the passions in general and of compassion in particular. I have argued that compassion is a risky and enfleshed practice that mobilises heightened and agonistic emotion which can be mobilised in large public events, like the Truth and Reconciliation Commission in South Africa, but which may also be practiced in any situation when we encounter those who suffer. I have made a case that compassion needs to be distinguished from feelings of sympathy (or even pity) and differs from charity or good works, which might enable us to purposively and practically alleviate the suffering of others. Compassion is a practice that necessarily involves risk, or contagion, for those who open themselves up to feeling for the suffering of others and is neither a reasonable nor a dutiful emotion. Compassion has traditionally been associated with religion, but as I have tried to demonstrate here, a secular logic can also sketch its commitments to an ethics of agonistic and affective inter-subjectivity. These insights lead me to conclude that we should reconsider the role of risky agonistic and affective practices and passions, like compassion, in a liberal and cosmopolitan global order, and make distinctions between such ethical practices and passions and emotions in general. Furthermore, we might reconsider what is at stake in such practices and how we might learn to practice them more skilfully.

Notes

1 Exemplary of this type of critical security studies, Claudia Aradua, in her article *The Perverse Politics of Four-Letter Words: Pity and Risk in the Securitisation of Human Trafficking*, critiques both a 'politics of pity' and a 'politics of risk' because they can be 'appropriated within a securitising discourse where migrants, boat people, asylum-seekers or trafficked women are integrated in a continuum of danger' (Aradau 2004: 252).

2 In his chapter *IR Theory Today*, Chris Brown discusses Terry Nardin's account of the difference between purposive and authoritative practices in terms of the differences between NATO or WTO whose purposive ethical associations are built around 'a concrete project (collective defence or the expansion of trade) and assumes common purposes amongst its members, (and) … international society (which) is an all-inclusive category whose practices are authoritative because they do not involve common purposes or a concrete project' (Brown 2001: 55).

3 In her book *Narrating Political Reconciliation: South Africa's Truth and Reconciliation Commission* (2008), Claire Moon offers an account of the TRC and how its norms and practices shaped the reconciliation industry. Moon details how the TRC transformed competing moral and political claims into a legal discourse and how through ritual practices of confession victims and perpetrators of the violence of apartheid were able to heal the wounds of this violence through practices of forgiveness. However, for Moon, the TRC produced new conflicts and failed to address both questions of justice and reparation, and the social inequality on which the political violence of South Africa is based.

4 Adam Phillips and Barbara Taylor understand kindness, from a psychoanalytic perspective, 'as being in solidarity with human need, and with the very paradoxical sense of powerlessness and power that human need induces' (Phillips & Taylor 2010: 117).

5 In her PhD thesis titled *Seeing Otherwise: Renegotiating Religion and Democracy as Questions for Democracy*, Lovisa Bergdahl makes the case that the ethical impact of the ambivalent practice of dissenting/constituting dialogue in education may be distorted and disabled by desire for consensus in educational systems committed to the rational protocols of the liberal and cosmopolitan order (Bergdahl 2010).

References

Aradau, Claudia. 'The Perverse Politics of Four-Letter Words: Risk and Pity in the Securitisation of Human Trafficking'. *Millennium Journal of International Studies*, Vol. 33, No. 2. 2004.

Arendt, Hannah. *On Revolution*. Harmondsworth. Penguin Books. 1973.

Audi, Robert (ed.). *The Cambridge Dictionary of Philosophy*. Second Edition. Cambridge. Cambridge University Press, 1995.

Beck, Ulrich. *World Risk Society*. Cambridge. Polity Press. 1999.

Bergdahl, Lovisa. *Seeing Otherwise: Renegotiating Religion and Democracy as Questions for Education*. Stockholm. Produced by the Education Department, Stockholm University. 2010.

Brown, Chris. *Understanding International Relations*. Second Edition. Basingstoke and New York. Palgrave Press. 2001.

Diprose, Rosalyn. *Corporeal Generosity: On Giving with Nietzsche, Merleau-Ponty and Levinas*. Albany. State University of New York Press. 2002.

Frost, Mervyn. *Constituting Human Rights: Global Civil Society and the Society of Democratic States*. London. Routledge. 2002.

Frost, Mervyn. *Global Ethics: Anarchy, Freedom and International Relations*. Abingdon and New York. Routledge. 2009.

Frost, Mervyn. 'Tragedy, Ethics and International Relations', Chapter 2 in Erskine, Toni and Lebow, Ned (eds). *Tragedy and International Relations*. Basingstoke. Palgrave Macmillan. 2012.

Kant, Immanuel. *Practical Philosophy*. Trans. Mary J. Gregor. Paul Guyer and Allen Wood(eds). Cambridge. Cambridge University Press. 1996.

Lash, S. 'Risk Culture', Chapter 2 in Adam, Barbara, Beck, Ulrich and Van Loon, Joost (eds), *The Risk Society and Beyond: Critical Issues for Social Theory*. London. Sage Publications. 2000.

Moon, Claire. *Narrating Political Reconciliation: South Africa's Truth and Reconciliation Commission*. London. Lexington Books. 2008.

Phillips, Adam and Taylor, Barbara. *On Kindness*. London. Penguin Books. 2010.

Rancière, Jacques. *The Politics of Aesthetics*. Trans. Gabriel Rockhill. London. Continuum Books. 2004.

PART II
SOCIOLOGY OF COMPASSION

4

TOWARDS A SOCIOLOGY OF COMPASSION IN WORLD POLITICS

Andrew Linklater[1]

Primo Levi stated that the 'Good Samaritan ethic' had no place in Auschwitz. There was no point extending a helping hand to those who would be dead within weeks – no profit in befriending those without 'distinguished acquaintances' or 'extra rations' that could be traded in exchange for acts of assistance. In that 'Hobbesian' condition, the norm was to allow 'the drowned' to 'drift by on their way to death'. Levi stressed that such behaviour seems shocking from the standpoint of ordinary morality. He added that faith in the Ten Commandments did not entirely disappear from the minds of the prisoners, but the general ethos stressed the pointlessness of compassion (Levi 2001: 39). The main imperative was to look after oneself.

Difficult questions arise about the conditions under which compassion plays a significant role in shaping social life.[2] They invite the comment that we do not have a sociology of compassion or much understanding about how to create one. Important as they are, Levi's reflections deal with a world that most people have the good fortune never to encounter; they may not seem to shed much light on 'normal states of affairs'. But the writings of Peter Singer and others prompt the observation that some of the same indifference to the survival of others in the death camps exists in relations between the rich and poor in world society today. Far from applying only to the camps, Levi's comments draw attention to two important themes for the study of compassion in world politics. They invite discussion of the conditions under which compassion 'stands a chance' in human affairs; more specifically, they raise the question of whether compassion requires forms of reciprocity that exist when peoples' lives are closely woven together in relations of mutual dependence. If that is the case then compassion is likely to be absent where it is most needed.

The following argument is that Elias's explanation of 'the civilizing process' provides a useful vantage point for reflecting on those questions. The first task is to highlight those dimensions of Elias's discussion of the process of civilization that are most relevant for a sociology of compassion in world affairs. Particular attention will be paid to the focus on rising levels of interconnectedness and their effect on how people became attuned to each other and how they came to identify with one another 'irrespective of social origins'. They did so within 'survival units' such as kinship groups, clans, empires and states that were locked in forms of competition that prevented the further widening of the scope of identification to include other peoples. As a result, feelings of compassion were largely confined to members of the same survival unit.

R ealist themes in Elias's writings were qualified by the contention that recent advances in human interconnectedness have replicated several features of the early phase of European state-formation. Societies that are mutually dependent have come under pressure to take greater account of each other's interests and to restrain their actions lest they weaken global political arrangements that are critical for their security. In that way, many become more attuned to each other. But are they any more likely to display compassion in relations with peoples who have nothing to give in exchange for assistance? Elias argued that there has been only a small increase in the level of compassion between different societies, and especially in the relations between rich and poor. Echoes of Enlightenment reflections on levels of compassion in relations between European and non-European peoples are worth noting in this context. Specific writings on compassion and sympathy in that period warrant consideration because of their focus on the challenges that came into existence as peoples became entangled in longer webs of interconnectedness and co-dependence. Some general comments about the foundations of a sociology of compassion in world politics are offered in conclusion, including the issue of how far compassion for others depends on other emotions such as a sense of collective shame on the part of 'civilized' peoples who fail to come to the assistance of others.

The civilizing process

The Civilizing Process (Elias 2000) provided a study of how, between the fifteenth and twentieth centuries, Europeans came to pride themselves on their level of civilization. It offered an account of how they began to think of themselves as more civilized than their medieval forebears and more advanced than 'savage' peoples around them. The discussion emphasized the unplanned emergence of state monopoly powers that checked the violent tendencies of late medieval or early modern peoples. External restraints that facilitated the pacification of society permitted the creation of longer and deeper webs of social and economic interconnectedness. The lives of individuals became more tightly interwoven as a result.

Structural changes were accompanied by the gradual transformation of psychological dispositions and drives. Internal restraints and higher levels of self-monitoring became more important relative to external constraints and the fear of punishment by state authorities. Those tendencies were linked with increasing mutual dependence, as each individual became more reliant on the rest for the satisfaction of needs by performing specialist tasks within a more complex social division of labour. People became better attuned to one another and more inclined to identify with, and to be respectful towards, each other irrespective of their differences, a process encouraged by 'diminishing contrasts' between the main social strata. More accustomed to peaceful relations, they became more likely to be disturbed by open displays of cruelty and violence, and also less willing to encounter anything that reminded them of their 'animal side'. As part of the remoulding of drives and sensibilities, they began to find the public slaughter of animals distasteful (the abattoir hid the practice 'behind the scenes'); they came to think that the killing of animals in blood sports was barbaric; and, for the same reasons, they no longer found pleasure in witnessing the public execution or humiliation of criminals.

Elias analysed the social conditions that pushed people in that direction in an unplanned manner, the point being to deflate false beliefs that civilization was part of the 'nature' of Europeans, a secure condition that was bound to survive the pressures should new fears and insecurities arise. Individual members of stable, pacified societies were compelled by the forces that tied them together to place strict restraints on impulses to threaten others, or to use violence against them, or to offend them or humiliate them. Attitudes towards the slaughter of animals were revealing. 'Civilized' people did not bring such killing to an end, but moved the 'distasteful' from public view. In the same way, death and the dying were hidden behind the scenes. Such practices revealed that identification with other persons was highly uneven between members of the same society. 'Civilized' attitudes to the dying reflected the broader reality that the 'established' strata did not display much compassion for the 'outsiders' in society who, because of power disparities, had little to offer in return (Elias 2010).

Elias used the term 'functional democratization' to describe a key aspect of the civilizing process: the condition in which approximate equalities of power and high levels of mutual dependence created incentives to moderate behaviour and to cooperate to preserve laws and institutions that were essential for security and prosperity (Mennell 2007: see Chapter 12 for a discussion of the opposing tendencies in modern societies, namely increasing 'functional de-democratization' and a corresponding decline of social solidarity). The same imperatives did not exist in relations with outsiders, who lacked the collective power to press their claims as well as the capacity to disrupt social arrangements should their demands be ignored or rejected. But it would be erroneous to suppose that compassion was little more than an instrument for minimizing threats to order and civility. Civilized people came to think that certain forms of violence were incompatible with the moral values of advanced societies; civilized self-images led significant numbers to oppose 'barbaric' practices and to sympathize with the victims. Members of civilized communities were so constituted that compassion for the suffering became part of their habitus. As noted, compassion did not flow evenly across the social strata, embracing all people in the same web of sympathies; it had a structure that reflected the distribution of power, status and wealth. Even so, the belief that they were compassionate rather than cruel, alert to the needs of other people rather than dismissive of them, became an important dimension of the self-image of civilized peoples.

Insider–outsider dualisms

Behaviour that was typical of medieval communities – the tendency of established groups to openly flaunt their superiority in their relations with the members of the lower strata – came to be seen as shameful or embarrassing in modern societies. Social taboos inhibited public expressions of supposedly innate cultural or class superiority (Wouters 1998). But collective attitudes towards migrants, refugees and asylum seekers in many locales indicate that the level of emotional identification is less strong when 'the established' perceive others as competing for scarce employment, as placing unfair demands on public services or as being in some other way parasitical on the host society. In those cases, some groups are branded with an outsider status because they have come from another society and are thought to identify with an alien culture, and because they are regarded as a threat to social harmony and integration.

Such attitudes towards foreigners, which are often infected with racial, ethnic or cultural stereotypes, cannot be disentangled from ancient struggles for power and security between independent political communities. The latter have been critical for the formation of national consciousness, and for the evolution of feelings of collective pride that stem from past glories in war. Displays of ethnocentrism may generate feelings of shame and embarrassment amongst the members of 'more civilized' groups who believe that their collective identity and moral attachments demand compassion for refugees, asylum seekers and other vulnerable outsiders. In their eyes, 'civilized' commitments require more even compassion flows. The same people may think that the creation of 'multicultural' societies must go hand in hand with a planned transition to 'post-national' communities that break down former hostilities between national groups; they may have cosmopolitan identities that emphasize the importance of extending solidarity and compassion across borders to assist outsider groups and to address global problems such as climate change that threaten the more vulnerable members of humanity. Those who think in that way are (significant) minorities in their societies; for the majority, the sense of identification with the nation-state (the crucial 'survival unit' in most regions of the world) remains strong. The desire to preserve national autonomy and cohesion, and to advance collective interests, is powerful, particularly where levels of mutual dependence are high. Attitudes to compassion are encapsulated by the slogan that 'charity begins at home', and by limited support for foreign aid and humanitarian assistance.

In his reflections on civilizing processes, Elias (1996) emphasized the role of 'insider–outsider dualisms' and 'the duality of nation-states' normative codes'. Those expressions captured the view that the members of one society are inclined to tolerate acts of violence against other societies that are generally regarded as morally unacceptable in relations within their own group. Especially when societies are locked in struggles for power and security, inhibitions against harming outsiders have been weaker than the taboos against injuring insiders. Where anxieties about security and survival run high, civilized restraints on violent harm against outsiders can dissolve quickly (in relations within as well as in relations between communities). The so-called 'war on terror' provided a reminder of how some strata within 'civilized' societies may decide that the taboo against torture is a moral luxury that clashes with more fundamental responsibilities to protect vital interests. Under such circumstances, compassion for the victims of torture, or support for the human rights of perceived enemies, then takes a back seat. It is also significant that the relaxation of social restraints on torture did not go unchallenged, and that elite discourse attempted to justify violations of global standards by defending 'civilized torture'. The contention was that torture need not violate 'civilized' norms but can display civilized compassion for enemies when there is no lasting physical damage to victims (equivalent to the loss of a vital body organ) or when it is subject to judicial review in accordance with civilized attachments to constitutional checks on executive power (Linklater 2007a).

The moral contortions of civilized societies with respect to debates over torture raise larger questions about how far compassion influences foreign policy. One finds here evidence of an older tension between the principles that the members of a society value in their relations with each other and the maxims which they regard as appropriate for dealings with other political communities – and specifically, the tension between duties to fellow citizens and obligations to non-citizens as fellow human beings (Linklater 2007b). Elias (1996) cited Bergson's writings to indicate that modern societies often seem pulled between competing moral imperatives in the foreign policy domain. He frequently defended a parallel to the realist thesis that states find themselves in security dilemmas, or 'double-bind processes' as he called them, when describing the consequences of power struggles that may endure until humanity is finally brought under the dominion of a world state. In his more pessimistic observations, he argued that little has changed in the history of international relations other than the methods of killing and the number of people involved (Elias 2007b: 129). Other observations – including the comment that the spread of information about Nazi atrocities led to widespread feelings of shock and revulsion – indicated that the civilizing process has influenced social attitudes to international relations. Elias suggested a contrast with classical antiquity where genocide was largely taken for granted, and indeed examples of the lack of compassion in relations between independent political community groups at different points in human history are easily compiled.[3] But he did not conclude that modern societies were significantly more civilized than those of the ancient world or more advanced morally than their distant ancestors in allegedly 'primitive' societies. As noted earlier, he emphasized that civilized restraints on force can crumble rapidly when societies are engaged in violent struggles where their very survival appears to be at stake – in which case behaviour that is little different from that of the ancients can become permissible. The aerial bombardment of German cities during the Second World War, and the use of the atomic bomb against Hiroshima and Nagasaki, revealed how such restraints can break down. Later government actions in response to such 'decivilizing processes' suggested an element of regret or shame about such actions that seemed incompatible with civilized self-images, though allegedly demanded by 'military necessity' at the time.[4] Several studies of the period in question have shown that constraints on force rest on the fragile reed of reciprocity, on the recognition that if the customary restraints are set aside, others will respond in kind.

Global civilizing processes

It is useful to consider what the English School theory of international society can contribute to laying the foundations for a sociology of compassion in world politics. The nature of its contribution is suggested by Butterfield's comment that a society of states depends on a complex labour of promoting mutual understanding and empathy, a term that falls short of the idea of compassion but draws attention to potentials for, as well as constraints on, significant levels of attunement and the widening of the scope of emotional identification in world politics.[5] Such orientations towards outsiders have been facilitated, Wight (1977) argued, where societies feel that they belong to the same civilization and are keenly aware of their differences from outlying regions populated by 'barbarians' or 'savages'. Analyses of societies of states shed light on levels of civility and on civilizing processes in world politics – from which a better understanding of the role of compassion may emerge (and which may make it easier for scholars at some future point to ascertain and explain how far levels of compassion have risen and fallen during the evolution of the modern states-system).

The realist dimensions of Elias's thought obscured the element of civility in world politics that has been explored in, for example, English School analyses of how the rules of war and the art of diplomacy contribute to international order even in the absence of a higher monopoly of power that can place restraints on state conduct. One of the authors he cited with reference to changing codes of conduct within civilized societies – François de Callières – wrote a major work on diplomacy which argued that each ruling aristocracy possessed court officials who could urge restraint in foreign policy and consideration for the interests of others.[6] Callières' perspective is noteworthy because it emerged in a period when the traditional aristocratic quest for national glory and for success in warfare had become counterproductive. So strategically interdependent had societies become that it was necessary, for reasons of self-interest, to tame aggressive impulses and to look to the sections of the nobility that had not been coarsened by engagement in war to promote respect for mutual restraint across the societies of Europe. It was important to rely more heavily on courtiers who could be trusted not to give offence in other European capitals, who could establish a reputation for honesty rather than for deceitfulness, and who could promote shared interests in peaceful co-existence by employing diplomatic skills that had been refined in the courts (Callières 1983 [1716]: 83).

Increasing strategic (or economic) interconnectedness between societies does not automatically lead to greater compassion for distant strangers. Peoples do not necessarily relish greater dependence on outsiders even though the levels of mutual reliance may be approximately equal. They may fear or resent the loss of control over their affairs that is the consequence of pressures to make compromises with, and concessions to, others, particularly their traditional rivals. But as Callières (1983 [1716]: 139) argued, the ability to enter into the minds of others, at least to the extent of understanding their standpoints and appreciating their hopes and fears, is an essential skill if societies are to deal with a principal feature of rising levels of strategic interconnectedness which is the capacity to inflict more destructive forms of harm over larger areas. A similar theme underpins the belief that mutual restraint and empathy, significant detachment from immediate interests, as well as foresight about how actions may affect other peoples are crucial for the survival of a society of states. Empathy, as noted earlier, is not the same as sympathy or compassion. But the analysis of the conditions that increase the social importance of empathic skills is significant for understanding the circumstances under which compassionate dispositions towards outsiders may develop. Specifically, it is necessary to understand how far peoples are bound together in relations of mutual dependence, and how their respective civilizing processes and related constructions of outsiders influence potentials for increasing empathy and compassion in relations between groups that have been separate from, and frequently divided against, each other.

Enlightenment reflections on compassion

The social demand for higher levels of controls over violent tendencies and for greater detachment and foresight in relations with other people was an important dimension of the civilizing process within European states. There was an overall trend towards widening the scope of emotional identification between people whose lives had become more closely interwoven and who were mutually dependent. The development of those features of the civilizing process highlighted the gulf between domestic and international politics. But some parallels with earlier patterns of European state-formation emerged in the system of states, even in the absence of a higher monopoly of power. They occurred in the relations between societies that had shared interests in controlling the power to harm. There were few counterparts in the relations with societies that did not possess the same capacity to inflict such injuries. Some observations about the reasons for the differences follow in conjunction with summary reflections on how Enlightenment thinkers responded to the moral challenges that resulted from advances in global interconnectedness in the colonial era.

Some aspects of the civilizing of conduct that emerged in the European states-system in the early eighteenth century were notoriously missing from encounters with 'savage' inferiors. Similar patterns of mutual dependence did not exist in relations between colonizing and indigenous groups – or they did not survive the first phase of exploration and colonization when settlers often depended on local communities for the satisfaction of basic needs (Cell 1979). What stood in the way of harmonious co-existence was the lack of the elements of reciprocity that exercised a civilizing effect on relations between the European powers. To spare their armies unnecessary violence and to ensure the safe return of captured troops, each state had an interest in reciprocated demonstrations of self-restraint (Parker 2002: 161). The 'durability' of their relationships – the virtual certainty 'that they will meet again' – underpinned such civility (Parker 2002: 167). Few such incentives to tame the exercise of power existed in contacts with less powerful groups in the non-European world.

But the moral implications of participation in lengthening webs of interconnectedness could not be ignored, and ethical reflections on the principles that should govern interactions between Europe's 'establishment' and non-European 'outsiders' moved to the centre of social and political theory during the Enlightenment.[7] Especially noteworthy are Adam Smith's reflections on the dominant emotional attitudes towards those with whom there is no 'connexion'. The same person, Smith (1982 [1759]: 136–7) observed, who is unable to sleep at night because of the knowledge that a finger is to be amputated the following day, will rest undisturbed knowing that some disaster has ruined the lives of millions of strangers several thousand miles away. Melancholy may be experienced because of such reminders of the power of fortune in human affairs. Indeed, and here Smith (1982 [1759]: 140) revealed the influence of Stoicism on his thought, people should not see themselves as 'separate and detached' individuals but as citizens of the world who feel sorrow over the misfortunes of others. Although they were required to balance their obligations to those in their immediate locales with cosmopolitan attachments, the fact remained that distant suffering could largely be ignored because it did not unsettle the routines of everyday life.

Smith's remarks on the bounds of compassion formed part of a larger argument that justice rather than benevolence is critical for the smooth functioning of societies (Smith 1982 [1759]: 86). Principles of justice revolved around the duty not to injure others unnecessarily – that is, around a version of the harm principle that has been at the heart of the criminal law in liberal societies for several decades. As critics have argued, the harm principle foregrounds negative duties not to injure others as opposed to positive duties to assist them (for further discussion, see the first two chapters in Linklater 2011). Smith's writings confirm the interpretation. Compassionate behaviour, he argued, may please the victims of suffering, but there is no entitlement in liberal societies to demand selfless behaviour over and above what is essential for the 'harmony of society' (Smith 1982 [1759]: 29, 95). While it is legitimate to condemn those who injure others needlessly, it is inappropriate to condemn citizens for failing to display abundant generosity (Smith 1982 [1759]: 121). Compassion or 'fellow feeling' was properly directed towards those who had been treated unfairly by people who placed self-interest above respect for the principles of justice. But as others observed, a certain gradation of concern was evident in responses to the violations of those standards. Commenting on the gulf between traditional moralities and the ethical questions that emerged as social relations were stretched across space, Lord Kames stated that compliance with the Stoic conviction that 'the first law of Nature regarding society (is) abstaining from injuring others' existed in 'different degrees'. In short:

> [...] an injury done to a man himself, provokes resentment in its highest degree. An injury of the same kind done to a friend or relation, raises resentment in a lower degree, and the passion becomes gradually fainter, in proportion to the slightness of the connection.
>
> (cited in Reibman 1987: 63–4)

Smith in particular posed the question of how the gradient of concern could become more even and universal. His answer, which echoes the explanation offered by the analysis of the civilizing process, was that lengthening social chains created pressures to develop a new kind of conscience. They made it necessary to strive to assess actions as if from the outside – that is, from the standpoint of those located much further along the webs of interconnectedness. They created compulsions to divide the self into two halves, one looking beyond the focus on self-interest in an attempt to judge personal conduct from the standpoint of an 'impartial spectator' (Smith 1982 [1759]: 110ff.). Evaluating behaviour in that way was essential to check the temptation to think only about personal needs and aspirations – to counteract that disposition that is the 'fatal weakness of mankind' and 'the source of half the disorders of human life' (Smith 1982 [1759]: 158). Exercises in 'self-distancing' were especially important to ensure that justice – and appropriate compassionate feelings – governed relations with those with whom there was no real 'connexion'. The clear implication was that people do not need such imaginative devices to underpin such moral dispositions in their interaction with family members or friends (Smith 1982 [1759]: 83). But in the case of widening social relations that do not rest on such emotional connections, those involved must acquire what Elias and Foucault (Foucault 1979) later regarded as central features of Western modernity, namely highly reflexive forms of self-monitoring and self-restraint, which Elias in particular linked with very long-term changes in the objects of shame or embarrassment. The importance of that argument is illustrated by Smith's observation that respect for justice and displays of 'fellow feeling' in relations with distant strangers were bound up with individual compulsions to avoid 'inner disgrace', and with the fear that an 'indelible stain' would result from failures to heed the promptings of an inner conscience (Smith 1982 [1759]: 137–8).

It is well known that liberals such as Smith believed that the expansion of commercial society had the potential to promote the requisite changes in moral psychology. The 'invisible hand' of the market economy could facilitate the development of just relations at the international level as it had done within nation-states. The conviction was that the interweaving of interests could have the civilizing effect of encouraging people to restrain the pursuit of self-interest lest they endangered the larger social order on which their prosperity depended (Elias 2000; Smith 1982 [1759]: 86, 230). Similar themes have run through the dominant liberal approaches to international relations, as is evident from analyses of the obsolescence of force between the stable, industrial powers as well as parallel studies of the liberal peace and related accounts of security communities that focus not only on shared national interests in the peaceful settlement of disputes but also on promoting 'we feeling' between the members of different societies.

Confidence in the progressive effects of the globalization of commerce has often been criticized for neglecting how social inequalities affect gradations of compassion. The issue is that compassion is more likely to flow between people who feel alike and who believe they have a largely similar fate – the corollary being that it is less likely to be directed towards those who are regarded as occupying fundamentally different social circumstances. Its prospects are limited where groups are powerless to influence the interests of those who are in a position to help them – where, as Levi stressed, the dominant do not depend on the vulnerable for the satisfaction of their interests, and where the weak have nothing to offer in exchange for assistance. When Smith discussed the vital importance of sympathy in binding people together, he stressed that what was critical was the ability to imagine what others were suffering, a faculty that is most developed when it is easy for those concerned to envisage succumbing to a similar fate. But that empathy with others which is critical if compassionate feelings are to develop is less likely to emerge when the gulf between one's circumstances and the conditions faced by others is so vast that it is hard to imagine falling victim to a similar experience (Barry 1980). Efforts to arouse compassion must then appeal to something other than the possibility or probability of having to live with identical or comparable suffering.

Enlightenment thinkers addressed that issue when they maintained that the lack of reciprocal interconnectedness is no excuse for cruelty, and when they implied that another's inability to damage the interests of the powerful strata was no reason for ignoring the social restraints that were usually honoured in relations between the members of 'civilized' groups.[8] Many *philosophes* expressed disgust with the uncivilized behaviour of settlers at the remote, ungoverned colonial frontier. Their conduct was a function of their location beyond the reach of the state's power; it indicated that they had been released from the civilizing restraints on violence and sexuality that existed in their homelands. Condemnation of their behaviour implicitly rejected any supposition that the 'durability' of reciprocal social relations was essential for the existence of civilized restraints; the apparent conviction that such constraints could be placed to one side when dealing with 'social inferiors' that had nothing to trade for benefits received was firmly rejected.

Of particular significance is Raynal's condemnation of the brutality of European adventurers and the indifference of colonial administrators to the suffering of those who were under their absolute control. The 'evisceration of human sympathy' was illustrated by the peculiar contradictions of the global era. The very people who abhorred the cruelty of their ancestors, and who could be moved to tears by dramatic representations of distress in the metropolitan theatres, could listen to descriptions of the suffering of slaves 'coolly and without emotion'; it was as if 'the torments of a people to whom we owe our luxuries are never able to reach our hearts' (cited in Muthu 2003: 109).

Several other eighteenth-century thinkers believed that the 'discourse of sentiment' might yet inspire Europeans to remove 'the contradictions of history' by ending ingrained indifference to distant suffering (Pocock 2005: 237). The discourse might promote support for the conclusion that cruelty is, as de Montaigne (1965) argued, the worst thing that civilized people can do. Raynal highlighted the contradictions of civilized societies – on the one hand, the pretence of compassion, on the other, the absence of humanitarianism towards the powerless and vulnerable. For a rather different thinker, John Wesley, that tension was most pronounced in the co-existence of 'civilized' prohibitions on taking possession of stolen goods with widespread apathy towards profiting from the degraded labour of enslaved persons. In his *Thoughts Upon Slavery*, he asked the captains of slave ships with their obsession with gold:

> What is your heart made of? Is there no such principle as compassion there? Do you never feel another's pain? Have you no sympathy, no sense of human woe, no pity for the miserable? ... And is your conscience quite reconciled to this? ... Can you see, can you feel, no harm therein?
>
> (Wesley 1958–9 [1872]: 77–8)

As already noted, a critique of unjust enrichment was at the heart of an argument that compared benefitting from colonial slavery with profiting from the receipt of stolen goods. The person who paid for commodities without displaying any desire 'to know how they are come by' was 'a partaker with a thief and ... not a jot honester than him'. But unjust enrichment from slavery was the greater evil because it was 'procured by means nothing near so innocent as picking of pockets, house-breaking, or robbery upon the highway' (Wesley 1958–9 [1872]: 78).

It is clear that Enlightenment thinkers addressed one of the key issues raised by the globalization of social and economic relations which Elias (2000: 379) summarized in this way: 'with Western society as its starting point, a network of interdependence has developed which not only encompasses the oceans further than any other in the past, but extends to the furthest arable corners of vast inland regions'. Movement in that direction created the need for an 'attunement of human conduct over wider areas, and foresight over longer chains of action than ever before' (Elias 2000: 379). Attunement can take many forms including the focus on how to control or outmanoeuvre adversaries. But the effects of the compulsions of interdependence may not be confined to strategic calculations. The greater interweaving of societies can prepare the way for 'progressions' in thinking from 'the standpoint of the multiplicity of people'; it can encourage advances in 'detachment' from traditional national perspectives in the course of learning how to adapt to, and accommodate, the interests of others. The overall process that is set in motion in that way may replace stereotyped representations of outsiders with more realistic understandings of them as fellow humans who also want to prolong life as long as possible with the minimum of pain and suffering (De Swaan 1995; Kilminster 2007: 128).

It is impossible to predict whether global interconnectedness and mutual dependence will reach a point where compassion levels become comparable to those that are found in the more harmonious societies of the present day. Arguably, that is one of the central questions – if not *the* central question – in studies of the social consequences of globalization. As noted earlier, societies often face competing pressures, but one dynamic revolves around the often begrudging acceptance of the pragmatic need for taking the interests of outsiders into account. That may lead to respect between equals, and indeed to concern for the welfare of other peoples. The social forces that create incentives to develop the most elementary kinds of attunement may become a bridge to more positive emotions including compassionate versions of cosmopolitanism. Levels of self-restraint, empathy and sympathy that emerged under conditions of mutual dependence may serve as models for conducting relations with less powerful groups. They may seem to many to define how the civilized should behave in their relations with all peoples, irrespective of power differences and without prior strategic calculations about whether displays of empathy and compassion are dictated by self-interest. But clearly many obstacles stand in the way.

Whatever the future holds, it is worth emphasizing that with rising levels of interconnectedness, more and more people are tied together by their hands and feet, by invisible forces that none control, that they pull each other this way and that without any collective understanding of where they are – or should be – heading (Elias 2007b: 77). Each group may hope to promote its interests without major concessions to others. Strong imperatives encourage some to remain attached to particularistic moral codes as peoples become entangled in longer chains of interconnectedness. But that may not be a sensible long-term strategy for the peoples involved, or one that contributes to mastering the processes that have thrown them together. Social systems that aim to arrange the structures and patterns of interconnectedness to suit their own interests invariably breed opposition and create dangers of conflict. Short-term goals may distract them from adopting political strategies that can promote more amicable relations with others; fierce competition to satisfy immediate interests may lead peoples to conclude that they are not guilty of compromising 'civilized values' but behaving as they must in order to survive. Such orientations can obstruct the realization that compassion is an important element in learning how to live with others and, when conducting relations with the less powerful groups in those lengthening chains of interdependence, in understanding how to live with themselves.

Concluding comments

It is important now to draw together the themes of this chapter in order to suggest how a sociology of compassion in world politics can be developed. Five points are advanced in conclusion. The first is that compassion is a natural moral emotion, not in the sense of being innate, as Rousseau and others thought, but because it is a universal property of all social systems. Even the most war-like cultures must display some degree of compassion towards infants in order to survive. All societies can recognize compassionate traits in others; that is one reason for their mutual intelligibility and one explanation of why they are capable, in principle at least, of expanding the scope of moral concern to include outsiders. The question is, under what conditions do enlargements of sympathy take place in the relations between independent political communities?[9]

Second, the plain reality is that feelings of compassion have usually been focused on other (key) members of the appropriate 'survival unit'. That is not to suggest that compassion has been highly prized in all societies, or to imply that expectations that compassion will be displayed towards weaker members have been universal (see Konstan 2001 on the ancient world). In many warrior societies, compassion is regarded as a sign of effeminacy and weakness. Appeals to the victorious army to show pity or mercy may incur contempt.[10] The ways in which people are inter-connected within modern societies, their reciprocal influence on each other, the forms of attunement which they are expected to have in order to function in the larger society and the movement towards basic respect for other persons as equals have created the context in which compassion has become a more valued social norm. Compassion flows clearly remain highly uneven within those societies. As in the societies of the past, a great deal hinges on the power balances between social strata, on the prevalent 'established-outsider' distinctions, on how far groups are dependent on one another and are compelled to exhibit consideration and respect. Growing inequalities within social democracies and in the wider world are revealing in this respect. Sympathy for the members of many subordinate strata has declined now that the dominant groups depend less on them for the satisfaction of their interests (see Chapter 12 in Mennell 2007).

A third observation is that in international history, competition for power, security and esteem between survival units has left little scope for compassion. In violent conflicts, societies often conclude that compassion is a luxury they cannot afford. But contemporary levels of interconnectedness – strategic, economic and social, environmental and so forth – have created pressures to exercise greater restraint in foreign policy, to think from the standpoint of others, and to acquire a degree of detachment from group norms that can pave the way for greater accommodation and compromise in external relations. Such developments may be the bridge to a condition in which compassion plays a role that exceeds that found in earlier periods of international history, but they provide no guarantee of progress in that direction, either in the relations between states or in the relations between the dominant and the dependent in the global economic and social system. The social compulsions of mutual dependence may nevertheless promote degrees of empathy and understanding – and elements of 'we feeling' – from which more compassionate orientations can develop.

The penultimate comment is that the current phase of global interconnectedness, which is marked by the greater significance of economic and social as opposed to strategic ties, owes much to the emergence of highly pacified communities that have made significant advances in removing force from their external relations. The globalization of social and economic relations would not have reached contemporary levels otherwise. Resentment at some of the consequences – and fear for economic security, collective identities and so forth – is evident in the attitudes and actions of many whose lives have been profoundly influenced by advances in the global interweaving of everyday circumstances. Uncertainties about the future and the sense of the loss of autonomy and control are often pronounced amongst the members of vulnerable groups who have been exposed to the consequences of rapid and radical social change. Resentment at refugees who are perceived as a threat to employment or as a drain on resources is one manifestation. The groups in question do not share the sense of opportunity that is felt by those who expect to profit from expanding circuits of commercial exchange. The widening gulf between those social strata does not augur well for the politics of compassion.

The final point is that the societies that promoted interconnectedness in the colonial era were forced to address the moral issues that were raised by incorporating outsider groups in European-dominated economic and political arrangements. Many social movements found in their civilized self-images the reasons for challenging and abolishing unnecessary violence and cruelty, the humiliation of other peoples, and the ruthless exploitation of their labour and resources. Opposition to the Atlantic slave trade and chattel slavery was a striking example of the modern 'campaign of compassion' that is designed to make dominant groups conform with the 'civilized' standards of self-restraint that are central to their collective identity and sense of social superiority (Sznaider 2001). Equivalent displays of moral concern are evident in transnational movements that attempt to protect vulnerable groups across the world from 'predatory globalization' (Falk 1999). It is too early to state with confidence that old social loyalties will be reshaped by advances in compassion; it is impossible to predict a global civilizing process in which sympathy for the vulnerable becomes one of the dominant propelling principles of world politics. The greater danger for some is a 'decivilizing process' – a coarsening of sensibilities amongst those who fear the effects of the globalization of social relations or amongst corporate organizations that are involved in competitions for success and survival in which there is little consideration for the vulnerable. Mutual dependence between groups has often been critical for the development of realistic and empathetic understandings of other peoples; it has been the spur to widening the scope of emotional identification within many nation-states and, to a degree, in the relations between some of the most interconnected societies. Where such pressures do not exist, the issue is whether countervailing power can be exercised by understandings that 'civilized' forms of life are incomplete and unworthy, or a source of shame or guilt, without an accompanying global politics of care and compassion.

Notes

1 I am immensely grateful to the anonymous reviewer for insightful criticisms and comments on an earlier draft of this chapter.

2 As for the meaning of compassion, the discussion here follows the *Oxford English Dictionary* definition of 'suffering with another', a notion that allows for an enormous range of practices that cannot be considered here.

3 Thucydides provided numerous examples of mass killing in the war between Athens and Sparta (Pouncey 1980). Roman brutalities against cities such as Carthage and Corinth are well known. As a general rule, in the ancient and medieval worlds, the fate of a defeated city depended on the wishes of the victorious commander. A city that surrendered stood a better chance of mercy; one that held out risked being subjected to several hours or days of mass murder, rape and plunder. Reflections on Roman warfare have stressed that a reputation for mercy (*clementia*) was often regarded as the key to ensuring quick surrender, but requests for mercy often met with contempt and derision. Such comments support the observation that compassion was not highly valued in the ancient world (Konstan 2001).

4 Towards the end of the war, Churchill distanced himself from the policy of aerial bombardment. Official attitudes to Bomber Command revealed a similar desire to distance the larger society from the more unsavoury dimensions of British military action (see Taylor 2004 for further discussion).

5 To illustrate the difference between empathy and sympathy: the torturer may empathize with a victim in order to obtain an understanding of the other that can lead to an effective cocktail of violent and non-violent inducements to reveal valuable information, but there may be no trace of sympathy in the encounter.

6 Late in life, Callières was appointed to the court of Louis XIV, and became *secretaire du cabinet* at Versailles, an office that involved supplying the secretary of state for foreign affairs with memoranda on the issues of peace and war (Keens-Soper and Schweizer 1983).

7 There is no space to develop this point here, but it is important to emphasize that the analysis of the civilizing process was designed to show that the forms of mutual dependence transformed the moral psychology of those involved, and especially attitudes to the shameful and embarrassing. But such changes did not only affect the conduct of those who were tied together in relations of co-dependence; they also influenced the ways in which the dominant groups behaved towards the less powerful and public debates about appropriate forms of 'civilized' behaviour. Changing moral sensibilities emerged amidst the pressures that resulted from closer interdependence between groups that could harm each other's interests, but they possessed a degree of 'relative autonomy' that invited the people involved to reflect on their responsibilities towards weaker and more vulnerable groups. Enlightenment reflections on the relationship between the colonizers and the colonized are a revealing expression of how changes in moral outlook in the relations between the mutually dependent in European societies influenced orientations towards the less powerful. Crucial was the emphasis on how the civilized should behave in order to remain true to their collective identity and shared values.

8 Smith supported efforts to bridge the gulf between the moral standards that were observed in relations within and in relations between states. But he argued that the gulf would never be closed entirely while people identified strongly with particular communities. Opposing Machiavellianism, he lamented the fact that efforts to disadvantage other societies can result not in the 'dishonour' that would provide evidence of a civilized society but in social approval and applause (Smith 1982 [1759]: 154–5, 217).

9 As noted elsewhere, Simone Weil argued that certain forms of compassionate assistance are easy to explain (Linklater 2011: Chapter 6). Routine patterns of socialization equip most people in functioning social systems with the capacity to empathize and sympathize with others – which can explain sympathy for an outsider who is in danger of dying from drought. Weil did not maintain that help is inevitable and automatic (and the members of one society may have many reasons for not acting compassionately towards

the members of another society). But Weil's writings prompt the conjecture that there have been many instances of rescue in different eras and regions that have been motivated by nothing other than a desire to help a desperate stranger that stems from the civilized norms of the community to which the rescuer belongs. It is clear, however, that the sense of solidarity with strangers and compassion towards the vulnerable in other societies have not been the governing force in world politics.

10 There is no space to consider this point, but for philosophers such as Nietzsche, pity or compassion are not core moral values. A recurrent theme is that pity is inextricably linked with a sense of superiority over the victims of suffering, with wielding power over them, and with little concern for their interests, as the victims define them. During classical antiquity and the European Middle Ages, compassion for the suffering was not associated with any programme of large-scale reform with the aim of organizing society around egalitarian principles. Significantly, modern forms of compassion are often judged by the extent to which they are genuinely responsive to others' needs rather than self-serving, and also by the degree to which they are committed to changing social arrangements that are in some way causally responsible for the plight of the vulnerable. Suspicions that humanitarian politics will lead to new forms of power over the pitied indicate that compassionate social movements are judged by more demanding ethical standards than in the past – although, in reality, there is often little expectation that the relevant movements can deliver significant social change (for further discussion, see Sznaider 2001).

References

Barry, B. (1980) Review of 'L. S. Scheleff, The Bystander: Behavior, Law, Ethics', *Ethics*, 90 (4), 457–62.

Callières, F. de (1983) [1716] *The Art of Diplomacy*. Leicester: University of Leicester Press.

Cell, J. (1979) 'The Imperial Conscience', in P. Marsh (ed.) *The Conscience of the Victorian State*. Hassocks and Sussex: Harvester Press.

de Montaigne, M. (1965) 'Of Cruelty', in *Essays*. London: Dent.

De Swaan, A. (1995) 'Widening Circles of Identification: Emotional Concerns in Sociogenetic Perspective', *Theory, Culture and Society*, 12 (2), 25–39.

Elias, N. (1996) *The Germans: Power Struggles and the Development of Habitus in the Nineteenth and Twentieth Centuries*. Cambridge: Polity Press.

Elias, N. (2000) *The Civilizing Process: Sociogenetic and Psychogenetic Investigations*. Blackwell: Oxford.

Elias N. (2007a) *An Essay on Time*. Dublin: University College Dublin Press.

Elias N. (2007b) *Involvement and Detachment*. Dublin: University College Dublin Press.

Elias, N. (2010) *The Loneliness of the Dying and Humana Conditio*. Dublin: University College Dublin Press.

Falk, R. (1999) *Predatory Globalization: A Critique*. Cambridge: Polity Press.

Foucault, M. (1979) *Discipline and Punish: The Birth of the Prison*. Harmondsworth: Penguin.

Keens-Soper, H. M. A. and K. W. Schweizer (1983) 'The Life and Work of François de Callières' (Introduction), in F. de Callières (1983) [1716] *The Art of Diplomacy*. Leicester: University of Leicester Press.

Kilminster, R. (2007) *Norbert Elias: Post-Philosophical Sociology*. Abingdon: Routledge.

Konstan, D. (2001) *Pity Transformed*. London: Duckworth.

Levi, P. 'Primo Levi in Conversation', in M. Belpoliti and R. Gordon (eds) (2001) *The Voice of Memory. Primo Levi: Interviews 1961–1987*. Cambridge: Polity Press.

Linklater, A. (2007a) 'Torture and Civilization', *International Relations*, 22 (1), 119–30.

Linklater, A. (2007b) *Critical Theory and World Politics: Sovereignty, Citizenship and Humanity*. Abingdon: Routledge.

Linklater, A. (2011) *The Problem of Harm in World Politics: Theoretical Investigations*. Cambridge: Cambridge University Press.

Mennell, S. (2007) *The American Civilizing Process*. Cambridge: Polity Press.

Muthu, S. (2003) *Enlightenment Against Empire*. Princeton: Princeton University Press.

Parker, G. (2002) 'The Etiquette of Atrocity: The Laws of War in Early Modern Europe', in G. Parker, *Empire, War and Faith in Early Modern Europe*. London: Allen Lane.

Pocock, J. G. A. (2005) *Barbarism and Religion: Volume 4, Barbarians, Savages and Empires*. Cambridge: Cambridge University Press.

Pouncey, P. R. (1980) *The Necessities of War: A Study of Thucydides' Pessimism*. New York: Columbia University Press.

Reibman, J. E. (1987) 'Kames's *Historical Law Tract* and the Historiography of the Scottish Enlightenment', in J. J. Carter and J. H. Pittock (eds) *Aberdeen and the Enlightenment*. Aberdeen: Aberdeen University Press.

Smith. A. (1982) [1759] *The Theory of Moral Sentiments*. Indianapolis: Liberty Fund.

Sznaider, N. (2001) *The Compassionate Temperament: Care and Cruelty in Modern Society*. London: Rowman and Littlefield.

Taylor, F. (2004) *Dresden: Tuesday 13 February 1945*. London: Bloomsbury.

Wesley, J. (1958/1959) [1872] 'Thoughts upon Slavery', in *The Works of John Wesley*, Volume 11. Grand Rapids, Michigan: Zondervan Publishing House.

Wight, M. (1977) *Systems of States*, Leicester: University of Leicester Press.

Wouters, C. (1998) 'How Strange to Ourselves are Our Feelings of Superiority and Inferiority', *Theory, Culture and Society*, 15 (1) 131–50.

5

COSMOPOLITAN POLITICAL INSTITUTIONS

Terry Macdonald

Introduction: the motivational problem for cosmopolitan political institutions

Recent philosophical debates on the topics of global justice and political legitimacy have furnished us with a rich set of moral arguments in favour of an array of cosmopolitan political institutions.[1] Proposed institutions range from those with the relatively modest aim of protecting some basic set of human rights more effectively than existing international institutions now achieve (Beitz 2009; Goodhart 2005; Gould 2004), through to those with the more ambitious aim of democratising some or all of the political decision-making undertaken beyond the boundaries of states (Held 1995; Archibugi 2008; Macdonald 2008). Despite the philosophical appeal of many of the justifications advanced for these institutions, all still face the challenge of demonstrating how the right kind of support for them could be *motivated*, as a means of establishing and sustaining the institutions in actual political practice.[2] This motivational problem extends beyond the undeniable difficulties of securing and sustaining political agreement on the *moral justifiability* of particular cosmopolitan political institutions. Even to the extent that political agreement can be reached in support of these institutions at the level of principle, there remains the additional challenge of motivating political action in *compliance* with the moral demand to support such institutions, given the fact that actors' moral beliefs are not always well aligned with their own political interests and broader behavioural dispositions.

Compliance with the norms of morally justified institutions can be achieved by harnessing motivations of a range of different kinds.[3] There are many ways of conceptually differentiating motivational 'types'; in the International Relations (IR) literature, it is common to distinguish motivations for supporting institutions by bundling them into three key categories, linked respectively to coercion, self-interest and morality (Hurd 1999; Hurrell 2007).[4] In this chapter I am concerned specifically with developing our understanding of the role that can be played by certain motivations that fall within the third – nominally 'moral' – category. For these purposes I define the broad category of moral motivations for supporting institutional norms as those that in some sense *'track' the moral justifiability* of those norms;[5] though in this chapter I do not attempt to examine the whole motivational set, but only those subsets that have been identified as especially important for supporting political institutions, and which I will shortly elaborate.

While coercion and self-interest can make crucial contributions to motivating support for morally justified political institutions (Keohane & Nye 2001; Gauthier 1986), moral motivations are of special importance because it is often thought that these can generate particularly *stable* support for morally justified institutions, of a kind that can sustain institutions even as background distributions of power and configurations of interests among actors shift with changing political circumstances (Rawls 1996; Buchanan & Keohane 2006). Assuming that favourably aligned coercive powers and configurations of interests are insufficient to motivate the development and stable maintenance of cosmopolitan institutions (at least under present political conditions), harnessing support from moral motivations seems critical to the political prospects for cosmopolitan institutions.

Our understandings of how moral motivations function psychologically and sociologically, and the political strategies and mechanisms that could assist to harness them in support of cosmopolitan institutions, could be greatly enhanced by rigorous empirical study. But for this we first need robust theoretical models to clarify concepts and generate hypotheses, which can then serve as *frames* for such empirical research. Whereas 'Realist' and 'Institutionalist' IR scholars have drawn on rich traditions of political and economic theory to develop sophisticated theoretical conceptions and hypotheses concerning the character of coercion- and interest-based motivations and their functions in supporting institutions (Morgenthau 1948; Waltz 1959; Keohane & Nye 2001), theoretical models of moral motivations in IR remain at a more embryonic stage of development. While some important contributions have been made by scholars drawing on sociological theory, the conceptions of moral motivation deployed in this work are still relatively thin – invoking but not philosophically unpacking sociological notions such as 'internalised' norms (Wendt 1999) and moral 'belief' (Hurd 1999; Buchanan & Keohane 2006). Because of this theoretical 'thinness', these conceptions are not accompanied by clear models of the internal psychological structure of these motivational mechanisms, or the sociological mechanisms and preconditions for their role in supporting political institutions.

More sophisticated theoretical models of the role played by moral motivations in supporting political institutions have been developed within the political philosophy literature, of which two are of particular note. The first of these is John Rawls's model of moral motivations as linked to the development of 'conception-based desires' to comply with morally justified institutional principles (Rawls 1999; Rawls 1996); the second is Martha Nussbaum's account of the role played in political life by moral motivations linked to emotions of 'compassion' (Nussbaum 1996; Nussbaum, 2001). In this chapter I aim to make some progress in our understanding of how the motivational problem might be effectively tackled for cosmopolitan political institutions by critically examining and contrasting the contributions and limitations of these two mechanisms of moral motivation for political institutions, and extrapolating some theoretical lessons for the cosmopolitan institutional case.

I proceed with this task by examining in turn the conception-based and compassionate models of moral motivation, highlighting their distinct dynamics and limitations as motivational supports for just political institutions. I argue that conception-based moral motivations embody an institutional *status-quo bias*, and so will tend to be more effective at generating stability within established institutional structures than propelling the creation of new (cosmopolitan) ones. Compassionate motivations are not hindered by the same degree of directly institutional status-quo bias, so have greater potential to support the development of new institutions; but compassionate motivations are limited in turn by their *partiality* – in particular, their need to be anchored in reasonably thick social relationships that generate strong non-moral motives for sustaining an attentive focus on the predicaments and suffering of others. A significant practical implication of this is that cosmopolitans may advance their institutional cause most effectively by harnessing compassionate partiality to the cause of cosmopolitan institutional development through an incrementalist institution-building process, rather than demanding immediately – or holding out for the implementation of – some comprehensive cosmopolitan institutional blueprint.

'Conception-based' moral motivations for supporting cosmopolitan institutions, and the problem of status-quo bias

Arguably the most influential account of moral motivation in recent political debates is that developed by John Rawls as part of his theory of justice for fundamental social institutions (Rawls 1999). One of Rawls's many contributions to the normative theory of political institutions is his argument for the importance of taking account of a special set of motivational considerations in the justification of political institutions, as a means for ensuring that just political institutions can achieve 'stability'. By 'stability' in this context, Rawls means that:

> however institutions are changed, they still remain just or approximately so, as adjustments are made in view of new social circumstances. The inevitable deviations from justice are effectively corrected or held within tolerable bounds by forces within the system.
>
> (Rawls, 1999: 401)

Rawls recognises the importance of a range of motivations in creating the 'forces within the system' that can hold political institutions together stably within a wider social order – including, perhaps most crucially, the forces of individual self-interest as aligned with the goods that political institutions promote. But prominent among these motivational forces, he argues, are 'moral sentiments' which 'are necessary to insure that the basic structure is stable with respect to justic.' (Rawls 1999: 401). In particular, he emphasises the fundamental importance of one specific type of moral motivation: the 'sense of justice shared by the members of the community' (Rawls 1999: 401) that is regulated by the political institutions in question. In his earlier work he describes this motivation as 'the desire to do what is just'. (Rawls 1999: 399). In his later work he characterises such motivations as 'conception-dependent desires', (Rawls 1996: 83), which he describes 'by saying that the principles we desire to act from are seen as belonging to, and as helping to articulate, a certain … conception, or a political ideal'. (Rawls 1996: 84). The relevant moral 'conceptions' here are full systems of moral principles for regulating institutional schemes, in which 'all the subordinate ideals are finally understood and organized into a coherent system by suitably general principles' (Rawls 1999: 419).

To be clear about the scope of his motivational argument, Rawls does not present this moral desire 'to do what is just' as a unified or comprehensive model of moral motivation (that is, a model of all the various motivations that can in some sense 'track' justificatory moral reasons, as distinguished from those grounded in self-interest or coercion rather than moral justifications). Rawls highlights and acknowledges the role played by a wider set of moral motivations in supporting political institutions, with particular emphasis on motivational responsiveness to social authority, and solidarities based on associational ties – both of which aid in the development of conception-based moral motivations, though their psychological contents and sociological functions remain distinct from it. (Rawls, 1999: 405–13). But despite recognising that 'conception-dependent desires' embody only one kind of moral motivation within a wider set, Rawls places the greatest emphasis on them in his theory on the grounds that they are the most crucial in generating stable support for just political institutions.

The reason that conception-dependent desires can provide uniquely stable support for just institutions, on Rawls's account, is that they *respond directly to the content of just institutional norms* (that is, they consist in the desire to support just norms), rather than responding (as do motivations of other kinds, such as interest-based prudential motivations) to some set of contingent and non-institutional, or 'background', social facts. Whereas motivations to support just institutions grounded in desires of other kinds – to promote self-interest, win social approval, and so on – are susceptible to weakening as the background social circumstances shift and change, Rawls argues that: •

> [o]nce a morality of principles is accepted …… moral attitudes are no longer connected solely with the well-being and approval of particular individuals and groups, but are shaped by a conception of right chosen irrespective of those contingencies.
>
> (Rawls 1999: 416)

But here we must highlight the important qualifier in this argument: as Rawls acknowledges, conception-dependent desires can only function to support just institutions 'once a morality of principles is accepted'; yet acceptance of a morality of principles is not in any way 'natural' or innate, but must be politically cultivated.

According to Rawls, a 'morality of principles' must be politically developed and cultivated in two respects. First, the *content of the moral conceptions of justice*, the support for which these desires motivate, must be politically constructed in such a way that they fit with the concrete institutions that they are intended to regulate, and the wider beliefs and desires of the individuals who are required to endorse them. On this point, Rawls is clear that the content of the moral conceptions supported by 'conception-dependent desires' is not dictated by '[h]uman nature and its natural psychology'; rather, the conceptions that we choose must 'meet the practical needs of political life', which means that its ideals 'must be ones that people can understand and apply, and be sufficiently motivated to honor' in particular historical and social contexts (Rawls 1996: 87). Second, the process of individual moral development in which people cultivate the specific moral motivation that is *the desire to act in accordance with these principles* must be itself politically cultivated. On Rawls's account, this can be achieved in general through the experience of living within just institutions, and in particular through appropriate moral education delivered to individuals raised within them (Rawls 1996).

In sum, Rawls claims that the efficacy of 'conception-dependent desires' in supporting political institutions is dependent upon two political conditions being successfully met: the development of contextually responsive and politically acceptable moral conceptions of just institutional principles; and the development, within populations subject to institutional norms embodying these principles, of the desire to comply with them simply *because* they are just. If this is correct, what follows for the question of how (if at all) moral motivations of this kind could plausibly be harnessed by present-day cosmopolitans in support of their favoured cosmopolitan institutional projects?

At this stage of the discussion it is instructive to introduce a distinction between two kinds of 'support' that moral motivations may be able to offer to just political institutions, and which institutional designers and reformers may aim to cultivate. First, just institutions may benefit from support from moral motivations to sustain the *stability* of just institutions once they have been established and set into operation. As we have just seen, this is the kind of support that is the focus of Rawls's discussion of moral motivation in his theory of justice. Within an already-just political society, in which institutions are regulated by some unified conception of justice, and the populations required to comply with these institutional norms have been raised and morally educated within this institutional scheme, Rawls's account explains how conception-dependent desires can motivate support for these principles and the institutions that instantiate them, and in doing so strengthen institutional stability.

But there is a second way in which just institutions may sometimes require support from moral motivations – and that is to drive the political action required to *establish and consolidate* their operation in the first instance. Arguably, it is this second kind of support that is of greater relevance for present-day cosmopolitans: whereas only a few thin elements of just cosmopolitan institutions now exist in a condition to benefit from stabilizing support, many more unjust institutions exist in need of either significant reform, or complete substitution by some new – more just – cosmopolitan alternative.

How can conception-dependent desires motivate action to create new institutions in conformity with just principles, in reform of an unjust status quo? Rawls offers no general theoretical answer to this question. In place of a general theoretical answer, he offers only a sketchy historical narrative about how he takes it that the motivational problem was solved in the establishment of the modern liberal-democratic societies to which his theory of justice is intended to apply (Rawls 1996). According to this narrative, just institutions developed first with the support of the motivational force of individual actors' self-interests, mediated by the exercise of political power to the extent that these interests were conflicting. Subsequently, once the institutions had been in place for long enough that populations had gained experience of living within them, as well as suitable forms of developmental moral education, Rawls claims they were able to shift to a stage of stability grounded on support from an 'overlapping consensus' of moral conceptions favouring the institutions, and the motivational force of the conception-dependent desires directed towards compliance (Rawls 1996).

Whether or not this narrative is accurate as an account of how liberal-democratic societies developed stable support for their institutions as a matter of historical fact, it offers little to help answer the more general question of how moral motivations could assist in getting cosmopolitan institutions off the ground in the first place, in lieu of initially favourable alignments of power and interest. Without existing just cosmopolitan institutions available to instil an acceptable and workable content to individuals' moral conceptions, and to provide the kind of moral education required to develop the requisite 'conception-dependent desires' associated with these conceptions, it is not evident how conception-dependent desires to comply with the institutional principles associated with a cosmopolitan ideal of justice can be produced through a developmental process of the kind sketched here by Rawls. In other words, this type of moral motivation appears (from Rawls's account of it) to be hampered by a problem of *institutional status-quo bias* – favouring stability over pro-justice cosmopolitan reform.

We can conclude from this that although Rawls's account shows how conception-dependent desires are useful in motivating stable support for particular justified institutions once they have already been institutionally established, it doesn't supply grounds for expecting that motivations of this kind can support the development of new cosmopolitan institutions, through reform from a status quo that is now so remote from the structure prescribed by cosmopolitan moral ideals. We therefore need to consider what other kinds of moral motivations might be able to do this work instead. More specifically, I will consider next: what might moral motivations based on emotions of *compassion* be able to contribute to this problem?

Compassionate moral motivations for supporting cosmopolitan institutions, and the problem of partiality

As noted earlier, Rawls does not claim that the 'conception-dependent desires' at the centre of his account of institutional stability constitute the full set of moral motivations available to support political institutions. In addition to the specific moral motivations linked to relationships of authority and solidaristic association, noted above, he recognises an important role for a broader set of 'moral emotions' in the experience of moral commitment, as well as in the processes of moral development that produce and sustain the 'conception-dependent desires' to do what is just (Rawls 1999: 420–9). Among these moral emotions, Rawls describes 'a natural sympathy with other persons' (Rawls 1999: 402), which sounds very much like what is commonly thought of as the emotion of compassion. Although Rawls recognises some role for compassion-like emotions in psychological moral experience and development, what he does not consider systematically is the possibility that moral emotions such as compassion may play some *direct* role in supporting political institutions – at least somewhat *independent* from their function as psychological and developmental props for the 'conception-dependent desires' that stabilise institutional commitments. This is the possibility I want to consider here.

We can find more rigorous analysis of the emotion of compassion, and of the possibility that such emotions might be able to generate substantive forms of motivational support for just political institutions, in Martha Nussbaum's writings on the role of compassion in political life (Nussbaum 2001; Nussbaum 1996). Here I critically examine her account of compassion to help assess how such emotions might be able to perform some of the motivational functions that Rawls's 'conception-dependent desires' are seemingly ill-suited for: contributing support to the initial *creation* of cosmopolitan political institutions, via institutional construction and reform from an unjust status quo.

On Nussbaum's characterisation, compassion is 'a painful emotion directed at another person's misfortune or suffering' (Nussbaum 1996: 31), which is contingent upon 'a certain sort of thought about the well-being of others' (Nussbaum 1996: 28). More specifically, this 'certain sort of thought' entails three beliefs:

> (1) the belief that the suffering is serious rather than trivial; (2) the belief that the suffering was not caused primarily by the person's own culpable actions; and (3) the belief that the pitier's own possibilities are similar to those of the sufferer. Each of these seems to be necessary for the emotion, and they seem to be jointly sufficient.
>
> (Nussbaum 1996: 31)

The role that compassion can play in supporting just political institutions, on this account, is a product of its special function of directing the force of individuals' motivations away from concern with their own personal interests or good, and towards a concern with the interests or good of others.[6] As Nussbaum puts it, compassion serves as 'a central bridge between the individual and the community; it is ...... our species' way of hooking the interests of others to our own personal goods' (Nussbaum 1996: 28). Compassion can motivate support for political institutions, then, to the extent that the institutions in question are judged by the pitier(s) to be instrumentally effective tools for achieving compassionate purposes (the alleviation of suffering), in a given case – or in the overall set of cases that the institutions in question aim to regulate.

Unlike the motivations associated with 'conception-dependent desires', compassionate motivations have no firm allegiance to any particular moral ideal of justice, or to the specific institutional principles that are entailed within it – except, perhaps, for the relatively thin moral principles that must be invoked to make judgements about the grounds for moral 'culpability', and thereby about whether or not a person's suffering has been caused by their own culpable actions in a given instance. The motivation of compassion consists in a desire to alleviate the suffering of some set of persons, not a desire to comply with any particular principles. Compassion-based support for particular institutions and their regulative norms will generally, then, be *contingent* in character – subject to additional judgements about the relative efficacy of alternative institutional arrangements in given contexts, and open to the possibility of abandoning established institutional norms and creating new ones should it turn out that the relevant forms and instances of suffering can best be alleviated by doing so.

This detachment from the demands of specific moral conceptions and principles may very well diminish the role of compassion as a moral motivation capable of lending strong support to the *stability* of established institutional norms, except in the subordinate role of supporting the development of 'conception-dependent desires'. But in relation to the distinct political problem of how moral motivations can lend support to the *creation of new* just institutions when established institutions are unjust – as is the primary need confronted by present-day cosmopolitans – the potential contribution of compassion appears much greater. The focus of compassionate desire on suffering persons rather than on institutional principles permits that if existing institutions are unjust, and fostering or failing effectively to prevent the kind of suffering to which emotions of compassion are responsive, then a compassionate actor will be motivated to seek new and more effective institutional instruments. In simple terms we can say that compassion is freer than 'conception-dependent desire' from significant *institutional status-quo bias* with respect to the content and scope of the institutional principles that will attract support.[7] Given what we have already established about the present motivational problem for cosmopolitan institutions, this points to grounds for viewing compassion as a particularly important kind of moral motivation in relation to the cosmopolitan case.

While compassion's relative insusceptibility to the problem of institutional status-quo bias has favourable implications for its capacity to support the development of cosmopolitan institutions, however, its motivational capacities are limited in other ways. Perhaps most significantly, they are limited by a tendency towards partiality – that is, to an 'unbalanced and inconsistent' (Nussbaum 1996: 43) compassionate concern for the suffering of different individuals, in a way that does not reflect any rational assessment of the relative importance of the respective individuals' suffering, the culpability of their actions in producing it, or the degree of similarity of the pitier's possibilities to those of the various sufferers. As Nussbaum characterises this problem of partiality, compassion:

> binds us to our own immediate sphere of life, to what has affected us, to what we see before us or can easily imagine. This means … that it distorts the world: for it effaces the equal value and dignity of all human lives, their equal need for resources and for aid in time of suffering.
>
> (Nussbaum 1996: 43)

This partiality constraint on the capacity of compassion to deliver robust motivational support for compliance with just principles is widely noted, and I take it that it is real and significant; it is also of particular salience in the case of cosmopolitan institutions, where any tendencies towards partiality will undercut the universalist and general moral demands of cosmopolitan institutional principles. But in order to understand the significance and implications of this limitation for cosmopolitan institutional development, it is useful to ask two further questions: what are the psychological or sociological grounds of this partiality in the operation of compassion, and how might they be overcome?

One possibility, proposed by Nussbaum, is that this partiality in the operation of compassion can be compensated for by feeding it through the rationalizing instrument of a principle-based institutional scheme: 'compassion can and should inform the structure of public institutions themselves, so that we do not need in every case to rely on the perfect compassion of individual actors' (Nussbaum 1996: 56). But in presenting this solution Nussbaum does not clearly identify the *mechanism* by which institutionalisation can moderate the distortions partiality infuses through compassionate moral action; she gives no developmental account of how institutions can come to be structured in a way that reflects a more impartial or systematic form of compassion than the individuals who have created the institutions – and who act through them and instantiate their principles – already themselves possess. Although Rawls supplies a clear account of a mechanism by which institutions can overcome compassionate partiality via the force of conception-dependent desires *once a just institutional scheme (embodying impartial moral principles) has already been established*, as we have just seen this does not address the issue of what moral motivations can impel the creation of just institutions in the first place. Merely appealing to the impartial structures of institutions in general, without an accompanying account of how the principles applied through the institutions can *come to be* impartially compassionate, does not present an adequate solution to the problem.

The issue can be captured succinctly thus: when the task for which we require compassion is that of making institutions (impartially) just, we cannot perform this task by calling upon just institutions to make compassion impartial. To do so would be to appeal to a causal circularity, and to invite political failure. This predicament prompts us to ask, then: are there any alternative strategies for harnessing compassion to the service of cosmopolitan institutional development, which can work effectively *despite* compassion's persistent partiality?

Harnessing compassionate partiality in support of cosmopolitan political institutions

One possible means of counteracting the problems caused by partiality in the operation of compassion, without denying the intractability of partiality itself, has been philosophically articulated by Richard Rorty (Rorty 1993). Rorty locates the source of partiality in contingent limitations in the scope of human imagination and identification – in which suffering others are not imagined and identified with as 'like us' in the ways necessary to trigger the motivating force of moral emotion. Rorty further proposes a corresponding political strategy through which this partiality can be overcome: *sentimental story-telling* undertaken on a cosmopolitan scale. Through this story-telling, the suffering of geographically and institutionally distant others is to be rendered vivid for political audiences, and drawn inside the scope of their collective imaginations and identities, thus bringing them into the kind of intimate psychological proximity with others that can trigger their compassionate emotion and subsequent action.

There is much merit both in Rorty's view of the psychological roots of compassionate partiality (as lodged in the limits of imagination and identification), and in the political strategy of sentimental story-telling that is derived from it. This is reflected in the wide application of such a strategy by many international non-governmental organisations (NGOs) working to promote, broadly speaking, 'cosmopolitan' humanitarian and human rights agendas. The advocacy materials disseminated by well-known NGOs such as Amnesty International (AI) and World Vision (WV), for example, have achieved great political and fund-raising successes through the use of compelling narratives woven around individual cases of human suffering (individual victims of human rights violations in the case of AI, and individual children in poverty, in the case of WV) as motivational hooks for harnessing compassionate support from their political audiences.[8]

But both this model of the sources of compassionate partiality, and the political strategies associated with it, have some serious limitations. To begin with the limitations of the political strategies: although forms of political advocacy based on this kind of sentimental story-telling can be highly effective to the extent that audiences can be engaged to listen to and remain attentive to the suffering depicted in the stories, audience attention can be fickle and inconstant, and often very hard to sustain over time (see Coicaud & Bell 2007 for case-studies and analysis of some such difficulties facing International NGOs). One reason for this is that the emotion of compassion involves the experience of sympathetic *pain*, and as such, over-indulgence in it can tend to deplete psychological resources and ultimately detract from the psychological well-being of the pitier. This problem is associated with a psychological phenomenon that has been given the label of 'compassion-fatigue' – a phenomenon noted within caring professions as well as among the audiences and prospective political supporters of cosmopolitan causes at the level of international politics (Moeller 1999). Because of the pain it involves for pitier as well as sufferer, compassion tends to induce not only the behavioural inclination to offer assistance, but also sometimes (more perversely) the inclination to turn away from the painful spectacle, and divert the gaze to less distressing sights. What follows from this is that while compassion can be effective at fostering care, it is not always so effective at fostering commitment; compassion can impel those who witness suffering to respond with moral concern, but it cannot in itself compel them to stick around to watch.

What is needed to facilitate the motivational functions of compassion, then, is not mere story-telling, but also some motivation (beyond the force of compassion itself) working to keep the attention of political actors consistently focused on the suffering of others, and to prevent them simply from turning away when the encounter becomes emotionally uncomfortable. To achieve this, the prospective pitier and the sufferer in need of assistance or care must be embedded in pre-existing social relationships of a kind that necessitate persistent *engagement* between the parties (involving both visibility and attentiveness), and from which they cannot readily extricate themselves. The social relationships that can supply such engagement will be of various kinds, but the most important of these will be: relationships of mutual care within families, friendships and (sometimes) local communities; and materially cooperative relationships aimed at mutually beneficial production and distribution of social goods.[9] Notice that I do not claim that all forms of social relationship will play important roles in satisfying the social preconditions for compassion; social relationships grounded in more abstract and communicative engagement (such as those based on intellectual or cultural exchange, or more spontaneous and transient social intimacies) will be less effective at anchoring the operation of compassionate emotion, insofar as these need not foster the visibility or focus on others' suffering that is crucial for the operation of compassion.

If the moral motivation of compassion is to operate robustly and reliably, then, it must hitch a ride, so to speak, on the motivational forces underpinning the establishment of the more materially grounded social relationships of reciprocal care and mutual interest within the global social order. In more general terms, we can say that the sources of partiality in the operation of compassion are not only psychological but also sociological. Partiality is due not only to the limited scope of sympathetic imagination, but also to the limited scope of concrete social relations that can motivationally sustain focus and attention on particular others, and these others' experiences of suffering.

This provisional understanding of the sociological dimension of compassionate partiality provides a basis, then, for reflection on the kinds of political strategies that might be effective in harnessing compassion in service of cosmopolitan institutional development. The most basic prescriptive corollary of this theoretical account of compassion is that cosmopolitans should work to hitch emerging institutions, and broader processes of institutional development, to the established social infrastructures of existing material social relationships – since it is here that the emotions of compassion capable of motivating support for new cosmopolitan institutions will be most likely to take anchor. This entails a general political strategy of working to build new institutions, better aligned with cosmopolitan principles, in an incremental fashion – beginning from inside existing social relationships and working out, rather than trying to impose a comprehensive cosmopolitan institutional scheme in some more top-down fashion.

This strategic recommendation will not come as news for any of the global justice advocates and activists who are already doing important work based on precisely this strategic template; the strategies favoured by my arguments here are those that many global justice activists working in the non-governmental sphere already routinely apply. One example of such a strategy can be found in the field of human rights promotion – an important institutional concern for cosmopolitans. Whereas 'top-down' or 'comprehensive' strategic approaches to human rights promotion would recommend placing focus on the status of human rights norms within the most high-level and fundamental institutions of the international system (aiming to incorporate human rights standards as constitutional norms within the international legal order), 'incrementalist' approaches instead target campaigns of institutional reform at particular companies, or within particular trade 'supply chain' networks or productive economic sectors (for detailed case-studies of such activist work, see Macdonald & Marshall 2010). Within these established social relationships it is easier to harness the motivational force of compassion (on the part of consumers, corporate shareholders, local governments and so on), and in doing so to gain political leverage for reformist campaigns that can subsequently be extended outwards – to wider sectors and international regulatory regimes – gathering moral motivation and political momentum as this process unfolds. But although the political strategies recommended on the basis of my theoretical analysis are not new, my arguments nonetheless contribute theoretical tools for understanding *why* these strategies work and are important, which may help both to refine strategies, and to increase momentum in the push along this strategic path.

Conclusions

My argument in this chapter has been developed in several stages, which can be summarised here briefly in conclusion. Motivations based on Rawlsian 'conception-dependent desires' can be effective at achieving stability within already-established political institutions, but not at motivating development of new political institutions based on non-institutionalised (or weakly institutionalised) moral conceptions, such as those of cosmopolitanism. Compassion appears to have greater potential to motivate support for new institutional development, but will operate most strongly and robustly when it is grounded in certain kinds of material social relationships, which provide non-moral motivations for participants to remain engaged with, and attentive to, the predicaments and painful experiences of others. Compassion can therefore most effectively be harnessed in support of cosmopolitan institutions through forms of strategic political action that embrace and work within the constraints of this socially grounded partiality, via the development of bottom-up and incremental institutional reforms.

One final and more general lesson we can draw from this analysis about the role of compassion in political life is that it would be mistaken to regard compassion as a wholly 'natural' moral emotion that can be expected to motivate remedial moral action through mere exposure to the (morally undeserved) suffering of others. Regarding compassion as a natural emotional experience would encourage the assumption that there are no *social preconditions* for its effective operation, to which political institutional-builders have both reason and opportunity to attend. This in turn would encourage the expectation that it should be possible to motivate individuals and political communities to support just institutions through some combination of principle-based moralising and sentimental story-telling – and that when these strategies fail there is nothing more to do than to condemn the moral failures of the individuals and groups involved.

If, instead, we accept the view I have presented here – that compassion in fact has some important social preconditions for its robust emotional functioning – then we can begin to see the motivational failures stymieing cosmopolitan institutional development as warranting a different kind of response. Instead of viewing present motivational failures as matters inviting sanctimonious judgement, and/or sceptical resignation to an unjust institutional status-quo, we can begin to engage with the motivational problem more as a challenge for active projects of strategic political advocacy and developmental institutional design. And since these strategies and designs are tasks over which cosmopolitans themselves can exercise a good deal of control, and on which a better job can in principle be done, this provides grounds for some tentative optimism about the prospects for successful development – over time – of cosmopolitan political institutions.

Notes

1 By 'cosmopolitan political institutions', I mean here to denote all institutions that: (a) have functions or effects that are characteristically 'political' in some established sense, such as exercising coercion (Valentini 2012), or exercising public political power (Hurrell & Macdonald 2012); and (b) are regulated by principles that are justifiable on some plausible account of cosmopolitan morality, where cosmopolitan morality is characterised, following Pogge & Bleisch (2002: 169), by commitments to individualism, universality and generality in the formulation of moral principles.

2 The general motivational problem for political institutions hinges on the assumption that institutions are constituted by multiple social actors linked together through norm-governed behavioural structures, and that such institutions therefore depend, for their establishment and stable operation, on the actors subject to their norms being sufficiently motivated to *comply*.

3 The notion of 'compliance' with cosmopolitan institutional norms could be specified in different ways, varying across three dimensions: first, the *range of actions* in support of

cosmopolitan political institutions with which compliance is sought; second, the *set of actors* whose compliant action is required; and third, the *extent* of compliant action (across the range of relevant actions and agents) that is regarded as sufficient to say that 'compliance' overall has been achieved. Here I largely bracket these questions, making only the general pragmatic assumption that compliance entails *whatever range of actions* (to create initially as well as to sustain institutions), by *whichever set of actors* (individual or collective, state or non-state) and with *whatever level of compliance* (between full compliance and full non-compliance) is required to achieve the effective and stable functioning of the particular cosmopolitan political institutions in question.

4 Hurd (1999) calls the third motivational category 'legitimacy', though I avoid using that term here as it is attributed diverse meanings across philosophical and sociological literatures, and so may confuse rather than clarify the questions at issue.

5 Here I bracket the question of how precisely the relationship between moral motivations and moral justifications should be specified, although I acknowledge that we would need to invoke some substantive philosophical account of this relationship to explain the precise sense in which motivations can be said to 'track' justifications, and in doing so count as 'moral' motivations. For important philosophical discussions of this question see Korsgaard 1996; Williams 1981 ('Internal and external reasons'); and Parfit 2011. This philosophical question can be bracketed for the present purposes because although this chapter is concerned in some sense with the character of moral motivations, it is the interface between moral motivations and political institutions, rather than the interface between moral motivations and moral justifications, that is the topic for analysis here.

6 Here I assume that any account of morality in general, or justice in particular, must incorporate some such concern with others, and that as such motivations of compassion orient a person towards some generic moral goals; this is the reason we can talk of compassion as a kind of 'moral' motivation. For the present purposes I do not need to commit myself to a more fine-grained account of the precise type of orientation towards others that morality consists in.

7 I qualify this statement with 'significant' since there will be some degree of status-quo bias, reflecting the extent to which status quo institutional norms shape the relatively thin moral principles that must be invoked to make judgements about the grounds for moral 'culpability' (remembering that one of the judgements underlying emotions of compassion concerns whether or not a person's suffering was caused by their own culpable actions in a given instance).

8 See *http://www.amnesty.org*, and *http://www.worldvision.org*, both accessed 31/08/2012.

9 Each of these relational types generates its own distinctive forms of moral motivation in addition to compassion – linked to moral solidarities of love and solidarity, and a sense of fairness or reciprocity, respectively. Here though I am not concerned with these social relationships as grounds for those other moral motives, but only with their role in providing anchors for the operation of emotions of compassion.

References

Archibugi, D. 2008. *The Global Commonwealth of Citizens: Towards Cosmopolitan Democracy*, Princeton, Princeton University Press.

Beitz, C. 2009. *The Idea of Human Rights*, Oxford, Oxford University Press.

Buchanan, A., & R. O. Keohane 2006. The Legitimacy of Global Governance Institutions. *Ethics & International Affairs*, 20, 405–37.

Coicaud, J., & D. Bell (eds) 2007. *Ethics in Action: The Ethical Challenges of International Human Rights Nongovernmental Organizations*, Cambridge, Cambridge University Press.

Gauthier, D. 1986. *Morals by Agreement*, Oxford, Oxford University Press.

Goodhart, M. 2005. *Democracy as Human Rights: Freedom and Equality in the Age of Globalization*, Abingdon, Routledge.

Gould, C. 2004. *Globalizing Democracy and Human Rights*, Cambridge, Cambridge University Press.

Held, D. 1995. *Democracy and the Global Order: From the Modern State to Cosmopolitan Governance*, Cambridge, Polity Press.

Hurd, I. 1999. Legitimacy and Authority in International Politics. *International Organization*, 53, 379–408.

Hurrell, A. 2007. *On Global Order: Power, Values, and the Constitution of International Society*, Oxford, Oxford University Press.

Hurrell, A., & T. Macdonald 2012. Global Public Power: The Subject of Principles of Global Political Legitimacy. *Critical Review of International Social and Political Philosophy*, 15: 553–71.

Keohane, R. O., & J. Nye 2001. *Power and Interdependence*, New York, Longman.

Korsgaard, C. M. 1996. *The Sources of Normativity*, Cambridge, Cambridge University Press.

Macdonald, K., & S. Marshall (eds) 2010 *Fair Trade, Corporate Accountability and Beyond: Experiments in Globalizing Justice*, London, Ashgate.

Macdonald, T. 2008. *Global Stakeholder Democracy: Power and Representation Beyond Liberal States*, New York, Oxford University Press.

Moeller, S. D. 1999. *Compassion Fatigue: How the Media Sell Disease, Famine, War and Death*, New York, Routledge.

Morgenthau, H. 1948. *Politics Among Nations: The Struggle for Power and Peace*, New York, Alfred A Knopf.

Nussbaum, M. 1996. Compassion: The Basic Social Emotion. *Social Philosophy and Policy*, 13(1): 27–58.

Nussbaum, M. 2001. *Upheavals of Thought: The Intelligence of Emotions*, Cambridge, Cambridge University Press.

Parfit, D. 2011. *On What Matters, Volume 2*, Oxford, Oxford University Press.

Pogge, T. W., & B. Bleisch 2002. World Poverty and Human Rights: Cosmopolitan Responsibilities and Reforms. *Ethical Theory and Moral Practice*, 6, 455–8.

Rawls, J. 1996. *Political Liberalism*, New York, Columbia University Press.

Rawls, J. 1999. *A Theory of Justice*, Oxford, Oxford University Press.

Rorty, R. 1993. Human Rights, Rationality, and Sentimentality. *In:* Shute, S. H. S. (ed.) *On Human Rights: The 1993 Oxford Amnesty Lectures*, New York, Basic Books.

Valentini, L. 2012. *Justice in a Globalized World: A Normative Framework*, Oxford, Oxford University Press.

Waltz, K. 1959. *Man, The State, and War*, New York, Columbia University Press.

Wendt, A. 1999. *Social Theory of International Politics*, Cambridge, Cambridge University Press.

Williams, B. 1981. *Moral Luck*, Cambridge, Cambridge University Press.

6

COMPASSION IN INTERNATIONAL RELATIONS

Mervyn Frost

Introduction

My intellectual project has been to bring to light the extent to which international relations is not well understood when it is viewed as a struggle for power by sovereign states, but is better understood as an ethical argument broadly construed. I have attempted to do this by building a theory which I have dubbed 'Constitutive Theory' (Frost 1996; Frost 2002). The theory sets out to demonstrate to readers that they are all participants in international relations and that as such they participate in the two major global practices of our time: the society of sovereign states and global civil society. It then seeks to bring to light what is involved in participating in these practices. I seek to do this from the internal point of view – that is from the point of view of those who participate in the practices. Many of the key features are usually hidden or tacitly assumed. In particular I have been concerned to demonstrate the ethical dimensions implicit in these practices. I start by highlighting what I take to be common to all social practices. In order to understand human action in any realm, we need to understand how actors are constituted as actors of a certain kind within a specific social practice with its associated 'rules of the game'. In all social practices (such as speaking English, playing football, bull fighting, participating in economic markets, family life, universities, the community of sovereign states and so on) the 'rules of the game', which may be tacit or explicit, specify what criteria need to be satisfied in order to become a participant, what menu of appropriate actions are open to participants, what actions are ruled out as mistakes or as inappropriate, and what misconduct would result in a participant being expelled from the practice. Social practices are underpinned by one or another ethical theory. 'Ethical theory' is here understood as that set of values that participants refer to in order to justify the practice as a whole, individual actions within it, and to which they refer when seeking to solve so-called 'hard cases'. In many social practices the underlying ethical theory is not completely settled and static, but portions of it are under ongoing discussion. These discussions are, one might say, the internal politics of the practice.

Practices and the emotions

Just as the social practices have built into them an ethical dimension, they also have built into them an emotional component. Participants in social practices, when learning how to participate, learn what emotions are appropriate within it. They also learn what emotions it would be appropriate to act on and what emotions are best not acted upon but rather contained. So, for example, rugby is an aggressive game. Participants learn that aggression is appropriate to participation in it. Giving the ball to the opponent as an act of generosity would be acknowledged as inappropriate. Chess is a competitive game and participants learn that competitiveness is an appropriate emotion while participating in it. Those participating in the Christian practice learn that loving one's neighbour is not only appropriate for Christian conduct, but is essential to it. In family life participants learn the importance of a whole range of emotions: love, loyalty, honour and so on. Not only do we learn what emotions are appropriate to each practice, we also learn what emotions are inappropriate in each case. Thus, for example, in competitive tennis we learn that losing a game on purpose out of compassion for one's opponent is inappropriate conduct, especially if one is playing in a competitive league. Similarly, losing one's temper during a match is considered out of order. In like fashion, participants in the practice of marriage know that marrying someone whom they hate would be an inappropriate thing to do.

At a very general level we might then say that social practices have built into them an emotional register. These emotional registers are often complex and their details are regularly disputed. For example, we can see in the chapter produced by Michael Ure for this volume how he sets out to untangle the complexities of the relationship between compassion, guilt, resentment and feelings about justice and injustice within a specific practice of ethical discourse. In university life, there is an ongoing debate about how emotions associated with friendship and love ought to be accommodated within the rules of the game of academic life in the relationships between staff and students.

How is all this relevant to the practices of international relations? A key point to make at the outset is that the major practices in international relations that I identified above are practices of practices. The system of sovereign states and global civil society are both global social practices that contain within themselves all other social practices, sporting, cultural, religious, scientific, educational and so on. Since these two are the practices of all practices, the ranges of practices contained within them are large and extremely diverse. The system of sovereign states contains within it, to mention but one class of diverse practices, all the practices associated with the many different religions in the world. Included here are those associated with Judaism, Christianity, Islam, Hinduism, Buddhism, animist religions and many others. Another important class of practices are all those to do with the multitude of diverse nations in the world. Other important classes of practices containing a wide diversity of practices are the class of cultural practices and the class of language practices. Within these classes of practices are a great diversity of ethical commitments and emotional registers. The participants in many of these define themselves in opposition to the other practices in the same class. Christians define themselves as 'not Jews', and so on. A central question to be asked here is: how have we managed to accommodate this great diversity of ethical commitments and emotional registers in the two major practices of practices in world affairs without there being a complete breakdown of order? A related question is: what emotional registers are components of these practices of practices?

Anarchical societies, ethics and emotions

The two fundamental global practices, the society of sovereign states on the one hand, and global civil society on the other, accommodate this great diversity within an anarchical structure. The anarchical structure of each is underpinned by a very specific set of ethical commitments and also by a specific emotional register that upholds and supports this accommodation of diversity. Let us examine the anarchical form more closely. An anarchy is an arrangement in which the participants are not under a centralised form of government and in which each participant is accorded a domain of liberty circumscribed by a strict boundary. Anarchy is to be distinguished from other forms of social organisation such as a state or empire which have a centralised form of rule. What is achieved in an anarchy is the accommodation of diversity through the maintenance of a set of liberties for the participants. In the society of sovereign states each state has available to it a set of freedoms associated with the word *sovereignty*. Although there is an ongoing discussion about what exactly is encompassed in this term, it is safe to say that, roughly speaking, each state is entitled to pursue its own domestic policies and its own foreign policies (Stankiewicz 1969; Bartelson 1995; Hinsley 1986). As always, these freedoms are subject to the constraint that each state respects, the right of other states to do the same. In such a system of free states it becomes possible to accommodate a wide range of diverse social, religious, cultural, national, educational and scientific practices (there are many others).

Similarly, global civil society is an anarchical arrangement. The participants in this society are individual men and women conceived of as the holders of human rights (in particular, first-generation rights). This, too, is an anarchical arrangement in that each participant is accorded a domain of freedom subject only to the constraint that he/she respects the freedoms of other participants. There is no central government. Within this practice there is an ongoing dispute amongst the participants about the precise list of rights that are considered to be protected within it. However, there is agreement on a core set of fundamental freedoms. What this anarchical order makes possible is, as was the case with the society of sovereign states, the protection of the values of freedom and diversity. Each rights holder is entitled to live his/her life in accordance with his/her individual choices. In this way ascetics can live side by side with hedonists, artists with technicians, hard-working people with lazy people and so on. The ethical underpinning of both of these anarchical societies is similar; both protect the values of freedom and diversity.

We must now turn to the questions: what is the emotional register embedded in each of these two anarchical practices? What emotions are appropriate to what states of affairs in these practices? What emotions within these practices are inappropriate both in themselves and as reasons for subsequent actions? We are well placed to seek answers to these questions because we are all participants in these practices. We have all in some measure learned how to participate in them. Since we are already participants, it follows that we must already have a stock of knowledge about the emotions appropriate to different states of affairs that emerge within them. More particularly, we must have some knowledge of the role that compassion plays in them.

What, then, do we know about the emotions appropriate to each? It seems to me that there are several core emotions that define the emotional registers of our global anarchical societies. These include, in summary form, at least the following: an emotional stance of tolerance towards fellow participants; a generally fearful stance towards serious threats to the stability of these anarchies; anger towards participants who infringe the freedom of fellow participants (through acts of aggression against free states, or through the abuse of other people's rights); and a sense of injustice towards those guilty of unjust conduct within the society of states or global civil society. Let us examine some of these in more detail. A full explication is beyond the scope of this chapter.

In the two practices of practices that I have described, as we have seen, a central value is the accommodation of a wide range of national and individual policies and goals in a stable and ordered system. For example, in the practice of sovereign states, many states institute internal arrangements and pursue national policies that are opposed and rejected by the governments and people of other states. Some states support religious ways of being and doing that are anathema to other states. The Saudi Arabian state upholds Islamic commitments whereas the British state has established within it a Christian church. Internal to many states are cultural practices that define themselves in opposition to those supported by other states. The method used to accommodate such diversity relies on the participants adhering to constraints on their behaviour and also constraints on their emotional responses towards one another. As indicated above, one emotion associated with this kind of constraining mechanism is tolerance. Actors in such systems have to learn, not positively to approve of all the other rival and antagonistic ethical, religious and cultural commitments, but positively to tolerate them, that is, to let them be. Thus, within the society of sovereign states, we might find that democratic states and socialist states disapprove fundamentally of those states that are not democratic or socialist; nevertheless, they are required to tolerate them. Similarly, Islamic states or fundamentalist Zionist ones are required to tolerate those that do not share their belief systems. Actors in this practice of practices are required to recognise that although they might dislike other regimes (religious, cultural, nationalist and so on), these emotions must be trumped by a higher order response of tolerance. They understand that such passions need to be restrained and made subservient to the feeling of tolerance. What must be stressed here is that tolerance itself is an emotional response which is appropriate to those occasions in the anarchical practices where one or more actors support positions that are objectionable to the other actors in the anarchy. Participants in this practice who fail to understand the appropriate occasions for a tolerant response must be understood to be participants who have not yet fully understood what is involved in being a participant in this practice.[1]

Similarly, in that anarchical practice that I have called 'global civil society' (GCS), individual rights holders might hate, loathe, resent, despise (and so on) the life choices taken by other rights holders (puritans despise the lazy, the libertarians have derision for the equalitarianism of the socialists and so on); nevertheless, as participants in this practice of practices, they will have developed the emotional response of tolerance which requires of them that they override their initial responses with one of tolerance. They are required to do this despite the fact that their own life choices within the sub-practices are built on ethical, religious and cultural commitments that are defined in opposition to those accepted by others. Thus, although Adam might dislike everything associated with Zionism (Islam, Christianity and so on), as a participant in GCS he is required to be tolerant towards those who hold these rival positions.

There may be some participants in these practices who have an emotional response to the successful working of these anarchies which is appreciative of the diversity displayed in their operation. They might experience the emotion of wonder and take delight in the range of different kinds of living together which takes place in these practices of practices.

Another emotion appropriate to these two anarchical practices is that of fear. Participants in them know that a central function of these practices is to accommodate diversity. They know, too, that the diverse elements contained within them include people who harbour emotions towards others in the anarchy that could easily override the tolerance requirement and spill over into destructive conflict. So, having an emotional response that is appreciative of the diversity that is protected by the anarchical society, they also fear what might happen were it to fail. Participants in these practices have learned that it is appropriate to experience an ongoing fear and anxiety about the possibility of the collapse of the anarchical order that makes the diversity possible. Another way of saying this is that in these practices there is an ongoing feeling of unease brought about by the ever-present risk of disorder or even breakdown.

Another emotion that is relevant to this discussion is that of respect. This is probably closely linked to the notion of tolerance. Individual states and individual rights holders, in order to participate successfully in these anarchical practices, need to show respect for the differences displayed by the other participants. New participants in these practices are required to respect difference.

What emotions are ruled out of order for participants in these practices? What passions and emotions are considered inappropriate? The answer is: all those emotions which might be lined up in opposition to the tolerance requirement, such as expansionist nationalist ones, fascist ones, racist ones, those associated with religious intolerance, those associated with cultural intolerance and so on. Recent history has exhibited many examples of states and individuals displaying these and also acting on them with more or less disastrous consequences. Participants who display these emotions have not yet fully mastered the emotional register appropriate to this practice.

Global practices and compassion

The question which we have to consider now is whether the emotional response of compassion is a component of the emotional register of the two anarchical orders under discussion. If it is, then we have to establish what is involved in having compassion for a fellow participant or participants. For the purposes of this discussion I understand 'having compassion' as 'being open to feeling the suffering and pain being experienced by other participants in a given practice and understanding that this openness is required for one's own well-being as a fully fledged ethical actor'.[2] To state the question in a different way: is it a requirement for participation in these practices that actors have compassion for others in the appropriate circumstances?

As a participant in both the practice of sovereign states and in global civil society, it seems to me that at present in the early phase of the twenty-first century, there is evidence that compassion is, indeed, a component of the emotional register of these practices. The evidence is widespread. In the society of sovereign states, it is to be found in the ever-wider acceptance by states that they should be moved by the suffering of other states after they have experienced famine, war, state failure, environmental disasters such as a tsunami or a volcanic eruption. The leaders and people of most states display their compassion on the occurrence of such events. They do this in what they say and do in response to such events. It would be odd indeed to find a state that turned away from such disasters with, metaphorically speaking, a shrug of indifference and a muttering of 'tough luck'. It seems to me correct to assert that participants in the society of sovereign states are required to understand what 'having compassion' entails and to know when it would be appropriate to exhibit it.[3] Further evidence in support of this is to be found in the setting up by the international community of states of the World Health Organization, the establishments of an international convention on the rights of the child, the putting in place of international laws of armed conflict and so on. In all these cases it seems reasonable to assume that these things were done in response to feelings of compassion among the participants in the system of sovereign states. The elaborate set of international laws and organisations put in place to deal with refugees (both asylum seekers and economic migrants) may be seen as a response to a similar set of feelings. The most well-documented instance of action following an expression of compassion is to be found in the process that led up to the abolition of the slave trade. Global responses to famines are similarly moved by feelings of compassion for the starving. In the contemporary world it is now well established, it seems to me, that to be a sovereign state requires of a state (both its leaders and its people) that it has compassion for the starving, the innocent harmed in war, those suffering loss from pandemics such as HIV/AIDS, those sold into slavery, those harmed in natural disasters, those who suffer in failed states and so on. A state that was not moved by compassion in such cases would be understood to be ethically unsound – ethically underdeveloped. None of this is to be taken as indicating that 'having compassion' necessarily leads to actions that ameliorate the pain and suffering in question. It may do so or may not. Indeed, there may be cases where an actor in these practices engages in courses of action which relieve pain and suffering, but which do not involve the actor who is doing good feeling compassion at all. Such actions are mere acts of charity.

Similarly, in GCS the rights holders who participate in it are similarly educated to feel compassion for rights holders elsewhere who are suffering through rights abuses of one kind or another. They are educated to feel empathy for the pain of those whose rights are being abused and to understand that having this feeling is what is required of a rights holder in good standing within the practice. Indeed, it is this 'fellow feeling' which provides the impulse for rights holders everywhere to be concerned that action be taken to rectify rights abuse wherever it happens. In those cases where we, as participants, have failed to have compassion for the victims of rights abuse, we rights holders feel ashamed about our own failure or the failure of others in this regard. Many actors in the international community have expressed this emotion about the community's failure to respond in time to prevent the massacre in Rwanda by the Hutu against the Tutsi.

For the state participants in the society of sovereign states and for the individual rights holders in GCS, the scope of compassion may be narrow or very wide indeed. An example of a narrowly focussed feeling of compassion might occur when a single state has compassion for the plight of a neighbouring state that has suffered a natural or man-made disaster of one kind or another. In contrast, many states together might have compassion for the plight of a majority of states in a region that are together suffering the effects of state failure or regional warfare. Similarly, an individual rights holder may have compassion for a single person who is suffering rights abuse, but on a much wider front, rights holders might be in compassion with the whole population of a country experiencing famine.

Being educated into the requirements of compassion within these two practices does not require participants to be in compassion with all those experiencing pain and suffering, wherever the suffering people may be, and at all times. Such a stringent requirement would be humanly impossible to fulfil. It would effectively require that states and individuals be in a Christ-like state of compassion all the time. Instead, what is required in the existing practices of world politics is an orientation towards the granting of compassion in cases of extreme pain and suffering. To whom compassion is given will vary from actor to actor. It might be conditioned by nearness to the sufferer, by a history of emotional closeness to the sufferer, and by economic, political and cultural factors. There is scope for a thoroughgoing discussion of who it is that most merits our compassion.

The analysis given here suggests that for participants in the two global practices that have been described in this chapter, knowledge of how and when to be compassionate is a requirement for all participants. The field of those to whom compassion might be extended is already global. The argument being offered here differs from that put forward by Andrew Linklater, who makes the case for educating people into being compassionate as a way of expanding the boundaries of moral concern beyond the narrow ones he perceives as existing today.[4] On the understanding of the practices that I am advancing in this chapter, the field of compassion for participants in these practices is already global. This is not some new emotion that has to be nurtured and expanded outwards to people who presently neither give it nor receive it. It is being given and received on a global and everyday basis already.

That an actor in the society of sovereign states or in global civil society is having/giving compassion for those suffering misfortunes of one kind or another, however, does not give us any detailed indication of what we ourselves, or others, should do to alleviate the suffering in question. What, from an ethical point of view, ought to be done (and by whom) to alleviate the suffering of those for whom one is feeling compassion? This is a question that requires starting and concluding an altogether different kind of argument, one that is in the first place ethical and which ultimately becomes political. The mere having of compassion does not indicate an answer to either the ethical or political questions.

In order to elucidate this claim, consider an instance of widespread famine in some part of the world (the famine that took place in recent times in North Korea might provide a useful example here). A clear majority of individuals and states worldwide had compassion for the state and the people of North Korea who were dying of starvation at the time. But this feeling, which was appropriate to the event, did not translate in any univocal way into a set of policies to relieve the suffering of the starving. Before doing anything at all, any global actor would have to consider a range of ethically charged accounts of the problem that needed to be addressed. Different accounts will indicate different responses to alleviate the problem. A first account might point out that the cause of the famine was to be found in the policies of the communist government. This ethically loaded evaluation would suggest that the right response should be directed towards changing the form of the North Korean state, putting in place a new constitution, a new government and a revised set of internal and international policies. It might further be suggested that the international community should actively engage in doing all of these things. A second ethically informed account might make the case that as North Korea is a recognised sovereign state, it ought to be allowed to arrange its internal constitution, government and policies as it sees fit, and that the appropriate response for the international community should be the narrow one of providing aid to the stricken state and its people. A third line of argument might point out that the plight of the North Korean state itself was caused by the ethically informed hostile reception given to it by the international community of capitalist states. This analysis would suggest that the long-term solution should be directed towards dismantling capitalism and those states currently supporting it. I have no doubt that there are many other possible interpretations of the causes of the famine (many of which would point to ethical failures by a whole range of actors) and the appropriate ethical response to the famine. This is not the place to consider all these rival interpretations. What I wish to highlight here is that having compassion for the starving people gives only the most limited guidance to those concerned about what ought to be done, given the circumstances. In seeking an answer to this question, difficult discussions will have to be had about the ethical values embedded in the global society of sovereign states within which North Korea is a participant; about the relationship between those values and the values embedded in global civil society which might point to the need to engage in humanitarian intervention of one kind or another; discussions about the appropriate form of constitution and also government that should be put in place in North Korea and so on. At the top level, thought would have to be given to the principles on which international aid is distributed and to the role of international organisations in the distribution of that aid. The only explicit action-guiding direction that follows from being in compassion with another, is that it requires the compassion giver to do what is ethically appropriate to alleviate the receiver's suffering. It does not indicate what this 'appropriate' action might be. The injunction 'be compassionate' is not a guide to action.

Finally, I wish to highlight what kind of failure is made when a participant in these practices fails to feel compassion in the appropriate circumstances. The failure is not that of having failed to 'do' the appropriate thing. It is not an ethical wrongdoing in the way that failing to honour a treaty commitment is. Thus it follows that a failure to feel compassion is not a failure to do one's duty (honour one's obligations), for one cannot dutifully feel compassion. A compassion failure reveals to the other participants in these practices a lack of ethical character, an inability to feel the emotions appropriate to a given set of circumstances. The charge is not that an actor did not do the right thing, but that the actor has displayed a lack of ethical education, that there are ways of being in the practice that the actor has not yet fully acquired.

Notes

1 They are like those sportsmen, women and children who continue to have tantrums in the middle of their sports matches.
2 It is distinct from mere sympathy, which is simply understanding the pain or suffering of another actor, but without any linking of this to one's own status as an ethical actor. For example, a tyrant might be able to feel sympathy for the suffering of those under his tyranny, but without any idea that having such co-feeling with the sufferer is constitutive of himself as a whole person.

3 Of course, states are not individuals and do not literally have feelings in the way that individual men and women do. But, the governments and citizens of states do, indeed, speak of feeling national pride and feeling the pain of injustice and of shame. In short, there is a discourse of emotions that we use when referring to states as actors in the society of sovereign states.

4 See his chapter in the current volume.

References

Bartelson, Jens. *A Genealogy of Sovereignty*. Cambridge: Cambridge University Press, 1995.

Frost, Mervyn. *Ethics in International Relations: A Constitutive Theory*. Cambridge Studies in International Relations. Cambridge: Cambridge University Press, 1996.

Frost, Mervyn. *Constituting Human Rights: Global Civil Society and the Society of Democratic States*. Routledge Advances in International Relations and Global Politics. London/ New York: Routledge, 2002.

Hinsley, F. H. *Sovereignty*. 2nd edition. Cambridge: Cambridge University Press, 1986.

Stankiewicz, W. J. *In Defence of Sovereignty*. London: Oxford University Press, 1969.

7

GUILT, ANGER AND COMPASSIONATE HELPING

Nicholas Faulkner

Compassion has oftentimes been viewed solely as an emotion, with no explicit need for 'compassionate' individuals to help those who are suffering (Cassell 2002). In contrast, recent scholarly work has reframed the definition of compassion, arguing that it must include some form of action (Whitebrook 2002 and Chapter 1 of this volume; Ben-Ze'Ev 2000). Following from these scholars, it seems that compassion arguably involves having both a sense of being moved by the suffering of another, and a desire to act to alleviate that person's suffering, presumably by helping in some way. Thus, if compassion is to be extended across national, ethnic, religious and cultural boundaries, members of any one group (national, ethnic, religious or otherwise) must be willing to act to help members of other groups. In short, they must engage in intergroup, compassionate helping. In this chapter, the roles of two emotions – guilt and anger – in motivating such intergroup compassionate helping are examined.

Social psychologists have had a long-running interest in examining the causes of helping behaviour, and have, in more recent years, directly investigated the causes of *intergroup* helping behaviour (Dovidio *et al.* 2006). As a result, a great deal of social psychological research is useful, at least in an instructive capacity, in theorising about how to expand compassionate helping. Despite its great promise, however, recent findings in social psychology on the effects of guilt and anger on intergroup helping have not been integrated into work on compassion. This chapter addresses this lacuna in existing literature by using research from social psychology to hypothesise about the effects of two emotions – guilt and anger – on compassionate intergroup helping. It argues that anger may be more effective than guilt in fostering such helping. While guilt tends to increase individuals' support for the abstract goal of compensation, it appears not to typically result in support for concrete action to help suffering outgroups. Anger, however, *does* tend to motivate concrete action.

The chapter proceeds as follows. First, the centrality of helping to the concept of compassion is highlighted. In this section, compassionate helping is defined as action that is taken to help a person or group that is suffering in some way. Second, the effect of guilt on compassionate helping is evaluated. In this section, the aetiology and definition of guilt is discussed, before reviewing evidence that suggests guilt increases commitment to the abstract goal of compensation, but does not uniformly lead to concrete action to help the suffering. Third, the effect of anger on compassionate helping is evaluated. As with guilt, the aetiology and definition of anger is first given, and is then followed by evidence demonstrating anger's ability to motivate concrete action. Finally, two reasons are given to explain why anger may be more effective than guilt in motivating compassionate helping.

The centrality of helping to compassion

According to Nussbaum (2001: 301), compassion is 'a painful emotion occasioned by the awareness of another person's undeserved misfortune'. For Nussbaum, however, while compassion is primarily an emotion, it also has a certain set of cognitive requirements associated with it:

> Compassion … has three cognitive elements: the judgement of *size* (a serious bad event has befallen someone); the judgement of *nondesert* (this person did not bring the suffering on himself or herself); and the *eudaimonistic judgement* (this person, or creature, is a significant element in my scheme of goals and projects, an end whose good is to be promoted).
>
> (Nussbaum 2001: 306)

Nussbaum is not alone in characterising compassion as an emotion accompanied by certain cognitive beliefs or appraisals. Cassell (2002: 440), for instance, has similarly argued that compassion is 'more complex' than other emotions, and requires: (a) knowledge that another is suffering; (b) 'identification with the sufferer'; and, (c) 'knowledge of what the sufferer is experiencing'.

Some theorists, however, have argued that compassion is more than merely an emotion accompanied by certain cognitive requirements. Instead, according to these scholars, compassion involves *acting* to help those who are suffering (Whitebrook 2002 and Chapter 1 of this volume; Ben-Ze'Ev 2000). Typically, those who argue that compassion involves acting to help some suffering other make a distinction between 'pity' and 'compassion'. Unlike Nussbaum (1996: 29) – who suggests that the words 'pity' and 'compassion' describe the same emotion – Whitebrook and Ben-Ze'Ev make a clear distinction between the two concepts. 'Pity', they claim, refers to an *emotion* experienced upon recognising the suffering of some other person or group. Contrarily, 'compassion' refers to *action* that aims to help those who are suffering, and that may follow from feeling pity.

While Ben-Ze'Ev and Whitebrook agree that 'pity' refers to emotion and 'compassion' to helping action, they do not explicitly agree on the extent to which helping action must be based on pity in order for it to be characterised as 'compassion'. Ben-Ze'Ev (2000: 328) rather ambiguously claims that compassion involves 'a willingness to become personally involved' and, compared to pity, 'involves far greater commitment to substantial help'. He does not, however, assert that help must be based on feelings of pity in order for it to be characterised as 'compassion'. Conversely, Whitebrook (2002: 530) argues that compassion 'should denote acting on the basis of feelings of pity, rather than simply feeling an emotion'. In short, Whitebrook claims that in order for helping action to be characterised as compassion, the help must 'follow from', or be based on, feelings of pity. In Chapter 1 of this volume, she emphasises the distinction between compassion viewed as emotion and compassion viewed as action. In doing so, Whitebrook implicitly suggests that helping action does not necessarily need to be based on pity in order to be characterised as compassion.

Following Whitebrook, I make a distinction between compassion as emotion, and compassion as action. I assume that action to help those who are suffering does not need to be based on feelings of pity in order to be characterised as 'compassionate helping'. Broadly following Ben-Ze'Ev (2000) as well, I characterise 'compassionate helping' as action that is taken to help a person or group that is suffering in some way. This action may or may not be based on feelings of pity. In what follows, I use empirical social psychological research to hypothesise about the effects of guilt and anger on compassionate helping.

Guilt

Similar to the term 'compassion', 'guilt' is also used in multiple and occasionally conflicting ways (Baumeister *et al.* 1994). One way to describe the distinct characteristics of guilt is to compare it to shame. In quotidian parlance, the terms 'guilt' and 'shame' are often used interchangeably. Guilt and shame, however, refer to 'distinct and distinguishable experiences' (Baumeister *et al.* 1994). Both guilt and shame are negatively valenced (thus painful) emotions, and both are evoked when one commits some form of transgression or wrongdoing (Tangney *et al.* 2007a, 2007b; Schmader & Lickel 2006). Guilt differs from shame, however, in the extent to which the global self is 'blamed' for the wrongdoing:

> Currently, the most dominant basis for distinguishing between shame and guilt centres on the object of negative evaluation and disapproval. Shame involves a negative evaluation of the global self; guilt involves a negative evaluation of a specific behaviour ... This differential emphasis on self ('*I* did that horrible thing') versus behaviour ('I *did* that horrible *thing*') gives rise to distinct emotional experiences associated with distinct patterns of motivation and subsequent behaviour.
>
> (Tangney *et al.* 2007b: 25–6)

Thus, according to Tangney *et al.* (2007b; 2007a), guilt is a painful emotion that arises when one negatively evaluates their *behaviour* (as opposed to themselves) after having committed a transgression. This definition describes *interpersonal guilt*: that is, guilt that arises when an *individual* commits some form of wrongdoing. There is, however, another form of guilt that seems relevant to the task of increasing inter-group compassionate helping: group-based guilt.

Group-based guilt (sometimes called collective guilt) arises when individuals feel personally or collectively complicit in the blameworthy actions of the groups to which they belong (Lickel *et al.* 2011; Iyer *et al.* 2004; Branscombe & Doosje 2004).[1] For example, white Australians may experience group-based guilt associated with the historical mistreatment of, and the current inequality facing, indigenous Australians (Leach *et al.* 2006, 2007). Similarly, Dutch citizens may experience group-based guilt associated with their nation's historical mistreatment of African slaves, or with the extent to which Jews were deported from Holland to Germany during the Second World War (Zebel *et al.* 2009). Since group-based guilt occurs between groups, it is worth examining further to determine to what extent it moti-vates compassionate helping across those groups. If group-based guilt does increase the extent to which one group helps another, then it may provide an effective basis for expanding compassionate helping internationally.

Theoretically, guilt should motivate helping

Theoretically, guilt is an emotion that should increase the inclination to make repa-rations for harm that you (or your group) have inflicted on another person or group (Doosje *et al.* 1998: 873). At the interpersonal level, guilt is associated with the inclination to make reparations for the harm that an individual has inflicted on another person (e.g. Barrett 1995; Frijda *et al.* 1989; Frijda 1986; Lewis 1993). At the intergroup level, some research is supportive of the contention that group-based guilt encourages some forms of intergroup helping. Importantly, however, not all research supports this contention: some, in fact, highlights the limitations of guilt as a motivator of intergroup helping. To frame this in terms of compassion, some (but certainly not all) social psychological research suggests that guilt may motivate some form of intergroup compassionate helping.

Guilt predicts support for apology, forgiveness and abstract compensation

Specifically, social psychologists have found that group-based guilt tends to moti-vate support for apologising to those who are suffering as a result of the actions of one's ingroup. In two studies, McGarty *et al.* (2005) tested this idea by examining white Australians' attitudes towards issuing an apology to indigenous Australians. White Australians may feel group-based guilt associated with their past poor treat-ment of indigenous Australians, and the persisting systemic inequality between the two groups. In both studies, McGarty *et al.* (2005) found that group-based guilt was a significant predictor of support for apology: white Australians who felt guilty for their group's role in causing harm to indigenous Australians were far more likely to support apologising to indigenous Australians. Moreover, the effect of guilt on support for apologising held even after statistically controlling for relevant socio-demographic variables, and perceptions of ingroup advantage. A similar association between guilt and apology at the interpersonal level has also been found previously (Roseman *et al.* 1994).

Group-based guilt is also linked to intergroup forgiveness. Hewstone *et al.* (2004) found that amongst a sample of students in Northern Ireland, group-based guilt predicted intergroup forgiveness. Protestants who felt guilty for the harm their group had done to Catholics were more likely to forgive Catholics. A virtually identical pattern of results was found amongst Catholics.

In addition to its likely effects on apology and forgiveness, group-based guilt also increases commitment to the abstract goal of compensation. For example, guilt about Holland's past colonisation of Indonesia predicted Dutch subjects' support for general government compensation to Indonesia (Doosje *et al.* 1998). Similarly, European Americans' group-based guilt associated with the advantages they enjoy relative to African Americans predicted support for the abstract goal of compensation (Iyer *et al.* 2003). In another series of studies, Gunn & Wilson (2011) investigated the extent to which collective guilt was positively associated with willingness to compensate. Specifically, they investigated whether non-Aboriginal Canadians who felt guilty for their group's historical mistreatment of Canadian Aboriginals were more likely to support offering Canadian Aboriginals compensation. Their measure of compensation, however, conflated measures of a general commitment to compensation (e.g. 'Should Aboriginals be compensated by Canada for the harms they endured in residential schools?') with specific concrete actions aimed at compensation (e.g. 'Which activities are you personally willing to partake in to ensure that the harms committed against Aboriginals in residential schools are redressed? Check beside all that apply: discuss with others, sign a petition, write a letter, take part in a protest/march, volunteer for groups aimed at improving conditions for Aboriginals, donate money') (Gunn & Wilson 2011: 1,479), thus making it impossible to determine whether guilt was associated with both abstract compensation *and* concrete action in their studies.[2]

Guilt does not typically predict concrete helping action

Earlier studies showing the positive effects of group-based guilt on apology, forgiveness and compensation understandably led researchers to have a generally positive view of guilt's ability to foster intergroup helping. More recently, however, an increasingly sceptical view of guilt's ability to motivate helping action has emerged (Lickel *et al.* 2011; Iyer & Leach 2010). According to this sceptical view, while guilt is associated with motivations to make reparations for wrongdoing, its narrow self-focus and low arousal make it rather limited in motivating genuine efforts to help outgroups (Leach *et al.* 2002, 2006; Thomas *et al.* 2009; Iyer & Leach 2010). Specifically, particularly when controlling for other emotions and relevant constructs, guilt has little to no association with the extent to which individuals engage in concrete helping action (e.g. Harth *et al.* 2008).

A number of studies have illustrated this claim. In one study, Iyer *et al.* (2003: Study 3) investigated European Americans' feelings and attitudes associated with their group's discrimination against African Americans. Results showed that group-based guilt about the discrimination predicted support for compensatory policies, but *did not* predict support for policies designed to increase opportunities for African Americans. Instead, they found, sympathy was a better predictor of these policies. In another study, Iyer *et al.* (2007: Study 1) found that guilt about the USA's occupation of Iraq did not predict any political action intentions amongst their American sample. They also found the same pattern of results amongst British citizens: guilt did not predict political action (Iyer *et al.* 2007: Study 2). Finally, Leach *et al.* (2006) found that non-Aboriginal Australians' guilt about systemic disadvantage facing Aboriginal Australians predicted support for the abstract goal of compensation, but did not predict support for concrete political action.

Guilt: an unreliable motivator of intergroup compassionate helping

Taken together, these findings suggest that guilt is unlikely to be an effective motivator of compassionate helping. If compassionate helping is to be expanded internationally, then individuals must engage in concrete acts to help suffering others, irrespective of national, religious, ethnic or any other group differences. While guilt seems to encourage individuals to support the abstract goal of compensating those who have been harmed, it does not seem typically to motivate concrete helping action. Furthermore, not only is guilt (when it is felt) only limitedly effective in motivating compassionate helping, it is also frequently not likely to be felt to begin with. If group-based guilt is to be experienced, the ingroup needs to be viewed as responsible for harming some other group (Branscombe & Doosje 2004; Branscombe *et al.* 2004; Mallett & Swim 2007). In many cases of suffering, those who are needed to engage in compassionate helping may not have harmed the suffering. Instead, the suffering may have been caused by natural causes (e.g. tsunamis, earthquakes etc.), or by some third party. In such cases, group-based guilt seems unlikely to arise in the first place.

Anger

In contrast to guilt, anger may be a more reliable motivator of intergroup compassionate helping. Anger is a high-arousal emotion (Rydell *et al.* 2008: Study 1; Lazarus 1991) that can occur when the cause of a negative outcome or state is attributed to factors that are under the control of some other individual or group (Weiner *et al.* 1982; Lazarus 1991). As such, anger can be directed towards particular individuals, or towards particular groups. There are, however, a range of types of anger that may occur when a negative outcome or state is, put simply, 'blamed' on some group or individual. Batson *et al.* (2007) make a distinction between three different forms of anger – personal anger, empathic anger and moral outrage – that may occur in such cases. Personal anger occurs when one's own interests have been harmed. Empathic anger occurs when a cared-for other person's interests have been harmed. Finally, moral outrage is a form of anger that occurs when one perceives that a moral standard has been violated. Batson *et al.* (2007) argue that distinguishing between these forms of anger may facilitate a better understanding of moral emotion and behaviour.

Leach *et al.* (2006) detail another form of anger: that which is directed towards one's own ingroup. This form of anger occurs when an individual becomes angry at their own ingroup for some harm that their ingroup has perpetrated against some other group. For example, European Australians may experience ingroup-directed anger in relation to their group's poor treatment of indigenous Australians.

Anger often leads to action against the focus of one's anger

While there are some differences in the action tendencies associated with each type of anger (see Batson *et al.* 2007), at least one tendency broadly exists across all four of the forms of anger just highlighted. Namely, when people become angry, they typically act to confront whomever their anger is directed towards. Many studies support this claim. One study of British soccer fan's reactions to the result of a match found that anger about the result predicted a desire to 'confront' and 'argue with' supporters of the opposing team (Crisp *et al.* 2007). In another study, East Germans who felt angry about their relatively disadvantaged position compared to West Germans were most keen to publicly protest (Kessler & Mummendey 2001). Similarly, (Mackie *et al.* 2000) found that anger directed towards an outgroup predicted the desire to take action against that outgroup. In another series of studies, anger felt by individual members of a harmed group predicted their desire to confront an outgroup that had harmed their group (Gordijn *et al.* 2006; Yzerbyt *et al.* 2003). In yet another study, anger predicted students' decisions to confront an authority in protest against fee increases (Stürmer & Simon 2009: Study 1).

Each of the studies just mentioned broadly examined the effect of *personal anger* on action against the person or group on which the anger was focussed. However, the desire to confront those whom anger is directed towards is not limited solely to personal anger. Indeed, the desire to confront harm-doers even occurs when individuals are angry at harm done to *outgroups*, rather than merely to themselves or their own groups. Van Zomeren *et al.* (2004) found that anger about an outgroup's unfair treatment by an authority predicted intentions to engage in actions to confront that authority.[3] Furthermore, Van Zomeren *et al.* (2004) found that anger was as strong a predictor of intentions to confront the authority in cases where an outgroup was harmed, as it was in cases where an ingroup was harmed. Similarly, in another series of studies, European Americans' anger at their own ingroup for its discrimination against African Americans was found to predict both abstract intentions to confront those responsible, and willingness to join a political group to confront those responsible (Iyer & Leach n.d.; Leach & Iyer n.d.). Similarly still, another study found that British citizens' anger at the US government's decision to invade Iraq predicted willingness to engage in political action to confront the government (Iyer *et al.* 2007: Study 2).

Taken together, these studies demonstrate that anger can motivate action against entities who have caused harm to one's self or ingroup or to some other individual or outgroup. This desire to confront those who are perceived to have caused harm may lead to some forms of compassionate helping. In particular, this would lead to compassionate helping in situations where anger is directed towards some group or individual who is causing some other group to suffer. For example, if anger is directed towards a dictator who is causing people in his or her country to suffer, then such anger may lead to actions to confront that dictator, thus potentially reducing the suffering he or she causes to his or her subjects.

Anger increases intergroup, ostensibly compassionate helping

While anger does cause individuals to confront the entity who is the focus of their anger, the effect of anger on compassionate helping does not seem confined merely to confronting some harm-doer. Instead, anger can motivate forms of concrete action that are intended to *directly* benefit those who are suffering (as opposed to confronting a harm-doer, which may only indirectly benefit the suffering). Montada & Schneider (1989), for instance, found that German citizens' moral outrage about inequality in their country predicted readiness to engage in a range of activities – including 'spending money' and 'joining an activity group' – to help the disadvantaged. In fact, of the emotions measured in Montada & Schneider (1989), moral outrage was the best predictor of helping. Moreover, the effect of moral outrage on helping tendencies remained significant even when controlling for a host of other emotions, including guilt, sympathy and fear.

Ingroup-directed anger also seems capable of motivating direct forms of intergroup compassionate helping. In two studies, Aarti Iyer and Colin Leach (Iyer & Leach n.d.; Leach & Iyer n.d.; also see Iyer & Leach 2010) measured the predictive effect of ingroup-directed anger on helping intentions. Their results revealed that ingroup-directed anger predicted intentions to compensate and make retribution. Specifically, European Americans' anger directed at their own ingroup for racial discrimination against African Americans predicted support for the abstract goal of compensation. The effect of anger on compassionate helping, however, does not appear to be confined merely to support for the abstract goal of compensation. Rather, anger also appears to motivate concrete action to help the suffering. Leach *et al.* (2006), for instance, found that non-Aboriginal Australians' anger about the systemic disadvantage faced by Aboriginal Australians predicted willingness for concrete political action (e.g. 'donate money to the cause' and 'help organize a demonstration'). Furthermore, a final study found that British citizens' anger about the decision to go to war in Iraq predicted political action (e.g. 'sign a petition', 'volunteer', 'attend a rally') aimed at: (a) compensating Iraq; (b) advocating withdrawal from Iraq; and, (c) confronting those responsible for going to Iraq (Iyer *et al.* 2007). In the same study, guilt was found not to predict any action tendencies.

In sum, anger seems capable of motivating two forms of compassionate helping. First, it motivates individuals to confront those who are causing harm. Second, at least in the case of ingroup-directed anger, it motivates concrete action to directly help those who are suffering.

Why anger may be more effective than guilt

The previous two sections of this chapter have highlighted evidence that suggests that guilt is largely ineffective in promoting concrete, direct action to help those who are suffering. In contrast, anger *does* seem capable of motivating concrete, direct forms of compassionate helping. But why might anger be more effective than guilt in motivating such action? While empirical research on this question is somewhat lacking, there are at least two possible explanations. The first explanation relates to the differential extent that guilt and anger are associated with physiological arousal. Guilt is typically characterised as a low-arousal emotion, whereas anger is characterised as a high-arousal emotion (Lazarus 1991). Indeed, a range of studies has demonstrated that anger increases blood pressure (Gambaro & Rabin 1969; Ax 1953; Schachter 1957), and that anger is typically felt as a higher-arousal emotion than guilt (Reisenzein 1994; also see Rydell *et al.* 2008). While empirical research is yet to validate the following claim directly, it appears that the high arousal associated with anger makes it capable of motivating 'the constructive, self-corrective action that the guilty want as a goal', but are not willing to act upon (Leach *et al.* 2006: 1,243).

A second possible explanation of why anger is more effective than guilt in motivating compassionate helping relates to the self–other focus of each emotion. Self–other focus determines which 'side' in a helping situation – either an individual's self/own group, or some suffering person/group – is most salient in an individual's mind when considering helping. To illustrate this, consider the example where a person in a relatively advantaged position is considering helping someone who is in a relatively disadvantaged position. This example is useful, as many cases of compassionate helping require advantaged groups (e.g. 'the rich') to help disadvantaged groups (e.g. 'the poor'). In such cases:

> When self-focused, the advantaged can be moved to pride or guilt in response to their privilege, depending on its perceived legitimacy. In contrast, focus-

ing on others can promote sympathy, moral outrage, or disdain toward the disadvantaged.

(Leach *et al.* 2002: 140)

Guilt is typically characterised as a self-focussed emotion (Hoffman 1976; Iyer *et al.* 2004; Leach *et al.* 2002; Thomas *et al.* 2009). As a result, individuals who feel guilt may be 'too wrapped up in their own misery to help the disadvantaged' (Leach *et al.* 2002: 145; Hoffman 1976). In other words, the self-focus of guilt can impede helping action, limiting it merely to 'tokenistic, top-down forms of symbolic action' designed primarily to assuage the helper's negative feelings (Thomas *et al.* 2009: 325; Iyer *et al.* 2004; McGarty *et al.* 2005).

In contrast, at least some forms of anger are not self-focussed. Moral outrage, in particular, as noted above, is an other-focussed response. Since it is other-focussed, it can promote action to help the suffering, rather than simply to assuage individuals' own negative emotional states (e.g. Montada & Schneider 1989). Not all forms of anger, however, are so clearly other-focussed. Personal anger, for instance, may be self-focused. One study hinting at personal anger's possible self-focus demonstrated that individuals who felt personal anger were willing to protest only when the protest provided an opportunity for catharsis of aggressive tension (Stürmer & Simon 2009). Moreover, the same study found that when participants were provided with a series of jokes designed to reduce anger, the relationship between anger and willingness to protest disappeared (Stürmer & Simon 2009: Study 2). In other words, people experiencing personal anger were willing to protest, but if they were given some well-designed jokes before being given the opportunity to protest, they no longer were willing to protest. While this suggests that anger is not uniformly other-focussed, it remains likely to be, on the whole, more other-focussed than guilt. As a result, anger seems more likely than guilt to motivate concrete forms of compassionate helping.

Conclusion

In this chapter, I have argued that anger appears more effective than guilt in motivating intergroup compassionate helping. In contrast to some authors who have written about compassionate action (e.g. Whitebrook 2002 and Chapter 1 of this volume), the arguments presented here have been based not solely on reason and appeals to like-minded theorists, but on empirical evidence from social psychology. This is important, at least for triangulation purposes, as doing this goes some way towards assessing the real-world effects of specific emotions on compassionate action in existing societies, something which may differ from the important, reason-based arguments about the effects of specific emotion presented by political and social theorists.

This chapter started by drawing on Whitebrook (2002 and Chapter 1 of this volume) and Ben-Ze'Ev (2000) to argue that helping is central to the concept of 'compassion'. It then examined the effects of guilt and anger on compassionate helping. Both experimental and observational research suggest that guilt increases abstract support for compensating those who have been harmed. This abstract support for compensation, however, does not necessarily translate to concrete helping action. Indeed, as the chapter has highlighted, many studies show that while guilt predicts abstract support for compensation, it often does not predict support for concrete action to help the suffering.

In contrast, anger has been shown to predict concrete action to directly help the suffering. Furthermore, it also predicts decisions to confront harm-doers, thus potentially indirectly helping those who are suffering at the hands of some harm-doer (e.g. a dictator, government authority or competing group). Thus, it appears anger is a more effective motivator of compassionate helping than guilt. There are a minimum of two reasons that at least somewhat explain why anger may be more effective than guilt in motivating compassionate helping. First, anger involves higher levels of physiological arousal than guilt. Second, anger appears to be, on the whole, more other-focussed than guilt, since guilt is very much a self-focussed emotion.

One limitation of this chapter is that it has not discussed the frequency and extent to which anger and guilt are experienced in response to the suffering of another person or group. Of course, if anger or guilt are to increase compassionate helping, then anger or guilt must first be felt. Future research could investigate the extent to which guilt and anger are experienced in response to another's suffering. What this chapter has demonstrated, however, is that interventions designed to increase concrete forms of compassionate helping would benefit by attempting to make potential helpers *angry* about another's suffering. Conversely, the utility of guilt in such interventions seems limited.

Notes

1 Earlier research overwhelmingly studied guilt at only the interpersonal level; that is, it studied guilt that arose from 'one's own *individual* behavior and wrongdoing' (Lickel *et al* 2011: 154, emphasis added). Recently, however, there has been an increased recognition that people 'can experience emotions on the basis of their self-categorization as group members' (Iyer and Leach 2010: 345; Iyer & Leach n.d.; Smith 1993). As such, the group-based guilt that individuals can feel in relation to their group's current or past transgressions, or in relation to their group's complicity in wide-scale injustice (Mallett & Swim 2007), has received increased attention amongst social psychologists.

2 However, given that the specific actions were strongly positively correlated with broad support for group compensation (Gunn & Wilson 2011: 1,479), one would expect (but cannot confirm) that guilt was positively correlated with both abstract support for compensation *and* support for taking concrete action.

3 It is worth noting, however, that more anger was experienced when an ingroup, rather than an outgroup, was the subject of the unfair treatment.

References

Ax, A. F. (1953) 'The physiological differentiation between fear and anger in humans', *Psychosomatic Medicine*, 15(5): 433–42.

Barrett, K. (1995) 'A functionalist approach to shame and guilt', in J. P. Tangney and K. Fischer (eds) *Self-conscious emotions: The psychology of shame, guilt*. New York: Guilford Press.

Batson, C. D., Kennedy, C. L., Nord, L. A., Stocks, E. L., Fleming, D. A., Marzette, C. M., Lishner, D. A., Hayes, R. E., Kolchinsky, L. M. and Zerger, T. (2007) 'Anger at unfairness: is it moral outrage?', *European Journal of Social Psychology*, 37(6): 1,272–85.

Baumeister, R. F., Stillwell, A. M. and Heatherton, T. F. (1994) 'Guilt: an interpersonal approach', *Psychological Bulletin*, 115(2): 243–67.

Ben-Ze'Ev, A. (2000) *The Subtlety of Emotions*. Cambridge: MIT Press.

Branscombe, N. R. and Doosje, B. (2004) 'International perspectives on the experience of collective guilt', in N. R. Branscombe and B. Doosje (eds) *Collective Guilt: International Perspectives*. Cambridge: Cambridge University Press.

Branscombe, N. R., Slugoski, B. and Kappen, D. (2004) 'The measurement of collective guilt: what it is and what it is not', in N. R. Branscombe and B. Doosje (eds) *Collective Guilt: International Perspectives*. Cambridge: Cambridge University Press.

Cassell, E. J. (2002) 'Compassion', in C. Snyder and S. J. Lopez (eds) *Handbook of Positive Psychology*. Oxford: Oxford University Press.

Crisp, R. J., Heuston, S., Farr, M. J. and Turner, R. N. (2007) 'Seeing red or feeling blue: differentiated intergroup emotions and ingroup identification in soccer fans', *Group Processes & Intergroup Relations*, 10(1): 9–26.

Doosje, B., Branscombe, N. R., Spears, R. and Manstead, A. S. R. (1998) 'Guilty by association: when one's group has a negative history', *Journal of Personality and Social Psychology*, 75(4): 872–86.

Dovidio, J. F., Piliavin, J. A., Schroeder, D. A. and Penner, L. A. (2006) *The Social Psychology of Prosocial Behavior*. Mahwah: Lawrence Erlbaum.

Frijda, N. (1986) *The Emotions*. Cambridge: Cambridge University Press.

Frijda, N., Kuipers, P. and Ter Schure, E. (1989) 'Relations among emotion, appraisal, and emotional action readiness', *Journal of Personality and Social Psychology*, 57: 212–28.

Gambaro, S. and Rabin, A. I., (1969) 'Diastolic blood pressure responses following direct and displaced aggression after anger arousal in high- and low-guilt subjects', *Journal of Personality and Social Psychology*, 12(1): 87–94.

Gordijn, E. H., Yzerbyt, V., Wigboldus, D. and Dumont, M. (2006) 'Emotional reactions to harmful intergroup behavior', *European Journal of Social Psychology*, 36(1): 15–30.

Gunn, G. R. and Wilson, A. E. (2011) 'Acknowledging the skeletons in our closet: the effect of group affirmation on collective guilt, collective shame, and reparatory attitudes', *Personality & Social Psychology Bulletin*, 37(11): 1,474–87.

Harth, N. S., Kessler, T. and Leach, C. W. (2008) 'Advantaged group's emotional reactions to intergroup inequality: the dynamics of pride, guilt, and sympathy', *Personality & Social Psychology Bulletin*, 34(1): 115–29.

Hewstone, M., Cairns, E., Voci, A., McLernon, F., Niens, U. and Noor, M. (2004) 'Intergroup forgiveness and guilt in Northern Ireland: social psychological dimensions of "The Troubles"', in N. R. Branscombe and B. Doosje (eds) *Collective Guilt: International Perspectives*. New York: Cambridge University Press.

Hoffman, M. L. (1976) 'Development of prosocial motivation: empathy and guilt', in N. Eisenberg (ed.) *The Development of Prosocial Behavior*. New York: Academic Press.

Iyer, A. and Leach, C. W. (Unpublished manuscript.) *Predicting European American's willingness to challenge systemic discrimination: the limits of group-based guilt*.

Iyer, A. and Leach, C. W. (2010) 'Helping disadvantaged out-groups challenge unjust inequality: the role of group-based emotions', in S. Stürmer and M. Snyder (eds) *The Psychology of Prosocial Behavior: Group Processes, Intergroup Relations, and Helping*. Oxford: Wiley-Blackwell.

Iyer, A., Leach, C. W. and Crosby, F. J. (2003) 'White guilt and racial compensation: the benefits and limits of self-focus', *Personality & Social Psychology Bulletin*, 29(1): 117–29.

Iyer, A., Leach, C. W. and Pedersen, A. (2004) 'Racial wrongs and restitutions: the role of guilt and other group-based emotions', in N. R. Branscombe & B. Doosje (eds) *Collective Guilt: International Perspectives*. New York: Cambridge University Press.

Iyer, A., Schmader, T. and Lickel, B. (2007) 'Why individuals protest the perceived transgressions of their country: the role of anger, shame, and guilt', *Personality & Social Psychology Bulletin*, 33(4): 572–87.

Kessler, T and Mummendey, A. (2001) 'Is there any scapegoat around? Determinants of intergroup conflicts at different categorization levels', *Journal of Personality and Social Psychology*, 81(6): 1,090–102.

Lazarus, R. (1991) *Emotion and Adaption*. New York: Oxford University Press.

Leach, C. W. and Iyer, A. (Unpublished manuscript.) *Rage against the machine? Perceived responsibility for injustice against an outgroup and willingness for political action*.

Leach, C. W., Iyer, A. and Pedersen, A. (2006) 'Anger and guilt about ingroup advantage explain the willingness for political action', *Personality & Social Psychology Bulletin*, 32(9):1, 232–45.

Leach, C. W., Iyer, A. and Pedersen, A. (2007) 'Angry opposition to government redress: when the structurally advantaged perceive themselves as relatively deprived', *The British Journal of Social Psychology*, 46(1): 191–204.

Leach, C. W., Snider, N. and Iyer, A. (2002) '"Poisoning the consciences of the fortunate": The experience of relative advantage and support for social equality', in I. Walker and H. Smith (eds) *Relative Deprivation: Specification, Development and Integration*. New York: Cambridge University Press.

Lewis, M. (1993) 'Self-conscious emotions: embarrassment, pride, shame, and guilt', in M. Lewis & J. Haviland (eds) *Handbook of Emotions*. New York: Guilford Press.

Lickel, B., Steele, R. R. and Schmader, T. (2011) 'Group-based shame and guilt: emerging directions in research', *Social and Personality Psychology Compass*, 5(3): 153–63.

Mackie, D. M., Devos, T. and Smith, E. R. (2000) 'Intergroup emotions: explaining offensive action tendencies in an intergroup context', *Journal of Personality and Social Psychology*, 79(4): 602–16.

Mallett, R. K. and Swim, J. K. (2007) 'The influence of inequality, responsibility and justifiability on reports of group-based guilt for ingroup privilege', *Group Processes & Intergroup Relations*, 10(1): 57–69.

McGarty, C., Pedersen, A., Leach, C. W., Mansell, T., Waller, J. and Bliuc, A. (2005) 'Group-based guilt as a predictor of commitment to apology', *The British Journal of Social Psychology*, 44(4): 659–80.

Montada, L. and Schneider, A. (1989) 'Justice and emotional reactions to the disadvantaged', *Social Justice Research*, 3(4): 313–44.

Nussbaum, M. (1996) 'Compassion: the basic social emotion', *Social Philosophy and Policy*, 13(1): 27–58.

Nussbaum, M. (2001) *Upheavals of Thought*. Cambridge: Cambridge University Press.

Reisenzein, R. (1994) 'Pleasure-arousal theory and the intensity of emotions', *Journal of Personality and Social Psychology*, 67(3): 525–39.

Roseman, I., Wiest, C. and Swartz, T. (1994) 'Phenomenology, behaviours, and goals differentiate discrete emotions', *Journal of Personality and Social Psychology*, 67: 206–21.

Rydell, R. J., Mackie, D. M., Maitner, A. T., Claypool, H. M., Ryan, M. J. and Smith, E. R. (2008) 'Arousal, processing, and risk taking: consequences of intergroup anger', *Personality & Social Psychology Bulletin*, 34(8): 1,141–52.

Schachter, J. (1957) 'Pain, fear, and anger in hypertensives and normotensives: a psycho-physiological study', *Psychosomatic Medicine*, 19(1): 17–29.

Schmader, T. and Lickel, B. (2006) 'The approach and avoidance function of personal and vicarious shame and guilt: comparing reactions to self-caused and other-caused wrong-doing', *Motivation and Emotion*, 30(1): 42–55.

Smith, E. R. (1993). 'Social identity and social emotions: Toward new conceptualizations of prejudice', in D. M. Mackie and D. L. Hamilton (eds), *Affect, cognition, and stereotyping: Interactive processes in group perception*. San Diego: Academic Press.

Stürmer, S. and Simon, B. (2009) 'Pathways to collective protest: calculation, identification, or emotion? A critical analysis of the role of group-based anger in social movement partici-pation', *Journal of Social Issues*, 65(4): 681–705.

Tangney, J. P., Stuewig, J. and Mashek, D. J. (2007a) 'Moral emotions and moral behavior', *Annual Review of Psychology*, 58: 345–72.

Tangney, J. P., Stuewig, J. and Mashek, D. J. (2007b) 'What's moral about the self-conscious emotions?' in J. Tracy, R. Robins and J. P. Tangney (eds) *The Self-Conscious Emotions: Theory and Research*. New York: Guilford Press.

Thomas, E. F., McGarty, C. and Mavor, K. I. (2009) 'Transforming "apathy into movement": the role of prosocial emotions in motivating action for social change', *Personality and Social Psychology Review*, 13(4): 310–33.

Van Zomeren, M., Spears, R., Fischer, A. H. and Leach, C. W. (2004) 'Put your money where your mouth is! Explaining collective action tendencies through group-based anger and group efficacy', *Journal of Personality and Social Psychology*, 87(5): 649–64.

Weiner, B., Graham, S. and Chandler, C. (1982) 'Pity, anger, and guilt: an attributional analysis', *Personality & Social Psychology Bulletin*, 8(2): 226–32.

Whitebrook, M. (2002) 'Compassion as a political virtue', *Political Studies*, 50(3): 529–44.

Yzerbyt, V., Dumont, M., Wigboldus, D. and Gordijn, E. (2003) 'I feel for us: the impact of categorization and identification on emotions and action tendencies', *The British Journal of Social Psychology*, 42(4): 533–49.

Zebel, S., Doosje, B. and Spears, R. (2009) 'How perspective-taking helps and hinders group-based guilt as a function of group identification', *Group Processes & Intergroup Relations*, 12(1): 61–78.

8

THE NEW SOCIAL POLITICS OF PITY

Iain Wilkinson

The cultural experience of so-called 'late' modernity is distinguished by an unprecedented expansion in our field of cultural vision (Jenks 1995). It is also recognised that in this development, large-scale acts of violence and extreme experiences of human suffering feature as routine components of media representations of the social world. John Thompson observes that via television and the internet, we are regularly brought into contact with forms of mass destruction that would be unknown to previous generations (Thompson 1995: 225–7). Similarly, when highlighting the peculiarity of the cultural landscapes we occupy, Michael Ignatieff observes that through modern media of mass communication we have become routine 'voyeurs of the suffering of others, tourists amid their landscapes of anguish' (Ignatieff 1999: 11).

Analysts claim that such experience is serving to radically transform our political outlooks and moral dispositions; and further, that this is made particularly evident in our interpretation and response to human suffering (Chouliaraki 2006; Tester 1994, 1999). It is very likely that the moral and political contradictions that now arise for people in connection with the experience of being positioned as remote witnesses of other people's suffering are without precedent. Luc Boltanski (1999) contends that the experience of being a 'detached observer' of human affliction creates a shared sense of political powerlessness and moral inadequacy; for we routinely find that we have no adequate means to respond to the imperative of action that the brute facts of suffering impress upon us. On a more critical footing, it is argued that, when repeated over time, such experience erodes our capacities for moral feeling and thereby makes it all too easy for us to dissociate ourselves from ties of responsibility towards others (Cohen 2001; Moeller 1999). Indeed, some suggest that the mass dissemination of the imagery of suffering 'normalises' a vivid awareness of human affliction in contexts that foreclose possibilities for participation in public debate and withhold the option of a compassionate engagement with human needs; and all the more so where this is packaged for us as forms of commercial news 'infotainment' (Biehl *et al.* 2007; Thussu 2007).

Whilst recognising these dangers, others would caution us to attend to the extent to which these developments have often been accompanied by new social arrangements for the institutional channelling of public sentiments of compassion toward a more responsive engagement with human problems on a grand scale (Hoïjer 2004; Tester 2001). It is argued that when focussing on the negative potential of the cultural arousal of our pity, critics often fail to attend to the scale and force of mass movements to care for the needs of strangers; and further, how this marks out our times as quite different to any others for which we have record (Wilkinson 2005). Organisations such as International Committee of the Red Cross, Oxfam, Save the Children, Médecins Sans Frontières and Amnesty International are unique to modern times and bear testimony to the fact that we dwell amidst social institutions and political cultures where, arguably, more is done to promote the sanctity of human life than ever before. Indeed, in the work of such organisations we may be witness to the institutional *realisation* of a 'cosmopolitan political community', which for most of the last two hundred years was thought of as no more than a utopian ideal (Beck 2006; Beck and Willms 2004: 176–94). On these grounds it can be suggested that we are still only just beginning to piece together an understanding of how the courting of humanitarian sentiment contributes to the large-scale institutional provision and funding of social care; and most certainly, we have not yet arrived in a position to judge the extent to which our social sympathies might be cultivated as a political virtue.

I am inclined to take seriously this latter view. I am, moreover, concerned to work to develop a more historically and sociologically elaborated account of modern humanitarianism and its presence within the social conditions and cultural experiences that we are made subject to. At the same time as I aim to devise a contribution to a critical sociology of humanitarianism, I also intend to pay heed to the cultural history and development of humanitarian forms of social inquiry. I approach the cultural artefacts of humanitarian campaign work both as objects for study and as holding value as a means to promote social understanding; particularly, where these serve to underline the ways social life takes place as an enactment of substantive human values. Indeed, here I am concerned to promote a conception of social life as an inherently moral experience; and further, as sets of meaningful relationships that greatly matter to people.

For these reasons I approach the attempt to document and explain the forms of human interaction that take place through sentiments of 'pity', 'compassion' and 'sympathy' as holding vital importance for the acquisition of social awareness and the arousal of social conscience. I aim to explore the ways such sentiments serve not only as a spur to social consciousness, but also, as bonds of social attachment and moral responsibility. To this end, my approach to social inquiry aims to recover eighteenth-century traditions of critical debate over the origins and bounds of 'social sympathy'; and further, it works to chart their development through the nineteenth and twentieth centuries and up to the present day. It marks an attempt to develop a new sociology of humanitarian sentiment and moral sensibility. It also aims to understand how sociological thinking might be rooted in and take its course from cultural responses to the problem of suffering.

This is a career project. In this chapter I outline some of the analytical terrain that is involved in this work and I also raise a couple of points for further argument and debate. First, I contend that where contemporary scholars devote the larger portion of their critical endeavour to initiating debates over points of definition and principle, they often go no further than to repeat moral concerns raised by cultural critics in the eighteenth and nineteenth centuries. It is possible to re-trace nearly three hundred years of critical inquiry into the virtue of moral sentiment; and this is often accompanied by sophisticated attempts to understand how our sentimental attachments to others might be fashioned for the purposes of social reform. I argue that, to critically evaluate the character and force of our contemporary social politics of pity, it is vitally important to recognise this as part of an extensive history of cultural debate over the ethics and bounds of modern humanitarianism.

Second, I argue that as part of this endeavour we need to be particularly attentive to how the problem of suffering features as part of our cultural *visualisation* of the social world; and further, to how this has changed over modern times. To this end I contend that it demands that we give privileged place to the task of understanding the ongoing development of our visual literacy of society. Indeed, where it may be argued that the development of social theory has suffered due to the 'denigration of vision' in Western cultures of critique, my work contributes to a counter-trend that aims to give due recognition to the role of visual experience in the advancement of critical thinking about society (Jay 1994). I hold to the view, however, that we are still only beginning to piece together an understanding of how to pursue this goal. We are still very much in the process of gathering an appreciation of the methodological difficulties involved in documenting the mediatised constitution of the cultural realities we inhabit. We have not gone very far towards applying this to sociological understanding. More often than not, sociology is left struggling to explain the influence of mass media over how we experience and relate to one another, let alone how media representations of the world might be appraised as forms of 'sociological knowledge'.

For these reasons, I hold there is still much work to be done in order to clear an analytical space that is adequate to explore our capacities for moral feeling. I further contend that we have yet to devise conceptual frameworks that are adequate to document and explain our contemporary social politics of pity. In what follows, I work with the understanding that progress towards these goals lies in clearing the ground for a new approach to questioning how the human social condition is made part of our moral imagination and an object of humanitarian social concern.

The forging of a controversy

At least as far as contemporary sociological theory is concerned, Luc Boltanski is generally recognised as having provided the most theoretically elaborated account of the social experience of being positioned by mass media as a witness to 'distant suffering' (Boltanski 1999; Chouliaraki 2006; Hoïjer 2004; Scannell 2004). Boltanski contends that, as a possible response to media representations of suffering, this is more accurately depicted as a form of 'pity' (Boltanski 1999). Drawing on earlier arguments advanced by Hannah Arendt in her famous essay on 'The Social Question' (1963), such a view holds that where 'compassion' connotes profound feelings of sympathy for and a strong identification with the situation of those 'in' suffering, by contrast, 'pity' lacks such emotional intensity and is more loosely configured as a moral conviction. When caught up in 'the passion of compassion', as Arendt puts it, it is most likely that people will have no patience or capacity for reasoned debate over points of ethical principle (Arendt 1963: 70–90). She claims that compassion is a 'boundless emotion' that drives rash decisions and inspires thoughtless actions. Whilst 'pity' invites debate over appropriate levels of social concern for those in suffering, by contrast, 'compassion' compels action and leaves no room for debate. As Boltanski emphasises, the possibility of responding to a person with 'pity' is a mark of our moral and social *distance* to them; one might feel 'pity' and at the same time lack any impulse, let alone the compulsion, to take actions to alleviate their suffering. With 'pity' there can and some might say *must* be politics. 'Pity' is loquacious, whilst 'compassion' does not lend itself to talk; rather, it is expressed in bodily gestures and passionate displays of care. Arendt warns:

> As a rule, it is not compassion which sets out to change worldly conditions in order to ease human suffering, but if it does, it will shun the drawn-out wearisome process of persuasion, negotiation, and compromise, which are the processes of law and politics, and lend its voice to the suffering itself, which must claim for swift and direct action, that is, for action with the means of violence.
>
> (Arendt 1963: 86–7)

Such analytical distinctions and critical viewpoints draw on a long tradition of public debate over the ways in which moral sentiment might serve as a civic virtue. At least as far as its philosophical lineage is concerned, this can be traced back to the latitudinarian theology of the seventeenth-century Cambridge Platonists (Crane 1934). In this context, humanitarian sentiment was promoted as a counter-reaction to the sectarian prejudices that fuelled the English Civil War and as a progressive riposte to the pessimism of Thomas Hobbes' political philosophy (Herdt 2001). It is in the eighteenth-century 'Enlightenment of Sympathy', however, that cultural critics made the most concerted efforts to understand how moral sentiment serves to endow us with our sociability and capacities for social solidarity (Frazer 2010). Indeed, here the very possibility of conceiving of ourselves as 'social beings' with a 'common humanity' was held to be relative to the depth, range and quality of our sympathetic attachments to others. In this respect, it was argued that the cultivation of social recognition and social understanding is sustained by the force of 'fellow feeling' (Mullan 1988).

Key figures in the Scottish Enlightenment such as Francis Hutcheson, David Hume and Adam Smith recognised 'social sympathy' as a form of moral experience in which we are set to encounter our ties of responsibility to others. Whilst by no means agreeing among themselves as to the means by or extent to which our 'moral sense' might be cultivated for the good of society, they all shared in the understanding that social life was founded on 'fellow feeling'; and further, that such sentiment has a positive role to play in the pursuit of civic virtue. Through their works it is also possible to detect an increasing concern to defend such views against the charge of political naivety. Whilst in his earlier address to the topic Hutcheson simply promotes the idea that our human thought and behaviours can be motivated by benevolence, through Hume's *A Treatise of Human Nature* ([1739–40] 1969) and *An Enquiry Concerning the Principles of Morals* ([1751] 1987) to Smith's *The Theory of Moral Sentiments* ([1759] 2006), it is possible to trace the development of a more conceptually elaborated analysis of the apparent frailties and partiality of our sympathetic attachments to others.

In this regard it is important to recognise that the suggestion that 'social sympathy' might serve as a morally progressive force for the good of society always courted controversy; and further, that this grew more heated as the century progressed. Francis Hutcheson's interventions were motivated by a concern to refute Bernard Mandeville's portrayal of humanity as fundamentally selfish in *The Fable of the Bees* ([1714] 1970) (Carey 2000; Sprague 1954). Furthermore, Adam Smith was moving to engage with outbreaks of critical concern surrounding 'the eighteenth-century cult of sensibility'; particularly those addressed to the extent to which feeling might be divorced from action. Indeed, on many accounts the period between 1780 to 1800 now stands out as the time where moral sentiment was taken up as a key matter for critical public debate. Here essayists such as Henry Mackenzie turned from an heroic portrayal of 'the man of feeling' to adopt a position of critique that condemns the 'enthusiasm of sentiment' as a clear danger to society. Mackenzie now warned that all too often sentimentalists are to be found 'talking of virtues which they never practice' and as being all too prepared to separate 'conscience from feeling' (Mackenzie [1771] 2001a; [1785] 2001b: 100). Similarly, albeit with the hope of rescuing moral sentiment as a public virtue, in the 'Preface' to his *Lyrical Ballads*, William Wordsworth condemned the 'degrading thirst after stimulation' that he witnessed in the popular enjoyment of sentimentalism (Wordsworth [1802] 2003: 10).

In addition to the widespread recognition that many people were more excited by the vicarious pleasures to be drawn from sentimentalism than by the possibility of making moral feeling a guide to the common good, it was also feared that the courting of high emotions in public life served as an incitement to violent conduct. Historical reviews of the period are now inclined to bring emphasis to the ways in which the fear that the French Revolution might spread to Britain consolidated the movement to erase sentiment from public affairs (Ellis 1996; Jones 1993). It was widely held that Robespierre had exploited a culture of unregulated sentimentality to initiate the Reign of Terror, and thereby had brutally exposed the potential for moral feeling to be co-opted for the purpose of mob rule. Indeed, William Reddy argues that more than any other factor at this time, it was the widespread belief, at least within governmental and elite intellectual circles, that an excess of moral feeling had fuelled a passion for revolutionary violence in France that subsequently led to it being cast as an anathema to civilized conduct and rational debate (Reddy 2000). On Reddy's account, moreover, it is in this counter-revolutionary move-ment to portray moral sentiment as an intellectual weakness and political vice that we find the origins of a cultural tradition wherein 'the Enlightenment' is portrayed, and indeed celebrated, above all as the harbinger of modern rationality. Thereafter, it became commonplace for civilised conduct to be identified with the extent to which a person behaves with a *dispassionate* regard for others; and where later com-mentators such as Arendt and Boltanski adopt a critical standpoint in which matters of sentiment are cast as a hindrance to reason, we should understand that this, as a view, is still very much coloured by the events of this time.

The rebellion of sentiment in social thought

In historical accounts of the rise of social science in the first half of the nineteenth century, it is now widely recognised that this was characterised by a culture of strict rationality; and indeed, that many of the pioneering attempts to render 'society' an object of scientific study were at the same time allied to gov-ernmental policies designed to impose stricter measures of rationalisation upon human conduct (Goldman 1983, 1991; Poovey 1995, 1998). Part of the expla-nation for this is sought in the extent to which the early practitioners of social science were driven by a 'moral aspiration' for *orderly* social reform. Indeed, on many accounts, at its origins sociological inquiry was politically conservative; and insofar as it was oriented towards the progressive development of society, it was largely utilitarian in its ethos and intent (Giddens 1976; Nisbet 1966).

Taking Edwin Chadwick's 1842 Report on *The Sanitary Condition of the Labouring Population* as her prime example, Mary Poovey argues that, at least as far as Britain is concerned, the official account of social life took on a highly abstract form (Poovey 1995:106–30). The intellectual validity and worth of social investigation was iden-tified in the extent to which it served as a means to translate social problems into numbers for statistical calculation. She argues that Chadwick pioneered a technical form of representation that, whilst working to present aggregated populations as an object for policy debate, also provided a means to 'disaggregate' the production of knowledge about the moral experience of social life. Here it became possible to engage in debate on social conditions as though they were 'objectively' removed from the bounds of morality and politics.

In this cultural setting, more sentimentally geared accounts of social life were decried as mere 'literature' along with the charge that they relied on excessively subjective interpretations of reality and experience (Lepenies 1988). In the senti-mental cast of their portrayal of the plight of people suffering extreme conditions of material poverty, they were, moreover, frequently identified as an obstruction to the implementation of 'sound policy' to discourage the 'undeserving poor' (Crocker 1987). Indeed, by the middle of the nineteenth century, it was widely recognised that, through their sympathetic accounts of people's social hardships and miseries, some 'humanitarian' writers were operating from a critical position that was designed to provoke the ire and consternation of establishment authorities. Moreover, it was frequently designed to question the morality of industrial capitalism and its favoured principles of political economy.

In 1844, the *Spectator* magazine called for the creation of a new political party to oppose 'laissez faire' by the 'rebellion of sentiment' (Roberts 2002: 258). In this setting, the novelist, political journalist and newspaper editor, Charles Dickens, was a figure of considerable influence. Indeed, when it comes to assessing the cultural politics of moral sentiment within mid-century Victorian culture, many are inclined to treat Dickens' work as the exemplar of the genre (Ledger 2007; Mason 2007; Poovey 1995: 155–81; Williams 1973: 218–9). It is widely understood that in his opposition to the cold-calculating statistical representation of social problems, Dickens sought to fashion a style of writing that evoked moral feeling and thereby a wider awareness of the moral values enacted within economic transactions and everyday social behaviours. In his satirical report on the annual meeting of the British Association for the Advancement of Science (1843) and in *Hard Times* (1854) in his caricature of Thomas Gradgrind, 'the man of facts and calculations', he makes clear his opposition to any form of symbolic representation that aims to deny attention being brought to the moral texture of social life as it is encountered in experience (Dickens [1843] 2009; [1854] 1995). As Mary Poovey notes, he decried the 'frightful empiricism' that holds that it is only in the contexts of its representation in the form of statistical laws that 'society' should be held up as an object for policy debate; for in this move individual human beings are all too easily 'obliterated' by numerical averages (Poovey 1993: 269). By contrast, in his journalism and novels, Dickens made it his mission to have his readers experience the sensation of sentimentality so as to raise the volume of public debate over the forms of moral experience that they were subject to, and see how in turn their actions were morally implicated in the discord of society (Mason 2007).

Similarly, in his 'letters' to the *Morning Chronicle* ([1849–50] 1971) and later book *London Labour and the London Poor* ([1861–2] 2010), Henry Mayhew did not shy away from making a moral appeal to social sympathy as part of his effort to document how people struggle to survive in insanitary urban conditions and on desperately low wages. Indeed, this was widely recognised as a major component of his 'success' in awakening the social conscience of the London middle classes. At the same time, it was identified by his critics as a primary reason to condemn his work. For example, following Mayhew's break from the *Morning Chronicle* in the summer of 1850 over the editorial censoring of his criticisms of 'free trade' and arguments in favour of protective tariffs, a fellow journalist, Angus Bethune Reach, reported on the incident by declaring:

> I am disposed to think ... that the editor of the *Chronicle* would have done well had he struck his pen through at least four of every eight columns of the disjointed lucubrations and melodramatic ravings of Mr Mayhew's sentimental draymen and poor artisans. Ever since Mr Mayhew's communications on the state of the poor attracted any attention, their author has kept summoning together public meetings of the classes among whom he had been mingling, apparently for no other purpose than to puff his own benevolent spirit.
>
> (cited in Thompson 1971: 39)

The suspicion that the literary attempt to arouse social sympathy was motivated by a project of self-aggrandisement or other insidious political motives was also voiced on many occasions as part of the critical response to the bestselling novel of the nineteenth century, Harriet Beecher Stowe's *Uncle Tom's Cabin* ([1852] 1994). It is widely held that the power of this work to awaken sympathy and direct moral feeling towards the plight of slaves was decisive to the anti-slavery cause; indeed, Jane Tompkins goes so far as to suggest that it is 'the most dazzling exemplar' of the power of literary sentimentalism to influence the course of history (Tompkins 1985: 125). At the same time, however, from the moment of its publication it attracted an inordinate amount of criticism. As Ted Hovet Jr notes, throughout the 1850s many reviewers sought to publicly condemn *Uncle Tom's Cabin* for its overly contrived and inaccurate portrayal of slavery, and at the same time moved to claim that Stowe revelled in her notoriety as a means to promote her career as a bestselling author (Hovet Jr 2007: 69). Through most of the twentieth century, moreover, at least within the field of American literary criticism, Stowe's writing was dismissed as morally degenerate, anti-intellectual, narcissistic and naively duplicitous. For example, in one of the more scathing dismissals of *Uncle Tom's Cabin*, James Baldwin claims that the overall effect of the book is to 'activate' and 'reinforce' the very oppression it sets out to decry. He writes:

> *Uncle Tom's Cabin* is a very bad novel, having, in its self-righteous, virtuous sentimentality, much in common with *Little Women*. Sentimentality, the ostentatious parading of excessive and spurious emotion, is the mark of dishonesty, the inability to feel; the wet eyes of the sentimentalist betray his aversion to experience, his fear of life, his arid heart; and it is always, therefore, the signal of secret and violent inhumanity, the mask of cruelty.
>
> (Baldwin 1949: 578–9)

On this account, Stowe should be condemned not only for propagating racial stereotypes, but also and above all for the sensational tone of her writing. For Baldwin, *Uncle Tom's Cabin* represents no more than a crude outburst of moral panic. He contends that Stowe's display of 'virtuous rage' and anguished dwelling upon acts of cruelty leaves no space for the development of critical thinking. He claims that the possibility of questioning society is denied by the passion of protest; and thereby, holds that Stowe unwittingly colludes in the maintenance of social structures and cultural attitudes that are implicated in the conditions that give rise to the violation of people's human rights.

An alternative view now holds that whilst *Uncle Tom's Cabin* deploys a morally odious form of racialism as a means to tell its story, we should still be concerned to work at understanding how it served to equip its readers with an expanded vision of the social world as well as the moral conviction whereby they were moved to accept an obligation to care for others. Accordingly, the greater danger here is that we fail to attend to the ways in which here, as well as on many other occasions, the cultivation of moral sentiment allowed for a mass awakening of social conscience on a scale that was previously deemed unimaginable. In this respect, it is with a greater concern to explain the role played by social sympathy within the cultivation of a sociological imagination and progressive movements for social change that we may venture to recover and critically reappraise the history of sentimentalism and its social politics of pity.

The social politics of pity

When working to understand why people might be motivated by moral feeling to care for distant others, Adam Smith held that this was limited by the social and cultural conditions under which we were made witness to their suffering. In this regard, moreover, he saw more cause to underline the frailties rather than strengths of our moral imagination and impulse. At one point he argued that, on being presented with news of a great disaster in China, a European may be moved to express his sorrow on behalf of the misfortunes of the Chinese people; but that nevertheless, he would quickly return to his own pleasures and:

> ... provided he never saw them, he will snore with the most profound security over the ruin of a hundred millions of his brethren, and the destruction of that immense multitude [would be] an object less interesting to him [a] paltry misfortune of his own.
>
> (Smith [1790] 2006: 132)

Elsewhere, he argued that when provoked by moral feeling, people tend to be caught up in a complex struggle to moderate their sympathies in line with how they understand themselves to be judged by others. For Smith, social behaviour is akin to a dramatic public performance in which we are concerned to win the approval of our audience (Marshall 1984). He further suggests that, in the majority of cases, it is more with a concern to look good in the eyes of our peers than from a genuine commitment to the welfare of others that we are provoked into action (Smith [1790] 2006: 113).

For many years now it has been possible to argue that Adam Smith greatly underestimated the extent to which social sympathy might be cultivated as an active force within the political arena. When devising his thesis, he was not in a position to reflect back on the history and development of modern humanitarianism and the many political campaigns that have sought to provide us with an education of compassion. Smith was alert to the fact that such work relied on media of cultural exchange such as novels and newspapers, and further, that our moral imagination was animated in connection to our capacity to visualise a person's social circumstances; particularly, how these involved them in the experience of suffering. He hardly began, however, to see how the symbolic representation of social suffering might be crafted to provoke our pity; and further, how humanitarianism organisations might work to channel the emotional response to 'distance suffering' into active programmes of social reform.

The inclusion of engravings of bodies in pain was an essential component of the earliest narrative attempts to evoke moral sentiment on behalf of the welfare of others (de Las Casas [1542] 1992). Indeed, some argue that the pictorial representation of human suffering was the 'ammunition' that did most to win public support for campaigns against the cruel treatment of women and children in the workplace and the enslavement of black people (Abruzzo 2011; Halttunen 1995; John 2006; Klarer 2005). It is also suggested that, more generally, when it came to recognising the experience of urban poverty, it was the enormous expansion in the cultural means to visually represent the lives of poor people on a grand scale that served to engage the public in debates over the need for social reform (Casteras 1995).

When taking stock of the cultural experience of modernity, we should recognise that on many occasions it has involved people 'in a sort of frenzy of the visible' which has induced quite dramatic awakenings to the reality of social worlds (Comolli 1980; Flint 2000). The great multiplication and dissemination of visual representations of society as well as the unprecedented expansion of the technological means to visualise human experience has radically transformed our capacity for self and social understanding. Moreover, it is also the case that in this history, humanitarian social reformers are often found operating in the vanguard of movements to develop and expand our social vision. This is certainly the case in Henry Mayhew's pioneering use of daguerreotypes to enhance his illustrative accounts of the lives of the London poor. In his pioneering use of flash photography to document the conditions of New York tenements in the 1890s, Jacob Riis also stands out as prime example of a humanitarian social activist, who, whilst pursuing his cause, cultivated his readers' sociological understanding of human experience (Riis [1890] 1997).

More recently, it is often through co-ordinated attempts to mobilise humanitarian sentiment on a grand scale that we have been alerted to the technological potential to visualise society in global terms; and further, for this to inspire global social consciousness and global bonds of sociality. In this respect, arguably, we are still only beginning to culturally decant the experience and impact of events such as 'Live Aid', the scale of the response to the 2004 Sumatra-Andaman earthquake tsunami or the speed with which international aid agencies gathered the resources to engage in the effort of saving lives in the aftermath of the 2010 Haiti earthquake. It is also the case, moreover, that we now find organisations such as Oxfam,

Amnesty International and Save the Children operating at the forefront of attempts to explore how so-called 'social media' might be used to forge political alliances and virtual communities actively committed to the pursuit of the means to combat human suffering. For example, Kate Nash argues that the possibilities afforded by new interactive communication media such as the internet and mobile phones for a two-way engagement between humanitarian campaign organisations and the public are creating a new 'cultural politics' where larger numbers of people than ever before in human history are actively involved in expressing their solidarity with the suffering of distant others (Nash 2008).

On these grounds, I suggest that the visualisation of the human experience of society is still much in the making. I also hold that we are still very much caught up in the process of realising the technological, cultural and institutional means to interpret and respond to this. We are not yet near to apprehending the range of possibilities for crafting moral sentiment in a pro-social direction. As yet we do not know how far it may be possible for people to be socialised into a sentiment-fired *practice* of care for others. Whilst courting many longstanding hazards relating to the potential for moral feeling to be driven along a course of ideological abuse, those operating with a social politics of pity are still in the process of discovering the cultural forms and terms of social interaction in which this serves the good of humanity. In this regard, there may be many more occasions where our capacity for social understanding will be re-made anew.

Concluding remarks

By the mid-nineteenth century, there was already a highly sophisticated 'economy of attention to suffering' (Spelman 1997: 1–14). In many instances, anti-slavery novelists and feminist pamphleteers were keenly alert to the many conflicts of interpretation as well as the wide range of political responses that might take place in response to their sentimental framing of social problems. Whilst working to 'educate' moral feeling so as to enable a sympathetic understanding of people's lives, they were very much aware that their style of writing was liable to court a great deal of controversy. For example, Elizabeth Clark notes that anti-slavery campaigners such as Theodore Dwight Weld and Lydia Maria Child devoted a considerable amount of energy to crafting texts that openly challenged those who would denounce them as mere purveyors of 'sensationalism' (Clark 1995). She claims that Weld and Child were not only concerned to appeal to the most 'scrupulous standards of proof' so as to combat sceptics' dismissal of their work, but also, that they sought to carefully temper their accounts of the violence done to slaves with detailed depictions of their friendships and family lives. Clark argues that, particularly following the success of *Uncle Tom's Cabin*, it was widely recognised that where readers' sympathies were engaged by 'fleshed out' accounts of slaves as 'whole people', then the depiction of their suffering would hold greater 'strategic value' as a means to shape public opinion in favour of the anti-slavery cause. Similarly, Karen Halttunen notes that whilst crafting their studies and reports, mid-nineteenth century humanitarian social reformers were also concerned to guard against the possibility that their readers would relate to the portrayal of human suffering as a sensational form of entertainment. In this respect, she argues that many were alert to the fact that by their critical praxis, they were 'caught in a contradiction of their own making'; namely, that while working to expose the 'obscenity' of unnecessary pain and violence, they might also make people inured to the shock of being a remote witness to human suffering, even to the point where some would treat the experience of gazing upon the pain of others as a gratuitous pleasure (Halttunen 1995).

Both Clark and Halttunen note that, in their concern to inform the emotional dispositions and practices of 'the public', most nineteenth-century social reformers were conversant with longstanding debates over the virtues of moral sentiment. It may be argued, furthermore, that they were more sensitive than we may ever be to the fact that their work was liable to court a hostile critical response. By their literary tactics, they were declaring themselves to be opposed to establishment politics and elite moral opinion. The courting of social sympathy was a radical act by which one was liable to be dismissed as a sensationalising self-promoter, a soft-hearted friend to the 'undeserving poor' or a revolutionary giving succour to violent protest and civil disorder. Yet this was a risk that they were prepared to take; for aside from embracing the fact that moral feeling matters in the conduct of social life, they remain convinced that it was an integral part of the attempt to understand the human social condition. In this regard, to take flight from social sympathy was tantamount to an abandonment of human social concern.

Past criticisms and current controversies are an insufficient guide to understanding the limits of possibility. The quest for the 'professional' accreditation of social science, particularly in the British and American academies, involved a concerted attempt to disassociate sociology from humanitarian movements of social reform (Lannoy 2004; Deegan 1981, 1988; Lengermann and Niebrugge-Brantley 2002; Turner and Turner 1990). On this setting, an ideology of rationalism often served to propagate an impoverished account of social life; particularly in terms of its embodied consequences and its effects as moral experience. The frequently gendered and racial hurt left by the drive to remove moral feeling from the work of sociology is contributing to a new movement to question how social bonds of sympathy may once again be studied both as an elemental part of the constitution of society and as a vital component of the attempt to research the human social condition as such. In domains of social inquiry inspired by feminist scholarship, American literary criticism, working-class studies and the medical humanities, there is now a widespread suspicion that there is a good deal of 'unfinished business' to be explored within the cultural politics of sentimentality (Berlant 2008).

By no means should this require us to forsake the attempt to understand the ways in which emotive portrayals of social life might serve to establish and sustain unequal power relations. We should also recognise that there are many occasions where our moral sense might be indulged to the cost of the effort to engage in critical thinking. It should, however, leave us prepared to treat social sympathy as a necessary component of social understanding. To this end, we might also initiate our sociological endeavour from the understanding that insofar as moral experience is strained from the record of social life, then it is rendered sterile as a means to attend to how society matters for people.

References

Abruzzo, M. (2011) *Polemical Pain: Slavery, Cruelty and the Rise of Humanitarianism*, Baltimore: The John Hopkins University Press.

Arendt, H. (1963) 'The Social Question' in *On Revolution*, Harmondsworth: Penguin.

Baldwin, J. (1949) 'Everybody's Protest Novel', *Partisan Review*, 16: 578–85.

Beck, U. (2006) *Cosmopolitan Vision*, Cambridge: Polity Press.

Beck, U. and Willms, J. (2004) *Conversations with Ulrich Beck*, Cambridge: Polity Press.

Beecher Stowe, H. ([1852] 1994) *Uncle Tom's Cabin*, New York: W. W. Norton & Co.

Berlant, L. (2008) *The Female Complaint: The Unfinished Business of Sentimentality in American Culture*, Durham: Duke University Press.

Biehl, J., Good, B., and Kleinman, A. (eds) (2007) 'Introduction: Rethinking Subjectivity', in *Subjectivity: Ethnographic Investigations,* Berkeley: University of California Press.

Boltanski, L. (1999) *Distant Suffering: Morality, Media and Politics*, Cambridge: Cambridge University Press.

Carey, D. (2000) 'Hutcheson's Moral Sense and the Problem of Innateness', *Journal of the History of Philosophy*, 38(1): 103–110.

Casteras. S. P. (1995) 'Seeing the Unseen: Pictorial Problematics and Victorian Images of Class, Poverty and Urban Life', in C. T. Christ and J. O. Jordan (eds) *Victorian Literature and the Victorian Visual Imagination*, Berkeley: University of California Press.

Chouliaraki, L. (2006) *The Spectatorship of Suffering*, London: Sage Publications.

Clark, E. B. (1995) 'The Sacred Rights of the Weak: Pain, Sympathy and the Culture of Individual Rights in Antebellum America', *The Journal of American History*, 82(2): 463–93.

Cohen, S. (2001) *States of Denial: Knowing About Atrocities and Suffering*, Cambridge: Polity Press.

Comolli, J. L. (1980) 'Machines of the Visible' in T. de Lauretis and S. Heath (eds) *The Cinematic Apparatus*, London: Macmillan.

Crane, R. S. (1934) 'Suggestions Towards a Genealogy of the "Man of Feeling"', *English Literary History*, 1(3): 205–30.

Crocker, R. H. (1987) 'The Victorian Poor Law in Crisis and Change: Southampton, 1870–1895', *Albion* 19(1): 19–44.

De las Casas, B. ([1542] 1992) *A Short Account of the Destruction of the Indies*, London: Penguin.

Deegan, M. J. (1981) 'Early Women Sociologists and the American Sociological Society: The Patterns of Exclusion and Participation', *The American Sociologist*, 16 (February): 14–24.

Deegan, M. J. (1988) *Jane Addams and the Men of the Chicago School, 1892–1918*, New Brunswick, NJ: Transaction Books.

Dickens, C. ([1843] 2009) *The Mudfog Papers*, Texas: Talamh Books.

Dickens, C. ([1854] 1995) *Hard Times*, London: Penguin Books.

Ellis, M. (1996) *The Politics of Sensibility: Race, Gender and Commerce in the Sentimental Novel*, Cambridge: Cambridge University Press.

Flint, K. (2000) *The Victorians and the Visual Imagination*, Cambridge: Cambridge University Press.

Frazer, M. L. (2010) *The Enlightenment of Sympathy: Justice and the Moral Sentiments in the Eighteenth Century and Today*, Oxford: Oxford University Press.

Giddens, A. (1976) 'Classical Social Theory and the Origins of Modern Sociology', *American Journal of Sociology*, 81(4): 703–29.

Goldman, L. (1983) 'The Origins of British "Social Science": Political Economy, Natural Science and Statistics, 1830–35', *The Historical Journal* 26(3): 587–616.

Goldman, L. (1991) 'Statistics and the Science of Society in Early Victorian Britain: An Intellectual Context for the General Register Office', *Social History of Medicine*, 4(3): 415–34.

Halttunen, K. (1995) 'Humanitarianism and the Pornography of Pain in Anglo-American Culture', *The American Historical Review*, 100(2): 303–34.

Herdt, J. A. (2001) 'The Rise of Sympathy and the Question of Divine Suffering', *Journal of Religious Ethics*, 29(3): 367–99.

Hoïjer, B. (2004) 'The Discourse of Global Compassion: The Audience and Media Reporting of Human Suffering', *Media Culture & Society*, 26(4): 513–31.

Hovet, T. Jr (2007) 'Harriet Martineau's Exceptional American Narratives: Harriet Beecher Stowe, John Brown and the Redemption of Your National Soul', *American Studies*, 48(1): 63–76.

Hume, D. ([1739–40] 1969) *A Treatise of Human Nature*, London: Penguin.

Hume, D. ([1751] 1987) *An Enquiry Concerning the Principles of Morals*, Indianapolis: Hackett Publishing.

Ignatieff, M. (1999) *The Warrior's Honour: Ethnic War and the Modern Conscience*, London: Vintage.

Jay, M. (1994) *Downcast Eyes: The Denigration of Vision in Twentieth Century French Thought*, Berkeley: University of California Press.

Jenks, C. (1995) *Visual Culture*, London: Routledge.

John, A. V. (2006) *By the Sweat of their Brow: Women Workers at Victorian Coal Mines*, London: Routledge.

Jones, C. (1993) 'Radical Sensibility in the 1790s', in *Reflections of Revolution: Images of Revolution*, A. Yarrington and K. Everest (eds), London: Routledge.

Klarer, M. (2005) 'Humanitarian Pornography: John Gabriel Stedman's *Narrative of a Five Year's Expedition against the Revolted Negroes of Surinam* [1796]', *New Literary History*, 36(4): 559–87.

Lannoy, P. (2004) 'When Robert E. Park was (Re) Writing "The City": Biography, the Social Survey, and the Science of Sociology', *The American Sociologist*, 35(1) 34–62.

Ledger, S. (2007) *Dickens and the Popular Radical Imagination*, Cambridge: Cambridge University Press.

Lengermann, P. M. and Niebrugge-Brantley, J. (2002) 'Back to the Future: Settlement Sociology, 1885–1930', *The American Sociologist* (Fall): 5–20.

Lepenies, W. (1988) *Between Literature and Science: The Rise of Sociology*, Cambridge: Cambridge University Press.

Mackenzie, H. ([1771] 2001a) *The Man of Feeling*, Oxford: Oxford University Press.

Mackenzie, H. ([1785] 2001b) 'Henry Mackenzie, The Lounger, No 20 (Saturday, 18 June 1785)', in *The Man of Feeling*, Oxford: Oxford University Press.

Mandeville, B. ([1714] 1970) *The Fable of the Bees*, Harmondsworth: Penguin.

Marshall, D. (1984) 'Adam Smith and the Theatricality of Moral Sentiments', *Critical Inquiry*, 10 (June): 592–613.

Mason, E. (2007) 'Feeling Dickensian Feeling', 19: *Interdisciplinary Studies in the Long Nineteenth Century*, (4): 1–19.

Mayhew, H. ([1849–50] 1971) *The Unknown Mayhew: Selections from the Morning Chronicle 1849–50*, E. P. Thompson and E. Yeo (eds), Merlin: London.

Mayhew, H. ([1861–2] 2010) *London Labour and the London Poor: A Selected Edition*, Oxford: Oxford University Press.

Moeller, S. (1999) *Compassion Fatigue*, London: Routledge.

Mullan, J. (1988) *Sentiment and Sociability: The Language of Feeling in the Eighteenth Century*, London: Clarendon Press.

Nash, K. (2008) 'Global Citizenship as Show Business: The Cultural Politics of Make Poverty History', *Media, Culture & Society*, 30(2): 167–81.

Nisbet, R. (1966) *The Sociological Tradition*, Heinemann: London.

Poovey, M. (1993) 'Figures of Arithmetic, Figures of Speech: The Discourse of Statistics in the late 1830s', *Critical Inquiry*, 19(2): 256–76.

Poovey, M. (1995) *Making a Social Body: British Cultural Formation 1830–1864*, Chicago: University of Chicago Press.

Poovey, M. (1998) *A History of the Modern Fact: Problems of Knowledge in the Sciences of Wealth and Society*, Chicago: Chicago University Press.

Reddy, W. M. (2000) 'Sentimentalism and its Erasure: The Role of Emotions in the Era of the French Revolution', *The Journal of Modern History*, 72(1): 109–52.

Riis, J. A. ([1890] 1997) *How the Other Half Lives*, London: Penguin.

Roberts, F. D. (2002) *The Social Conscience of the Early Victorians*, Stanford: Stanford University Press.

Scannell, P. (2004) 'What Reality Has Misfortune?', *Media, Culture & Society*, 26(4): 573–584.

Smith, A. ([1790] 2006) *The Theory of Moral Sentiments*, New York: Dover Publications.

Spelman, E. V. (1997) *Fruits of Sorrow: Framing Our Attention to Suffering*, Boston: Beacon.

Sprague, E. (1954) 'Francis Hutcheson and the Moral Sense', *The Journal of Philosophy*, 51(24): 794–800.

Tester, K. (1994) *Media Culture and Morality*, London: Routledge.

Tester, K. (1999) 'The Moral Consequentiality of Television', *European Journal of Social Theory* 2(4): 469–83.

Tester, K. (2001) *Compassion, Morality and the Media*, Buckingham: Open University Press.

Thomas, K. (1983) *Man and the Natural World: Changing Attitudes in England 1500–1800*, London: Penguin.

Thompson, E. P. (1971) 'Mayhew as Social Investigator' in *The Unknown Mayhew: Selections from the Morning Chronicle 1849–50*, E. P. Thompson and E. Yeo (eds), Merlin: London.

Thompson, J. B. (1995) *The Media and Modernity: A Social Theory of the Media*, Cambridge: Polity Press.

Thussu, D. K. (2007) *News as Entertainment: The Rise of Global Infotainment*, London: Sage.

Tompkins, J. (1985) *Sensational Designs: The Cultural Work of American Fiction*, Oxford: Oxford University Press.

Turner, S. P. and Turner, J. H. (1990) *The Impossible Science: An Institutional Analysis of American Sociology*, Newbury Park, CA: Sage.

Wilkinson, I. (2005) *Suffering: A Sociological Introduction*, Cambridge: Polity Press.

Williams, R. (1973) *The Country and the City*, London: Hogarth.

Wordsworth, W. ([1802] 2003) 'Preface to *Lyrical Ballads*' in *Wordsworth and Coleridge Lyrical Ballads and Other Poems*, Ware: Wordsworth Editions Ltd.

PART III

CRITICAL COMPASSION

9

COMPASSION AND THE STOLEN GENERATIONS

Joanne Faulkner[1]

In May 1997, *Bringing Them Home*, the Human Rights and Equal Opportunity Commission's report on removed Aboriginal children, was tabled in the Australian Federal Parliament. The report represented the culmination of two years' gathering of testimony from individuals who were separated from their families by state agencies. Its authors, Sir Ronald Wilson and Professor Mick Dodson, chose to preserve the witnesses' accounts in their own words rather than paraphrasing them. The effect of this choice is a profoundly moving document: presented in the first-person voice, the testimony of *Bringing Them Home* is addressed to the reader directly, and, as such, stages anew the distress and trauma of those who tell their stories. The report appeals to readers' sense of compassion, and is intended to motivate a desire to act in accordance with such compassionate feeling. This gesture recalls a tradition of understanding political subjectivity that has roots in modern thought from Hutcheson to Rousseau. It bids its audience to access a part of the self that resonates with the vulnerability all humanity shares, but to which some are materially more exposed than others. It appeals to a capacity to internalize the other's suffering that has been fostered by liberal political culture since the eighteenth century. The effects of such internalization, however, are not straightforward.

For while it is clear that *Bringing Them Home* was emotionally poignant, less certain is whether it resulted in tangible improvement in material and political conditions for indigenous Australians. These conditions have arguably worsened since 1997, despite numerous gestures of sympathy tendered towards the 'stolen generations' by politicians and the Australian public alike.[2] This complicates the modern assumption that compassion engenders appropriate humanitarian action. In the case of the various policies enacted in the name of Aboriginals' protection, there may even be grounds for the suspicion that expressions of sympathy exhaust themselves in fine rhetoric; or worse, give rise to further injury through a perverse desire for the spectacle of others' suffering. For it is one thing to arouse feelings of vulnerability in moral bystanders. It is still another feat of the imagination to productively respond to such feelings.

This chapter addresses the dual roles of compassion and the aesthetic imagination in negotiating social inequality, particularly reconciliation. *Bringing Them Home* brought into the sphere of public life a new collective identity, making visible for the first time the 'stolen generations'. In so doing, it also brought to light lies of omission through which mainstream Australian identity had hitherto been formed. Various responses in the community ensued, ranging from identification to denial.[3] Yet even to the extent that compassion prevails, a disconnect between compassionate identification with indigenous people and recognition of their political agency is evident. Jacques Rancière's account of aesthetics as a 'distribution of the sensible' through which the political becomes possible serves as a useful term of art in understanding this disconnect. According to Rancière, modes of representation both open and delimit what (and whom) the community recognizes as politically salient. For Rancière, an analogy or metaphor not only *renders intelligible* a political concept: crucially, the representation – *and the quality of the addressee's response to it* – also gives form to the conceivable variety of ethical and political relationship (Rancière 2004).

With this 'distribution of the sensible' in mind, I wish here to examine the quality of political subjectivity and community that has emerged from Australians' engagements with *Bringing Them Home*, among other discourses about Aboriginality. The 'stolen generations' report prompted feelings of sympathy for a previously unrecognized category of people, and in this sense provoked a 'redistribution of the sensible'. Such sympathy was enabled by an identification: non-Aboriginal, middle-class readers were brought to a realization about a suffering at the heart of Aboriginality, by themselves feeling that suffering as if it were their own. The imminent danger of such identification, however, is that a difference in power and privilege between addresser and addressee may remain unrecognized. The situations of Aboriginal and white Australians are not equivalent; and so, if a redistribution of the sensible were to take place in response to *Bringing Them Home*, there would need first to be an effort on the part of the report's audience to realize that this suffering *is not their own* – that, to the contrary, they are beneficiaries of Aboriginal dispossession.

My contention is that until this asymmetry is adequately (and publically) addressed – and the complicated and problematic potentialities of sympathetic identification acknowledged – appreciation of the specific interests and agency of indigenous people will continue to be remote to most Australians. In order to demonstrate the potential failure of sympathetic identification to comprehend difference, I will contrast the optimism of Enlightenment philosophy regarding sympathy with the contemporaneous, but more sceptical, elaboration of identification developed by Donatien Alphonse François de Sade. Sade's writing teaches the extent to which modern subjects enjoy a sense of their own interiority by means of passionate engagement with others' suffering. Moreover, Sade places radically into question the presumption of much Enlightenment thought that the social is grounded in an hegemony of desires and sympathies. In this light, the onus is on recipients of *Bringing Them Home* to respond in ways that open a space for interests, demands and identities that likely contradict – rather than feed into – their own. It is hoped that a modified adoption of Sade's critical engagement with modern moral discourses will suggest a redistribution of the political sensible that will render more visible indigenous alterity.

The problem this chapter addresses, then, concerns how non-indigenous Australians might find a way to *identify* with the 'stolen generations' without thereby minimizing such injustice (with the judgement that 'I suffer along with you'), or infantilizing Aboriginal people and rendering them passive victims. In the light of Sade's critique of the political aesthetic of compassion, how, in other words, can we prevent compassion from becoming narcissistic? Before turning to Sade, let's first consider the roles of a sensationist epistemology and aesthetic, and of dramatic representation, in eighteenth-century articulations of compassion.

Compassion and liberal political virtue

The idea that compassion should guide politics is a modern invention, coextensive with an aesthetic revolution in both philosophical and artistic practice. The seventeenth and eighteenth centuries witnessed the birth of a heightened sensitivity – even a new *sensibility* – regarding the suffering of others, in response to changes to social order, technology, the rise of Empire and the expansion of trade within and between economies. Increased social mobility meant interpersonal relationships required a foundation other than those hierarchies grounded in the power of church and monarchy. Existing meaning-giving structures were now less binding, as power and wealth were redistributed according to the imperatives of a budding individualism. A shift in emphasis to the individual as an economic unit saw with it a shift in what was taken as indicative of social status: from 'birth' or bloodline, to 'work' and the management of the self.

These social shifts were witnessed by a democratization of aesthetics well exemplified by the invention of the 'novel'. Rather than drawing from a repository of traditional plots, Defoe's *Robinson Crusoe* focused instead on the daily events and thoughts of an individual (Watt 1960: 13). Through this aesthetic form, the life of an 'ordinary man' became visible in all its quotidian detail. This new 'realism' in storytelling was in concert with developments in philosophy following Locke, as Crusoe discovers his relation to the world and to himself through his senses. *Robinson Crusoe* demonstrated the process of accrual of knowledge by emphasizing the engagement between experience and the ideas of an individual man, stripped of his connections with conventional society. Defoe tutored his reader in this new – and rather acquisitive – conception of 'man's' relationship to the world. As evidenced by Crusoe's rapport with his 'man Friday', however, the place of sympathy in this vision of natural humanity was still obscure; and for Locke compassion is not inborn but must be taught (Locke 2004: I, 3).

Yet in empiricist philosophy after Locke, compassion became a significant feature of 'natural man', and a critical device for negotiating new social, economic and subjective frontiers, accounted for within the terms of a sensationist epistemology and aesthetic. For Hume, 'benevolence' is instinctual, a *passion* rather than an *idea*.[4] Accordingly, the passions provide important information about the context of moral judgement that would be lacking were one to have recourse to reason alone.[5] Compassion is central to human relations for Hume because it pertains to pain: an irreducible aspect of bodily experience shared by all, and stronger in its effect than pleasure.[6]

When Hume comes to explain the mechanism through which others' pain is communicated and causes compassion, however, he turns to the theatre stage of entertainment – so that enjoyment becomes pivotal to this process:

> … these feelings, being delightful in themselves, are necessarily communicated to the spectators, and melt them into the same fondness and delicacy. The tear naturally starts in our eye on the apprehension of a warm sentiment of this nature: our breast heaves, our heart is agitated, and every humane tender principle of our frame is set in motion, and gives us the purest and most satisfactory enjoyment.
>
> (Hume 1975: §VII, 207)

In an instance of what Rancière calls 'an aesthetic regime of politics', then, the subject of compassion is positioned as a discerning, sensual spectator of suffering, and the sufferer as an object of ambivalent enjoyment.

The manner in which the eighteenth-century theatre arranged relations between actors and audience contributed already to the range of possibilities available for imagining social bonds. The introduction of the proscenium post-reformation separated players from audience, casting the performance as spectacle, and instituting a division between 'action' and 'passion' also evident in philosophy. For example, we find Smith and Rousseau also identifying the *spectator* as the focus of awareness about compassion.

For Smith, using the theatre and spectatorship as metaphors for ethical engagement served a number of purposes. The first was didactic: this 'scene' was rhetorically vivid for his intended readership of bourgeois theatregoers, and so readily illustrated to them the concepts he wished to convey. By referencing a familiar situation, Smith was able to evoke the 'proper' critical disposition for moral judgement: one of detached engagement. His account of sympathy doubled as a lesson in how to enjoy theatre: a spectator should be emotionally engaged enough to attend to the situation of the 'actor', yet also sufficiently detached to judge objectively. Charles Griswold frames this in terms of theatre criticism:

> … the critic is not objective or impartial by virtue of suppressing emotional response, or what Smith calls 'sympathy'. The critic's impartiality also depends on the ability to refine, through careful reflection, his evaluative responses …
>
> (Griswold 1999: 68)

Smith's theatrical metaphor thus communicates the phenomenology of sympathy, which demands both a connection to the actor and a reflective distance from their situation. Only through such distance, according to Smith, is moral judgement possible.

Second, the theatre analogy appeals to Smith's epistemological assumptions. The subject of empirical philosophy is one whose experiences are impressed upon them from without – so that such a subject is analogous to the spectator of a play. Yet Smith also assumed that impressions made upon individuals by their environment – including their *social* world – are in common. Smith perceived the social world to be like an ordered stage, possessing the coherence, structure and momentum of a theatrical narrative. For Smith, the proscenium, or 'fourth wall', remains intact: the imagined 'impartial spectator' comprehends the ethical situation *in its entirety* because they are not implicated by it, just as a sensitive audience can adjudge of the motivations and propriety of a character *because* of their separation from the action. This figure, then, performs a great deal of work in stabilizing Smith's vision of 'society', and account of sympathy. For Smith, one is able to respond to others' joys and pains appropriately because at bottom, society operates according to the regular and harmonious desires of the individuals of which it is composed. Because, it is assumed, we are all similarly attuned to a common world, the notion that we also resonate with each other's suffering in a compassionate manner appears uncomplicated.

If at stake, for Smith, was an affective social harmony married to individualism, its measure was the efficacy of the 'impartial spectator': the regard of the other he bid each to internalize as a means of self-regulation. This figure further deepened Smith's commitment to the theatrical metaphor: if 'all the world is a stage' (as was a mainstay of aesthetically oriented eighteenth-century moral philosophy), then, for Smith, so was the interiority of the subject. For, not only do 'I' perceive and judge the moral probity of others' actions and responses – and not only does the other perceive and judge mine – but moreover, I regard *myself as if I were another*, and adjust my comportment appropriately. Accordingly, the self in pain calibrates its expressions of suffering to suit the tastes of its witnesses, whose point of view is internalized by reflective imagination. The actor solicits the other's compassionate attention by playing down his anguish, so as not to alienate the onlooker's sympathy with discomfiting 'displays' of agony. Each thus becomes spectator and spectacle in one.[7]

The significance of the unseen, impartial spectator becomes clearer once we consider the social milieu of these audiences, consisting of middle-class subjects: the social spectator *par excellence*. The middle class occupies that station 'between the Mean and the Great', most conducive, according to Defoe, to happiness because it is least exposed to hardship of the lowborn or 'embarrass'd with the Pride, Luxury, Ambition and Envy of the upper Part of Mankind' (Defoe 1993: 5). Those who comprise the middle class may conceive of themselves as self-made, autonomous and modest individuals. Yet the middle way also designates comfort, a self-conscious distance from vulnerability and a paradoxical relation between work and enjoyment, guilt and pleasure. Being removed from the hardship of the lower orders and from the vices of aristocrats, they are afforded a social niche in which to cultivate a modest leisure. And in this leisure, the middle class came to practise sensitivity to others' suffering.

Rousseau is more critical than Smith of this leisure and the arts that fill it, wary of the stylization of affect that accompanies the cultivation of aesthetic sensibility. Nonetheless, Rousseau contributes to this cultivation through his own novels,[8] and thereby to a 'distribution of the sensible' through which middle-class experience, as a mode of practice and of perception, was fostered. His 'second maxim' concerning pity, and the remarks following it, reveal the peculiar historical conditions of this niche. And, again, the exchangeability of experience is emphasized:

> We never pity another's woes unless we know we may suffer in like manner ourselves… I know nothing so fine, so full of meaning, so touching, so true as these words. … Why have kings no pity on their people? Because they never expect to be ordinary men. Why are the rich so hard on the poor? Because they have no fear of becoming poor. Why do the nobles look down upon the people? Because a nobleman will never be one of the lower classes.
>
> (Rousseau 1974: 185)

For Rousseau, compassion requires the ability perfectly to identify with the other, so that we can easily imagine ourselves to be exchanged into their place.[9] The better to elucidate the position 'in-between' that has the freedom to identify with others' lot, Rousseau continues with a cross-cultural example. He describes the middle-class situation by projecting it upon 'the other', through whom the uncertainty of the 'station-between' great wealth and scarcity is illuminated:

> Why are the Turks generally kinder and more hospitable than ourselves? Because under their wholly arbitrary system of government, the rank and wealth of individuals are always uncertain and precarious, so that they do not regard poverty and degradation as conditions with which they have no concern; to-morrow, any one may himself be in the same position as those on whom he bestows alms to-day.
>
> (Rousseau 1974: 185)

Rousseau's dicta that 'all men are born poor and naked … liable to the sorrows of life' and that 'man's weakness makes him sociable' (Rousseau 1974: 182–3) also demonstrate an instability of circumstance belonging to the middle class that would enable them more readily to imagine themselves in the position of another. The available modes of sociability, according to Rousseau, are either envy (in the face of others' happiness) or pity (in the face of their suffering), as one glances either up or down the social scale to one's own potential future. Rousseau captures the ambivalence of the bourgeois subject regarding their fellows, as well as the sense of vulnerability belonging to the middle-class condition. Insofar as men are not self-sufficient and compare themselves to others, Rousseau prefers pity to envy:

> Pity is sweet, because, when we put ourselves in the place of one who suffers, we are aware nevertheless of the pleasure of not suffering like him. Envy is bitter, because the sight of a happy man, far from putting the envious in his place, inspires him with regret that he is not there.
>
> (Rousseau 1974: 182)

For Rousseau as for Smith, the middle-class subject constructs their 'sensibility' specularly. Looking always to the lot of other stations to which they either aspire or avoid, the middle-class subject senses their belonging to community by means of an internal resonance with others' suffering. Others' sorrow thus serves the inner life of the individual, who prides himself/herself on the ability to feel. For Rousseau, indeed, an awareness of suffering – and that, *this time*, it is not 'I' who suffers – becomes the defining trait of middle-class experience: a precarious security (or 'frail happiness') built on a tendency for comparison with others (*amour propre*) Rousseau both detests and attempts to cultivate (Boyd 2004: 524; Orwin 1997: 309).

Suffering is, then, a rarefied thing in this context: viewed from a safe distance and mediated by the arts. In *Émile*, Rousseau counsels how to instruct an adolescent in the art of feeling compassion for fellow men. The purpose of these lessons, however, is to develop Émile's character, by redirecting the sexual feelings and envy to which adolescence is prone (Rousseau 1974: 193–6). The proto-citizen Rousseau grooms in Émile is instructed in a particular aesthetic comportment to others. Rousseau conceives compassion as an interiority acquired through witnessing suffering; and the pleasure derived from not being in the place of the sufferer is also a source of guilt. The object of Émile's education, however, is *a particular response to suffering* rather than its alleviation. Suffering is a resource for Émile's affective and moral training, and as important a lesson as learning to feel is the maintenance of a distance from misfortune (Rousseau 1974: 192). Rousseau is mindful of the limits of compassion, and careful that his pupil shouldn't be overwhelmed by the magnitude of suffering in the world, lest he become enslaved to it (Boyd 2004: 532).

The emphasis on theatrical metaphors and spectatorship we find in Hume, Smith and Rousseau is instructive of the meaning of compassion for their shared cultural milieu. A primary element of the value of compassion for them – indeed, the very manner in which it was fostered – was the display of a sympathetic sensibility. It was not enough to *feel* compassion; one should also be *seen to feel* compassion, as a mark of one's character and propriety. By the publication of Rousseau's *Julie* – which famously excited its readers to hysteria (Darnton 1984: 215–51) – crying had become an inter-subjective activity: a public demonstration of one's virtue and sensibility, and so also a well-cultivated social skill (van Elferen 2007; Copjec 1999). Eighteenth-century literature took up the mantle of educating the emotions by putting protagonists through torments calculated to make readers feel their painful bonds with the frailest humanity. John Mullan recounts, in this vein, a letter to Samuel Richardson that assiduously records the violence of the reader's response to his novel, *Clarissa*:

> I verily believe I shed a pint of tears … When alone in agonies would I lay down the Book, take it up again, walk about the Room, let fall a Flood of Tears, wipe my Eyes, read again, perhaps not three Lines, throw away the Book crying out excuse me good Mr Richardson, I cannot go on …
>
> (quoted in Mullan 1997: 119)

This reader identified with Clarissa's suffering, and then bid Richardson to bear witness to her appropriated agony – all the while reflecting upon her performance of pity in the letter, as if in a mirror. In these crude ecstasies of agony the reader appropriated an enjoyment, and performed her 'self' as a caring, moral subject.

The desired outcome of such an education was to refine sensitivity to pain and others' suffering. But more than this, the aim was to translate these pangs of sympathy into a language and narrative form that shapes a socially connected, yet self-possessed, individual, and prefigures both today's humanitarian discourse and (a quite 'sadistic') enjoyment of reality television. This aesthetic form shaped conscience in terms of passive spectatorship, so that an emphasis falls on appropriate subjective response and discourse, rather than action and the support of vulnerability. Significantly, it is in these pangs of enjoyment of sympathy, celebrated by the novel, that the Marquis de Sade found a niche through which to critique liberal society and the Christian morality that it reinvests with a new political and economic meaning. And it is here that we may also situate the ambivalent responsiveness of Australians to the suffering of indigenous people.

Sade's enlightenment

It is said that Sade 'greatly admired' Rousseau's 1761 epistolary novel *Julie, or the New Héloïse* (Rousseau 1997). The appeal of *Julie*, as with other novels of its kind, was the emotional attachment readers were able to form to its protagonist, whose moral deliberations were followed with acute attention. It is not difficult to discern a relation of influence between Rousseau and Sade's writing: his companion books, *Juliette* and *The New Justine*, both contain titular references to Rousseau's novel. But Sade doffs his cap to 'conduct books' in general, most notably Richardson's *Pamela, or Virtue Rewarded*. His relation to these works is not simple emulation. Sade implicitly critiques the interests they serve through a mocking, excessive repetition of their rhetorical practices. Up-ending the presumption that virtue is most natural or worthwhile, Sade produces a critical pastiche of *Pamela* by subtitling *Juliette* '*The Prosperities of Vice*' and *Justine* '*Good Conduct Well Chastised*'. Sade sets out to educate his reader in the perversities of Nature, which rewards vice rather than virtue; and conjectures that mothers will prescribe his *Philosophy in the Bedroom* as mandatory reading for their daughters.

In this manner, Sade picks up the threads current within eighteenth-century elaborations of sympathy discussed thus far: sensation, spectatorship, individuality and enjoyment. If compassion originates in a corporeal connection between self and other – established through witnessing, and culminating in an increased interiority through which subjects explore their individuality – Sade unsettled such complacent interiority. Concerned to limit solipsistic tendencies within empiricism, Smith had grounded the civil society of free individuals in sympathy. But in so doing he reduced the range of capacities and appetites individuals could express. Smith's favoured metaphor is telling in this regard. The theatre space organizes Smith's conception of the social sphere: self-contained and regulated by the 'impartial spectator', whom each internalizes as their conscience. Sade, conversely, unhinged the key terms of compassion discourse from the imperative for social stability and hegemony.[10]

Because for Sade there is no 'invisible hand' and no 'impartial spectator', there are only rival subjects with competing and disorganized desires. Social space for Sade is local rather than universal, akin to parlour theatrics rather than Smith's public stage: 'For Sade, the object of vision has no independent integrity. Its significance is shaped by the desiring of the observer' (Shapiro 2002: 121). Instead of the internalized normativity enshrined by Smith's dialectic of spectator and spectacle, Sade explores the idea of ethical relation through the enjoyment subjects take witnessing the spectacle of others' suffering. Sade interrogates the value of the social affects, so that whilst Rousseau praises modesty for its natural innocence, for Sade modesty is 'a refinement of lust' (Frappier-Mazur 1996: 110, Hénaff 1999: 127–30) – merely a sublimated mode of seduction. Likewise, pity is for Sade an enfeebling, useless emotion.[11]

Of interest is the effect of these reversals on the reader's interiority. Sade's parodic narrative frustrates expectations regarding the course of the plot, increasing in depravity rather than virtue by means of a repetitive series of orgies that plunder the esteemed traits: modesty, maternity and innocence. *Justine* presents an improper radicalization of the sympathetic identification esteemed by modern Europeans, whereby sexual enjoyment is procured through the other's suffering. An orphaned child, Justine lands from one abusive situation to another: her incorruptible innocence serving both as an enticement to the libertine to despoil her and as a locus of identification (and ambiguous enjoyment) for the reader. Sade's inversion of the conduct narrative schools the reader in an obverse potentiality of the 'natural passions' of men. For Sade nature is not inherently good, and nor is passion epistemically uncomplicated. Rather, nature is as prone to destroy as to create; and passion – more specifically *com*passion – is sheep's clothing for a bourgeois instrumentality.

If, through his perverse performance of Enlightenment thinking, Sade played out the unwelcome implications of sympathetic identification, he also inhabited his role as author parodically and ambiguously. For instance, he never settled on a final version of *Justine*, which was always in the process of being rewritten, one apparently finished edition serving as draft for the next. Further, Sade dissociates himself from the views espoused by his protagonists – stating at the beginning of the work that their triumph over virtue only sharpens readers' sympathy for Justine. And elsewhere Sade demurs on the question of authorship of *Justine* altogether, suggesting that the work 'is but the final paroxysm of a diseased imagination' (Sade 1965: 154). We might also conjecture, a *contagious* imagination. For readers are left with Sade's disturbing images, uncertain what they mean and how to purge them, or even what their own emotional response to these images is or should be: revulsion, boredom or enjoyment?[12]

Significantly, by muddying his own relation to the narrative, Sade assigns responsibility for *Justine's* ethical implications to the reader. While Rousseau and Richardson were available to answer for their books, the author of *Justine* strategically obviated such responsibility, leaving that volatile bundle – *Justine* – uncontained, to wreak havoc on the reader's delicate interiority. The philosophical libertines of *Justine* offer no guidance in this regard. The book's plot is driven by Justine's compulsion to tell her history of abuse to apparently good men with whom she seeks refuge. Each time her confidante listens to her sympathetically before again betraying, ridiculing and sexually violating her. We would take from this monotonous procedure that the wounded innocence embodied by Justine's testimony is unsuccessful. Virtue *is* well chastised, and the libertine's sympathy gains him a better purchase upon her rather than bringing salvation. Like the bourgeois subject of Smith's philosophy, by working continually upon her interiority, Justine delivers herself all the more surely to the norms that would govern her.

Through its various distorting repetitions and dislocations, then, Sade's text disorients its readers, implicating them in the crimes against Justine by means of the sympathy Sade had so deliberately stirred in them. By leading the reader to doubt her own affective states, Sade invokes a situation in which *no one* can be held to account for what happens to Justine, and yet everyone is culpable – implicated in her suffering through their emotional relation to it. Sade thus re-stages the confusion of identifications and disavowals evoked by the humanitarian situation, and places sympathy under suspicion. By redrawing individualism in the absence of a socially cohesive affect, and by refocusing the element of spectatorship the cultivation of compassion demands, Sade exposes the shadowy residues of inequity within democratic society. For Sade, in this murky ethical field, there is but one thing left to do: enjoy!

Sade, then, as surely as Smith and Rousseau, is engaged in a project of education of the emotions – albeit a less prescriptive approach to education. Let's now explore the lessons we can take from Sade with respect to the report on the stolen generations.

Significances of sympathy in *Bringing Them Home*: after Sade

In writing *Bringing Them Home*, Wilson and Dodson responded to a yawning absence of Aboriginal representation in Australian political and cultural life. Whereas every event of moment seems to occasion another reworking of the question of Australian national identity, the perspectives and experiences of indigenous Australians are continually overlooked, as if this very neglect might even constitute Australian identity (Nicolacopoulos and Vassilacopoulos 2002). Into this void, Dodson and Wilson issued *Bringing Them Home*. An impressive number of statements provide sites of sympathetic identification through which the protracted history of paternalistic policy governing the lives of indigenous people is allowed to unfold. Survivors' accounts of deprivation and abuse document personal experiences of removal from traditional lands and family, physical and sexual abuse in institutional and foster care, forced labour, prohibition of language, strictly managed marriage and the withholding of wages. Government correspondence showing the cold calculations of policies concerted toward breeding out Aboriginality[13] is set against this testimony. Through this juxtaposition of suffering and paternalistic indifference, the authors build a strong case for a national apology and financial compensation to Aboriginal people.

Yet a further wager of the report was that by bringing the stories of the 'stolen generations' into the public record, the survivors of these policies might be restored to a *new* Australian community, constituted through the inclusion of Aboriginal stories. The goal was to achieve recognition for Aboriginal historical experience, by rendering this trauma in terms accessible to the Australian public. Testimony is thus charged with the task of mediating a troubled relation by *translating* the testifier's experience into a language that is shared – bringing the victim/witness and perpetrator into the same arena, so promoting mutual understanding through a process of internalization. Situated within an already established linguistic and legal context, the testimony provides a conventional frame to neutralize the damaging effects of fear and violence. Testimonial language and practice promise to shelter the survivor from the vicissitudes of others' desires, and repair them to an equal footing under law. It was hoped that, once this testimony had become part of the common language, Aboriginal self-determination could be conceivable.

We might pause here to reflect on the effects of this strategy in terms of Rancière's distribution of the sensible, and the political imperative to alter the frame of perception so that new voices may be heard. We could ask, in this vein: Did *Bringing Them Home* shift the parameters of representation, or did it simply apply to representations of relation (or a 'partition of the sensible') already available to the mainstream community? The short answer is that it did both, and while it appears we have maintained the status quo, there remain as-yet unrealized potentialities for intra-Australian relations suggested by *Bringing Them Home* that it is beholden on Australians to put into practice.

First, by adhering to the formal structures governing the space of testimony, the report, arguably, protected the mainstream community from the unstable effects of those for whom it speaks, containing the vengeance that might render *white* Australians vulnerable. According to this view, the report stages an encounter between the stolen generations and those in whose name they were removed; but the testimonial form of address has allowed the non-indigenous community to position themselves as (impartial) spectator and judge rather than as accused, thus escaping responsibility for the other's suffering. Furthermore, there is a risk that the objectives of the report compromise and limit the kinds of subjective experience that can be represented: where, for instance, indigenous ways of parenting might be distorted in order to build a relation of *identification* between Aboriginal and European Australians. Such domestication need not have been imposed by the report's authors: as Smith shows, when acting on the public stage, the subject curtails their expression of suffering so as not to exceed the degree necessary to elicit the spectator's compassion. Soliciting the other's recognition, the actor trains his/her style of address to suit his/her witness. Were the report's mandate simply to bring Aboriginal subjectivity into the fold of the mainstream community, this would suppose a notion of social harmony of which there are good reasons to be wary: this assumed model of reconciliation is insufficiently demanding of the *dominant* culture.

However, second – and most critically – *Bringing Them Home* can be read far more radically, as a paradigm altering discourse, to the extent that it forces a recognition of what it would mean for Aboriginal interests to be *included* in 'Australian identity': *an identity previously established on the destruction of Aboriginal experience*. By these lights, *Bringing Them Home* does, indeed, compel a change of the political–aesthetic regime, by reckoning a part that previously was not counted. This inconvenient significance of the report is already available to any reader who realizes the responsibility of being addressed by such testimony. The reflections above regarding Sade's ambiguous 'gift' to his reader may assist in thinking through this responsibility.

Recall that, by obscuring his authorial responsibility for *Justine*, Sade upset the reader's assumed role in relation to Justine's plight: because 'no one' was accountable for the text, *everyone* was rendered culpable, implicated in an ambivalent enjoyment of their situation of spectatorship in relation to her. Likewise, those to whom the testimony of the 'stolen generations' is addressed must also realize that they are implicated in indigenous suffering by virtue of being its audience: by virtue, in other words, of being an individual with the capacity to feel sympathetic in response to the suffering of another. This relation speaks to a demurral familiar to the sphere of contemporary Australian politics, but best exemplified by the former Prime Minister John Howard's claim that present Australians and governments cannot be held responsible for the actions of past generations.[14] We might respond to this sentiment that, as presently no one is accountable, all non-indigenous Australians are equally as culpable, by virtue of the spectacle that continues to unfold around them, in their newspapers, on their television screens, in their streets and parliaments.

The realization of such responsibility is necessarily disorienting: it places one in a position of *vulnerable* identification, rather than an identification that appropriates the other's suffering to an enjoyment of one's own interiority. Sade had recognized the confusion of identity between self and other in the spectacular humanitarianism engendered by testimony. The demand on the sufferer to offer herself to the benefactor as a spectacle domesticates her: installing within her the gaze of the more powerful subject. The testifier's proneness to harm furnishes the very significance of testimony, and delimits the manner in which they can exist within a community. Framed thus, indigeneity risks being reduced to a dependent identity, awaiting either appropriate recompense or further exploitation. Sade's co-option of his reader's desire by virtue of their sympathetic response, conversely, is key to fabricating a 'new community', in which it cannot be taken for granted who is subject to whom.

Sade's insight was that the relation of identification that permits compassion also yields an enjoyment of the other: a *jouissance* through which the 'actor' facilitates for the spectator an intimate experience of their pangs of conscience. By focusing critical attention on the aesthetic frame of compassion, Sade demonstrated the spectator's affective investments in the scene of the other's vulnerability. Through it they are able to experience their own vulnerability at a repudiating, depoliticized distance. To take a lesson from Sade that it's uncertain he would 'authorize', what is needed is for the 'spectator' to take responsibility for their enjoyment, and perhaps even to open themselves, in their vulnerability, to the other's enjoyment: to the demands of competing desires that both constitute and potentially threaten community.

Thinking 'reconciliation' with Rancière

When news broke in 2007 of endemic child abuse in Northern Territory Aboriginal communities, then-Prime Minister Howard was quick to describe the situation as a 'Hobbesian nightmare', thus signalling the need for sovereign action.[15] He may well have called it a 'Sade-ian boudoir'. For most chilling about the Northern Territory Emergency Response (NTER, also known as the NT Intervention) was the ease with which Howard was able to mobilize images of suffering first delivered by *Bringing Them Home*, to the task of further disempowering Aboriginal people – and the bipartisan approval with which this 'response' was met.[16] The problem was not that Australians had not been able to identify with the testimonies of the 'stolen generations'. Indeed, after the report was tabled, Parliament briefly became a theatre of grief that would rival any eighteenth-century parlour: politicians openly wept as testimonial accounts were read into Hansard. In the broader community, National Sorry Day was informally instituted, Sorry Books were signed, and this upsurge of compassion eventually culminated in a 'walk for reconciliation' across Sydney Harbour Bridge. The high point was the national apology: a formal admission by the sovereign of wrongdoing, which promised to be deeply productive for reconciliation.

This promise is largely yet to be actualized, however, as ever more paternalistic 'solutions' to what is seen as an 'Aboriginal problem' are tendered in the place of genuine efforts to include and recompense indigenous people. The problem is not so much a deficit of sympathetic identification with others' suffering. Indeed, indigenous communities have themselves come to be identified with suffering, reduced in the public imagination to their vital needs. Following Rancière's critique of political philosophy in *Dis-agreement*, as delimiting in advance who and what can be deemed politically significant, such a deeming of Aboriginality to vital need is politically dangerous. Indigenous disadvantage is relegated, according to this analysis, to what Aristotle called *pathos* – an animal life that feels only pleasure and pain – as distinct from *logos*, which is the higher order *human* life, recognized as political (Rancière 1999: 2). What's needed is a challenge to this 'partition of the sensible': the terms according to which life asserts its political relevance, and relations between indigenous and non-indigenous Australians are structured. For such a redistribution to take place, the roles of 'actor' and 'spectator', 'sufferer' and 'benefactor', must be unsettled, so that both terms may register as *active* rather than passive: both implicated in the vulnerability of the other and in the capacity to respond to such vulnerability.

The staging of the 'Aboriginal plight' in the media for the most part encourages a spectacular regard for indigenous life. During the child-molestation panic that precipitated the NT Intervention,[17] newspaper front pages were splashed with the most abject images photographers could capture: of children playing in the dirt, the air thick with flies; drunk old men or smashed teenagers, desperate and hopeless.[18] Aboriginal life was represented as unfortunate, and readers were shocked that such depravity had occurred out of sight of urban/eastern Australia. The policies that were subsequently enacted on their behalf, and which were broadly accepted as necessary (for the sake of the children), did not recognize indigenous agency or specificity, or even the shared history between indigenous and non-indigenous Australians (and the state) that has led to such endemic poverty and family breakdown. The solution to the 'Aboriginal problem' which *The Australian* has consistently proposed, *pace* Howard, is the abandonment of cultural traditions and adoption of liberal individualism: assimilation rebooted.

Importantly, this spectacular treatment of indigenous issues avoids responsibility for the colonial relationship that engendered (and continues to engender) inequity. It has encouraged a narcissistic regard for Aboriginal suffering, whereby that suffering is appropriated to a middle-class sense of virtue. Such humanitarianism through spectatorship fails to address the extent to which others' predicament is connected to one's own life and practices – as well as privilege. But moreover, this situation also fails to acknowledge the active part of the spectator in the shaping of narrative, and the relations of 'actor' to 'audience'. As Rancière puts this:

> Why identify 'looking' with 'passivity' if not by the presupposition that looking means … being separated from the reality that is always behind the image? Why identify hearing with being passive if not by the presupposition that acting is the opposite of speaking, etc.? … [These oppositions] are what I call a partition of the sensible, a distribution of places and of capacities or incapacities attached to those places. … There is *capacity* on one side and *incapacity* on the other.
>
> (Rancière 2007: 277)

By these lights, we might ask what it would take for the spectators of Aboriginal disadvantage to 'emancipate' themselves and the Indigenous Other so that both are on the 'side' of capacity? One avenue for achieving this emancipation would be to seek out alternative representations of Aboriginality put forward by indigenous people such as Gary Foley, Jackie Huggins, Aileen Moreton-Robinson; or by art-ists' collectives such as 'proppaNOW'.[19] For Rancière, this movement would start, however, with the acknowledgement that being a spectator, listener or reader implicitly involves action through interpretation. Readers and witnesses have the power to redistribute the sensible – to interpret the world, and thereby also to transform it (Rancière 2007: 277) – as readily as do authors and activists. Accordingly, the interpretation of images of suffering found in the news media, as well as *Bringing Them Home, cannot* be indifferent or inactive. Rather, we are implicated in them through our own histories and interests; through our own interpretations that, in turn, influence the stand we take in relation to the suffer-ing they depict; and, ultimately, through our own *in*action.

Sade's lesson, too, had been that the enjoyment of suffering drawn from spec-tacular compassion implicates all: this is why Smith and Rousseau both drew limits around pity, for fear that it would capture the onlooker within the other's suffering. Yet if Australian identity is to be opened up to the critical perspectives it currently excludes, it is imperative that non-indigenous Australians should open themselves to being captured by their *ontological other*'s suffering: the Aboriginal other, whose dispossession presently constitutes Australian national identity. Australians are obligated, as addressees of *Bringing Them Home*, to risk feeling a sense of respon-sibility for the Australian story of violence and expropriation that implicates all. They are, likewise, obligated to ask themselves what it would mean to acknowledge the dividends they have taken from indigenous disadvantage. Is there scope in the public arena for the expression of an Aboriginal *jouissance*: for the demand of a pleasure – land, money and respect – from the remainder of the community? And is there scope for the broader community to yield to such *jouissance*: to count the part that previously had no part, and thereby include indigenous people in the community *on their own terms*? This encounter may be the next challenge of reconciliation.

Notes

1 I would like to thank Paul Muldoon for his generosity in providing comments on an early draft of this chapter, which were invaluable in reviewing and clarifying the ideas expressed herein. The comments provided by an anonymous reviewer have also been extremely helpful and challenging to me, and I am indebted to that individual for their generous yet critical engagement with my work.

2 The sense that the standing of indigenous people in Australia has degenerated rather than improved is captured by responses to the Northern Territory intervention, to which we will turn later in this chapter. See Dodson (2007), Stringer (2007), Maddison (2009: 12–18), and Hinkson (2007). At the time of writing, new legislation has recently passed through both houses of federal parliament (Stronger Futures in the Northern Territory Bill 2011) that further entrenches the intervention, and continues to suspend the Anti-discrimination Act.

3 Most notably, Keith Windschuttle's campaign against stolen generation discourse, as well as other conservative critics largely connected to *Quadrant* magazine (Windschuttle 2009, 2010). Windschuttle especially objects to the use of the term in schools. See Vasek and Perpitch (2009).

4 Passions are for Hume more diffuse, and more easily conjoined with other affections and ideas, whereas ideas are 'endowed with a kind of impenetrability, by which they exclude each other, and are capable of forming a compound by their conjunction, not by their mixture' (Hume 1968: 'Of Benevolence and Anger', §VI, 366).

5 It appears evident that the ultimate ends of human actions can never … be accounted for by *reason*, but recommend themselves entirely to the sentiments and affections of mankind, without any dependence on the intellectual faculties. Ask a man *why he uses exercise*; he will answer, *because he desires to keep his health*. If you then enquire, *why he desires health*, he will readily reply, *because sickness is painful*. If you push your enquiries farther, and desire a reason *why he hates pain*, it is impossible he can ever give any. This is an ultimate end, and is never referred to any other object.

(Hume 1975: I, 293. Emphases in original.)

Freud takes up this modern account of the role of pleasure and pain in motivating human behaviour in the form of the 'pleasure principle'.

6 Hume thus accounts for sympathy as a contagion of affect between individuals:

We have a lively idea of every thing related to us. All human creatures are related to us by resemblance. Their persons, therefore, their interests, their passions, their pains and pleasures must strike upon us in a lively manner, and produce an emotion similar to the original one; since a lively idea is easily converted into an impression. If this be true in general, it must be more so of affliction and sorrow. These have always a stronger and more lasting influence than any pleasure or enjoyment.

(Hume 1968: 369)

7 The sufferer lowers 'his passion to that pitch, in which the spectators are capable of going along with him' (Smith 1976: I.iv.2.22; see also Marshall 1986: 174).

8 Like Plato, in the *Discourse on the Arts and Sciences* Rousseau expresses a wariness of the arts, depicting them as agents of the corruption of morals; and, in his *Letter to D'Alembert*, too, Rousseau targets the theatre specifically as a corrupter of virtue, eliciting as it does false emotion (Marks 2007: 729). Again like Plato, however, he uses the arts to inculcate his readership with good morals (Kelly 1997). *Émile* itself is a literary dramatization of a child's education using a hybrid form of philosophical treatise and novel.

9 Note that Smith directly contradicts this argument: exchangeability is not a prerequisite of sympathy for Smith, which is why a man can sympathize with a woman in childbirth (Smith 1976: VII.iii.I.4).

10 As Michael J. Shapiro argues:

[Sade's] view of the social … departs from the mainstream tendency to harmonize the self with the order. The social for Sade is an irreconcilable problem. Social space, given the moral imperatives that define it, cannot help but frustrate any individual self and the possibility of producing ethical bonds among selves.

(Shapiro 2002: 126)

11 For Rousseau, conversely, pity functions in nature as laws and morals do in society, regulating our relations with others 'from within' rather than from without. (Rousseau 1992: 38)

12 For a discussion of the contagion of affect, from Sade to his reader, see Faulkner 2007.

13 See in particular part 2 of *Bringing Them Home*, which documents the history of policies of removal; and Manne 2001: 10–11, 38–40.

14 Howard stated, in response to Federal Parliament's apology to the stolen generations in 2008, 'I do not believe as a matter of principle that one generation can accept responsibility for the acts of earlier generation'. (Quoted in Davies (2008).)

15 See John Howard's speech, 'To Stabilise and Protect' at <www.abc.net.au/news/opinion/speeches/files/20070625_howard.pdf> (accessed 23 February 2009).

16 In the name of abused Aboriginal children, Howard demanded a carte blanche to introduce a raft of radical measures to the most underprivileged and remote communities in Australia: including the quarantining of welfare payments to all in the community, compulsory health checks of all children and mandatory reporting by health carers of any known childhood sexual activity, including between consenting teenagers. These measures called for the suspension of the anti-discrimination act (see Altman and Hinkson 2007 and Maddison 2009).

17 I call the concern for child abuse a 'panic' because, while certainly indigenous children are more vulnerable to sex abuse than non-indigenous children in Australia, evidence that there was an out-of-control problem in Northern Territory Aboriginal communities has not been borne out since the NTER has been in place. One legal scholar writes:

> The anticipated increase in prosecutions for child sex offences has not eventuated, and communities have perceived little or no change in the safety and wellbeing of Aboriginal children. Indeed, the negative impacts of the intervention may have, in some cases, further damaged the health and wellbeing of communities.
>
> (Billings 2009: 37)

18 As Aileen Moreton-Robinson writes:

> The media had prepared the white Australian imaginary [for the Intervention] by utilising a discourse of pathology that entailed constantly reporting negative stories of Indigenous dysfunction, corruption, neglect and sexual abuse to elicit white virtue and possessive investments in citizenship.
>
> (Moreton-Robinson 2009: 68; see also MacCallum and Reid 2012)

19 'ProppaNOW' includes artists such as Vernon Ah Kee, Richard Bell, Andrea Fisher, Tony Albert and Bianca Beetson. Their work attempts to open up new ways to imagine indigeneity, and its relation to mainstream Australian culture, through what is at times very confronting imagery (Neale 2010). ProppaNOW were profiled on the ABC radio national program, *Awaye!* <http://www.abc.net.au/rn/awaye/stories/2010/2870224.htm> (accessed 20 May 2012).

References

Altman, J. and Hinkson, M. (2007) *Coercive Reconciliation: Stabilise, Normalise, Exit Aboriginal Australia*, Melbourne: Arena Publications.

Billings, P. (2009) 'Still Paying the Price for Benign Intentions? Contextualising Contemporary Interventions in the Lives of Aboriginal Peoples', *Melbourne University Law Review* 33 [1], 1–38.

Boyd, R. (2004) 'Pity's Pathologies Portrayed: Rousseau and the Limits of Democratic Compassion', *Political Theory* 32 [4]: 519–46.

Copjec, J. (1999) 'More! From Melodrama to Magnitude', in J. Bergstrom (ed.) *Endless Night: Cinema and Psychoanalysis, Parallel Histories*, Berkeley: University of California Press.

Darnton, R. (1984) *The Great Cat Massacre: And Other Episodes in French Cultural History*, London: Penguin Books.

Davies, A. (2008) 'Apology was a mistake, says feisty Howard', *The Age*, 12 March 2008, <http://www.theage.com.au/articles/2008/03/11/1205125911264.html> (accessed 18 May 2012).

Defoe, D. (1993) *Robinson Crusoe*, 2nd edition, M. Shinagle (ed.), New York: W. W. Norton & Company.

Dodson, P. (2007) 'What Ever Happened to Reconciliation?', in Jon Altman and Melinda Hinkson (eds) *Coercive Reconciliation: Stabilise, Normalise, Exit Aboriginal Australia*, Melbourne: Arena Publications, pp. 21–29.

Faulkner, J. (2007) 'The Vision, the Riddle, and the Vicious Circle: Pierre Klossowski Reading Nietzsche's Sick Body through Sade's Perversion', *Textual Practice* 21 [1]: 43–69.

Frappier-Mazur, L. (1996) *Writing the Orgy: Power and Parody in Sade*, trans. G. C. Gill, Philladelphia: University of Pennsylvania Press.

Griswold, C. L. (1999) *Adam Smith and the Virtues of Enlightenment*, Cambridge: Cambridge University Press.

Hénaff, M. (1999) *The Invention of the Libertine Body*, trans. X. Callahan, Minneapolis: University of Minnesota Press.

Hinkson, M. (2007) 'Introduction: In the Name of the Child', in Jon Altman and Melinda Hinkson (eds) *Coercive Reconciliation: Stabilise, Normalise, Exit Aboriginal Australia*, Melbourne: Arena Publications, pp. 1–12.

Human Rights and Equal Opportunity Commission (1997) *Bringing Them Home: Report of the National Inquiry into the Separation of Aboriginal and Torres Strait Islander Children from Their Families*, Sydney: Sterling Press. <http://www.hreoc.gov.au/pdf/social_justice/bringing_them_home_report.pdf> (accessed 8 June 2012)

Hume, D. (1968) *A Treatise of Human Nature*. London: Oxford University Press.

_____ (1975) 'Enquiry Concerning the Principles of Morals', in P. H. Nidditch (ed.) *Enquiries Concerning Human Understanding and Concerning the Principles of Morals*, Oxford: Clarendon Press.

Kelly, C. (1997) 'Rousseau and the Case against (and for) the Arts', in C. Orwin and N. Tarcov (eds) *The Legacy of Rousseau*, Chicago: The University of Chicago Press.

Locke, J. (2004) *An Essay Concerning Human Understanding*, Adelaide: University of Adelaide. <http://ebooks.adelaide.edu.au/l/locke/john/l81u/> (accessed 8 June 2012)

MacCallum, K. and Reid, H. (2012) 'Little Children and Big Men: Campaigning Journalism and Indigenous Policy', *Australian Journalism Review*, 34 [2]: 71–84.

Maddison, S. (2009) *Black Politics: Inside the Complexity of Aboriginal Political Culture*, Sydney: Allen & Unwin.

Manne, R. (2001) *In Denial: The Stolen Generations and the Right. Quarterly Essay 1*. Melbourne: Schwartz Publishing.

Marks, J. (2007) 'Rousseau's Discriminating Defense of Compassion', *American Political Science Review* 101 [4]: 727–39.

Marshall, D. (1986) *The Figure of Theater: Shaftesbury, Defoe, Adam Smith, and George Eliot*, New York: Columbia University Press.

Moreton-Robinson, A. (2009) 'The Good Indigenous Citizen: Race War and the Pathology of Patriarchal White Sovereignty', *Cultural Studies Review* 15[2]: 61–79.

Mullan, J. (1997) 'Feelings and Novels', in R. Porter (ed.) *Rewriting the Self: Histories from the Renaissance to the Present*, London and New York: Routledge.

Neale, M. (2010) 'Learning to be proppa: Aboriginal artists collective ProppaNOW', *Artlink* 30[1]. <http://www.artlink.com.au/articles/3359/learning-to-be-proppa-aboriginal-artists-collecti/> (accessed 20 May 2012)

Nicolacopoulos, T. and Vassilacopoulos, G. (2002) 'Racism, Foreigner Communities and the onto-Pathology of White Australian Subjectivity', in A. Moreton-Robinson (ed.) *Whitening Race: Essays in Social and Cultural Criticism*, Canberra: Aboriginal Studies Press.

Orwin, C. (1997) 'Rousseau and the Discovery of Political Compassion', in C. Orwin and N. Tarcov (eds) *The Legacy of Rousseau*, Chicago: The University of Chicago Press.

Rancière, J. (1999) *Dis-agreement: Politics and Philosophy*, trans. J. Rose, Minneapolis: University of Minnesota Press.

_____ (2004) *The Politics of Aesthetics: The Distribution of the Sensible*, trans. G. Rockhill, London and New York: Continuum.

_____ (2007) 'The Emancipated Spectator', *Art Forum* [March issue]: 271–80.

Rousseau, J.-J. (1974) *Émile*, trans. B. Foxley, London: Dent.

_____ (1992) *Discourse on the Origin of Inequality*, trans. D. A. Cress, Indianapolis: Hackett Publishing.

_____ (1997) Julie, or the New *Héloïse: Letters of Two Lovers who Live in a Small Town at the Foot of the Alps*, trans. P. Stewart and J. Vaché, Hanover, NH: Dartmouth College Press.

Sade, D. A. F. de (1965) *The Complete Justine, Philosophy in the Bedroom, and Other Writings*, R. Seaver and A. Wainhouse (eds), New York: Grove Press Inc.

Shapiro, M. J. (2002) *Reading 'Adam Smith': Desire, History, and Value*, Oxford: Rowman & Littlefield Publishers, Inc.

Smith, A. (1976) The Theory of Moral Sentiments, Oxford: Clarendon Press.

Stringer, R. (2007) 'A Nightmare of the Neocolonial Kind: Politics of Suffering in Howard's Northern Territory Intervention', *Borderlands* e-journal 6 [2]. <http://www.borderlands. net.au/vol6no2_2007/stringer_intervention.htm> (accessed 8 June 2012).

Van Elferen, I. (2007) '"Ihr Augen Weint!": Intersubjective Tears in the Sentimental Concert Hall', *Understanding Bach* 2: 77–94.

Vasek, L. and Perpitch, N. (2009) 'Rabbit-Proof Fence Grossly Inaccurate: Keith Windschuttle', *The Australian*, 13 December, <www.news.com.au/entertainment/movies/rabbit-proof-fence-grossly-inaccurate-keith-windschuttle/story-e6frfmvr-1225809985321> (accessed 14 May 2010).

Watt, I. (1960) *The Rise of the Novel: Studies in Defoe, Richardson and Fielding*, London: Chatto & Windus.

Windschuttle, K. (2009) 'The Stolen Generations 1881–2008' in *The Fabrication of Aboriginal History*, Volume Three, Sydney: Macleay Press.

_____ (2010) 'Why There Were No Stolen Generations', *Quadrant Online* [LIV]: 1–2. <http://www.quadrant.org.au/magazine/issue/2010/1-2/why-there-were-no-stolen-generations> (accessed 24 May 2010)

10

PHILOCTETES AND THE POLITICS OF RESCUE

Paul Muldoon

> O my country, and you unsleeping gods, if you have any pity still, bring
> vengeance, vengeance, late though it be, on all my persecutors!
>
> (Sophocles, *Philoctetes*, lines 1,039–41)

Since the publication of her magnum opus, *Upheavals of Thought*, Martha Nussbaum
has been at the forefront of efforts to build democratic and cosmopolitan forms
of solidarity on the basis of a shared vulnerability to suffering. Unpersuaded that
the safe and privileged citizens of the world will concern themselves with the fate
of distant or unknown others simply out of an abstract concern for their human
dignity, she has invested her intellectual energies in spruiking compassion as an
ethical motivator. Nussbaum proceeds on the basis that compassion is among the
more reliable of the moral sentiments, that the sight of others in pain is likely to
elicit projects of helping because it puts people in mind of their own, all too human,
vulnerability to suffering. At the same time, she is acutely aware that compassion is
a notoriously partial emotion whose ethical potential is restricted by its tendency
to stick 'close to home'. Her attention has thus naturally turned to the question
of how compassion might be cultivated in such a way that it generates more reliable responses to distant suffering. In this endeavour, Nussbaum has appealed to
tragic drama as an indispensable tool of civic education. From her perspective, such
works of art can help to expand the boundaries of compassion by encouraging
their audience to see that they share similar possibilities with people different from
themselves and are equally vulnerable to disasters and misfortunes. By learning (or
re-learning) how to see like the audience at a Greek tragedy, Nussbaum hopes that
the citizens of democratic states will come to understand when their compassion is
warranted, and feel obliged to alleviate the suffering of others regardless of where
they are located.

For the purposes of this chapter I intend to put to one side the question of whether it really is possible to re-learn how to think like an audience at an Ancient Greek tragedy. Whether the festival of the Great Dionysia actually did promote the 'habits of wonder' that Nussbaum associates with tragic drama and whether these effects might somehow be replicated in the context of modern mass media raises more complex questions about the relationship between art and politics than I can hope to pursue here.[1] What I aim to do instead is to concentrate on one of Nussbaum's favoured examples from Greek tragedy, Sophocles' *Philoctetes*, to problematise the connection she asserts between compassionate imagining and political judgement. The chapter is divided into three parts. In the following section I give a brief outline of Nussbaum's conception of compassion as 'sympathetic vision' and the political significance she attaches to it. Next I draw the connection she establishes between pity and politics into doubt by questioning whether the experience of shared suffering that is constitutive of compassion might not distort political judgement rather than improve it. Turning to Sophocles' *Philoctetes*, I illustrate how the phenomenology of pain has a tendency to create an unconditional sense of obligation towards the suppliant, effectively blinding those befriended in suffering to the claims of the political world. In the final section of the chapter, I attempt to redeem the political potentialities of compassion by approaching the *Philoctetes* as a drama about the eponymous hero's struggle to deal with the past. I argue that in cases of historical injustice, the unconditional sense of obligation that arises from the experience of compassion can provide an invaluable, if still deeply fraught, method of political re-integration.

Invisibility, sympathetic vision and tragedy

Nussbaum's political theorising starts from the assumption that 'just institutions' are a necessary, but not a sufficient, condition of a 'decent society'. Since even the best institutions need support to preserve their stability over time and many civic roles leave actors broad discretion, the education of citizens into certain habits of thinking remains a critical task in any liberal democracy (Nussbaum 2001: 403–4). The primary focus of Nussbaum's work, at least since the publication of *Upheavals of Thought*, has thus been less the 'institutions and procedures' that make up the basic structure of society than the 'quality of vision' fostered through the political culture (Nussbaum 1999: 266). Of particular concern for Nussbaum is the kind of systemic social blindness that refuses recognition to groups both within and beyond the polity, effectively consigning them to invisibility. As she illustrates through her subtle analysis of Ralph Ellison's novel *Invisible Man*, the refusal of recognition that is definitive of the social outcast ultimately finds its source in a 'defect of imagination'. In Ellison's America it is, of course, the black man who remains unrecognised, rendered invisible in his humanity by a 'biochemical accident' to the epidermis. Yet, as Nussbaum points out, in a society whose 'inner eyes are so deficient', the 'accident of invisibility' can easily befall any human being (Nussbaum 1999: 261).

If the principles of justice embedded in the basic structure of society are to work effectively, therefore, they need to be supported by a public culture that is able to identify and correct these defects of imagination.

It is in this context that Nussbaum seeks to rehabilitate compassion as a political virtue. In her Aristotelian account, compassion is not so much an involuntary feeling that spreads in the manner of a contagion as a cognitive understanding based on certain reflective judgements: first, that the suffering inflicted upon a victim is significant or has 'size'; second, that the suffering is undeserved or, at the very least, much greater than what is deserved, and finally that we share certain human possibilities with the suffering person such that we believe similar misfortunes might easily befall us (Nussbaum 2001: 305–16). Nussbaum is the first to concede that these judgements often go wrong and that there will be situations in which onlookers feel no compulsion to help others despite the fact that their compassion is genuinely warranted. Yet in emphasising the cognitive dimension of the emotion, Nussbaum exposes its connection with the visual powers of imagination and understanding in such a way as to make its political potential manifest. In her highly ocular account, underscored by frequent use of visual metaphors, compassion becomes equated with a kind of 'sympathetic vision' that penetrates into the hidden, interior world of others. Compassion, as she construes it, helps us to establish a connection with outcasts and strangers by imaginatively exposing their 'invisible life' and allowing us to appreciate their struggles and trials as potentially our own (Nussbaum 1999: 257).

By defining compassion as an imaginative power, a way of seeing that deepens our understanding of others, Nussbaum is able to side-step criticisms that the emotion is too closely connected to particular, existential encounters to have any general political efficacy.[2] As sympathetic vision, compassion enjoys a certain degree of autonomy from the specific instances of co-suffering to which it remains phenomenologically tied, making it susceptible to analysis (and cultivation) as a dimension of political culture. As Nussbaum freely admits, however, compassion can only be expected to play a positive role in shaping public culture if its inherent tendency towards partiality can be overcome. Her desire to rehabilitate compassion as a political emotion thus takes the form of a critical engagement with the long-standing objection – one dating back at least as far as the Stoics – that 'we cannot build a stable and lasting concern for humanity on the basis of such a slippery and uneven motive' (Nussbaum 2003: 12). As Nussbaum is the first to acknowledge, compassion always 'begins from where we are'. The sentiments that inspire projects of helping and which mark compassion as a truly political emotion are characteristically aroused by things and persons *we* see as important or invest with significance. This leaves open the possibility that we will remain untroubled by the suffering of those beyond our immediate 'circle of concern'.[3] As Nussbaum points out, '[a]ll kinds of social barriers – of class, religion, ethnicity, gender, sexual orientation – prove recalcitrant to the imagination, and this recalcitrance impedes emotion' (Nussbaum 2001: 317). If compassion is to serve the democratic and cosmopolitan project, therefore, the imaginative capacities of citizens will need to be expanded beyond those with whom they already identify.

The vehicle that Nussbaum privileges for this task of expanding the imagination is 'narrative art' and, more specifically, Ancient Greek tragic drama.[4] This emphasis upon the classical tragic genre rests upon a number of factors. It is in part a function of the fact that tragic drama foregrounds generic human predicaments that all of us have reason to expect and to fear: illness, loneliness, hunger, old-age, oppression, loss, betrayal and death. By exposing these scenes of human disaster, tragedy forces us to recognise how our very humanness makes us vulnerable to suffering (Nussbaum 2001: 409). The attraction to tragedy is in part also based on the fact that the theatre of Dionysus successfully combined 'disaster with dignity'. More than simply exposing loss and pain as an inescapable fact of human life, according to Nussbaum, tragic drama reveals the complexity of particular situations, exposing individuals, not just as victims, but also as agents. If spectators of these dramas become intensely concerned with the fate of the suffering heroes, it is precisely because they can recognise them as agents, struggling to preserve their dignity in the face of personal and political misfortune (Nussbaum 2001: 408–9). Finally, tragic drama recommends itself as a political tool because it was, from the very outset, a civic institution that played an interrogatory role in the life of Athenian citizens.[5] Tragic theatre created an empathic and reflective space in which Athenian citizens could develop a sense of compassion for those who suffer undeservedly and explore the complexities of political judgement. For Nussbaum, it is precisely this reflective space of empathy and judgement that needs to be recovered in contemporary democracies. 'By thinking like the audience at an ancient Greek tragedy,' she writes, 'we may possibly move closer to building a community that does indeed "foster the dignity and well-being of all persons within its borders"' (Nussbaum 1998: 8).

Nussbaum is, of course, by no means alone in assuming tragic theatre played (and can still play) a critical role in the education of democratic citizens. The fact that contemporary democratic societies lack a comparable civic institution to the Great Dionysia has not deterred critics from appealing to the tragic festival as a model of reflective space, distinct from both the urgent decisionism of politics and abstract contemplation of philosophy, in which the problems connected to civic life can be exposed and explored.[6] For the purposes of this chapter, however, I intend to put aside the very broad question of the political potentialities of tragic theatre in favour of a more narrow discussion of what one tragic play, Sophocles' *Philoctetes*, might have to tell us about the relationship between politics and pity. Nussbaum returns to the *Philoctetes* again and again in her discussions of compassion, highlighting the way in which the play encourages its audience to feel compassion for the eponymous hero and to take a stand against his exploitation at the hands of the Greek commanders. In the following section I seek to bring out some of the less appealing aspects of compassion by focusing on its tendency to create unconditional obligations. My primary argument is that Nussbaum's conception of compassion as 'sympathetic vision' leads her to treat imaginative identification with the suppliant as an ethical and political achievement *in and of itself* – as if there was no need to evaluate the merits and implications of such identification in each case. Missing from such an approach is any understanding of the way in which the phenomenology of pain can work to distort perspectives and characters, blinding those befriended in suffering to the claims of the political world. Drawing attention to Sophocles' subtle illumination of the phenomenon of pain, I expose the potential for both the wounded suppliant and the compassionate onlooker to become enclosed within a private world of suffering, disconnected from the wider political community and the responsibilities that come with civic life.

Sophocles' *Philoctetes* and the phenomenology of pain

Sophocles' *Philoctetes* recommends itself as a vehicle for exploring the political potential of compassionate imagining for two main reasons. The first has to do with the deeply abject state of its eponymous hero. On the way to Troy, the hapless Philoctetes trespasses upon a sacred shrine and is bitten on the foot by the venomous serpent that guards the sanctuary. Repulsed by his ulcerous wound and disturbed by his ill-omened cries, the commanders of the expedition abandon him on the desolate island of Lemnos, where he remains for ten lonely, desperate years. His reversal in fortune could not be more marked. On Lemnos, Philoctetes is deprived of the private associations of the *philia* and the public associations of the *polis* that are simultaneously the mark and the vehicle of civilisation (Segal 1981: 296). This 'son of a high-born house' has thus come to live the life of a wild and solitary castaway, 'more like a savage creature / Than a man' (Segal 1981: 223–4).[7] Philoctetes keeps himself alive by his magical bow – a gift from his friend and patron Heracles – but the lack of surplus in his economy of life draws him towards that most fragile of states 'where man strays on the territories of animal' (Worman 2000: 15; Segal 1981: 293; Morwood 2008: 68; Nussbaum 1976: 41). To compound matters further, his festering wound, foul rags and wild cries make him repellent to behold. Though the sailors who stop at the island from time to time offer him alms, nobody wants to take him home (Segal 1981: 310–11). For all intents and purposes, in other words, Philoctetes is the abject suppliant *par excellence*, a figure of fear and disgust who is simultaneously dependent upon others for his rescue and vulnerable to further abuse.[8]

The second reason why the *Philoctetes* recommends itself as a study in compassion relates to the absence of any political or familial ties connecting the characters. All the action of the play takes place on the deserted island of Lemnos and involves characters that are unrelated to one another by blood (Hall 2012: 8). Unique in this respect within the tragic genre, the play locates its principal actors in an empty, lawless space, remote from both the public arena of the Greek camp and the private domicile of the kinship group. On Lemnos, as Edith Hall has astutely noted, 'there are no cities, institutions, lawgivers, judges, priests, prophets, or other authority figures to provide frameworks for the action' (Hall 2012: 7–8; see also Segal 1981: 292; Carter 2007: 77). The civilised, rule-governed, spaces of the *polis* and the *oikos* are kept in the background, leaving the characters free to work out their responsibilities towards one another independently of any pre-existing, binding norms. In a highly self-conscious way, then, Sophocles deploys the dramatic device of the deserted island to contrive an encounter between human beings *as human beings*. By locating Philoctetes in a space beyond law and duty, he sharpens the problem of responsibility and response in the face of human suffering. Owed nothing by way of political or familial obligations, the wounded hero presents an unrefracted ethical trial for all who encounter him, a true test of the excellence of their 'inner eyes'.[9] Audiences of the *Philoctetes* can thus readily observe what, if any, power compassion has to overcome antipathy and disgust and mark their own responses to the wounded hero against those of the various characters in the play.

These ethical trials are set up by a strange twist of events at Troy. Ten years after having abandoned him on Lemnos, the Greeks learn through an oracle that they cannot secure victory at Troy without Philoctetes and his magical bow. Odysseus and Neoptolemus, the son of Achilles, thus embark on a mission to bring the wounded hero back to the Greek camp. Anticipating that Philoctetes will be too embittered to respond to persuasion, Odysseus plans an elaborate deception. Capitalising on the naivety of his young, still impressionable, companion, the crafty Odysseus enlists Neoptolemus in a plan to ensnare Philoctetes in a web of lies. Knowing how desperate Philoctetes is to leave the island, Neoptolemus sets out to lure him to the ship on the pretext he is being offered a passage home. Everything proceeds according to plan, until Philoctetes is overcome by a savage attack of pain and asks Neoptolemus to guard his bow. As Philoctetes falls into a relieving sleep, the chorus encourages Neoptolemus to seize the opportunity that fate has presented and steal away with the bow. Increasingly unsettled by his feelings of compassion, however, Neoptolemus finds himself unable to proceed. As Philoctetes awakes, he reveals the deception and is on the point of handing him back the bow before Odysseus' intrusion briefly stays his hand. Odysseus and Neoptolemus return to the ships with the bow, exciting Philoctetes' fear that he is about to be abandoned a second time. Ultimately, however, it is Neoptolemus' compassion for Philoctetes that assumes priority in his ethical 'calculations'. Against Odysseus' pleadings and threats, he resolves to return the bow, hoping that he might still persuade his newly won friend to make the journey to Troy of his own volition. When Philoctetes refuses, Neoptolemus relents and agrees to honour his earlier (though at that time disingenuous) promise to grant him a passage home.

In Nussbaum's reading of the play, it is Neoptolemus' compassionate, non-instrumental response to Philoctetes that establishes the ethico-political norm to be followed. In line with a widely shared view, Nussbaum treats Odysseus as a pitiless statesman who justifies his shameless exploitation of Philoctetes' vulnerability by reference to the higher political goal of victory at Troy. Instrumental through and through, Odysseus does not even perceive his attempt to deceive Philoctetes as morally reprehensible. From his perspective, whatever is good for the community (and, of course, himself) is *ipso facto* also just. Nussbaum juxtaposes this proto-utilitarian approach to the suppliant against the far more humane attitude personified by the chorus. Where Odysseus 'shows no interest in Philoctetes as a person', writes Nussbaum, the chorus of common soldiers attempt to 'vividly and sympathetically imagine the life of a man whom they have never seen' (Nussbaum 1999: 258). In a moving passage, close to the beginning of the play, the chorus evinces a remarkable capacity to picture the life of this 'stranger and outcast', marking the ways in which fate has stripped him of all the things that make life worthwhile. Later on, as Nussbaum would have it, 'this kind of vivid imagining prompts [Neoptolemus to make] a political decision against using Philoctetes as a tool' (Nussbaum 1999: 259). Awakened to their common humanity by this story of suffering, Neoptolemus decides he can no longer participate in the deception and must show Philoctetes the respect of telling him the truth. Not only is Nussbaum persuaded that this is the right response to the suppliant, she assumes that 'the audience' is also being 'led to believe this a politically and morally valuable result'. '[B]y showing the public benefits of the very sort of sympathy it is currently awakening in its spectators', she writes, 'the drama commends its own resources as valuable for the formation of decent citizenship and informed public choice' (Nussbaum 1999: 258–9).

Nussbaum's valorisation of the compassionate, non-instrumental response to the suppliant chimes with a common reading of the play, according to which the friendship struck up between the compassionate onlooker (Neoptolemus) and the wounded suppliant (Philoctetes) forms an ethico-political relation akin to that which Foucault discusses under the rubric of the 'care of the self' (Foucault 1986; Foucault 2005). Sophocles' *Philoctetes* is often understood as struggle between Odysseus and Philoctetes over Neoptolemus' soul in which the young man grows in personal integrity or, as Foucault would have it, learns to 'care for himself', through his encounter with the wounded hero (see Tessitore 2003: 78; Nussbaum 1976: 40). On this view, Philoctetes inadvertently assumes the role of the moral educator who prepares the fatherless Neoptolemus as a future leader by freeing him from the corrupt political style of Odysseus. As Foucault argues, in the Greek (as distinct from the Roman) world, the care of the self had nothing to do with the withdrawal of the individual from political life. On the contrary, the practice of caring for the self was an instantiation of a pedagogical relation in which *ephebes* were educated into the virtuous use of the power they were destined to wield in the city-state. To care for the self was to engage in a reflexive activity under the guidance of a teacher in which one turned one's attention towards oneself in order to render one's soul fit for the role of governing others (Foucault 2005: 37–9, 82–3).[10] In this case, it is Philoctetes' supplication that provides the catalyst for the young Neoptolemus to cast his gaze back upon himself, reflecting in disgust on his participation in the deceit of a wounded man.[11] By awakening his compassion, in other words, Philoctetes brings Neoptolemus (and presumably the citizens in the audience) to an awareness of the need to exercise power in an ethically responsible way.

The way in which this encounter plays out would, however, seem to place a question mark over both its status as an 'ethico-political' relation and the idea that it leads to a 'politically and morally valuable result'. A strong argument could certainly be made that Neoptolemus mounts a critical challenge to Odysseus' pitiless utilitarianism, according to which anything that produces a good outcome for the community is considered just. As Hall points out:

> Neoptolemus is the only one of the Greek party who takes Philoctetes seriously as a social being with intact "human rights", entitled to expect complete candour in his interlocutors and to have his opinion about his own future consulted and respected regardless of how irrational it may seem.
>
> (Hall 2012: 13)

Rather than exploit his vulnerability for political gain (as does Odysseus) or try to pass him off with charity (as do the occasional visitors to the island), Neoptolemus interacts with him as if he were a fully enfranchised subject, possessed of all the rights to which he has no authoritative claim. Yet the suggestion that the audience will or should perceive Neoptolemus' compassionate response to Philoctetes as a *political* achievement is undermined by the fact that it jeopardises the public interest in victory at Troy.[12] As Tessitore points out, much of the dramatic urgency of the mission to retrieve Philoctetes derives from the fact that 'the fate of the entire Greek expedition at Troy hangs in the balance' (Tessitore 2003: 61). Either Philoctetes and his bow will be brought to Ilium or the Greeks will be forced to capitulate. By revealing Odysseus' deception, Neoptolemus effectively consigns the decade-long Greek campaign to failure. The merit of this disregard for the collective interest is made even more dubious by the fact that Neoptolemus' series of decisions (from exposing the deception to agreeing to take Philoctetes home) also jeopardise Philoctetes' interest in a cure for his wounds. In short, while Neoptolemus' compassionate response to the wounded suppliant appears admirable from a certain, strictly ethical, point of view, it does not seem to be in the best interests of any of the parties (Tessitore 2003: 82; Nussbaum 1976: 47).[13]

If Sophocles is teaching the audience a lesson about compassion, therefore, it would appear to be a much more ambiguous one than Nussbaum acknowledges in her recent work. At the same time as the experience of compassion brings Neoptolemus to a sense of his ethical responsibility to the wounded suppliant, it encourages him to override vital public and private considerations. By agreeing to 'rescue' Philoctetes in the (seemingly irrational) way that he wants, Neoptolemus denies the Greeks the victory they should win over the Trojans, prevents the wounded hero from receiving the cure of Asclepius at Troy, exposes his countrymen to the risk of a retaliatory attack from the Greek army, and, last but not least, places his own life in peril. Once his compassion is aroused, in other words, the 'tender-hearted' Neoptolemus seems to lose any sense of where to stop. As Hall notes, '[t]he support which pity creates in him becomes unconditional' (Hall 2012: 12). Cold-hearted as it appears, therefore, Odysseus' instruction to Neoptolemus 'not to look' at Philoctetes in case his compassion be aroused makes a certain, albeit uncomfortable, political sense (*Philoctetes*, lines 1,068–9). Unlike his naïve companion, Odysseus seems all too aware of the danger of what

Hall refers to as the 'transformative power of pity' (Hall 2012: 12). Indeed, a more generous reading of the Odyssean character might in fact see in his pitiless disregard for the feelings of the wounded suppliant a wise insurance against the tendency of compassion not simply to motivate, but to motivate to excess.

Arguably, the excessive, unconditional nature of Neoptolemus' response to Philoctetes as suppliant is Sophocles' way of pointing to the intoxicating, de-politicising effects of shared pain. No stranger to suffering, Sophocles gives vivid representation to the phenomenon of pain throughout the play, exposing its distance from the phenomenon of politics.[14] Two aspects of this phenomenology of pain bear special note. In the first place, pain has no language through which to establish a communicative relation. Ironically enough, given the entire drama is devoted to the experience of suffering, the eponymous hero of the *Philoctetes* describes his pain as 'unspeakable'. This ambiguous characterisation is in one sense quite literally true. When Philoctetes suffers a severe attack from his wounded foot, he screams out in agony, making noises that are closer to 'bestial howls' than 'human converse'. To draw upon the well-known Aristotelian distinction, his pain has 'voice' (cries, groans, grunts), but not 'speech' (words, grammar, meaning), depriving him of the one 'gift' that distinguishes the political animal and secures his membership in the *polis* (Aristotle 1996: 13).[15] Philoctetes' pain is, however, also unspeakable in the other, less literal, sense of being incommunicable. While Sophocles attempts to represent the terrible agony of the suppliant aurally and visually throughout the play, it remains an inaccessible, subjective experience, beyond measure or quantification. Consequently, as Hall points out:

> … [t]he communication between sufferer and the witness, despite the witness's best intentions and efforts, is thoroughly deficient. Philoctetes has great difficulty explaining to Neoptolemus what the matter is, and Neoptolemus has equal difficulty in understanding the nature and extent of the problem.
>
> (Hall 2012: 15)

Second, pain, whatever its immediate cause, is experienced as torture, stripping those subject to its torments of their agency. In the *Philoctetes*, Sophocles grants pain an existence independent of the eponymous hero and represents it as a vicious aggressor without ever denying that it springs from the venom of a serpent rather than the hand of a human. In his powerful, still deeply arresting, metaphor, pain becomes a 'devouring beast', a gluttonous predator that does not simply attack the wounded hero, but consumes his person and his persona. As Segal makes clear, the metaphor of the devouring beast speaks to both the exterior character and savage intensity of physical suffering. For the wounded hero the pain 'is itself animate', a beast of prey that hunts him down and gorges on his body, pushing him to the very limits (and beyond) of human endurance (Segal 1981: 292, Worman 2000: 7). Sophocles repeatedly underlines the fact that this experience of pain as torture cripples Philoctetes in mind as well as body, his dragging gait providing an apt analogy for his loss of mental agility. Time and time again Philoctetes reveals his inability to move around a problem and evaluate it from different angles so as to reveal the best course of action. Thus, in the face of the chorus' well-intentioned and objectively accurate advice that it is in his best interests to accompany them to Troy, the wounded hero first sends them away in disgust and then begs them to return. Cognisant of their growing frustration with his refusal of help, he tells them 'I don't know what I am saying. / Pain drowns my senses' (*Philoctetes*, lines 1,193–5). Philoctetes' senseless resistance to the one course of action that everyone else knows is for the best is not perhaps entirely without its own logic (a point I come back to in the next section). Yet it does tend to confirm the supposition, articulated by the chorus earlier in the play, that the pain of his wound has driven the pitiful hero '[p]retty near out of his mind' (*Philoctetes*, lines 174–5).

The more we are inclined to see Neoptolemus' encounter with Philoctetes as an encounter with pain, the less we are inclined to see it as productive of an ethico-political relation in which communication and agency play a critical role. Nussbaum, as we have seen, skirts around this problem by connecting Neoptolemus' compassion to the narrative effort the chorus makes earlier in the play to sympathetically imagine the wretched life of the man he is yet to meet. As Worman has noted, however, it is less the 'estranged voice of pain' than the 'voice of pain up close' that impacts most deeply upon the *ephebe* (see Worman 2000: 20–9)[16]. In the critical scene of the play, the so-called moment of 'turning' or 'reversal', it is not Philoctetes' story, but his cries of agony, that have the transformative effect. Instructively, Neoptolemus' feelings of pity overwhelm him at the very moment when the speech of the suppliant fails, when Philoctetes can no longer carry on in conversation and descends into raw, animal-like noise. At this moment, the young man is himself overcome, literally taken over, by a terrible pain, setting up a clear correspondence between the physical torture that strikes at the suppliant and the emotional torture that strikes at his saviour. As Worman would have it, this experience of co-suffering gives rise to a kind of 'feverish identification' in which Neoptolemus begins to echo Philoctetes' 'vocabulary of disease' (Worman 2000: 27–8). Overcome by pity, the young man uses precisely the same words to describe his emotional anguish as Philoctetes' uses to describe his physical distress. In a perverse, but nonetheless illuminating, way, therefore, the intensity of the relation between the two men is grounded, not in communication, but in an experience of torture.

Contra Nussbaum, this experience of shared, torturous pain appears to distort rather than sharpen Neoptolemus' judgement, rendering him incapable of thinking from the standpoint of more than one other. Initially, as Tessitore points out, Neoptolemus' feelings of compassion conduce to paralysis (*aporia*) because they actually bring to consciousness a previously unrecognised (or perhaps consciously buried) dilemma. As his pity for Philoctetes is aroused, he is momentarily unable to decide whether to tell him the truth, thereby making himself a traitor to the Greek cause, or continue with the deception, thereby making himself a traitor to his better nature (Tessitore 2003: 80). At this point, in other words, he still seems to appreciate that he has a dilemma to resolve, that he must choose between two meritorious options and will be accused of being 'false' whether he speaks or holds his tongue (*Philoctetes*, lines 908–9). The more his pity takes hold, however, the more he appears to lose the critical space from which to evaluate the relative merits of the claim Philoctetes' makes upon his common humanity and the claim the Greek army makes upon his common citizenship. Odysseus' violent intrusion into this space of deliberation momentarily draws Neoptolemus back to the political world and the imperative of military victory. Yet as the young man marches back to the ship, bow in hand, the cries of the suppliant keep ringing in his ears, drowning out the distant voices of the Greek army marooned on the shores of Troy.[17] Without giving an account of his reasoning, Neoptolemus suddenly informs Odysseus that he intends to return the bow to Philoctetes to make amends for the wrong he has done. In the face of this alarming turn of events the incredulous Odysseus, speaking on behalf of the collective interest, justifiably characterises this 'decision' as either a sign of madness or a joke.

While the pitiless Odysseus hardly seems like a model to follow, therefore, it is not clear that the compassionate Neoptolemus secures a more morally *and* politically valuable result. When Odysseus accuses him of 'acting like a fool', Neoptolemus responds by saying '[j]ustice is sometimes better than wisdom' (*Philoctetes*, lines 1246–7). To Odysseus the response scarcely makes any sense: 'Justice!', he exclaims, 'To throw away what I have helped you to win?' (*Philoctetes* lines 1,248–9). But this is, of course, precisely the point. Where Odysseus thinks *justice* in relation to the interest an action serves (in this case the interest of the political community in victory), Neoptolemus thinks *justice* in relation to the integrity of the action itself. His compassionate response to Philoctetes constitutes justice, at least in his mind, precisely because it is not tied to an instrumental concern of any kind. If ethical purity or poetic beauty were the only measures of action, Neoptolemus' position would be difficult to fault. Yet it is hard to see how it can be integrated into a conception of politics where the problem of interest (configured either as the search for a common interest or as the need to adjudicate between competing interests) is ineradicable. Tellingly, the more Neoptolemus tries to do the right thing by the suppliant, the further he moves away from anything that serves an interest. By agreeing to take the wounded hero home, he condemns the Greek cause at Troy, consigns Philoctetes to a life of agony and torment, and exposes his countrymen and himself to reprisal from his former allies. Indeed, as Tessitore points out, the most likely outcome of 'Neoptolemus's decision' is that it 'will perpetuate and extend to himself the unhappy and desperate situation in which Philoctetes now finds himself' (Tessitore 2003: 82). For all his compassion (indeed because of his compassion), in other words, the young man doesn't actually seem to help anyone.

Rather than express a certain complementarity between pity and politics, therefore, the *Philoctetes* seems to point to a deep, and potentially irresolvable, tension between the ethical demands of humanity and the political demands of community. On the one side sits the unconditional compassion of the friend, who naively responds to the painful appeals of the suppliant, however irrational they may be (Neoptolemus), while on the other side sits the pitiless utilitarianism of the statesman, who brutally disregards individual suffering in the name of protecting the interests of the political community (Odysseus). By the end of the play Philoctetes has won the battle for Neoptolemus' soul and been rewarded with his friendship and unconditional loyalty. But this victory does nothing to resolve the impasse between pity and politics that sits at the heart of the play. As Tessitore points out, the upshot of Neoptolemus' compassion for Philoctetes is not a more decent politics, but the 'complete renunciation of politics' (Tessitore 2003: 82). It could, of course, be objected that the intervention of the demi-god Heracles in the final scene of the drama, according to which Philoctetes and Odysseus are placed back on their destined path to Troy, points to the possibility of harmonising the competing obligations of humanity and community. However, the fact that Sophocles calls upon this *deus ex machina* only seems to underline the fact that no reconciliation between a concern for humanity and a concern for community is possible *at the human level*. In Tessitore's persuasive account, 'the conflict exposed by this drama remains intact beneath the play's surface resolution' (Tessitore 2003: 83). To the extent that Sophocles can be said to be delivering a message to the audience, it would appear to be that feelings of compassion are as likely to endanger the political as to ennoble it.

Coming to terms with the past

The analysis I have provided so far has been focused upon the way the play's characters react to the repellent Philoctetes and the social rift this opens up between Odysseus and Neoptolemus. Though radically opposed, one to the other, the responses of each of these characters seems inadequate. While Odysseus' pitiless utilitarianism is too insensitive, Neoptolemus' unconditional compassion is too unworldly. Spectators of the tragedy are thus left with a certain sense of *aporia*: neither concern for one's *polis* nor concern for one's *philia* offers a pathway through the dilemma at the heart of the play. A slightly different perspective on this problem opens up, however, once our attention turns to Philoctetes and his reactions to the reactions others have to him. In this section, I approach Philoctetes from a slightly different angle, treating him less as an abject suppliant in need of rescue than as a resentful hero preoccupied with avenging the 'injustice' done to him in the past. When the play is examined from this perspective, it is not the struggle between Odysseus and Neoptolemus, but the struggle within Philoctetes that takes centre stage. As the characters around him adopt their positions, Philoctetes also positions himself in relation to them, implicitly and explicitly asking what kind of action on their part might suffice to bring about reconciliation. Clearly the fact that it takes the intervention of the demi-god Heracles to secure Philoctetes' political re-integration does not speak highly of the power of human beings to overcome divisions and deal with the past. Yet, as I attempt to demonstrate, Neoptolemus' expression of unconditional compassion is far from irrelevant to Philoctetes' belated decision to return to the fold and go to Troy. On the contrary, I argue that the young man succeeds in breaking into Philoctetes' resentment by reversing the order of priority previously assigned to the individual and the collective.

In contrast to the Greek commanders, who make the politically logical decision to sacrifice one man for the sake of the community, Neoptolemus makes the ethically perfect (which is, at the same time, the ethically mad) decision to sacrifice the community for the sake of one man.

The action in the *Philoctetes*, as with all tragedies, is over-determined by the past and, more specifically, the ill-fated visit to Chyrse, where the eponymous hero unwittingly trespasses on the sacred shrine. As a matter of strict causality, all of Philoctetes' suffering can be traced back to this accident of fate. Had it not been for the misadventure at Chyrse, Philoctetes would not have disrupted the religious observances of the army and the commanders would not have found it necessary to abandon him on the deserted Lemnos. In the mind of the abandoned hero, however, his social isolation is less a consequence of the injury he sustains at Chyrse than a fresh injury in its own right (Hall 2012: 9–10).[18] With some justification, Philoctetes regards himself not simply as the subject of a misfortune, but as the victim of an injustice.[19] The double significance this lends to Philoctetes' 'wound' plays out in his relations with the returning Greek party and is expressive of what divides him from them. While his interlocutors proceed on the basis that his suffering has a single aetiology ('the anger of Chyrse', as Neoptolemus puts it), Philoctetes distinguishes between the contingencies of fate ladled out by the gods and the wrongful acts perpetrated by human beings.[20] From this distinction emerge two sharply opposed accounts of responsibility. Whereas the returning Greeks see no need to look any further than the mischief of the gods, Philoctetes blames Odysseus and the sons of Atreus for everything he has gone through (*Philoctetes*, lines 314–5). In an altogether conspicuous way, therefore, the play brings the question of Philoctetes' sense of injustice into focus. Spectators of the play inevitably find themselves speculating on the extent to which Philoctetes' resentment is justified and, just as importantly, what kind of action is required to shift it.

Clues to Philoctetes' subjective understanding of his situation are littered through his speech. In her psychoanalytically inflected article, 'Infection in the Sentence', Worman shows that it is not just the hero's injury, but also his perception of his injury, that registers symptomatically in his language. Philoctetes, she writes, suffers a peculiar kind of 'leakage from his wounds to his words', such that his speech 'shudders disturbingly between heroic lament and bestial howls' (Worman 2000: 2). Though vastly different in nature, each of these modes of expression is understood to constitute a verbal abnormality indicative of a kind of disease. Where Philoctetes' much-remarked 'bestial howls' point to the depth and intensity of his physical pain, his 'heroic lament' points to the depth and intensity of his psychological disturbance. As Worman points out, long years of exile on the deserted island of Lemnos have denied the wounded hero the 'curative effects of verbal communication', making his speech 'heavy with suffering' (Worman 2000: 10–11). When he is not struck dumb by an attack of his illness, he speaks in deeply lyrical and melancholic tones: 'his voice resounds with disaster and loss' (Worman 2000: 21, 29). Rarely a vehicle for direct communication with others, Philoctetes' speech belongs to a private world of suffering where the memories of the past strike like the wound on his foot, each assault as vivid and as painful as it was when first inflicted. In his first encounter with Neoptolemus, he bitterly recalls the moment when he awoke on Lemnos to find his companions had deserted him: 'think what I felt, lad / Waking to find them gone; what an awakening!' (*Philoctetes*, lines 277–8). Ten years later, his betrayal at the hands of the Greek commanders remains his central psychological reference point – the moment when he was lost to the world and the world was lost to him.

Throughout the drama, Philoctetes appears as a melancholic hero, grieving end-lessly for all that he formerly held dear: his homeland, his friends, his father (who he fears he will never see again), and his former noble, heroic self.[21] As soon becomes clear, however, the underlying cause of his melancholic state, its traumatic catalyst, is not the rupture of these all-too-human attachments, but the loss of a world in which good is rewarded and evil punished, a world in which the gods make sure that the scheming Odysseus and the sons of Atreus get their due (Tessitore 2003: 74–5, 84). For ten years (and in the face of his rude awakening), Philoctetes has clung to the frail hope of this divine justice to come. If he has managed to go on despite all his hardships, it is only because he still believes the moment will arrive when the gods will finally avenge the 'injustice' perpetrated upon him by the Greek commanders.[22] For all his apparent conviction, however, Philoctetes is plagued by doubt, causing his allusions to the justice of the gods to swing wildly between bitter disappointment and blind faith. When he finally comes face to face with Odysseus he cries out:

> May the gods destroy you! How often have I prayed it. But the gods have no good gifts for me; and there you stand, rejoicing in life, while every breath I draw is agony and torment, my sufferings your sport.
>
> (*Philoctetes*, lines 1,020–1,024)

Only a few lines later he renews his attack upon Odysseus, this time with greater hope for the result he desires: 'Go to your miserable death, as surely you will, for what you did to me, if there is any justice in heaven. Ay, and I know there is' (*Philoctetes*, lines 1,035–7). For Philoctetes the justice that never comes must yet still come. All the while, however, he is forced to confront the abysmal reality of the indifference of the gods, who have not only let him suffer undeservedly for ten years, but taken the best and left the worst among the commanders at Troy. As he learns from Neoptolemus, the noble Ajax, Achilles and Patroclus are dead and gone, while the evil Odysseus, Agamemnon and Menelaus survive and prosper.[23]

Philoctetes' uncompromising attachment to justice is what defines him as a hero, but it is also what prevents him from engaging as a political being and working through the 'pain of things gone by' (Segal 1981: 317). His incapacity for thinking politically is borne out by the fact he can neither entertain the possibility that his abandonment on Lemnos was justifiable under the circumstances nor countenance the thought that the collective interest in victory outweighs his own personal inter-est in justice.[24] As far as he is concerned, his own claim for amends (read vengeance) trumps everything else. Indeed one of the clearest indices of his uncompromising stance can be found in the fact that Philoctetes places himself completely beyond the reach of the definitive political art of persuasion. As he spitefully confesses to the young Neoptolemus, he would rather listen to the serpent that poisoned him than suffer the 'subtle words' of that beguiling statesman Odysseus (*Philoctetes*, lines 628–32). Ironically enough, however, it is Philoctetes' stubborn resistance to persuasion that necessitates Odysseus' devious (though still fully political) use of language. Had the wounded hero only been more open and more reasonable, more willing to listen to reason, there would have been no need for Odysseus to resort to deception. On the face of things Tessitore would thus seem to be right to conclude that Philoctetes is wedded to a standard of justice that 'makes political participation impossible' (Tessitore 2003: 82; see also Nussbaum 1976: 40, 42).[25] His justice is too perfect or, at any rate, too absolute to find a place within the inherently compromised world of politics, where wrongdoing of some kind or another appears to be the price of doing anything at all. For him, it is moral uprightness, not communal membership, which provides the criteria for differentiating between people. He thus arrives at the politically untenable position of perceiving Odysseus and the Atridae as his enemies instead of the Trojans.

More than simply turning his friends into enemies, however, Philoctetes' faith in divine justice makes him an enemy to himself. The more he clings to the expectation of the vengeance that never arrives, the more he deepens his own isolation and anguish. At various points in the play, Philoctetes either prioritises revenge over recovery or incorrectly equates the two, thereby closing himself off from the very compassion he seeks to elicit from his visitors. When Philoctetes refuses Neoptolemus' earnest entreaties to seek healing at Troy, his newly won friend chastises him for becoming complicit in his own suffering:

> Each one of us must live the life god gives him; / It cannot be shirked; but there is no excuse, / Nor pity, for those who choose to cling to suffering / And hardship of their own making, as you would do.
>
> (*Philoctetes*, lines 1,348–51)

Philoctetes is not, of course, insensitive to Neoptolemus' friendship and, by this point in the play, has genuine concern for his welfare. How, he asks, evidently troubled by his own stubbornness, can he turn deaf ears to such a 'kind counsellor'? (*Philoctetes*, lines 1,349–50). These moments of self-castigation notwithstanding, Philoctetes is compelled to keep resisting his kind counsellor because the pity he really covets is not that of his fellow man (which manifests in helping), but that of the gods (which manifests in revenge). In his bitter exchange with Odysseus, Philoctetes begs the unsleeping gods, if they have 'any pity still', to 'bring vengeance, vengeance, late though it be, on all my persecutors!' (*Philoctetes*, lines 1,039–43). Moments later he draws an explicit connection between the death of his enemies and the end of his pain, saying 'if I might but live to see them perish, I could believe my torture ended' (*Philoctetes*, lines 1,043–4).

As the play unfolds, then, Philoctetes emerges as a traumatised subject who is yet to integrate his experience of abandonment. Rather than work to resolve his problem communicatively, the wounded hero anaesthetises his pain, first, by affecting a rage violent enough to overwhelm his hurt; second, by locating an agent who he can hold responsible for his suffering; and finally, by seeking to get revenge upon that agent at all costs (see Brown 1995: 68). It is entirely consistent with this symptomatic structure of resentment that Philoctetes should have become a wholly reactive character, incapable of engaging in self-constituting action. Almost every decision he makes in the play relates to his obsessive desire to get even with Odysseus and the Atridae. Even after he is befriended by the young Neoptolemus, his entire libidinal energy remains invested in getting revenge upon his 'enemies' and there is nothing he will not sacrifice, including his own life, in order to prevent Odysseus from achieving his political goal (*Philoctetes*, lines 1,004–5). However, as his internal and external audience begin to appreciate, Philoctetes' desire for revenge is less a balm for his suffering than a symptom of it. The more he plunges into the pool of righteous rage, the more he deepens his own suffering and alienation. 'Heroic lament' is his solace for justice denied, but it does nothing to help him come to terms with the past. On the contrary, such impotent wailing merely cuts him off from the lives and needs of others, leaving him, like the dishonoured Achilles, 'trapped in a carapace of self-regarding and inflexible emotion' (Morwood 2008: 72).

To see the wounded hero in this light is to become cognisant of the extent to which his path to recovery is contingent upon a process of self-transformation. As Segal underlines:

> Philoctetes cannot return to the human world with the burden of hatred and bitterness symbolised by the mysterious wound. He must come to terms with the past, with the society that rejected him, and with the gods from whom the wound originates.
>
> (Segal 1981: 317)

For Philoctetes, this does not simply mean giving up his attachment to an impossible justice, but dealing with the problem for which this attachment serves as compensation: his lingering fear of betrayal. In the scene preceding Heracles' intervention, where the wounded hero seems to waiver as to whether to accept Neoptolemus' advice to sail to Troy, it is his fear of being harmed again that appears uppermost in his mind: 'It is not the thought of what is past that sours me, / But what is yet to come. I can foresee it. / The soul that has conceived one wickedness / can nurse no good thereafter' (*Philoctetes*, lines 1,356–9). Philoctetes' fear of a repetition of the past is, on any reasonable account of things, well justified. Odysseus clearly feels so little compunction about having once abandoned the crippled man on a deserted island that he is willing to do it again. The only difference is that this time he doesn't even seem to baulk at depriving Philoctetes of his life-sustaining bow. Neoptolemus has, by his stage in the play, shown himself to be of a different, more noble, character. But his earlier role in Philoctetes' deception has created a lingering feeling of distrust. When, towards the very end of the play, Neoptolemus attempts, in all sincerity, to convince Philoctetes that he will find people at Troy who will heal his foot and set him free, the wounded hero responds by saying: 'Do you mean that, serpent's tongue?' (*Philoctetes*, line 1,375).

It is indicative of the depths to which Philoctetes' distrust runs that the demi-god Heracles is needed to persuade him to Troy. Instructively, Heracles offers nothing to Philoctetes by way of inducements that haven't been offered to him before. At different points in the play, Odysseus and Neoptolemus have foretold of the prizes of healing and immortality that are to be his on returning to Troy, yet together and individually they have been unable to lure him back to the Greek cause. If the demi-god succeeds where they have failed, therefore, it can only be because he brings reliability to the promises they have already made. There are, of course, manifold reasons why Philoctetes might be more inclined to trust Heracles than his fellow Greeks, even ones like Neoptolemus who were not party to his original betrayal. Heracles is at once a god-like figure, a great warrior, a patron and a friend. Above all else, however, he is the victim of an analogous disease who remains indebted to Philoctetes for having lit the pyre that relieved him of his suffering. Unlike the members of the Greek party, he can justly claim to know something of what Philoctetes has been through, to have suffered as he suffered and to be genuinely motivated to return the gift that he was once given. Philoctetes greets Heracles as 'The very voice / that I have longer to hear!' because it is the one voice he knows he can trust without reservation (*Philoctetes*, lines 1,444–5). He obeys it because it restores to him a memory of an event that not only precedes the trauma of abandonment, but reminds him of the possibility of self-transformation.

However, it would be wrong to assume that Neoptolemus' compassionate response to Philoctetes is inconsequential to his attempt to deal with the past. Heracles does not make his appearance until Neoptolemus has already agreed to honour his promise to take Philoctetes home to Malis and they are about to set sail. The timing is critical, but not necessarily for the reasons that might first be assumed. There is, of course, a powerful sense in which Heracles must appear when he does because all the available political strategies for getting Philoctetes to Troy (strategies both foul and fair) have been exhausted, leaving the Greek forces on the brink of a monumental military catastrophe. On this pessimistic reading, Heracles' inter-vention speaks to the impossibility of reconciliation and the limits of our human powers in dealing with the past. Yet, it could also be argued that Neoptolemus' willingness to sacrifice the Greek cause at Troy is precisely what is needed in order to break into Philoctetes' melancholic state of resentment and distrust. As James Morwood points out, the ease with which Philoctetes is persuaded by Heracles to join his comrades in Troy has struck many critics as psychologically unconvincing. If the appearance of the demi-god is needed to bring Philoctetes around, it must also be the case that he is 'emotionally ready' to listen to his exhortation (Morwood 2008: 72). Following Segal, then, it might reasonably be concluded that it is the trust Neoptolemus helps to renew in human friendships that enables Philoctetes to reopen his converse with the divine – the divine that lives, not only on Mount Olympus, but also in himself (Segal 1981: 297). By responding to his suffering with unconditional compassion, in other words, Neoptolemus ignites Philoctetes' god-like capacity for self-overcoming.

Psychologically, according to Morwood, Philoctetes is cured while still on the island because his desire for revenge has given way to a willingness to engage with the world: 'He has come to terms with his past and discovered that he has a future' (Morwood 2008: 72–3). As he bids farewell to Lemnos, Philoctetes looks to speed his voyage to Troy, obedient to his fate, to his friends and to Zeus (*Philoctetes*, lines 1,464–7). Yet the happy resolution achieved by Heracles' intervention at the end of the play would surely not have blinded the audience to the extraordinary scene that precedes it where Neoptolemus 'decides' to abandon the political community to its fate at Troy. In this precipitous moment, all the suffering of ten years of war, all the heroes who have gone to their death or been driven into madness, is outweighed by one man's desire to take his suffering home. The lesson, it seems, if tragedy can ever be said to offer such a lesson, is that a trust once broken can only be renewed by a gesture that transfigures through its very excess. If this is indeed what Sophocles has in mind, then the stakes of rescuing wounded subjects mired in the injustices of the past would appear to be very high indeed. Only an unconditional compassion, a compassion willing to sacrifice the entire community for the sake of a single man, would appear to be sufficient to resolve the internal struggle of the aggrieved, tipping them towards reintegration rather than revenge. The story of Philoctetes suggests that pity for the one can be a means towards the good of many. Troy does fall after all. But if Sophocles allows compassion to serve the political in this story of suffering, it is only by putting it at risk.

Notes

1 Working along similar lines, J. Peter Euben has made some interesting, albeit speculative, comments on the potential for comedic television to play a similar interrogatory role in contemporary society as Aristophanic comedy in Ancient Greece (Euben 2003: 64–85).

2 In *On Revolution*, Arendt argued that:

> Compassion, by its very nature, cannot be touched off by the sufferings of a whole class or a people or, least of all, mankind as a whole. It cannot reach out farther than what is suffered by one person and still remain what it is supposed to be, co-suffering.
> (Arendt 1963: 80)

3 In 'Compassion and Terror' Nussbaum asserts that her concern is fundamentally the same as Adam Smith's: 'our difficulty keeping our minds fixed on the sufferings of people who live on the other side of the world' (see Nussbaum 2003: 12).

4 'Narrative art', writes Nussbaum, 'has the power to make us see the lives of different people with more than a casual tourist's interest' (Nussbaum 1999: 267). In contrast to snapshots of human misery, which tend to promote voyeurism or indifference or both, good stories, vividly told, bring out the full complexity of lives remote from our own. Incidentally, Nussbaum's implicit privileging of narrative over image in the cultivation of compassion gains support from Susan Sontag's evocative analysis of the iconography

of suffering in *Regarding the Pain of Others*. 'A narrative seems likely to be more effective than an image', writes Sontag, '[p]artly it is a question of the length of time one is obliged to look, to feel' (Sontag 2003: 110). Whatever the merit of this distinction between narrative and image, however, the medium of story-telling remains central to the project of educating compassion in public culture. Nussbaum is in no doubt that the deep understanding of others made possible by story-telling will prove beneficial to political interaction and political judgement. By allowing other people to appear as 'spacious and deep', she writes, story-telling provides 'an essential preparation for moral and political interaction'. She goes on to argue:

> Habits of empathy and conjecture conduce to a certain type of citizenship and a certain form of community: one that cultivates a sympathetic responsiveness to another's needs, and understands the way circumstances shape those needs, while respecting separateness and privacy.
>
> (Nussbaum 1999: 272–273)

5 As Nussbaum, suggests, 'a tragic poem was assumed to be part of the political and moral life of the polis, offered with a view to learning and to action' (Nussbaum 2003: 27).

6 See for instance Euben 1990; Janover 2003; Goldhill 2004.

7 On this point about the civilising power of the polis and the oikos see Segal 1981: 296.

8 As Segal points out, Philoctetes' 'eagerness to leave his lonely condition makes him vulnerable to deception and manipulation' (Segal 1981: 297).

9 As James Morwood has noted, Philoctetes 'sets a challenge to the play's characters – how will they react to so repellent a figure? – and thus serves as a touchstone to illuminate their moral qualities' (Morwood 2008: 69).

10 Based on his reading of Plato's *Alciabiades*, Foucault concludes that '[t]hose who must take care of themselves are the young aristocrats destined to exercise power' (Foucault 2005: 82).

11 As Neoptolemus painfully acknowledges: 'All is disgust (duschereia) whenever a man leaves his own nature to do things that ill befit it' (902–3).

12 Later in the chapter I suggest that there is in fact a second, though less commonly recognised, political problem at stake in the play: the injustice of Philoctetes' abandonment.

13 As Nussbaum notes:

> It is of the greatest interest to note that for Neoptolemus acting justly seems to mean not simply acting in Philoctetes' interests – for surely to coerce him to return to Troy and be healed would clearly be in his interests, as well as those of Neoptolemus, Odysseus, and all the army.
>
> (Nussbaum 1976: 47)

14 The conception of politics presupposed here is based on two minimal conditions: (i) that it is an arena in which relations are constituted through the medium of speech and (ii) that it is an arena in which individuals must operate as agents; i.e. with deliberative capacities and the power to make decisions effective.

15 As Nancy Worman indicates, Philoctetes' convulsive, ill-omened cries simultaneously mark him as a wild, strange creature (*agrios* and *deinos*) and provide the pretext for his expulsion from the political community. For the Greek army, his speech is not simply infected, but also infectious; and his abjection on the deserted island of Lemnos serves as a kind of linguistic quarantine that protects the polis from contamination (Worman 2000: 4–9).

16 The first phrase refers to the representation of Philoctetes' plight given by the Chorus, while the second refers to Neoptolemus' physical encounter with the fallen hero and his bout of extreme pain (see Worman 2000: 20–29).

17 Presumably the audience, further removed from the experience of pain, are in a position to recognise that Neoptolemus has lost his sense of perspective. Yet as Edith Hall has pointed

out, Philoctetes' suffering seems to dominate everything else. While the play 'asks the proto-Utilitarian question of whether the suffering of a single individual should be allowed to outweigh the interests of the whole community', the thing the spectator remembers at the end of all this 'intellectual questioning' is Philoctetes' screams (Hall 2012: 5).

18 According to Edith Hall:

> Philoctetes has also become obsessed by the question of who is responsible for his suffering, on an incorrect and paranoid impulse blaming the Atridae (who did abandon him but did not actually cause his injury). This is an incorrect reaction to a wholly correct perception on his part – that his problem is quite as much social as physiological.
>
> (Hall 2012)

I proceed on the basis that the correctness or incorrectness of Philoctetes' reaction is open for debate.

19 Late in the play, Philoctetes even goes so far as to describe 'the evil-hearted sons of Laertes', Agamemnon and Menelaus, as his 'murderers' (*Philoctetes*, line 1,354).

20 There are numerous indications of this differentiation in the play. It is made particularly explicit, however, when Philoctetes addresses Odysseus, saying 'may you perish for the injustice you did to his man here ...' (*Philoctetes*, lines 1,035–39). Instructively, when Worman is discussing Philoctetes' illness she differentiates between the 'internal aggressor' (Philoctetes' inflamed foot) and the 'external aggressors' (the Greek leaders) (Worman 2000: 30).

21 In his essay 'Mourning and Melancholia', Freud revealingly suggests that '[t]he complex of melancholia behaves like an open wound' (Freud 2005: 212)

22 As Nussbaum ironically notes:

> [t]he gods have been deaf to his pleas for ten years – and yet the conviction that they do care for justice and will punish wrongdoing remains almost unquestioned in Philoctetes' mind, as though this alone had enabled him to hold out.
>
> (Nussbaum 1976: 42)

23 Upon hearing this bad news from Neoptolemus, Philoctetes mournfully asks:

> Does nothing evil ever die? It seems
> A special providence protects all such.
> I think the gods delight to turn away
> All deep-dyed villains from the door of death
> And hale in all the good men. Why, then, why
> Praise we the gods, when, while we praise,
> We find them evil?
>
> (*Philoctetes*, lines 447–52)

24 As Nussbaum herself acknowledges:

> Though it strikes us and the Chorus as horrible that, despite his innocence of wrongdoing, he was treated so callously by those who owed much and were to owe more to his services, there is little doubt that such callousness on the part of the leaders was right from a utilitarian viewpoint.
>
> (Nussbaum 1976: 31)

25 In her earlier, more extended discussion of the play, Nussbaum similarly acknowledges the problematic nature of Philoctetes' notion of justice: 'Philoctetes comes to light as the completely apolitical man, obsessed with self-interest and subjective concerns ... He regards himself not as part of a general cause, but as the focus of a divinely inspired retributive project' (Nussbaum 1976: 40).

References

Arendt, Hannah (1963) *On Revolution*. London: Faber and Faber.

Aristotle (1996) *The Politics and the Constitution of Athens*, ed. by Stephen Everson. Cambridge: Cambridge University Press.

Brown, Wendy (1995) *States of Injury: Power and Freedom in Late Modernity*. Princeton: Princeton University Press.

Carter, David (2007) *The Politics of Greek Tragedy*. Exeter: Bristol Phoenix Press.

Euben, J. Peter (1990) *The Tragedy of Political Theory: The Road Not Taken*. Princeton: Princeton University Press.

____ (2003) *Platonic Noise*. Princeton: Princeton University Press.

Foucault, Michel (1986) *The Care of the Self*. Harmondsworth: Penguin Books.

____ (2005) *The Hermeneutics of the Subject: Lectures at the College de France 1981–1982*. New York: Picador.

Freud, Sigmund (2005) *On Murder, Mourning and Melancholia*. London: Penguin Books.

Goldhill, Simon (2004) *Love, Sex and Tragedy: How the Ancient World Shapes Our Lives*. Chicago: University of Chicago Press.

Hall, Edith (2012) 'Ancient Greek Responses to Suffering: Thinking with Philoctetes', in J. Malpas and N. Lickiss (eds), *Perspectives on Human Suffering*. New York: Springer.

Janover, Michael (2003) 'Mythic Form and Political Reflection in Athenian Tragedy', *Parallax* 9(4): 41–51.

Morwood, James (2008) *The Tragedies of Sophocles*. Exeter: Bristol Phoenix Press.

Nussbaum, Martha (1976) 'Consequences and Character in Sophocles' *Philoctetes*', *Philosophy and Literature*, 1(1): 25–53.

____ (1998) 'Victims and Agents', *Boston Review: A Political and Literary Forum* 23(1). http://new.bostonreview.net/BR23.1/nussbaum.html (accessed 16 August 2013)

____ (1999) 'Invisibility and Recognition: Sophocles' *Philoctetes* and Ellison's *Invisible Man*', *Philosophy and Literature*, 23(2): 257–83

____ (2001) *Upheavals of Thought: The Intelligence of the Emotions*. Cambridge, Massachusetts: Harvard University Press.

____ (2003) 'Compassion and Terror', *Daedalus*, 132(1): 10–26.

Segal, Charles (1981) *Tragedy and Civilisation: An Interpretation of Sophocles*. Cambridge, Massachusetts: Harvard University Press.

Sontag, Susan (2003) *Regarding the Pain of Others*. London: Penguin Books.

Sophocles (1953) *Electra and Other Plays*. Translated by E. F. Watling. Harmondsworth: Penguin Books.

Tessitore, Aristide (2003) 'Justice, Politics, and Piety in Sophocles' *Philoctetes*', *Review of Politics* 65(1): 61–88.

Worman, Nancy (2000) 'Infection in the Sentence: The Discourse of Disease in Sophocles' *Philoctetes*', *Arethusa* 33: 1–36.

11

PITY, COMPASSION, AND FORGIVENESS

David Konstan

Let me begin with a confession – the first stage on the way to appealing for compassion and forgiveness (and usually followed by an apology and promise of reform): I am not a political scientist, but a student of classical Greece and Rome. My research on compassion and related ideas has been historical, an analysis of how ancient concepts compare to our own. I have written a book on pity in the classical world and early Christianity, another on the emotions of the ancient Greeks, in which I discuss, among other sentiments, anger and the assuaging of anger, as well as love and hatred, and still another book on the origins of the modern conception of forgiveness (Konstan 2001; Konstan 2006; Konstan 2010).[1] In this brief chapter, I should like to draw upon classical ideas that are broadly within the semantic neighborhood of compassion to suggest some distinctions among these and related concepts that may be useful in evaluating the role of compassion in politics today. I do not, of course, mean to legislate the meaning of words on the basis of some presumed historical or, still worse, etymological considerations. The notions conveyed by such terms as compassion, sympathy, pity, forgiveness, clemency, humaneness, benevolence, and reconciliation, as well as phrases such as the assuaging of anger and the renunciation of vengeance, are not neatly bounded, and there are broad areas of overlap and combination. Still, some sense of how these ideas relate to classical Greek and Roman concepts that map, sometimes only roughly, onto the modern categories may help to clarify our thinking about the role of such sentiments in the contemporary world.

If we look to early Greek ideas that correspond to compassion, as it is understood today, the nearest, and certainly the most common, is pity, or, more strictly, *eleos*, the ancestor, by way of the longer form *eleomosunê*, of the English "alms." Aristotle defines pity as "a kind of pain in the case of an apparent destructive or painful harm in one not deserving to encounter it," and which, he adds, "one might expect oneself, or one of one's own, to suffer, and this when it seems near"

(*Rhetoric* 2.8, 1385b13–16). Two things stand out in this definition: first, we feel pity only for those whose misfortune is underserved; and second, we feel pity only for those kinds of adversity to which we ourselves are vulnerable. Pity is thus a decidedly moral emotion, involving a judgment of the causes of another's suffering; people who have brought suffering upon themselves do not deserve our pity (for example, criminals who are brought to justice and must pay the penalty). What is more, pity seems to have an egoistic dimension: if we are in no way susceptible to the misfortune we perceive in another, we will not experience the kind of anxiety that is, apparently, a precondition for pity. One consequence of this view is that the gods (or God) will not be given to pity, at least in the case of most forms of human misery, to the extent that they are immune to such distress.[2] But neither can those wholly in despair feel pity, for they no longer expect anything worse to happen to them. The direct experience of suffering *per se* does not make us more susceptible to feeling pity for others, according to Aristotle (in contrast to what is often assumed today).

Aristotle offers some further qualifications of the idea of pity. For example, he affirms that we do not pity those who are very close to ourselves, such as family members or intimate friends. This too follows from his definition, for pity is aroused at misfortune that "one might expect oneself, or one of one's own, to suffer." We note first that we do not pity our own misfortune – Aristotle's formula does not allow, it would appear, for self-pity – since, when we ourselves are suffering, we are no longer expecting to do so; it is our vulnerability to hardship that allows us to pity, not the current experience of it. A consequence of this account is that, although pity depends on our susceptibility to adversity, we feel it only when we are not actually in the same situation as those we pity: pity presupposes a difference in condition between subject and object, the capacity to regard another's suffering from the vantage point – never wholly secure – of our own well-being. It is this feature of pity, it would seem, that lends to the sentiment a note of condescension, and has led in modern times to a rejection of pity as a basis for fellow feeling, especially in connection with various supposed disabilities. But if we cannot feel pity for ourselves, since then both the pitier and the pitied will be in the same condition, neither can we feel it for those who are "our own," in Aristotle's phrase; the point is that we treat those dearest to us as extensions of ourselves, and so we suffer along with them – and hence lose that difference in circumstance that is a precondition for pity. As Aristotle famously put it in the *Nicomachean Ethics*, friends are another self.

In connection with intimate relationships, including that with our own selves in the case of self-love, Aristotle avoids the term *eleos*, and avails himself of alternative expressions such as (in Greek) *sullupeisthai*, *sunalgein*, and *sunakhthesthai*, all of which mean to "condole" or "feel pain together" with another. Correspondingly, for the sharing of positive sentiment, Aristotle uses the terms *sunkhairein*, *sunêdesthai*, and similar compounds that are again marked by the prefix *sun-*, or "with" (the Latin equivalent is *con-*), words that indicate we feel pleasure with the other person. This sense of sharing in the feeling of the other, that is, in the immediate pain or pleasure that a dear one is experiencing, is in contrast to pity, where we do not experience what the other feels but rather a pain induced by our sense of vulner-ability to a comparable misfortune in the future. To put it another way, pity does not involve sharing the sentiment of others, for that would only occur when they were themselves feeling pity and we pitied them precisely for that – surely not a typical case. There is, however, a part of pity that we can share with the pitied – that is, the raw sensation of pain that enters into Aristotle's definition and which, isolated from the larger moral and other conditions that are stipulated for pity, is presumably much the same for pitier and pitied.

The *sun-* words (transliterated in English as *syn-* or, before a labial, *sym-*) that we have identified above bring us close to a conception of sympathy, which derives from the Greek word *sumpatheia*. Yet the latter term is relatively rare in the vocabu-lary of the classical period, and most often refers to coordinated events such as the motion of stars and affairs on Earth. In later Greek, and particularly among Christian writers, the term comes to supplement pity (*eleos* or *eleomosunê*), in part because the latter had acquired something of the sense of "mercy" (it is often translated as such) and lost some of the quality of an emotion. There is a comparable evolution in Latin from the notion of *misericordia*, which corresponds most directly to the Greek *eleos*, to *compassio*, a term that first appears in Christian literature and is, of course, the ancestor of the English "compassion." Now, sympathy in the modern construal of the term involves identification with another, precisely the capacity to share the other's sentiment fully, irrespective of the circumstantial distance that Aristotle installed between the pitier and the pitied. Edmund Burke, for example, writes that "sympathy must be considered as a sort of substitution, by which we are put into the place of another man, and affected in many respects as he is affected" (Burke 1990: 41), and David Hume insists that the thought of another's passion may acquire "such a degree of force and vivacity, as to become the very passion itself" (Hume 1906: 317). We may note here that such a conception of sympathy, while it misses the element of aloofness or disdain to which the idea of pity is subject, also lacks the moral element that was, for Aristotle and most of his contemporaries, cen-tral to the idea of pity. If we share entirely in the feelings of another, what happens to the idea of desert? Are we to suffer with the condemned criminal, irrespective of the justice of the case? Is compassion independent of ethical judgment?

These questions come alive in particular with respect to the idea of forgive-ness, which has become central to psychological, judicial, religious, and political discourse in the past few decades, to the extent that declarations of regret or remorse and petitions for forgiveness can be found almost daily in the press. Forgiveness implies forgoing vengeance, and while it is possible to adopt an attitude of com-miseration with all, irrespective of desert, and out of a kind of cosmic sympathy be willing to be reconciled with our enemies or persecutors unconditionally, asking nothing of them either previously or in return, for most of us such a blanket pardon of offenses, without regard to the moral state of the offender, seems either beyond our power or, seen differently, is tantamount to exonerating the wrongdoer and in some sense condoning the crime.[3] Should compassion always govern our responses – and if so, is it constrained by moral considerations, which might justify an abiding anger or resentment for wrongs suffered and foreclose the option of forgiveness or reconciliation?[4] It was worries such as these that led ancient thinkers to insist that pity not be eviscerated of its ethical or judgmental content, and so be casually extended even to those who deserve their suffering.

The historian Polybius, who lived for many years as a hostage in Rome during the first half of the second century BC, wrote a history of Rome from 220–146 BC, in which he sought to persuade his fellow Greeks of the extraordinary power and good qualities of the Roman Republic. At one point, when dealing with hostilities in his own home territory of Arcadia, Polybius pauses to explain why he has chosen not to follow the account of the historian Phylarchus for these events, even though many find him a trustworthy source. Polybius affirms that Phylarchus was out to show the cruelty of the leaders who sacked the city of Mantinea, and so he emphasized the terrible misfortunes that its population suffered, which, he says, elicited the tears of Greeks everywhere (2.56.6). In order to rouse the sentiment of pity and, Polybius says, render his readers sympathetic (*sumpatheis*) to his version of the story, Phylarchus described how women bared their breasts and tore their hair, while everyone, men, women, children, and the elderly, wept and lamented as they were led off to slavery (2.56.7). Polybius insists that history, as opposed to tragedy, is not supposed to shock but to recount the truth, however prosaic it may be. "Apart from this," Polybius adds, "Phylarchus simply narrates most of his reversals, and provides no reason or character traits; but without these it is impossible to feel pity rationally [*eulogôs*] or be angry responsibly [*kathêkontôs*] at any event" (7.56.13; cf. the historian Dio Cassius 51.15.2, who observes that Antony and Cleopatra "pitied irrationally [*alogôs*]"). Yes, Polybius allows, it is terrible for free men to be beaten, but if this is punishment for starting a battle without warrant, then we regard it as justified; so too with killing another person, as when we catch a thief or adulterer in the act. The critical distinction in all such cases resides not in the acts themselves, but rather in the reasons and characters of the actors.

Polybius, then, like Aristotle, adopts a cognitivist approach to emotion, in which an evaluation of motives and context is essential to the very nature of an emotion. In Polybius' account, however, the criterion is prescriptive: neither the actors in the narrative nor the reader *should* be moved by good or bad fortune as such. Polybius then applies his principle to the fate of the Mantineans. When they were conquered four years earlier, they were treated with great humanity (*philanthrôpia*, 2.57.8); no people, Polybius says, had ever encountered kindlier enemies. But then they changed allegiance, and when the opportunity presented itself, they slit the throats of the enemy garrison, in violation, Polybius says, of the laws common to all mankind (2.58.6). This is why they inspired, and should inspire, not pity but extreme anger (2.58.8), and no one should feel the least sympathy for their plight.

When it came to war, judicial trials or political quarrels and battles, the emotional response to one's opponent or sympathizers typically ranged between pity for those whose misfortune was thought to be undeserved and anger toward those who were deemed to have violated their obligations and commitments. Needless to say, anger was most often directed against enemies, whether public or personal, who were accused of betrayal or else of contravening the universal norms of proper behavior; pity, in turn, tended to be reserved for the sufferings of those on one's own side, who were naturally enough supposed to be in the right. There was, nevertheless, room for generosity of spirit, and victors could spare at least some of the conquered, if they thought they were innocent of wrongdoing. The point here is not so much to approve or condemn the behavior of the ancient Greeks and Romans (though by and large it left much to be desired in respect to the humane treatment of opponents), but rather to observe that, where emotion entered the realm of politics, the discourse took the form of an opposition between anger and pity, both of which were conceived in moral terms. People were surely moved also by bare compassion, irrespective of ethical judgment; after all, this is exactly what Polybius accused Phylarchus of feeling, or at all events of eliciting in his readers, thereby winning sympathy for what Polybius regarded as an unjust cause (Polybius and Phylarchus were, unsurprisingly, on different sides in the conflict). But Polybius could expect his readers to respond with understanding to the way he cast his argument against his rival; the Aristotelian conception of pity was dominant in the ideology of his time.

Can it ever be right to massacre an entire population, or reduce it to slavery, however wrong or treacherous they might have been? Mass exterminations of the sort were not uncommon in classical antiquity; indeed, at the end of the Peloponnesian War, in which Athens was defeated by a coalition of states under the leadership of Sparta, some of the victorious allies, we are told, including Thebes and Corinth, pushed for the annihilation of the Athenians; they were spared only because the Spartans thought that Athens would be useful as a counterweight in case their current allies turned against them (Xenophon *Hellenica* 2.2.19–20). Pity was a weak reed on which to depend after intense hostilities, and it may seem that some deeper disposition to compassion, and a recognition of the limits of revenge, however justified it might appear, are needed to prevent such extreme atrocities. Modern experience of genocide nevertheless suggests that the discourse of compassion has not necessarily fared better than the ancient way of thinking. To some extent, indeed, even the ideology of human rights as a basis for universal respect, which might be thought to substitute for the less rigorous motive of sympathy, may work against general solidarity, since where passions run high, extreme violence may be justified by casting the enemy as less than human – as vermin, beasts, and the like, and so not deserving of regard.[5] It is noteworthy that the language of dehumanization is largely absent from classical histories, despite the chilling manner in which they recount massacres.

If we think of compassion as a generalized sentiment of identification with others, particularly when they are afflicted by some woe, few today are likely to disagree that it is a good thing, or if they do dissent, it is because they regard the others as unworthy of fellow feeling: where deep-seated racism is not a factor, then people may imagine, for example, that the poor have not done enough to lift themselves out of poverty, or may find some other reason for withholding generosity from those who are less well off. The sheer magnitude of suffering in the world may inhibit what may seem like useless anguish on behalf of others, not to mention the danger of a misguided kind of benevolent activism, which may do more harm than good. If we leave aside such limitations upon a universal altruism, the situations in which the practical exercise in compassion is possible commonly involve a sense of injury and the desire, or need, to overcome it by extending fellow feeling to one's erstwhile antagonist. And this takes us into the territory of forgiveness.

In an emotional economy predicated on anger for unjustified offenses and pity for unmerited suffering, there is little room for forgiveness: one can either demand recompense in some form or other for the harm done, or else recast the offense as excusable and so not deserving of punishment. Excuses may come in various forms, but in antiquity all are basically reducible to the premise that the offense in question was in some sense unintentional or involuntary (of course, one may have misjudged the situation and subsequently discover that no wrong was done, but that is a distinct case). Thus, Aristotle writes in the *Nicomachean Ethics*, *sungnômê* – the Greek term most commonly rendered as "forgiveness" but which, as we shall see, rather means something like "understanding" – is appropriate when people act either under external compulsion or in excusable ignorance of the facts or circumstances (1109b18–1111a2). As he puts it:

> ... since virtue concerns emotions and actions, and praise and blame are due in the case of voluntary acts, whereas *sungnômê*, and sometimes pity [*eleos*], are due in the case of involuntary acts, it is obligatory for those investigating virtue to define what is voluntary and what is involuntary.
>
> (1109b30–4)

and Aristotle goes on to observe: "it is believed that involuntary acts are those that occur either by force or through ignorance." This is not to say that Aristotle offers easy ways to evade responsibility for one's actions. He raises, for example, the case in which a tyrant who has power over one's parents and children orders one to commit some wrong or shameful deed, circumstances that we might regard as compulsory. Aristotle acknowledges that there is some ambiguity as to whether an act performed under such conditions is indeed voluntary, and he concludes that "such actions are mixed," but he immediately adds that "they rather resemble voluntary ones" (1110a11–12). And if voluntary, then they merit punishment, not pardon.

Now, Aristotle's *sungnômê* is not what is meant by "forgiveness" today, at least in the most common acceptation of the term. We do not typically say: "You meant no harm, and only acted under absolute constraint or out of an excusable lack of knowledge of the circumstances, and so I forgive you." We forgive, if we forgive at all, instances of genuine wrongdoing, that is, the kind of action that elicits anger in the ancient scheme of things, not pity or kindness. Aristotle also remarks that for some actions, "praise is not given, but *sungnômê* may be, when someone does things one ought not to do on account of circumstances that are beyond human nature and which no one could endure" (3.1, 1110a23–6). If we imagine someone betraying a secret after a long process of torture, we might conclude that such an act, though strictly speaking wrong and subject to punishment, may be excused insofar as no one, we might imagine, could withstand such treatment. Still, what Aristotle is providing here are grounds for exoneration, not forgiveness; forgiveness responds to a deliberate offense, not one where responsibility is in some measure diminished.

Forgiveness, however, is not merely a matter of giving over a desire for punishment or vengeance, or the wish to see justice done. Such unconditional compassion may be perceived as a virtue or an ideal, but it may also be seen as coming dangerously close to exoneration, as I remarked earlier.[6] Subjectively, it may be desirable to give over resentment and not to harbor hard feelings, which can certainly get in the way of personal serenity and well-being. Objectively, however, there are good reasons for granting forgiveness only when the wrongdoer acknowledges the error, exhibits a sense of remorse, and gives evidence of having changed in some fundamental way that guarantees that the act will not be repeated in the future. Forgiveness on these terms requires a sincere apology and what we may call a change of heart in the offender; only on this condition is forgiveness properly granted. Undiscriminating compassion can do as much harm as good; indeed, a strong case has been made that God himself, as conceived both in the Hebrew Bible and the New Testament, does not grant forgiveness unconditionally (cf. Griswold and Konstan 2012).

Conditional forgiveness, however, raises problems of its own. How is one to judge whether the remorse expressed by the offender is sincere, and a sign of a genuine change of heart? Is so total a moral transformation indeed possible for anyone? And if all the indications confirm that a wrongdoer has indeed undergone such a change, is the offended party now obliged to forgive? If not, does this not grant extraordinary power to the injured person – to accept or reject a sincere petition for reconciliation, or to demand gestures so humiliating that they are tantamount to punishment rather than a foreswearing of revenge? And are there crimes so grave that forgiveness is out of the question, or even immoral? Given the dilemmas that seem to be attached to the very concept of forgiveness, we may well ask where and why such a cultural practice arose – the more so, inasmuch as classical thinkers, to all appearances, did not develop a comparable discourse but put forward various strategies for excusing misbehavior as a basis for reconciliation.

The place to look for forgiveness in the context of the ancient Greek and Roman world is, above all, the Bible, and indeed the Bible does not disappoint in this regard. But it is remarkable that forgiveness, whether in the Hebrew Bible or the New Testament, is principally – some would argue exclusively – the province of God. What is lacking is any sustained interest in interpersonal forgiveness. In the Hebrew Bible, God forgives his chosen people when they backslide or disobey his injunctions, but he does so only when there are sufficient signs of repentance and a return to his ways. In the New Testament and in early Christian writers, there is a greater emphasis on original sin and the fallen state of mankind, from which one can be redeemed only through faith and by the grace of God. Now, there is no fooling God, so the question of sincerity does not arise in this context, though of course one may honestly repent and then lapse again into sin. As for the possibility of a genuine change of heart, this is just what acquiring faith means: a renewal or rebirth, the casting off of the old Adam and the emergence of a new self. This kind of forgiveness is inherent in the Christian idea of faith. But clearly it is a gift from God, not something that a human being can bestow on another.

This is not the place to set out in detail the arguments that show that forgiveness in the Jewish and Christian traditions was properly understood as God's prerogative. But there may have occurred to readers the famous passage from the Sermon on the Mount (Matthew 6:12): "Forgive us our debts, as we also have forgiven our debtors," which recurs in a slightly different form in the Gospel of Luke (11:4), where Jesus urges us pray that God "forgive us our sins, for we ourselves forgive everyone who is indebted to us." The term for "forgive" here is not *sungnômê* (or the related verb), as in Aristotle, but rather *aphiêmi*, literally "to release" or, in the case of debts, "to remit." In English, we speak of forgiving a debt, without necessarily implying that the debtor is guilty of wrongdoing (or defaulting) or that an apology is due; it is the creditor's right simply to cancel the debt in a spirit of generosity or affection, without an exhibition of remorse and change of heart on the part of the other. Of course, it is not in our power to forgive sins, as the text in Luke has it; this is the domain of God, who can wipe away sin – strike it from the books, as it were – in the same way that human beings can forego collecting on a loan. However, whereas one earns God's forgiveness through faith and repentance, as well as by good actions in this world (for example, releasing those who are indebted to us), it is not for us mortals to insist on such manifestations of remorse and moral transformation. Forgiveness in this deeper sense is not relevant to interpersonal transactions.

When did forgiveness descend, as it were, from heaven and take up residence on earth, as a process or exchange between human beings? I have argued (Konstan 2010) that this change occurred very late in Western history, indeed not before the Enlightenment, when the possibility of a moral transformation came to be detached, at least partially, from its theological context and was seen as a strictly ethical, as opposed to religious, reform. One of the thinkers who bears responsibility for this change is Immanuel Kant. Thus, Joanna North (1978), writes: "Kant seems to think that through … a positive change of heart a person can become a 'new man.' The sinful person he once was will be punished while the new person he has become will not." What we see here, I believe, is a kind of secularization of conversion. If such a moral revolution is possible, apart from faith, we may now require evidence of it as a condition for granting forgiveness to someone who has wronged us. But such a demand brings with it the moral conundrums indicated above, and along with these another, more metaphysical quandary. For, as North observes of Kant's "new man":

> This ingenious solution creates many problems of personal identity, and makes forgiveness redundant. If I repent, and in so doing, become a new man, asking for forgiveness seems to be a matter of asking for a response aimed at a person who no longer exists. But if this is really so, then there

can be no point in asking for forgiveness, and the person who is asked for
forgiveness can only aim his response at a metaphysical shadow.

(North 1978)

We can, of course, separate compassion from forgiveness and the entire complex
of apology, remorse, and change of heart on the part of the offender; but we have
seen that unconditional compassion carries with it its own moral difficulties. One
can perhaps forgive, or at least pardon, without any special sense of compassion:
presidents pardon political allies who have been accused of wrongdoing, and it
may be strategic to overlook the offenses of others if we are convinced that there
is no danger that they will repeat the crime in the future, irrespective of any pain
they may feel, whether it is pangs of conscience or simply unanticipated consequences of their misbehavior (for instance, time in prison). Whether such methods
of reconciliation count as forgiveness is perhaps debatable. Julie Fitness, in an article
entitled "Betrayal, Rejection, Revenge, and Forgiveness: An Interpersonal Script
Approach" (2001), writes: "a truly contrite offender must take full responsibility for
the offence." "Sincere apologies," Fitness explains, "imply that an offender is feeling guilt." What is more, "the pain of guilt … motivates atonement and a desire to
make the suffering partner feel better." We feel an "empathic distress in response to
the pain" that we have caused, according to Fitness, and this in turn will "motivate
remorseful behaviors and attempts to restore the relationship." Fitness is looking
principally at betrayals in intimate relationships, such as infidelity in a marriage,
where partners can, or imagine that they can, read the signs of the other's internal
state of mind, and desire such confirmation of a change of heart. But an analogous
pattern is often at work in the case of more distant relations.

Compassion is not limited to forgiveness scenarios, and few will oppose the cultivation of sensibility to the plight and sufferings of others, whether in the personal
or the political sphere. But how to translate this sentiment into practical and ethical
action is by no means self-evident. If the forgiveness script has its limitations and its
history, compassion itself, in the sense of identification with another's pain and suffering, has not always held the high place among moral sentiments that it seems to enjoy
today. Its role in Enlightenment thought is due at least in part to a new conception of
human beings as individuals, effectively monads, who apprehend the world around
them exclusively through information provided by the senses; sympathy was a means
of transcending one's private world, a special faculty that allowed us to bridge the
distance between ourselves and others that seemed like a precondition for sociability.
Alternative approaches to the social nature of human beings, which see individualism
as a product of culture rather than a natural, pre-social condition, may look to other
motives as the basis for interpersonal harmony and reconciliation.

In subjecting the idea of compassion to a historical analysis and critique, I do
not mean in the least to impugn its value in the modern world. Needless to say, we
live within the emotional and ethical parameters of our time, as these have been
both inherited and transformed under new conditions of social life. The chapters in this book offer various case studies in the role of compassion, and amply

demonstrate its importance as well as possible limitations in the political sphere. In these comments, I hope merely to have outlined something of the background to our contemporary concern with compassion, and to have indicated that even so humane a principle and sentiment may be bounded by a specific historical and cultural horizon.

Notes

1 This chapter is based largely on the results of these more detailed studies, and the reader is kindly asked to consult them for full references to sources and bibliography. See also Kaster 2005 for related Roman values and emotions.
2 Homeric gods are not wholly invulnerable: for example, they may suffer at the death of their mortal children; but the gods were most often conceived of as aloof from human misery, and philosophers of all schools insisted on their perfect happiness.
3 For an especially lucid discussion, see Griswold 2007.
4 On the legitimacy of sustained anger, see Brudholm 2008.
5 See, for example, Smith 2011.
6 For a more positive account of unconditional forgiveness, see Bash 2007.

References

Bash, Anthony. 2007. *Forgiveness and Christian Ethics*. Cambridge: Cambridge University Press.

Burke, Edmund. 1990. *A Philosophical Enquiry into the Origin of our Ideas of the Sublime and the Beautiful*. Oxford: Oxford University Press.

Brudholm, Thomas. 2008. *Resentment's Virtue: Jean Améry and the Refusal to Forgive*. Philadelphia: Temple University Press.

Fitness, Julie. 2001. "Betrayal, Rejection, Revenge, and Forgiveness: An Interpersonal Script Approach," in M. Leary (ed.), *Interpersonal Rejection*. New York: Oxford University Press, pp. 73–103.

Griswold, Charles L. 2007. *Forgiveness: A Philosophical Exploration*. Cambridge: Cambridge University Press.

Griswold, Charles, and David Konstan, eds. 2012. *Ancient Forgiveness*. Cambridge: Cambridge University Press.

Hume, David. 1906 (orig. 1739–40). *A Treatise of Human Nature*, L. A. Selby-Bigge (ed.). Oxford: Oxford University Press.

Kaster, Robert A. 2005. *Emotion, Restraint, and Community in Ancient Rome*. Oxford: Oxford University Press.

Konstan, David. 2001. *Pity Transformed*. London: Duckworth.

Konstan, David. 2006. *The Emotions of the Ancient Greeks: Studies in Aristotle and Classical Literature*. Toronto: University of Toronto Press.

Konstan, David. 2010. *Before Forgiveness: The Origins of a Moral Idea*. Cambridge: Cambridge University Press.

North, Joanna. 1978. "Wrongdoing and Forgiveness." *Philosophy* 62: 499–508.

Smith, David Livingston. 2011. *Less than Human: Why we Demean, Enslave, and Exterminate Others*. New York: St. Martin's Press.

12

COMPASSION AND TERROR

Martha C. Nussbaum

The name of our land has been wiped out.

Euripides, *Trojan Women*

Not to be a fan of the Greens or Blues at the races, or the light-armed or heavy-armed gladiators at the Circus.

Marcus Aurelius, *Meditations*

1

The towers of Troy are burning. All that is left of the once-proud city is a group of ragged women, bound for slavery, their husbands dead in battle, their sons murdered by the conquering Greeks, their daughters raped. Hecuba their queen invokes the king of the gods, using, remarkably, the language of democratic citizenship: "Son of Kronus, Council-President [*prytanis*] of Troy, father who gave us birth, do you see these undeserved sufferings that your Trojan people bear?" The Chorus answers grimly, "He sees, and yet the great city is no city. It has perished, and Troy exists no longer." Hecuba and the Chorus conclude that the gods are not worth calling on, and that the very name of their land has been wiped out.

This ending is as bleak as any in the history of tragic drama – death, rape, slavery, fire destroying the towers, the city's very name effaced from the record of history by the acts of rapacious and murderous Greeks. And yet, of course, it did not happen that way, not exactly: this story of Troy's fall is being enacted, some six hundred years after the event, by a company of Greek actors, in the Greek language of a Greek poet, in the presence of the citizens of Athens, most powerful of Greek cities. Hecuba's cry to the gods even casts Zeus as a peculiarly Athenian official – president of the city council.

So the name of Troy wasn't wiped out after all. The imagination of its conquerors was haunted by it, transmitted it, and mourned it. Obsessively the Greek poets returned to this scene of destruction, typically inviting, as here, the audience's compassion for the women of Troy and blame for their assailants. In its very structure the play makes a claim for the moral value of compassionate imagining, as it asks its audience to partake in the terror of a burning city, of murder and rape and slavery. Insofar as members of the audience are engaged by this drama, feeling fear and grief for the conquered city, they demonstrate the ability of compassion to cross lines of time, place, and nation – and also, in the case of many audience members, the line of sex, perhaps more difficult yet to cross.

Nor was the play a purely aesthetic event divorced from political reality. The dramatic festivals of Athens were sacred celebrations strongly connected to the idea of democratic deliberation, and the plays of Euripides were particularly well-known for their engagement with contemporary events. *The Trojan Women'* s first audience had recently voted to put to death the men of the rebellious colony of Melos and to enslave its women and children. Euripides invited this audience to contemplate the real human meaning of its actions. Compassion for the women of Troy should at least cause moral unease, reminding Athenians of the full and equal humanity of people who live in distant places, their fully human capacity for suffering.

But did those imaginations really cross those lines? Think again of that invocation of Zeus. Trojans, if they worshipped Zeus as king of gods at all, surely did not refer to him as the president of the city council; *prytanis* is strictly an Athenian legal term. So it would appear that Hecuba is not a Trojan but a Greek. And her imagination is a Greek democratic (and, we might add, mostly male) imagination. Maybe that's a good thing, in the sense that the audience is surely invited to view her as their fellow and equal. But it still should give us pause.

Did compassion really enable those Greeks to comprehend the real humanity of others, or did it stop short, allowing them to reaffirm the essential Greekness of everything that's human? Of course compassion required making the Trojans somehow familiar, so that Greeks could see their own vulnerability in them, and feel terror and pity, as for their own relations. But it's easy for the familiarization to go too far: they are just us, and we are the ones who suffer humanly. Not those other ones, over there in Melos.

America's towers, too, have burned. Compassion and terror now inform the fabric of our lives. And in those lives we see evidence of the good work of compassion, as Americans make real to themselves the sufferings of so many people whom they never would otherwise have thought about: New York firefighters, that gay rugby player who helped bring down the fourth plane, bereaved families of so many national and ethnic origins. More rarely our compassion even crosses national boundaries: the tragedy led an unprecedented number of Americans to sympathize with the plight of Afghan women under the Taliban.

Yet at the same time, we also see evidence of how narrow and self-serving our sense of compassion can sometimes be. Some of us may notice with new appreciation the lives of Arab Americans among us – but others regard the Muslims in our midst with increasing wariness and mistrust. I am reminded of a Sikh taxi driver describing how often he was told to go home to 'his own country' – even though he came to the United State as a political refugee from the miseries of police repression in the Punjab. And while our leaders have preached the virtues of tolerance, they have also resorted to the polarizing language of 'us' versus 'them,' as they marshal popular opinion to pursue a war on terrorism.

Indeed, the events of September 11 make vivid a philosophical problem that has been debated from the time of Euripides through much of the history of the Western philosophical tradition. This is the question of what to do about compassion, given its obvious importance in shaping the civic imagination, but given, too, its obvious propensity for self-serving narrowness. Is compassion, with all its limits, our best hope as we try to educate citizens to think well about human relations both inside the nation and across national boundaries? So some thinkers have suggested. I count Euripides among them, and would also include in this category Aristotle, Rousseau, Hume, and Adam Smith. Or is compassion a threat to good political thinking and the foundations of a truly just world community? So the Greek and Roman Stoics thought, and before them Plato, and after them Spinoza and (again) Adam Smith.

The enemies of compassion hold that we cannot build a stable and lasting concern for humanity on the basis of such a slippery and uneven motive; impartial motives based on ideas of dignity and respect should take its place. The friends of compassion reply that without building political morality on what we know and on what has deep roots in our childhood attachments, we will be left with a morality that is empty of urgency – a 'watery' concern, as Aristotle put it.

This debate continues in contemporary political and legal thought. In a recent exchange about animal rights, J. M. Coetzee invented a character who argues that the capacity for sympathetic imagination is our best hope for moral goodness in this area. Peter Singer replies, with much plausibility, that the sympathetic imagination is all too anthropocentric and we had better not rely on it to win rights for creatures whose lives are very different from our own.[1]

I shall not trace the history of the debate in this chapter. Instead, I shall focus on its central philosophical ideas and try to sort them out, offering a limited defense of compassion and the tragic imagination, and then making some suggestions about how its pernicious tendencies can best be countered – with particular reference throughout to our current political situation.

2

Let me set the stage for the analysis to follow by turning to Smith, who, as you will have noticed, turns up in my taxonomy on both sides of the debate. Smith offers one of the best accounts we have of compassion, and of the ethical achievements of which this moral sentiment is capable. But later, in a section of *The Theory of Moral*

Sentiments entitled "Of the Sense of Duty," he solemnly warns against trusting this imperfect sentiment too far when duty is what we are trying to get clear.

Smith's concern, like mine, is with our difficulty keeping our minds fixed on the sufferings of people who live on the other side of the world:

> Let us suppose that the great empire of China, with all its myriads of inhab-itants, was suddenly swallowed up by an earthquake, and let us consider how a man of humanity in Europe, who had no sort of connexion with that part of the world, would be affected upon receiving intelligence of this dreadful calamity. He would, I imagine, first of all, express very strongly his sorrow for the misfortune of that unhappy people, he would make many melancholy reflections upon the precariousness of human life, and the vanity of all the labours of man, which could thus be annihilated in a moment.... And when all this fine philosophy was over, when all these humane senti-ments had been once fairly expressed, he would pursue his business or his pleasure, take his repose or his diversion, with the same ease and tranquility, as if no such accident had happened. The most frivolous disaster which could befal himself would occasion a more real disturbance. If he was to lose his little finger tomorrow, he would not sleep tonight; but, provided he never saw them, he will snore with the more profound security over the ruin of a hundred millions of his brethren, and the destruction of that immense multitude seems plainly an object less interesting to him, than this paltry misfortune of his own.

That's just the issue that should trouble us as we think about American reactions to September 11. We see a lot of 'humane sentiments' around us, and extensions of sympathy beyond people's usual sphere of concern. But more often than not, those sentiments stop short at the national boundary.

We think the events of September 11 are bad because they involved *us* and *our* nation. Not just human lives, but *American* lives. The world came to a stop – in a way that it rarely has for Americans when disaster has befallen human beings in other places. The genocide in Rwanda didn't even work up enough emotion in us to prompt humanitarian intervention. The plight of innocent civilians in Iraq never made it onto our national radar screen. Floods, earthquakes, cyclones, the daily deaths of thousands from preventable malnutrition and disease – none of these makes the American world come to a standstill, none elicits a tremendous outpouring of grief and compassion. At most we get what Smith so trenchantly described: a momentary flicker of feeling, quickly dissipated by more pressing con-cerns close to home.

Frequently, however, we get a compassion that is not only narrow, failing to include the distant, but also polarizing, dividing the world into an 'us' and a 'them.' Compassion for our own children can so easily slip over into a desire to promote the well-being of our children at the expense of other people's children. Similarly, compassion for our fellow Americans can all too easily slip over into a desire to make America come out *on top* and to subordinate other nations.

One vivid example of this slip took place at a baseball game I went to at Comiskey Park, the first game played in Chicago after September 11 – and a game against the Yankees, so there was heightened awareness of the situation of New York and its people. Things began well, with a moving ceremony commemorating the firefighters who had lost their lives and honoring local firefighters who had gone to New York afterwards to help out. There was even a lot of cheering when the Yankees took the field, a highly unusual transcendence of local attachments. But as the game went on and the beer began flowing, one heard, increasingly, the chant "U-S-A. U-S-A," a chant first heard in 1980 during an Olympic hockey match in which the United States defeated Russia. In that context, the chant had expressed a wish for America to humiliate its Cold War enemy; as time passed, it became a general way of expressing the desire to crush an opponent, whoever it might be. When the umpire made a bad call against the Sox, a group in the bleachers turned on him, chanting "U-S-A." From 'humane sentiments' we had turned back to the pain in our little finger.

With such examples before us, how can we trust compassion and the imagination of the other that it contains? But if we don't trust that, what else can we plausibly rely on to transform horror into a shared sense of ethical responsibility?

I shall proceed as follows. First, I shall offer an analysis of the emotion of compassion, focusing on the thoughts and imaginings on which it is based. This will give us a clearer perspective on how and where it is likely to go wrong. Second, I shall examine the countertradition's proposal that we can base political morality on respect for dignity, doing away with appeals to compassion. This horror proposal, at first attractive, contains, on closer inspection, some deep difficulties. Third, I will return to compassion, asking how, if we feel we need it as a public motive, we might educate it so to overcome, as far as we can, the problem that Smith identified.

More than a warm feeling in the gut, compassion involves a set of thoughts, often quite complex.[2] We need to dissect them, if we are to make progress in understanding how it goes wrong and how it may be steered aright. There is a good deal of agreement about this among philosophers as otherwise diverse as Aristotle and Rousseau, and also among contemporary psychologists and sociologists who have done empirical work on the emotion.[3]

Compassion is an emotion directed at another person's suffering or lack of well-being. It requires the thought that the other person is in a bad way, and a pretty seriously bad way. (Thus we don't feel compassion for people's loss of trivial items like toothbrushes and paper clips.) It contains within itself an appraisal of the seriousness of various predicaments. Let us call this *the judgment of seriousness.*

Notice that this assessment is made from the point of view of the person who has the emotion. It does not neglect the actual suffering of the other, which certainly should be estimated in taking the measure of the person's predicament. And yet it does not necessarily take at face value the estimate of the predicament this person will be able to form. As Smith emphasized, we frequently have great compassion for people whose predicament is that they have lost their powers of thought; even if they seem like happy children, we regard this as a terrible catastrophe. On the other side, when people moan and groan about something, we don't necessarily have compassion for them: for we may think that they are not really in a bad predicament. Thus when very rich people grumble about taxes, many of us don't have the slightest compassion for them: for we judge that it is only right and proper that they should pay what they are paying – and probably a lot more than that. So the judgment of seriousness already involves quite a complex feat of imagination: it involves both trying to look out at the situation from the suffering person's own viewpoint and then assessing the person's own assessment. Complex though the feat is, young children easily learn it, feeling sympathy with the suffering of animals and other children, but soon learning, as well, to withhold sympathy if they judge that the person is just a crybaby, or spoiled – and, of course, to have sympathy for the predicament of an animal who is dead or unconscious, even if it is not actually suffering.

Next comes *the judgment of nondesert*. Hecuba asked Zeus to witness the undeserved sufferings of the Trojan women, using the Greek word *anaxia*, which appears in Aristotle's definition of tragic compassion. Hecuba's plea, like Aristotle's definition, implies that we will not have compassion if we believe the person fully deserves the suffering. There may be a measure of blame, but then in our compassion we typically register the thought that the suffering exceeds the measure of the fault. The Trojan women are an unusually clear case, because, more than most tragic figures, they endure the consequences of events in which they had no active part at all. But we can see that nondesert is a salient part of our compassion even when we do also blame the person: typically we feel compassion at the punishment of criminal offenders, to the extent that we think circumstances beyond their control are at least in good measure responsible for their becoming the bad people they are. People who have the idea that the poor brought their poverty upon themselves by laziness fail, for that reason, to have compassion for them.[4]

Next there is a thought much stressed in the tradition that I shall call *the judgment of similar possibilities*: Aristotle, Rousseau, and others suggest that we have compassion only insofar as we believe that the suffering person shares vulnerabilities and possibilities with us. I think we can clearly see that this judgment is not strictly necessary for the emotion, as the other two seem to be. We have compassion for nonhuman animals, without basing it on any imagined similarity – although, of course, we need somehow to make sense of their predicament as serious and bad. We also imagine that an invulnerable god can have compassion for mortals, and it doesn't seem that this idea is conceptually confused. For the finite imaginations of human beings, however, the thought of similar possibilities is a very important psychological mechanism through which we get clear about the seriousness of another person's plight. This thought is often accompanied by empathetic imagining, in which we put ourselves in the suffering person's place, imagine their predicament as our own.

Finally, there is one thing more, not mentioned in the tradition, which I believe must be added in order to make the account complete. This is what, in writing on the emotions, I have called *the eudaimonistic judgment*, namely, a judgment that places the suffering person or persons among the important parts of the life of the person who feels the emotion. In my more general analysis of emotions, I argue that they are always eudaimonistic, meaning focused on the agent's most important goals and projects. Thus we feel fear about damages that we see as significant for our own well-being and our other goals; we feel grief at the loss of someone who is already invested with a certain importance in our scheme of things. Eudaimonism is not egoism. I am not claiming that emotions always view events and people merely as means to the agent's own satisfaction or happiness. But I do mean that the things that occasion a strong emotion in us are things that correspond to what we have invested with importance in our account to ourselves of what is worth pursuing in life.

Compassion can evidently go wrong in several different ways. It can get the judgment of nondesert wrong, sympathizing with people who actually don't deserve sympathy and withholding sympathy from those who do. Even more frequently, it can get the judgment of seriousness wrong, ascribing too much importance to the wrong things or too little to things that have great weight. Notice that this problem is closely connected to obtuseness about social justice, in the sense, for example, that if we don't think a social order unjust for denying women the vote, or subordinating African Americans, then we won't see the predicament of women and African Americans as bad, and we won't have compassion for them. We'll think that things are just as they ought to be. Again, if we think it's unjust to require rich people to pay capital gains tax, we will have a misplaced compassion toward them. Finally, and obviously, compassion can get the eudaimonistic judgment wrong, putting too few people into the circle of concern. By my account, then, we won't have compassion without a moral achievement that is at least coeval with it.

My account, I think, is able to explain the unevenness of compassion better than other more standard accounts. Compassion begins from where we are, from the circle of our cares and concerns. It will be felt only toward those things and persons we see as important, and of course most of us most of the time ascribe importance in a very uneven and inconstant way. Empathetic imagining can sometimes extend the circle of concern. Thus Batson has shown experimentally that when the story of another person's plight is vividly told, subjects will tend to experience compassion toward the person and form projects of helping. This is why I say that the moral achievement of extending concern to others needn't antedate compassion, but can be coeval with it. Still, there is a recalcitrance in our emotions, given their link to our daily scheme of goals and ends. Smith is right: thinking that the poor victims of the disaster in China are important is easy to do for a short time, but hard to sustain in the fabric of our daily life; there are so many things closer to home to distract us, and these things are likely to be so much more thoroughly woven into our scheme of goals.

Let us return to September 11 armed with this analysis. The astonishing events made many Americans recognize with a new vividness the nation itself as part of their circle of concern. Most Americans rely on the safety of our institutions and our cities, and don't really notice how much they value them until they prove vulnerable – in just the way that lovers often don't see how much they love until their loved one is ill or threatened. So our antecedent concern emerged with a new clarity in the emotions we experienced. At the same time, we actually extended concern, in many cases, to people in America who had not previously been part of our circle of concern at all: the New York firefighters, the victims of the disasters. We extended concern to them both because we heard their stories and also, especially, because we were encouraged to see them as a part of the America we already loved and for which we now intensely feared. When disaster struck in Rwanda, we did not similarly extend concern, or not stably, because there was no antecedent basis for it: suffering Rwandans could not be seen as part of the larger 'us' for whose fate we trembled. Vivid stories can create a temporary sense of community, but they are unlikely to sustain concern for long, if there is no pattern of interaction that would make the sense of an 'us' an ongoing part of our daily lives.

Things are of course still worse with any group that figures in our imaginations as a 'them' against the 'us.' Such groups are not only by definition non-us, they are also, by threatening the safety of the 'us,' implicitly bad, deserving of any misfortune that might strike them. This accounts for the sports-fan mentality so neatly depicted in my baseball story. Compassion for a member of the opposing team? You've got to be kidding. "U-S-A" just means kill the ump.

3

In light of these difficulties, it is easy to see why much of the philosophical tradition has wanted to do away with compassion as a basis for public choice and to turn, instead, to detached moral principles whose evenhandedness can be relied on. The main candidate for a central moral notion has been the idea of human worth and dignity, a principle that has been put to work from the Stoics and Cicero on through Kant and beyond. We are to recognize that all humans have dignity, and that this dignity is both inalienable and equal, not affected by differences of class, caste, wealth, honor, status, or even sex. The recognition of human dignity is supposed to impose obligations on all moral agents, whether the humans in question are conationals or foreigners. In general, it enjoins us to refrain from all aggression and fraud, since both are seen as violations of human dignity, ways of fashioning human beings into tools for one's own ends. Out of this basic idea Cicero developed much of the basis for modern international law in the areas of war, punishment, and hospitality.[5] Other Stoics used it to criticize conventional norms of patriarchal marriage, the physical abuse of servants, and many other aspects of Roman social life.

This Stoic tradition was quite clear that respect for human dignity could move us to appropriate action, both personal and social, without our having to rely at all on the messier and more inconstant motive of compassion. Indeed, for separate reasons, which I shall get to shortly, Stoics thought compassion was never appropriate, so they could not rely on it.

What I now want to ask is whether this countertradition was correct. Respect for human dignity looks like the right thing to focus on, something that can plausibly be seen as of boundless worth, constraining all actions in pursuit of well-being, and also as equal, creating a kingdom of ends in which humans are ranked horizontally, so to speak, rather than vertically. Why should we not follow the countertradition, as in many respects we do already – as when constitutions make the notion of human dignity central to the analysis of constitutional rights,[6] as when international human rights documents apply similar notions.

Now it must be admitted that human dignity is not an altogether clear notion. In what does it consist? Why should we think that all human life has it? The minute the Stoic tradition tries to answer such questions, problems arise. In particular, the answer almost always takes the form of saying, Look at how far we are above the beasts. Reason, language, moral capacity – all these are seen as worthy of respect and awe at least in part because the beasts, so-called, don't have them, because they make us better than others. Of course they wouldn't seem to make us better if they didn't have some attraction in themselves. But the claim that this dignity resides equally in all humanity all too often relies on the better-than-the-beasts idea. No matter how we humans vary in our rational and moral capacities, the idea seems to be, the weakest among us is light-years beyond those beasts down there, so the differences that exist among us in basic powers become not worth adverting to at all, not sources of differential worth at all. Dignity thus comes to look not like a scalar matter but like an all-or-nothing matter. You either have it, or, bestially, you don't.

This view has its moral problems, clearly. Richard Sorabji has shown how it was linked with a tendency to denigrate the intelligence of animals;[7] and of course it has been used, too, not only by the Stoics but also by Kant and modern contractarians to deny that we have any obligations of justice toward nonhuman forms of life. Compassion, if slippery, is at least not dichotomous in this way; it is capable of reaching sympathetically into multiple directions simultaneously, capable, as Coetzee said, of imagining the sufferings of animals in the squalid conditions we create for them.

There is another more subtle problem with the dignity idea. It was crucial, according to the Stoics, to make dignity radically independent of fortune: all humans have it, no matter where they are born and how they are treated. It exerts its claim everywhere, and it can never be lost. If dignity went up or down with fortune, it would create ranks of human beings: the well-born and healthy will be worth more than the ill-born and hungry. So the Stoics understood their project of making dignity self-sufficient as essential for the notion of equal respect and regard.

But this move leads to a problem: how can we give a sufficiently important place to the goods of fortune for political purposes once we admit that the truly important thing, the thing that lies at the core of our humanity, doesn't need the goods of fortune at all? How can we provide sufficient incentive for political planners to arrange for an adequate distribution of food and shelter and even political rights and liberties if we say that dignity is undiminished by the lack of such things?[8] Stoic texts thus look oddly quietistic: respect human dignity, they say. But it doesn't matter at all what conditions we give people to live in, since dignity is complete and immutable anyway. Seneca, for example, gives masters stern instructions not to beat slaves or use them as sexual tools (*Moral Epistle* 47). But as for the institution of slavery itself? Well, this does not really matter so much, for the only thing that matters is the free soul within, and that cannot be touched by any contingency. Thus, having begun his letter on slavery on an apparently radical note, Seneca slides into quietism in the end, when his master scornfully says, "He is a slave," and Seneca calmly replies, "Will this do him any harm? [*Hoc illi nocebit?*]"

Things are actually even worse than this. For the minute we start examining this reasoning closely, we see that it is not only quietistic – it is actually incoherent. Either people need external things or they do not. But if they do not, if dignity is utterly unaffected by rape and physical abuse, then it is not very easy, after all, to say what the harm of beating or raping a slave is. If these things are no harm to the victim, why is it wrong to do them? They seem not different from the institution of slavery itself: will they really do him any harm, if one maintains that dignity is sufficient for eudaimonia, and that dignity is totally independent of fortune? So Seneca lacks not only a basis for criticizing the institution of slavery, but also for the criticism his letter actually makes, of cruel and inhumane practices toward slaves.

Kant had a way of confronting this question, and it is a plausible one, within the confines of what I have called the countertradition. Kant grants that humanity itself, or human worth, is independent of fortune: under the blows of "step-motherly nature" goodwill still shines like a jewel for its own sake. But external goods such as money, health, and social position are still required for happiness, which we all reasonably pursue. So there are still very weighty moral reasons for promoting the happiness of others, reasons that can supply both individuals and states with a basis for good thoughts about the distribution of goods.

The Stoics notoriously deny this, holding that virtue is sufficient for eudaimonia. What I want to suggest now is that their position on human dignity pushes them strongly in this direction. Think of the person who suffers poverty and hardship. Now either this person has something that is beyond price, by comparison to which all the money and health and shelter in the world is as nothing – or she does not have something that is beyond price. Her dignity is just one part of her happiness – a piece of it that can itself be victimized and held hostage to fortune; her human dignity is being weighed in the balance with other goods and it no longer looks like the thing of surpassing, even infinite worth, that we took it to be. There are, after all, ranks and orders of human beings; slavery and abuse can actually change people's situation with regard to their most important and inclusive end, eudaimonia itself.

Because the Stoics do not want to be forced to that conclusion, they insist that external goods are not required for eudaimonia: virtue is sufficient. And basic human dignity, in turn, is sufficient for becoming virtuous, if one applies oneself in the right way. It is for this deep reason that the Stoics reject compassion as a basic social motive, not just because it is slippery and uneven. Compassion gets the world wrong, because it is always wrong to think that a person who has been hit by misfortune is in a bad or even tragic predicament. "Behold how tragedy comes about," writes Epictetus, "when chance events befall fools." In other words, only a fool world mind the events depicted in Euripides' play, and only fools in the audience would view these events as tragic.

So there is a real problem in how, and how far, the appeal to equal human dignity motivates. Looked at superficially, the idea of respect for human dignity appears to provide a principled, evenhanded motive for good treatment of all human beings, no matter where they are placed. Looked at more deeply, it seems to license quietism and indifference to things in the world, on the grounds that nothing that merely happens to people is really bad.

We have now seen two grave problems with the countertradition: what I shall call *the animal problem* and what I shall call *the external goods problem*. Neither of these problems is easy to solve within the countertradition. By contrast, the Euripidean tradition of focusing on compassion as a basic social motive has no such problems. Compassion can and does cross the species boundary, and whatever good there may be in our current treatment of animals is likely to be its work; we are able to extend our imaginations to understand the sufferings of animals who are cruelly treated and to see that suffering as significant, as undeserved, and to see its potential termination as part of our scheme of goals and projects.[9]

As for the problem of external goods, compassion has no such problem, for it is intrinsically focused on the damages of fortune: its most common objects, as Aristotle listed them in the *Rhetoric*, are the classic tragic predicaments: loss of country, loss of friends, old age, illness, and so on.

But let us suppose that the countertradition can solve these two problems, providing people with adequate motives to address the tragic predicaments. Kant makes a good start on the external goods problem, at least. So let us imagine that we have a reliable way of motivating conduct that addresses human predicaments, without the uneven partiality that so often characterizes compassion. A third problem now awaits us. I shall call it *the problem of watery motivation*, though we might well call it *the problem of death within life*.

The term 'watery motivation' comes from Aristotle's criticism of Plato's ideal city. Plato tried to remove partiality by removing family ties and asking all citizens to care equally for all other citizens. Aristotle says that the difficulty with this strategy is that "there are two things above all that make people love and care for something, the thought that it is all theirs, and the thought that it is the only one they have. Neither of these will be present in that city" (*Pol.* 1262b22–3). Because nobody will think of a child that it is all theirs, entirely their own responsibility, the city will, he says, resemble a household in which there are too many servants so nobody takes responsibility for any task. Because nobody will think of any child or children that they are the only ones they have, the intensity of care that characterizes real families will simply not materialize, and we will have instead, he says, a 'watery' kind of care all round (*Pol.* 1262b15).

If we now examine the nature of Stoic motivation, I think we will see that Aristotle is very likely to be correct. I shall focus here on Marcus Aurelius, in many ways the most psychologically profound of Stoic thinkers. Marcus tells us that the first lesson he learned from his tutor was "not to be a fan of the Greens or Blues at the races, or the light-armed or heavy-armed gladiators at the Circus" (1.5). His imagination had to unlearn its intense partiality and localism; his tutor apparently assumed that already as young children we have learned narrow sectarian types of loyalty. And it is significant, I think, that the paradigmatic negative image for the moral imagination is that of sports fandom: for in all ages, perhaps, such fandom has been a natural way for human beings to express vicariously their sectarian loyalties to family, city, and nation. It was no accident that those White Sox fans invoked the hockey chant to express their distress about the fate of the nation.

The question is whether this negative lesson leaves the personality enough resources to motivate intense concern for people anywhere. For Marcus, unlearning partiality requires an elaborate and systematic program of uprooting concern for all people and things in this world. He tells us of the meditative exercises that he regularly performs in order to get himself to the point at which the things that divide people from one another no longer matter. One side of this training looks benign and helpful: we tell ourselves that our enemies are really not enemies, but part of a common human project:

> Say to yourself in the morning: I shall meet people who are interfering, ungracious, insolent, full of guile, deceitful and antisocial.... But I,... who know that the nature of the wrongdoer is of one kin with mine – not indeed of the same blood or seed but sharing the same kind, the same portion of the divine – I cannot be harmed by any one of them, and no one can involve me in shame. I cannot feel anger against him who is of my kin, nor hate him. We were born to labor together, like the feet, the hands, the eyes, and the rows of upper and lower teeth. To work against one another is therefore contrary to nature, and to be angry against a man or turn one's back on him is to work against him.[10]

Notice how close these thoughts are to the thought-content of a greatly extended sort of compassion. Passages such as these suggest that a strong kind of even-handed concern can be meted out to all human beings, without divisive jealousy and partiality; that we should see ourselves not as team players, not as family members, not as loyal citizens of a nation, but, most essentially, as members of the humankind with the advancement of our kind as our highest goal.

Now even in this good case problems are lurking: for we notice that this exercise relies on the thoughts that give rise to the animal problem and the external goods problem. We are asked to imagine human solidarity and community by thinking of a 'portion of the divine' that resides in all and only humans: we look like we have a lot in common because we are so sharply divided from the rest of nature. And the idea that we have a common work relies, to at least some extent, on Marcus's prior denigration of external goods: for if we ascribed value to external goods we would be in principle competing with one another, and it would be difficult to conceive of the common enterprise without running into that competition.

But I have resolved to waive those two difficulties, so let me do so. Even then, the good example is actually very complex. For getting to the point where we can give such concern evenhandedly to all human beings requires, as Marcus makes abundantly clear, the systematic extirpation of intense cares and attachments directed at the local: one's family, one's city, the objects of one's love and desire. Thus Marcus needs to learn not only not to be a sports fan, but also not to be a lover. Consider the following extraordinary passage:

> How important it is to represent to oneself, when it comes to fancy dishes and other such foods, "This is the corpse of a fish, this other thing the corpse of a bird or a pig." Similarly, "This Falernian wine is just some grape juice," and "This purple vestment is some sheep's hair moistened in the blood of some shellfish." When it comes to sexual intercourse, we must say, "This is the rubbing together of membranes, accompanied by the spasmodic ejaculation of a sticky liquid." How important are these representations, which reach the thing itself and penetrate right through it, so that one can see what it is in reality. (VII.3)[11]

Now, of course, these exercises are addressed to the problem of external goods. Here as elsewhere, Marcus is determined to unlearn the unwise attachments to externals that he has learned from his culture. This project is closely connected to the question of partiality, because learning not to be a sports fan is greatly aided by learning not to care about the things over which people typically fight. (Indeed, it is a little hard to see how a Kantian project can be stable, insofar as it teaches equal respect for human dignity while at the same time teaching intense concern for the externals that go to produce happiness, externals that strongly motivate people not to treat all human beings equally.) In the Marcus passage, however, the link to partiality seems even more direct: for learning to think of sex as just the rubbing of membranes really is learning not to find special value or delight in a particular, and this extirpation of eroticism really does seem to be required by a regime of impartiality.

But getting rid of our erotic investment, not just in bodies, but in families, nations, sports teams – all this leads us into a strange world, a world that is gentle and unaggressive, but also strangely lonely and hollow. To unlearn the habits of the sports fan we must unlearn our erotic investment in the world, our attachments to our own team, our own love, our own children, our own life.

Marcus suggests that we have two choices only: the world of real-life Rome, which resembles a large gladiatorial contest (see Seneca *Delra* 2.8), each person striving to outdo others in vain competition for externals, a world exploding with rage and poisoned by malice; or the world of Marcus's gentle sympathy, in which we respect all human beings and view all as our partners in a common project whose terms don't seem to matter very much, thus rendering the whole point of living in the world increasingly unclear.[12]

And this means something like a death within life. For only in a condition close to death, in effect, is moral rectitude possible. Marcus repeatedly casts life as a kind of death already, a procession of meaningless occurrences:

> The vain solemnity of a procession; dramas played out on the stage; troops of sheep or goats; fights with spears; a little bone thrown to dogs; a chunk of bread thrown into a fish-pond; the exhausting labor and heavy burdens under which ants must bear up; crazed mice running for shelter; puppets pulled by strings .... (VII.3)[13]

(This, by an emperor who was at that very time on campaign in Parthia, leading the fight for his nation.) And the best consolation for his bleak conclusion also originates in his contemplation of death:

> Think all the time about how human beings of all sorts, and from all walks of life and all peoples, are dead.... We must arrive at the same condition where so many clever orators have ended up, so many grave philosophers, Heraclitus, Pythagoras, Socrates; so many heroes of the old days, so many recent generals and tyrants. And besides these, Eudoxus, Hipparchus, Archimedes, other highly intelligent minds, thinkers of large thoughts, hard workers, versatile in ability, daring people, even mockers of the perishable and transitory character of human life, like Menippus. Think about all of these that they are long since in the ground.... And what of those whose very names are forgotten? So: one thing is worth a lot, to live out one's life with truth and justice, and with kindliness toward liars and wrongdoers. (VI.47)

Because we shall die, we must recognize that everything particular about us will eventually be wiped out: family, city, sex, children – all will pass into oblivion. So really, giving up those attachments is not such a big deal. What remains, and all that remains, is truth and justice, the moral order of the world. So only the true city should claim our allegiance.

Marcus is alarming because he has gone deep into the foundations of cosmopolitan moral principle. What he has seen is that impartiality, fully and consistently cultivated, requires the extirpation of the eroticism that makes life the life we know – unfair, uneven, full of war, full of me-first nationalism and divided loyalty.[14]

So, if that ordinary erotic humanity is unjust, get rid of it. But can we live like this, once we see the goal with Marcus's naked clarity? Isn't justice something that must be about and for the living?

4

Let me proceed on the hypothesis that Marcus is correct: extirpating attachments to the local and the particular delivers us to a death within life. Let me also proceed on the hypothesis that we will reject this course as an unacceptable route to the goal of justice, or even as one that makes the very idea of justice a hollow fantasy. (This is Adam Smith's conclusion as well: enamored as he is of Stoic doctrine, he thinks we must reject it when it tells us not to love our own families.) Where are we then?

It looks as if we are back where Aristotle and Adam Smith leave us: with the unreliability of compassion, and yet the need to rely on it, since we have no more perfect motive.

This does not mean that we need give up on the idea of equal human dignity, or respect for it. But insofar as we retain, as well, our local erotic attachments, our relation to that motive must always remain complex and dialectical, a difficult conversation within ourselves as we ask how much humanity requires of us, and how much we are entitled to give to our own. Any such difficult conversation will require, for its success, the work of the imagination. If we don't have exceptionless principles, if, instead, we need to negotiate our lives with a complex combination of moral reverence and erotic attachment, we need to have a keen imaginative and emotional understanding of what our choices mean for people in many different conditions, and the ability to move resourcefully back and forth from the perspective of our personal loves and cares to the perspective of the distant. Not the extirpation of compassion, then, but its extension and education. Compassion within the limits of respect.

The philosophical tradition helps us identify places where compassion goes wrong: by making errors of fault, seriousness, and the circle of concern. But the ancient tradition, not being very interested in childhood, does not help us see clearly how and why it goes especially wrong. So to begin the task of educating compassion as best we can, we need to ask how and why local loyalties and attachments come to take in some instances an especially virulent and aggressive form, militating against a more general sympathy. To answer this question we need a level of psychological understanding that was not available in the ancient Greek and Roman world, or not completely. I would suggest (and have argued elsewhere) that one problem we particularly need to watch out for is a type of pathological narcissism in which the person demands complete control over all the sources of good, and a complete self-sufficiency in consequence.

Nancy Chodorow long ago argued that this narcissism colors the development of males in many cultures in the world.[15] Recent studies of teenage boys in America, particularly the impressive work of Dan Kindlon and Michael Thompson in their book *Raising Cain*, have given strong local support to this idea.[16] The boys that

Kindlon and Thompson study have learned from their cultures that men should be self-sufficient, controlling, dominant. They should never have, and certainly never admit to, fear and weakness. The consequence of this deformed expectation, Kindlon and Thompson show, is that these boys come to lack an understanding of their own vulnerabilities, needs, and fears – weaknesses that all human beings share. They don't have the language to describe their own inner worlds and are by the same token clumsy interpreters of the emotions and inner lives of others. This emotional illiteracy is closely connected to aggression, as fear is turned outward, with little understanding of the implications of aggressive words and actions for others. Kindlon and Thompson's boys become the sports fans who chant "U-S-A" at the ump, who think of all obstacles to American supremacy and self-sufficiency as opponents to be humiliated.

So the first recommendation I would make for a culture of respectful compassion is a Rousseauian one: it is, that an education in common human weakness and vulnerability should be a very profound part of the education of all children. Children should learn to be tragic spectators and to understand with subtlety and responsiveness the predicaments to which human life is prone. Through stories and dramas, they should learn to decode the suffering of others, and this decoding should deliberately lead them into lives both near and far, including the lives of distant humans and the lives of animals.

As children learn to imagine the emotions of another, they should at the same time learn the many obstacles to such understanding, the many pitfalls of the self-centered imagination as it attempts to be just. Thus, one should not suppose that one can understand a family member, without confronting and continually criticizing the envy and jealousy in oneself that pose powerful obstacles to that understanding. One should not imagine that one can understand the life of a person in an ethnic or racial group different from one's own, or a sex different from one's own, or a nation, without confronting and continually criticizing the fear and greed and the demand for power that make such interactions so likely to produce misunderstanding and worse. What I am suggesting, then, is that the education of emotion, to succeed at all, needs to take place in a culture of ethical criticism, and especially self-criticism, in which ideas of equal respect for humanity will be active players in the effort to curtail the excesses of the greedy self.

At the same time, we can also see that the chances of success in this enterprise will be greater if the society in question does not overvalue external goods of the sort that cause envy and competition. The Stoics are correct when they suggest that overvaluation of external goods is a major source of destructive aggression in society. If we criticize the overvaluation of money, honor, status, and fame that Seneca saw at Rome and that we see in America now, then we may encourage people to pursue other, less problematic external goods, including love of family, of friends, of work, even, to a certain extent, of country. If people care primarily for friendship, good work, and – let's even hope – social justice, then they are less likely to see everything in terms of the hockey match and more likely to use Marcus's image of the common project. Because my vision is not a Stoic one, there will still be important sources of good to be protected from harm, and there will still be justified anger at damage to those good things. But a lot of occasions for anger in real life are not good or just, and we can do a lot as a society to prune away the greedy attachments that underpin them.

After *Raising Cain*, Kindlon wrote a book on rich teenagers in America.[17] It is an alarming portrait of the greed and overvaluations of a certain class in our nation, and its tales of children who humiliate others because they don't go on the same expensive ski vacations or have the same expensive designer clothes are a chilling illustration of how overvaluation is connected to destructive violence. There is a great deal to say about how education could address such problems, but I shall not go into that here.

Instead, I want to turn back to Euripides, reflecting, in concluding, on the role of tragic spectatorship, and tragic art generally, in promoting good citizenship of the sort I have been advocating here. Tragedies are not Stoic: they start with us 'fools' and the chance events that befall us. At the same time, they tend to get their priorities straight.

Thus, the overvaluations I have just mentioned are usually not validated in tragic works of art. The great Athenian tragic dramas, for example, revolve around attachments that seem essentially reasonable: to one's children, city, loved ones, bodily integrity, health, freedom from pain, status as a free person rather than a slave, ability to speak and persuade others, the very friendship and company of others. The loss of any of these is worthy of lamentation, and the dramas encourage us to understand the depth of such loss and, with protagonists, to fear it. In exercising compassion the audience is learning its own possibilities and vulnerabilities – what Aristotle called "things such as might happen" – and learning that people different in sex, race, age, and nation experience suffering in a way that is like our way, and that suffering is as crippling for them as it would be for us.

Such recognitions have their pitfalls, and I have identified some of them in talking about *The Trojan Women*. We always risk error in bringing the distant person close to us; we ignore differences of language and of cultural context, and the manifold ways in which these differences shape one's inner world. But there are dangers in any act of imagining, and we should not let these particular dangers cause us to admit defeat prematurely, surrendering before an allegedly insuperable barrier of otherness.

When I was out in the rural areas of Rajasthan, visiting an education project for girls, I asked the Indian woman who ran the project (herself an urban woman with a Ph.D.) how she would answer the frequent complaint that a foreigner can never understand the situation of a person in another nation. She thought for a while and said finally, "I have the greatest difficulty understanding my own sister."

There are barriers to understanding in any human relationship. As Proust said, any real person imposes on us a "dead weight" that our "sensitivity cannot remove." The obstacles to understanding a sister may in some instances be greater than those to understanding a stranger. At least they are different. All we can do is trust our imaginations, and then criticize them (listening if possible to the critical voices of those we are trying to understand), and then trust them again. Perhaps out of this dialectic between criticism and trust something like understanding may eventually grow. At least the product will very likely be better than the obtuseness that so generally reigns in international relations.

As Euripides knew, terror has this good thing about it: it makes us sit up and take notice. Tragic dramas can't precisely teach anything new, since they will be moving only to people who at some level already understand how bad these predicaments are. But they can awaken the sleepers by reminding them of human realities they are neglecting in their daily political lives.

The experience of terror and grief for our towers might be just that – an experience of terror and grief for our towers. One step worse, it could be a stimulus for blind rage and aggression against all the opposing hockey teams and bad umpires in the world. But if we cultivate a culture of critical compassion, such an event may, like Hecuba's Trojan cry, possibly awaken a larger sense of the humanity of suffering, a patriotism constrained by respect for human dignity and by a vivid sense of the real losses and needs of others.

And in that case, it really would turn out that Euripides was right and Hecuba was wrong: the name of the Trojan land was not wiped out. It lives, in a work of the imagination to which we can challenge ourselves, again and again.

Notes

1 J. M. Coetzee, *The Lives of Animals*, ed. Amy Gutmann (Princeton, NJ: Princeton University Press, 1999).

2 I am drawing on an analysis of compassion for which I argue at greater length in Nussbaum, *Upheavals of Thought: The Intelligence of Emotions* (New York: Cambridge University Press, 2001), chaps. 6–8.

3 C. Daniel Batson of the University of Kansas should be mentioned with honor here, because he has not only done remarkable empirical work, but has also combined it with a conceptual and analytic clarity that is rare in social science research of this type. See in particular *The Altruism Question* (Hillsdale, NJ: Lawrence Erlbaum, 1991). Candace Clark's sociological study is also exemplary: *Misery and Company: Sympathy in Everyday Life* (Chicago: University of Chicago Press, 1997).

4 Clark's empirical survey of American attitudes finds this a prominent reason for the refusal of compassion for the poor.

5 See my "Duties of Justice, Duties of Material Aid: Cicero's Problematic Legacy," *Journal of Political Philosophy* 7 (1999): 1–31.

6 Germany is one salient example. In a forthcoming book, James Whitman describes the way this central notion has constrained legal practices in Europe generally, especially in the area of criminal punishment. Dignity, he argues, is a nonhierarchical notion that has replaced hierarchical orders of rank.

7 Richard Sorabji, *Animal Minds and Human Morals: The Origins of the Western Debate* (Ithaca, N.Y.: Cornell University Press, 1993).

8 I deal with this question at greater length in "Duties of Justice," and also in "The Worth of Human Dignity: Two Tensions in Stoic Cosmopolitanism," in *Philosophy and Power in the Graeco-Roman World: Essays in Honour of Miriam Griffin*, ed. Gillian Clark and Tessa Rajak (Oxford: Oxford University Press, 2002), 31–49.

9 See Coetzee, *The Lives of Animals*, 35: "There are people who have the capacity to imagine themselves as someone else, there are people who have no such capacity (when

the lack is extreme, we call them psychopaths), and there are people who have the capacity but choose not to exercise it."

10 II.i, trans. G. Grube (Hackett edition). Cf. also VI.6: "The best method of defense is not to become like your enemy."

11 Based on the translation in Pierre Hadot, *The Inner Citadel: The Meditations of Marcus Aurelius*, trans. Michael Chase (Cambridge, MA: Harvard University Press, 1998), with some modifications.

12 It is significant that this adopted emperor did not, as the movie *Gladiator* shows us, make a principled rational choice of the best man to run the empire. In real life, Marcus chose his worthless son Commodus, tripped up yet once more by the love of the near.

13 Translation from Hadot/Chase.

14 One might compare the imagery of ancient Greek skepticism. Pyrrho, frightened by a dog (and thus betraying a residual human attachment to his own safety) says, "How difficult it is entirely to divest oneself of the human being." Elsewhere he speaks of the skeptic as a eunuch, because he lacks the very source of disturbance.

15 Nancy Chodorow, *The Reproduction of Mothering* (Berkeley, CA: University of California Press, 1978).

16 Dan Kindlon and Michael Thompson, *Raising Cain: Protecting the Emotional Life of Boys* (New York: Ballentine Books, 1999).

17 Dan Kindlon, *Too Much of a Good Thing: Raising Children of Character in an Indulgent Age* (New York: Miramax, 2001).

13

THE THEATER OF CLEMENCY

Dorothy Noyes[1]

> Many a prince who has averted his countenance from melancholy for a single
> unfortunate person has at the same time given the order for war, often from
> a vain motive.
>
> (Kant 1764)

Just after the conclusion of the Seven Years' War, Immanuel Kant published his
treatise *On the Observation of the Feeling of the Beautiful and the Sublime.* This exposition of familiar eighteenth-century aesthetic categories offers an experiential
foundation for his later thinking on ethics and indeed for liberal politics at large.
Kant describes the antinomies of scale that structure modern Western perceptions
of the social world: the intimate scale at which we encounter others face to face,
and the grand, sublime scale that forces us to generalize or to ignore particulars,
standing at a distance as we attempt to grasp the whole.

In this framework, compassion is a natural consequence of intimacy, while the
grand scale is more problematic. Kant's example of the prince who knows how to
compartmentalize echoes contemporary observations about Frederick II of Prussia,
famously compassionate to individuals and ruthless to collectivities. Kant simultaneously anticipates a twentieth-century political proverb: "The death of one man is
a tragedy; the death of a million men is a statistic."[2] The example invokes a recurrent
set of tensions in Western political thought between the private and the political,
passive feeling and positive action, particular attention and generalization, and the
executive as individual and as sovereign representative. In this chapter, I explore
how these tensions are played out in a European dramatic tradition, and how they
are revealed to shape compassion's conditions of possibility.

The beauty of compassion finds an ambiguous counterpart in the realm of the
sublime: clemency. While compassion is an emotion available to anyone in any social
relationship, clemency is a formal right that can be exercised only by a sovereign

upon a subject: the pardoning of a sentenced criminal. Indeterminate in meaning but conspicuous as an exceptional public act, any exercise of clemency provokes discussion about the private feelings and interests that lie beneath it. Its performative, ceremonial character lends itself to theatrical representation. The event of clemency, which brings scales into collision as it reaches down from sovereign to subject, became a privileged theme in early modern opera and spoken drama for the staging of debates over the appropriate relationship between feeling and policy.

The true public sphere of early modern Europe, theater, played out scenarios of social possibilities before a diverse audience. One long-lived and widely distributed scenario deals with the sovereign's rite of passage from common humanity into divine monarchy. This literal sublimation (a concept antedating Freud by many centuries) is effected through an act of clemency. Emerging from absolutist propaganda and playing itself out with the mass spectacles of Fascism, the theater of clemency reached its apex between the French Revolution and the July Revolution of 1830. Bringing sentimental, liberal, and utilitarian thought into dialogue, the tradition cumulatively defines the conditions under which compassion can foster sustained political learning and suggests that these are incompatible with the form of the modern state.

Between compassion and self-mastery

Kant's celebrated suspicion of compassion begins in a critique of theatricality. His first argument against classifying compassion as a virtue appears in the early aesthetic treatise, *On the Observation of the Feeling of the Beautiful and the Sublime* (1764). Kant notes that misfortune on the tragic stage awakens *teilnehmende* (sympathetic or participatory) sentiments in the spectator, who "is gently moved and feels the dignity of his own nature." But as he begins to sort out the ethical implications of aesthetic effects, Kant raises objections of scale and of utility to the cultivation of compassion. We weep for a "suffering child, an unhappy though upright woman" but receive unmoved the report of a great battle with the general suffering entailed.

> For it is not possible that our bosom should swell with tenderness on behalf of every human being and swim in melancholy for everyone else's need, otherwise the virtuous person ... with all this good-heartedness would nevertheless become nothing more than a tenderhearted idler.
>
> (Kant 2011 [1764]: 19, 22–3)

Kant's irony is surely directed at the new "bourgeois tragedy" of the 1750s, practiced to great public success by Lessing and Diderot. Featuring the misfortunes of ordinary people in the contemporary world, these dramas were explicitly intended to provoke *Teilnehmung* and *Mitleid* (compassion) in the spectators. Communicated across the audience through tears, these feelings would generate social bonds extending into everyday life. Lessing defended a focus on domestic concerns and on "those, whose circumstances come closest to our own" in lieu of the public political themes, noble protagonists, and antique or exotic settings of older tragedy: "A state is much too abstract an object for our feelings" (Lessing 2010 [1767]: 251). Bourgeois tragedy, like the larger sentimental culture of which it was a formulation, "transfers the seat of the social from the public to the private sphere" (Fleming 2009: 69–70), with the consequence that the public sphere and the category of the political are rendered at best uninteresting, at worst inauthentic. Thus if we looked only at the sentimental tradition, we might well conclude that compassion is incompatible with modern state politics, citing Kant in support. And given the early Lessing's insistence on theater as a vehicle to create and celebrate communal feeling among the already like-minded, we might join the critics (most famously Nietzsche) who see theatrical compassion as the root of bourgeois complacency and ultimately of virulent nationalism in Germany (Fleming 2009: 43–4).

But the eighteenth century saw the elaboration of another, seemingly more conservative variety of theatrical reflection on compassion, which I am calling the theater of clemency. An evolving theme rather than a genre, this textual tradition explores the clash of public duty and private feeling, addresses the challenge of compassion without identification, and asserts the value of the political sphere while pointing out its dangers. It can be understood as staging precisely the antinomies Kant identifies, for Kant is not creating a new aesthetics, but spelling out the ethical implications of an established set of distinctions, which I schematize in Table 13.1.

The theater of clemency explores the political implications of the clash of scales. An act of clemency is, on the face of it, sublime. A ruler extends pardon to a condemned and sentenced criminal in the power of the state. If forgiveness is an informal communal process of reweaving a torn social fabric, clemency works from above and offers formal reincorporation to the formal offender. When the criminal has committed *lèse-majesté*, the sovereign must overcome personal feeling and interest to grant the pardon. His claim to inhabit a higher sphere is correspondingly enhanced.[3] In the early modern period, clemency was believed to have the same exemplarity as the contrary performance of punishment, and, for that matter, the performance of heroic theater. In all of these performances, the public display

TABLE 13.1 Kant's antinomies

	Beautiful	*Sublime (Erhabene, lit. "elevated")*
Scale	Intimate/proximate/particular	Grand/distant/general
Relation to the audience	Egalitarian, same	Hierarchical, other
Ego investment	Happiness; fulfillment of natural inclinations	Dignity; self-mastery
Rational response	Recognition, identification	Admiration (*Bewunderung*)
Affective spectrum	Love–compassion–contempt	Esteem–respect–fear
Desired effect	Social engagement	Emulation of exemplar
Genre	Comedy (and bourgeois tragedy)	Tragedy (traditional)

of noble or terrifying actions would create a strong impression on spectators and inspire them to virtuous conduct that would sustain the political order.

To be sure, acts of clemency have long been suspect precisely *as* theater. Ever since Julius Caesar first codified clemency as a political strategy, political leaders down to the American presidents who pardon turkeys on Thanksgiving Day have been thought to stage shows of clemency as distractions from the broader exercise of tyranny or precisely to emphasize their sovereign power of exception over the rule of law (Fiskesjö 2003; Sarat 2005). Clemency is inherently dramatic as a disruption of normative routine, breaching the law that the sovereign exists to uphold. Its meaning and import are thus indeterminate: any single act can be variously attributed to political calculation, personal interest, or godlike pity. But the Stoic tradition of ethical education, and particularly Seneca with his thankless task of preaching self-mastery to the young Nero, nonetheless singled out clemency as an *inclinatio animi*, a disposition of the soul to pity and generosity, that could and should be cultivated in monarchs (Konstan 2005). With the rise of absolutism in Europe, this stoic tradition was revitalized in princely education and princely flattery on the part of subjects hoping for gentle treatment; conversely it was revitalized in the language of monarchical legitimation, and again its importance as show was critical: "Clemency is the most beautiful sign / That makes the universe recognize a true monarch," declares the Empress Livie in Corneille's 1639 *Cinna*; Montesquieu echoes the language in 1748, calling clemency "the distinguishing characteristic of monarchs" (De l'esprit des lois: VI.xxi), a practical necessity for a regime type in which nobles are motivated by honor rather than fear or virtue. The great jurist Cesare Beccaria highlighted the problematic relationship between the exceptional display of clemency and ordinary princely conduct, observing acidly in 1764 that clemency "has often been deemed a sufficient substitute for every other virtue in sovereigns" (Beccaria 1983 [1775]: 98).

By the eighteenth century, clemency was a reified aspect of monarchical self-presentation, particularly important in managing the contradictions of enlightened absolutism. Reformers like Beccaria denounced real acts of clemency as threats to the emerging rule of law, ideally to be replaced by more humane and comprehensive legal systems that would require no exceptions. Clemency was abolished in France after the Revolution and not restored until Napoleon (Moore 1991: 98). But despite Enlightenment faith in abstract principle, less radical democratic regimes preserved the executive's prerogative of pardon, in part precisely because of its theatrical character. In 1788, Alexander Hamilton's language echoed that of the sentimental stage, pitting the beauty of compassion against the sublimity of justice: "The criminal code of every country partakes so much of necessary severity, that without an easy access to exceptions in favor of unfortunate guilt, justice would wear a countenance too sanguinary and cruel" (Federalist Paper 74). Hamilton's discussion of clemency's uses and dangers implicitly acknowledges that, in democracies, the management of appearances that influence public feeling is as important as the application of principle.

Hamilton defended political theatricality on pragmatic grounds and I defend actual theater as a source of political insight for similar reasons.[4] Even Kant acknowledged that although neither the self-gratifying disposition of compassion nor the other-directed sense of honor can be considered virtues, both drive more people to virtuous actions than does the universal love for mankind (Kant 2011 [1764]: 25). Motives and intentions are ultimately incalculable, and as we know from contemporary political life, there is in any case no straight line from admirable "values" to humane outcomes. If ethics is about principles, politics is about forms: patterns to be shared, communicated, and reproduced so that power can be effectively and sustainably exercised. Eighteenth and nineteenth century censors understood this, paying closer attention to the exemplifications of theater than to the abstractions of philosophy. When he built the Berlin Staatsoper as almost his first action on acceding to the Prussian throne in 1740, Frederick II repeated the period commonplace that theater served "à réformer les moeurs" (Oschmann 1991). This we might translate not with its disembodied contemporary derivatives as "to reform morals," but more concretely as "to reshape manners." Theater models the *how* as much as the *what*, staging the social processes through which diverse actors set into a common predicament negotiate their conflicts and compromises. Moreover, theatrical attendance was a social process in its own right, bringing nobles and bourgeois, women and servants, and often royalty into a common space of mutual visibility. At once more hierarchical and more inclusive than Habermas' famous coffeehouses, the theater constituted the true public sphere of the period, recognized as such by both reactionaries and reformers. It was aesthetically and socially pluralist: themes, devices, artists, and spectators circulated among court operas, bourgeois tragedies, and plebeian *Singspiele*. Like coffeehouses, theaters were attended regularly and routinely. They thus constituted a zone of cumulative embodied reflection as particular themes were endlessly replayed and revised in new works. Lessing argued that because theater created collective experiences that worked on the hearts, minds, and bodies of spectators sitting among their fellow citizens, it was the ideal site for the inculcation of *com*-passion, feeling together.

Born in the heroic spectacle of Baroque theater, the theater of clemency complicated this communal experience of feeling by placing the drama at a historical, social, and geographical remove from the present. This was a matter of prudence before patrons and censor but also one of aesthetic decorum, the achievement of sublimity. Court-commissioned tragedies and *opera seria* were typically set in the ancient world, drawing on Roman historians to bring insights from the exemplary state with which contemporary monarchs claimed both symbolic and literal continuity. Prose tragedies for more bourgeois audiences often turned to neighboring countries and to the sixteenth century, when the modern state began to take shape. To northern Europeans, the most important neighbor for the purposes of reflection was Spain, home to the greatest empire since the Roman. Spain offered not a straightforward narrative of rise and decline, but a confusing simultaneity of reaction and modernity, state power and state fragility. A proximate rather than a remote Other, Spain was close enough to home, institutionally and culturally, to provide what we might call a subjunctive space for political reflection: an arena for counterfactual and hypothetical experimentation.

The theater of clemency is inaugurated by Corneille's *Cinna, ou la clémence d'Auguste*, premiered in 1639 as Louis XIII and Richelieu sought to discipline the French nobility and win the monopoly of honor as well as of sovereignty. It plays itself out in Verdi's two supreme operas of clemency denied by a prison state: *Don Carlos* (1867) and *Aida* (1871), composed in the shadow of Prussian power and European imperialism, and is finally travestied in Puccini's *Turandot* (1926) as Fascism conscripts emotion for mass spectacle. I examine three influential works at the tradition's turning point: Mozart's *La Clemenza di Tito*, commissioned for a Habsburg coronation in 1791, the immediate aftermath of the French Revolution; Schiller's *Don Carlos* (1787, revised 1805), a longer-meditated reflection on the dark side of ruler humanity, originally conceived for the new National Theater in Mannheim; and Hugo's *Hernani* (1830), a work of deliberate provocation whose riotous premiere served as prelude to the July Revolution.

At the core of each drama is a crisis for an absolute monarch. Confronted with the perpetrator of a revolt against the state and his own person, he must decide whether to execute the offender. The decision is not self-evident for a variety of reasons that still today condition the granting of pardons: there are mitigating factors to the offender's guilt, the ruler has a personal tie to the offender, the offender has a power base or a grievance with public legitimacy, or finally because, as Seneca told Nero, if Augustus had condemned every vanquished rebel, he would have had nobody left to rule. The dramas offer qualifying variations on Corneille's happy ending, in which the sovereign overcomes his predatory, vengeful, or simply human impulses and masters himself by pardoning his challenger. The ruler's dilemma reveals the larger contradiction between the ruler's humanity and the ideology of divine kingship (which gradually mutates into that of impersonal representation). At the same time, it marks a rite of passage for the society as a whole, from the feudal cycle of interpersonal violence into the stable hierarchy of absolutist rule. Both the personal tension and the historical transition give an opening to democratizing pressures informed by newer ideologies: sentimentalism, which sees the foundation of the state in the human sympathy of friendship and companionate marriage; liberalism, with its relocation of sovereign authority to the autonomous individual; and utilitarianism, with its generalizing tendency. These conflicting political pressures give the clemency theme continuing relevance even after the collapse of the *ancien régime*. For the contradictions in executive power continue, torn precisely between sympathy, autonomy, and utility; moreover, there is no unilinear transition into democracy. Personal power and despotism persist or are reinvented, while the Enlightenment machinery of state sometimes evolves into Weber's iron cage. Beauty can be perverted into Fascist kitsch, compassion into nationalist hysteria; sublimity and *Bewunderung* can lead to the scorched earth beneath totalitarian imaginings.

The clemency dilemma forces the two scales to meet. As presented in this tradition, an act of clemency can break a cycle of violence. Gratuitous, a gift without expectation of return, it can convert the negative reciprocity of revenge into virtuous emulation that disperses itself through the society. But this only works where communications are open and multidirectional, where interpersonal social attention is sustained. The dramas play out the political challenges to these conditions. They further suggest the necessary, though dangerous, objectifications of these interpersonal processes in statecraft. Mozart, informed by the sentimental tradition, shows us how particularist compassion may be scaled up to provide collective benefit, though at a dangerous psychological cost to the ruler. Schiller, thinking through liberalism, shifts the emphasis of the Kantian imperative to propose that political progress requires us to treat others as ends in themselves, but *also* as a means to more general ends. This balance of humanity and efficiency is not easily maintained. In Hugo, who reconsiders Napoleon's utilitarianism, interpersonal emotion is relegated to the local domain, cut off from large-scale political calculus as the state builds upwards. The consequence is a growing asymmetry between the center and the periphery of empire – not incidentally a future motor of humanitarian disaster.

Mozart: from exemplarity to reciprocity

By the eighteenth century, *opera seria*, a genre performed in Italian and German courts at carnival time, was the privileged ritual for the production of sovereignty (Feldman 2007). Designed to provoke a succession of contrasting emotions and to astonish the listener with the virtuosity of castrato singers whose high, powerful voices transcended nature, opera gave musical expression to the struggle between passion and control and suggested the sovereign's own supernatural status. The famously musical Frederick II of Prussia commissioned several operas on the subject of clemency, including an adaptation of *Cinna*, and drafted his own libretti presenting the self-mastery and eventual patriotic mercy of Roman dictators better known for arrogance and cruelty. One final chorus confirms the threatening undertone of absolutist clemency: "Celebrate the liberty that Silla *returns to us* / He is greater in conquering himself / Than in having conquered our enemies."[2]

No soft case himself, Frederick was nonetheless the period's most accomplished orchestrator of public emotion; he proclaimed himself the "Anti-Machiavel" and Bismarck would later sneer at his *"Gefühlspolitik."* Well read in the new French sentimental thought, outside of the opera house the skeptic Frederick cultivated not his divinity but his human *sensibilité* as a basis for rule, shifting register downward from the sublime to the beautiful. He defined his relationship to his subjects as one of mutual love and perhaps inaugurated the now-familiar public stance of the leader as a man in sympathy with the common people, seizing the eighteenth-century equivalent of photo opportunities on the battlefield or in visits to conquered Silesia, circulated through prints and anecdotes (Frevert 2012). Like the Hapsburg Joseph II and other rulers of the period, Frederick accepted massive numbers of petitions from humble subjects, often receiving them face to face as he traveled on horseback through his territories. The selective positive response to a petition became the equivalent of clemency performance for the humblest classes, in which the king's compassionate attention would overcome bureaucratic neglect, the biases of the legal system, and most immediately the oppressive impositions of local nobles. Luedtke makes a case for genuine, if far from perfect, communication between people and sovereign through this mechanism, in which initiative from below could occasionally prevail (Luedtke 1999).

Enlightened absolutism's attempt to bridge the gulf between baroque sublimity and bourgeois sentimentalism found its fullest expression in Mozart's *La Clemenza di Tito*, composed in haste at the end of his life in 1791 for the Prague coronation of the new Holy Roman Emperor. Reworking the much-set libretto of the court poet par excellence Pietro Metastasio, the opera enacted monarchical legitimation at a particularly tricky moment. As Grand Duke of Tuscany, Leopold II had made Tuscany the first state in Europe to suppress the death penalty; now faced with noble rebellion around the empire in the aftermath of Joseph II's reforms, he had to draw back, and had just restored serfdom in Bohemia. Leopold had inherited a rhetoric of "clementia austriaca," deployed whenever nobles were restless or unpopular ministers were retained (Berry 2007: 331); and as the brother of Marie Antoinette but the ruler of a rival power he stood in a particularly uncomfortable relation to the events of 1789.

La Clemenza di Tito looks back reflexively on the cliché that royal clemency has become. "Reduced to a true opera," in Mozart's words, Caterino Mazzolà's revision of the libretto concentrated on the interplay between two major themes in all of Mozart's operas: sovereign clemency and interpersonal forgiveness.[5] The integration of comic or *buffa* opera's bourgeois themes and musical devices into an *opera seria* did not impress the coronation audience – oral tradition recalled the new empress dismissing it as "German filth" – but the broader Prague public attending subsequent performances received it with enthusiasm, and *Tito* was the most esteemed of Mozart's operas from the time of his death to around 1830, by which time its optimistic reconciliation of political scales was no longer conceivable.

The Roman emperor Titus (reign 79–81 AD) was integral to the clemency topos: he was celebrated across the early modern period as the very model of the generous ruler, relieving disaster victims and putting on lavish games for the people. Metastasio's libretto opens at the point where earlier dramas conclude: at the request of the Senate, Tito has renounced the love of a foreign princess, conquering passion for the sake of the Patria. Auguste's famous concluding assertion in *Cinna* – "Je suis maître de moi comme de l'univers," endlessly reworked in *seria* libretti, appears here at the beginning of the opera, as the patrician Annio reports the dismissal of Berenice: "Tito ha l'impero e del mondo e di sé." In contrast, the disgruntled princess Vitellia, whose father has been dethroned by Tito and who has been disappointed in her expectation of becoming his consort, refers to him sarcastically in the very first scene as "this clement hero." She is already conspiring to have him assassinated, manipulating her lover Sesto to conquer his loyalty and avenge her. The opera poses, therefore, the challenges that arise *after* the usual happy ending. How does a ruler maintain a genuinely benevolent disposition over time, given ongoing incentives to behave tyrannically? And how can the enlightened ruler become exemplary for a nobility still caught up in the feudal code of honor and revenge? The proffered solution is to cultivate generalized compassion through reflective mutual attention.

The opera presents a general pattern of interpersonal mimesis, working for both good and ill. Virtuous examples prompt virtuous emulation, but the negative reciprocity of affront and revenge is just as powerful. Both work through proximity and visual attention. Sesto's obsession with Vitellia's beauty leads him to treachery, while his friend Annio preaches the remedy: "Return to Tito's side ... and amend your past error with repeated proofs of fidelity." This Beccarian notion of criminal reform through the inculcation of new habits (as practiced in Leopold's Tuscany) is energized by a focus on the exemplary prince, but in *Tito* a thicker texture of social attention is also called for. Gazing must be supplemented by dialogue, the sharing of knowledge, and reflection. The opera is seeded with exhortations to turn back and look at another person in order to forestall hasty action. Many are directed by the desperate Sesto to the negative exemplar Vitellia: his very first address to her is "Pensaci meglio" (think better of it). When characters do listen to new information and revise their intentions at the request of another person, the social benefits are greatly enlarged.

A sequence in Act One establishes this pattern while also transforming the sovereign exemplarity of *opera seria* into a multidirectional social process. In revising Metastasio, Mozart and Mazzolà greatly increased the number of sung ensembles, bringing the conversational character of *buffa* opera to a hierarchically organized genre in which musical prominence reflected social prominence and individuals expressed their emotions in solitary arias. Instead, Mozart flanks the most ceremonial scene of the opera with seemingly trivial duets focused on the love of Sesto's sister Servilia and his friend Annio – the *seconda donna* and *secondo uomo* in casting terms, the lowest-ranking principals in the piece. Implicitly, the sublime is enabled by the beautiful.

The intimate duets affirm the horizontal solidarities that will make conflict resolution possible. In the first, Sesto agrees to Annio's request for his sister's hand, and the two men sing with one voice asking heaven to conserve their friendship. (Schiller creates a similar scene between the childhood friends Don Carlos and Posa, which Verdi will turn into a more famous duet.) There ensues a public scene in which Tito refuses a temple in his honor and proposes that the tributes of the provinces be spent instead on disaster relief for Vesuvius victims. With this revision, he confirms his sublimation of private feeling into generalized benevolence as well as his desire to refuse the role of god on earth. Tito then calls Annio and Sesto aside to announce that since he cannot have love he too will have friendship, and reduce the "infinite space that the gods placed between" himself and his subject Sesto by marrying Servilia.

Suppressing their horror, Annio and Sesto raise no objection, and the anguished Annio goes to give Servilia the news, resolving to follow Tito's example of self-mastery. She demands that he remain to explain the situation and comfort her.

Metastasio's two exit arias are now conflated into a Mozartian invention: the "duet of influence," in which one character introduces an idea, a second character repeats it, a passage of dialogue ensues, and the two then recapitulate the main idea together (De Médécis 2002). Today the example we know best is *Don Giovanni's* "La ci darem la mano." But in the early years of the nineteenth century when *Tito* was Mozart's most highly valued opera, the duet "Ah, perdona al primo affetto" was also its most widely circulated number – its accessibility to middle-class performers being precisely the point (Senici 1995: 9). The duet's musical and thematic structure encapsulate the opera's pedagogy of mutual listening and responsive reform.

Annio sings a sad verse apologizing for his incautious expression of love, the force of long habit. Servilia follows his melodic and thematic lead, but makes a revision: he was her first love, and will also be her last. The tune already sounds more cheerful in her brighter soprano. She has carried them from the past to the future, and now Annio sings on a rising line of his present delight at hearing the "accenti" of his beloved, the distinctiveness of her voice folding towards his. She mirrors him with a decorated falling exclamation, and their voices intertwine ecstatically: "The more that I listen to your senses / The more my ardor grows." Aroused and not wholly logical, the lovers express the kinesthetic character of the "mutual tuning-in process" that Alfred Schütz declared to be the constitution of society in interaction (Schütz 1951). At last they recapitulate the main melody together in close harmony: the conclusion is not sorrowful but exultant.

Further strengthened by this affirmation, Servilia goes to tell Tito that she will marry him faithfully if he wishes, but wants first to "make clear to [him] a secret": her heart belongs to Annio. Tito renounces her instantly and declares he will marry Vitellia instead (having, in any case, no particular interest). He praises Servilia and Annio for their willingness to sacrifice self-interest for love – a sentimental revision of his own Stoic sacrifice of love for country: "I want to tie so worthy a knot, so that the fatherland will have more citizens equal to you both." In an enthusiastic aria he wishes that every heart around him were so sincere, so that rulers could understand what was happening around them. He draws the moral of this sequence of scenes dramatizing the good results of open lines of communication, which have prevented an unhappy outcome for all concerned. To strengthen the point, there follows immediately a disastrous communication failure and a concomitant return to negative reciprocity. Vitellia sarcastically congratulates Servilia on her coming elevation, and Servilia, irritated, returns this hostility with a pert remark that fails to make Vitellia's error clear to her. This leads Vitellia to launch the revolt and bring them all nearly to disaster.

In the second act, Sesto is arrested as the author of the revolt. When Vitellia learns that, contrary to all her assumptions, Sesto has not betrayed her (revising a chain of negative reciprocity that has now captured Tito himself), her attention is finally caught, and as the others rush off to the arena, she finally responds to Sesto's initial plea: "I'll follow you; let me *think* first." But once again it is Servilia who spurs the transformation of sentiment into useful action: "If you have nothing but tears for him, all your crying will be useless." Emulating Servilia's own frankness, Vitellia will confess to Tito her protagonism in the conspiracy – not, like Corneille's noble conspiratress Émilie, to claim the glory, but to save Sesto's life: an ordinary human motive prompted by compassion. Thus Servilia becomes the most powerful agent in the opera despite being its structurally weakest character, whose cast position, musical personality, and even name place her among the servant and peasant soubrettes of opera buffa. Servilia inaugurates an exemplarity that works uphill.[6] Recall that in this period the custom of plebeian petitions to the monarch, bypassing the intervening layers of nobility and bureaucracy, was represented as a catalyst for reform (Berry 2007: 335; Luedtke 1999). By the same token, the alliance of Servilia's communication and Tito's top-down compassion can transform the characters in between: Vitellia, trapped in the old cycle of vengeance; the too-respectful Annio; and the *primo uomo* Sesto, torn between the old and the new political orders. Mozart's *Tito* thus complicates opera seria's sublime construction of exemplary sovereignty with a sentimental, buffa focus on the domestic virtues. It emphasizes musically the idea that education cuts both ways. Bourgeois friendship and companionate marriage, pillars of sentimental political thought, will remain central concerns of the theater of clemency; so will the transparency and communication of which they are the icons.

But before we affirm the sentimental solution to the problem of sovereignty, we must remember the title character, who ultimately does not succeed in removing the distance between himself and his subjects. Tito is excluded from the conjugal love, if not the friendship, that is now seen as the foundation of the state. He must live on a higher scale. In Metastasio's fuller libretto, he declares "I want no other / bride than Rome: my children will be / the subject peoples." This is in keeping with his turn from particular to general goods, but it makes a modern ear uneasy.

Tito's incessant clemency in the most imprudent circumstances and his obsession with living up to his fame by granting it on all possible occasions take a new light from his repeated insistence on the "torment" that results from his ascent to the "sublime throne." Forced literally to become a god, Tito sublimates his human anguish at losing Berenice in endless acts of benevolence: "If you keep me from being generous, what do you leave me with?" Later faced with punishing Sesto, he concludes, "let me not abandon the usual path," and affirms his decision for clemency in the opera's most old-fashioned aria, a *da capo* structure that concludes with repetition of the initial assertion and a march-like coda emphasizing the effortful self-control by which gentleness is sustained. By the end of the opera, his very identity is threatened. Now that his best friend and his prospective bride are both revealed as traitors, he sees the exemplary system in collapse. This is no longer an interpersonal struggle but a conflict of abstractions: "We'll see which is more constant, the perfidy of others or my clemency." He ends up throwing off the idiom of friendship and compassion in which he forgave Sesto as a man while pardoning him as a sovereign: now he assumes the godlike mask he had earlier tried to refuse. *Cinna* concludes with the emperor declaring "Auguste a tout appris, et veut tout oublier." Tito reaffirms this Stoic paradigm: "Let it be known in Rome / that I am the same, and that I / know all, absolve everyone, and forget everything." But in an opera so insistent on the value of shared knowledge and particular attention, this final assertion of generalized forgetting is a regression from reform to repetition.

Schiller: feeling as tyranny and impotence

Tito's qualified optimism that the scales can be bridged to produce a virtuous circle between social compassion and princely clemency is undone in Schiller's verse drama *Don Carlos*. In this complex text, completed in 1787 and given final revision in 1805,[7] Schiller blends two genres, the Stoic plot of the sovereign's education and Lessing's bourgeois tragedy, placing each in a new setting as a kind of experiment. The old heroic plot is translated from ancient Rome to the Spain of Philip II and the Black Legend, a context in which the outcome of sublimation will not be clemency and political reform but tyranny and political impotence. The sentimental plot becomes, as Schiller called it, "a family portrait in a princely household" – a court setting in which we see impulses of affection thwarted by etiquette, intrigue, and the competition for power. Not openness but secrecy and self-protection are the principles of survival. Schiller invokes Kant's language to discredit the solution of enlightened absolutism: along with companionate marriage and friendship, compassion cannot scale upward without destabilizing rule. But Schiller also shows Kant's generalizing ethical prescriptions failing to hold up against either particular feeling or the grand machinery of state.

Like *Tito*, *Don Carlos* opens at the moment when the princely hero has been forced to renounce love for the good of the state: his promised bride Elisabeth has been married to his father Philip instead. But the Infante is showing the strain, and the King is worried. Both the Queen and his friend the Marquis of Posa, just returned from the rebellious Flemish provinces, call on Carlos to pitch his ambitions higher: "Love is your office … Bring it to your future realms / And feel, instead of the stabs of conscience, / The joy of being God. Elisabeth / was your first love. Let Spain / be the second," urges the Queen, echoing the absolutist idiom we heard in *Tito*. Posa makes the same plea in modern terms, and as the Kantian liberal voice of the play, has himself jumped scale without benefit of sovereignty: "For I do not stand here as … the playmate of the boy Carlos. / A deputy of all humanity, / I embrace you." Posa reminds him of his former commitment to free Flanders from Spanish tyranny, asking whether the Prince's "sublime heart / has forgotten to beat for humanity." Through the course of the play, Posa and Elisabeth struggle in vain to push Carlos up the Platonic ladder from romantic passion to the defense of freedom. But Carlos is trapped in the sentimental idiom and his bursts of heroic resolution, lacking any plan for implementation, fizzle into hysteria. He cares only for love – that of Elisabeth, of Posa, even of his father, who listens appalled as Carlos insists on the beauty of tears that create sympathy between men.

Posa already inhabits the sublime end of this modern continuum: he too speaks of *Mitleid* and *Mitgefühl*, of friendship and the voice of nature, but he is more interested in generalized benefits. When Philip tries to reward him for his service to the state, Posa insists "I enjoy the laws" and refuses to be a "prince's servant." He exhorts the king to "restore humanity's lost nobility" in the sublime Kantian sense: the citizen should have no particular loyalties, but only "his brother's equally honorable rights."

King Philip dismisses both Posa's liberalism and the sentimentalism of Carlos as youthful raving; in fact, each threatens him. Conscious of the split between King and man in himself, he nonetheless fails to keep the levels separate, reigning through the old particularist idiom that creates political corruption. *Gnade* (grace) in Philip's language is not the divine grace of clemency, but debased into payment for favors. Contemptuous of the courtiers thus bought off, he is struck with admiration when Posa dares to speak his mind freely. But rather than accepting Posa's argument for general benevolence, he takes it as a mark of Posa's own uniqueness, his singular ability to rise above the plane of common men. He knows how to respond only by offering larger *Gnaden*, more exceptional privileges, in the hope of securing Posa's friendship.

The King's yearning for friendship, like that of Tito, is born in part of marital frustration. The King's inadvertent love for Elisabeth, married to cement an alliance, is expressed in jealousy, and any feeling for his son is overridden by envy of his youth and fear of his rivalry. Rather than feeling compassion for others, he wants it for himself, and Posa points out the contradiction for one who has become a god on earth: "*You* need [*brauchen*] sympathy! ... But since you have / cast men down to play them like strings on an instrument / Who will share harmony with you?" All displaced onto Posa, his affections unhinge him when he learns that Posa has been conspiring with Carlos to liberate Flanders: the shocked courtiers report, "The King has wept!" The tears praised by Carlos as the compassionate tokens of humanity are, for a divine monarch, an indicator of disintegration.

After Posa's murder, Carlos not only refuses the once longed-for gesture of feeling from his father, but declares before the whole court that the king has won neither Posa's love nor his political services. Posa died to save Carlos; moreover "You imagined yourself to rule him – and you were / An obedient tool of his high designs ... Your scepter was the plaything of his hands." Philip is in every sense unmanned by Carlos' revelations. In contrast to the positive sublimation urged as remedy for Carlos' frustrated love, Philip embraces sovereign power as enlarging the scope of his revenge, while failing to overcome his particular hatred of his own son:

> The world
> is still, for an evening, mine. I will
> so use it for this evening, that after me
> For ten generations no more plants
> Will grow on this scorched earth. He [Posa] brought
> Me as a sacrifice to humanity, his idol.
> Humanity will atone to me for him! – And now –
> With his puppet I'll begin.

Mozart's opera ends with a declaration of general clemency. Schiller's play moves toward conclusion with a declaration of general, even cosmic tyranny, given the scale of an empire "on which the sun never sets" and in which the Church rules nature. But Philip's own humanity, impaired as it is, prevents him from sustaining that leap of scale. Reduced to a "kleiner Mensch," the king calls in his final desperation for the Grand Inquisitor to restore control.

In the despotic situation, Carlos' compassion is hardly less destructive than Philip's self-pity: feeling leads at best to chaos. Neither is sovereign over himself, much less his empire. The real political alternatives are presented by Posa and the Grand Inquisitor.[8] Their competing visions of the instrumentalization of persons for the good of the state reminds us that Kant's *Foundations of the Metaphysics of Morals* was published in 1785, squarely in the middle of the drama's five-year composition process. Posa's "sublime example," as Philip calls it, is precisely that of the famous second formulation of the categorical imperative: "Act in such a way that you deal with [*brauchst*] humanity, whether in your own person or in that of anyone else, always at the same time as an end, never only as a means." Posa imagines balancing the two ends through the Kantian prescription of the general love of mankind. "A new state, the godlike offspring of a friendship" will be born – as the author of the "Ode to Joy" himself envisioned in the years prior to the Terror – but within it immediate affections will not distract from the needs of a distant suffering province. Posa believes that compassion can be scaled up.

Admitting that he has contemplated using Philip's favor to supplant Carlos as de facto future ruler, Posa is a far more viable candidate, exercising self-control of a kind unknown to father or son. He wrestles with his impulse to subordinate persons entirely to policy, as when he renounces the efficient but "barbarisch" solution of killing the indiscreet princess of Eboli to protect his project of reform. But as with the modern technocrats he anticipates, his temptation is to place too much faith in his own theories, and while Philip imagines himself as a musician playing men like strings on a lute, Posa is still more dangerously in love with the idea of himself as the "sculptor" who can shape a more perfect reality. He tries to shape Carlos in a way that Carlos' feebler clay cannot hold; trying to manipulate the king amid the complex secrecies of the court environment, he crafts a plot that collapses under its own intricacy, regressing into particularist intrigue. Elisabeth reproaches Posa for having used her without the consent she is now ready to grant, and also recognizes the pointlessness of his self-sacrifice for Carlos, condemning it precisely as theatrically "sublime," done to excite *Bewunderung* (we recall the "vain motive" of Kant's prince). On the contrary, it is the single moment in which compassion rather than ambition overrides his judgment. Even Posa falls off both sides of the Kantian tightrope: the superhuman sublime and the human beautiful cannot meet sustainably in the universal love of mankind.

Posa reproaches the King in Kantian terms: "Men to you are usable [*brauchbar*], nothing more." But this is the lesson of the Grand Inquisitor when Philip comes before him like a child to be scolded for his irresponsible surrender to compassion: "When you whimper about sympathy, have you not raised the world to be your equal? ... Men are / For you only numbers, nothing more." In excoriating the King for not delivering Posa immediately to their hands, he rejects the humane argument for sovereign clemency: "If one man may find grace, by what right can you sacrifice a hundred thousand?" No individual trumps the reason of state.

Both Posa, the apostle of progress, and the Grand Inquisitor, the guardian of reaction, know that men are mortal and limited; systems matter more for the long reach and the long term. Posa's solution is the law: a public transparent system under which all are the same. Transparency is of course no feature of the Spanish court, with its old-fashioned spying, gossip in the corridors, and compromising letters. The play is set in the claustrophobic palace; even its final scene involves overhearing and discovery: nothing changes despite the crisis at the heart of things. This kind of secrecy fosters generalized fear and a conspiratorial instinct from which Posa himself is not exempt. At the end he laments not having been open with Carlos about his intentions, and several characters make fatal mistakes because of bad information. So far, so much like the empire of *Tito* before its reformation. But there is another kind of secrecy revealed at the end of the play, and it is more dangerous still to the public welfare. Where law is a public apparatus, the order of the Inquisition is that of the efficient surveillance state. The Inquisition has known everything all along, biding its time so as to seize Posa at the climactic moment and make a public example of him. The designs of Posa are as nothing to this silent passionless machinery. There never was a hope for the liberal alliance of private feeling to large-scale reform.

Hugo: utilitarian clemency and the marginalization of feeling

If *Don Carlos* takes us straight towards the police state, Hugo's 1830 *Hernani, ou l'Honneur castillan* offers a more differentiated view of political change, staging the birth of a center–periphery split in which sublime scorched-earth generalities will coexist with stagnant particularisms. The setting remains sixteenth-century Spain, but earlier, in 1519: we get the plot of *Cinna* reworked as the prelude to *Don Carlos*. Not the old man Philip II but his father Charles V is on the throne, aged nineteen, in the year of his election as Holy Roman Emperor. His power is expanding rather than contracting, optimistic rather than defensive. He is Posa born into the sovereign's role: predatory like Philip, calculating for utility like the Inquisitor, but also good-humored, unwilling to waste life needlessly, and a liberal for himself if not for others. Hugo sets the imperial rise of Charles – recognizably a figure of Napoleon in a moment when French liberals were reconstructing his myth – against a narrative of generational conflict. This was understood to encode the struggle for power as the Restoration monarchy intensified its repression (including the prohibition of Hugo's own last play after the young poet, like Posa, refused to be bought off with favors from the monarch). Declaring the play's famous Romanticism to be "liberalism in literature," Hugo orchestrated a riot to call attention to its premiere, and later claimed this as the rehearsal for the July Revolution five months afterwards (Ledda 2008; Laforgue 2009).

Spain itself is represented in a moment of political consolidation and a shift from the feudal to the monarchical order even as Charles himself ascends to a higher plane of political organization. The *peuple* as embodiment and motor of the spirit of history appear in both Hugo's preface and Charles' musings, but they remain offstage (Laforgue 2009: 79). Rather, like *Tito* and *Don Carlos*, the play dramatizes the struggle between different forms of power among those who already possess it. Each form offers a different economy of social interaction. The feudal mode is governed by the honor code of reciprocity: the duties of hospitality and revenge override all human feeling or personal interest. The royal mode that replaces it is dominated by a pettier code of interested reciprocity, in which the loyalty of courtiers is purchased by largesse and undermined by envy. The imperial mode, in which the ruler must learn to contend alone with nations and abstract forces of history, transcends and negates humanity. An act of clemency – not a move in a reciprocal gift exchange but rather an undeserved grace from above – bridges Charles' passage from the second mode to the third as he ascends to quasi-divine status.

The titular hero Hernani, his beloved Doña Sol, and her jealous uncle and would-be husband, the duke Ruy Gomez Silva, are trapped in the old world of *l'honneur castillan*. Endlessly crossing his arms and blocking the door while he jabbers on about the golden age of the Cid, Gomez was recognized by the audience as a figure of Bourbon reaction. But the young lovers, despite the uninhibited lyricism of their passion, have no alternative to offer: they spend the entire play rehearsing their *Liebestod*. Creatures of the periphery, the three belong to Aragón, the kingdom united by marriage to Castile and subordinated de facto, struggling to hang on to its feudal privileges. Gomez clings to the portraits of his ancestors in his mountain castle; Hernani, whose father was executed by Charles' father as a traitor, is still further removed from the political center in his temporary status as an outlaw and bandit. They no longer pose the threat to rule that Mozart's Vitellia and Sesto pose: Brooks says that the character Hernani is "tragedy become melodrama without realizing the change" (Brooks 1984 [1976]: 98). As they play out their interpersonal and internal conflicts between love, honor, and revenge, they hold on to less and less, and the outcome of their opposition to Charles is determined from the very first act. "And when I have the world?" asks Charles. "Then I will have the tomb," says Hernani. Still more than Vitellia, the three are caught up in the cycle of unreflective negative reciprocity, as well as being blind to self-interest. Over and over, they attempt to sacrifice themselves for one another when it can do no good, misunderstand one another when the possibility of happiness arises, refuse to escape when the opportunity offers itself. They never listen and never think: rather than opening themselves to compassion, they remain automatons of the honor code.

Charles rarely listens either, but he is a rapid calculator and an intelligent man. Like us – though unlike Hugo's Romantic public – he rolls his eyes at the highminded folly of the feudal protagonists and refuses to dignify it with recognition; like Philip, he is contemptuous of his less highminded courtiers. An ironic pragmatist, he partakes of what the liberal idealist Mme de Staël condemned as Napoleon's "utilitarianism," but this works for good as well as ill: he refuses to execute either Hernani or Gomez when nothing important can be gained by it, and although he abducts Doña Sol, he does not rape her. Struck by her contempt, in Act III he begins to think.

The fruits of this come in the fourth act, as Charles waits by the tomb of Charlemagne in Aix-la-Chapelle to surprise the conspirators planning to assassinate him before he can be elected emperor. But this shift of scene and scale forestalls any *Tito*-like birth of communication within his own realm. Rather, Charles holds a conversation with Charlemagne: not a real ancestor, like the portraits to whom Gomez is always talking, but a chosen exemplar who can advise him how to "enlarge his soul to the measure of his fortune." He turns from strategizing his election to a serious consideration of the responsibilities of empire and the dangers of climbing the "moving pyramid of states and kings." Half-whimsically entering the tomb, he asks to be shown how to "conquer and to rule" those below him, with their petty rivalries, and whether to punish or to pardon.

When he emerges, startling the now-arrived conspirators as the seeming specter of Charlemagne, cannonades outside the chapel simultaneously proclaim him emperor. His men come forward and Charles now has Hernani, Gomez, and a throng of noble malcontents in his power. Sol is also brought in: she and Hernani repeat their ritual of mistrust and reconciliation. Charles observes, "I need to give the world a lesson." After Sol throws herself at his feet begging for clemency, Charles thinks a moment, lifts her up, and hands her to Hernani. He restores to Hernani his name and ducal possessions and takes the Order of the Golden Fleece from his own neck to place it around Hernani's. He grants a blanket pardon to the conspirators, and with the exception of Gomez glowering in a corner, the scene ends with a universal "Gloire à Carlos!"

Charles turns back to Charlemagne's effigy to see whether the fine tableau has passed the test: "Are you pleased with me?"

> Did I understand the voice that speaks in your tomb?
> Ah! I was alone, lost, alone before an empire,
> A whole world shouting and threatening and conspiring,
> The Danes to punish, the Holy Father to pay,
> Venice, Suleiman, Luther, Francis I,
> A thousand jealous daggers already glowing in the shadows,
> Pitfalls, reefs, enemies uncounted,
> Twenty peoples, each enough to daunt as many kings,
> Everything rushed, everything pressing, everything to be done at once.
> I implored you, "Where should I begin?"
> And you answered: "My son, with clemency!"

There is policy, to be sure, in the procuring of internal order among peoples and their quarreling feudal lords. Charles subdues grudges and historic resentments with incorporation into empire, buys off the petty-minded with largesse, and offers a lesson in self-control to those capable of receiving it. At the same time he teaches himself that his own cares are now higher:

> Extinguish yourself, young heart full of flame!
> Now let the spirit rule, so long troubled by you.
> Your loves henceforth, your mistresses, alas!
> Are Germany, Flanders, and Spain.

Charles cannot now afford the distraction of human feeling. Revising the earlier ironic "clemency" in which he pardons Gomez by taking Sol, he makes a disinterested sacrifice of the woman he loves to Hernani and the general peace. It is not the former honor-driven reciprocity but an act of grace, the godly equivalent of human compassion. This removes him still further from ordinary men, and his manner is now literally imperious, rebuffing an elderly grandee who presumes upon having known him in infancy. We hear the echo of Tito taking Rome for his bride, but with the more worrying image of multiple *maîtresses*, and at that reference to Flanders we cannot help thinking of the ominous outcome we know from Schiller. Charles' passions have perhaps not been effaced but generalized, and will no longer have the check of interpersonal responsibility, for as "the keystone of the vault" Charles now speaks only to Charlemagne and Charlemagne only to God. The violence initially threatened to Doña Sol may now be wrought upon whole countries.

For the moment, however, Charles' subjects benefit from his indifference. Having accidentally bestowed a title on his grasping retainer Don Ricardo in Act I, and inadvertently addressed him as a grandee at the beginning of Act IV, he now deliberately names him the chief of his household security. Less ambiguously, like Tito, he "forgets the names" of the conspirators, who, it is to be hoped, will learn his lesson and forget their own grudges and historical resentments, spreading his grace further. Hernani is less impressed when Charles says he has forgotten about the rivalry between their two fathers, observing "The one whose flank is bleeding has a better memory," but even he says at act's end, "Who is it then, who changes us all like this?"

Having given his lesson with the other gifts, the mobile Charles now departs from the stage. In contrast to the grounding of the other characters, his act of clemency has "definitively separated the space of power from the space of love" (Laurent 2009: 100). This is not only nineteenth-century liberalism's rejection of sentimentalism for a narrower view of self-interest (Reddy 2000), but even anticipates neoliberalism's conversion of every locality into periphery. In the new, superhuman mode of power, Charles has become at once transcendent and nowhere, and the stage is no longer the center of the political universe as in *Clemenza*, but the space of those left behind, where the ignoble instrument Ricardo maintains order (Laurent 2009: 98). Not surprisingly, the emperor's lesson is accordingly short-lived. The drama does not end with "Gloire à Carlos!": there is an Act V, Hernani's wedding back in Saragossa. Charles is absent: a courtier observes that he is preoccupied with Luther and the Ottoman emperor; the drunken Ricardo boasts of what he would do to Luther, and the courtiers resume their envious carping at Hernani's sudden elevation.

For the courtiers, Charles' transformation has not proven exemplary: they note the difference in him, but continue to merit contempt themselves. One might have more hope for the idealistic feudal characters. And at first Hernani seems to have his eyes opened, renouncing his revenge and throwing away his dagger; his once divided soul is now "only love." But even in him we see no real learning: it is subtraction rather than synthesis. His old role as bandit is over, but his only future is to become a courtier, living on largesse with the once-despised "golden sheep to hang around his neck" (Laforgue 2009: 80). The sovereign's gratuitous clemency raises the giver but degrades the receiver: without some kind of equality there can be no meaningful emulation.

Gomez, in holding on to his feudal principles, holds also on to his dignity; but Charles has not changed him at all: "Unlike him, I have not forgiven." After the wedding, when the lovers are alone and Sol is still perversely delaying consummation with conversation, Gomez sounds the fatal horn that summons Hernani to fulfill his vow and take his life in payment for violating the duke's hospitality. Sol tries falling at his feet, but unlike Charles, this figure of feudal revenge denies clemency. Hernani has no solution to propose. Torn between the insistent Sol and the inexorable Gomez, he is pulled straight back into the dilemma of love and honor. Although Charles revises his earlier actions, the others can only repeat themselves, and this time the proposed self-sacrifices are accomplished, not as edifying examples but as suicides leaving no survivors (Ledda 2008: 174). While Charles is away ruling the world, the Spanish periphery kills itself off, endlessly replaying *Le Cid*.

In *Tito*, the cycle of revenge is overcome by political learning that comes from mutual interpersonal attention. *Hernani* explores the same possibility, developing the demonstration that learning is not durable without continuous reinforcement. This cannot exist when the ruler is removed from interaction, and still less in the absence of a democratic community of compassion, such as was potentially formed among Carlos, Elisabeth, Posa, and their sympathizers. An isolated act of clemency transforms nothing.

The Inquisition's all-seeing apparatus in *Don Carlos* gives way in *Hernani* to a more realistic account of power on the grand scale. Sovereigns never fully control the lower levels or the remote outposts: they ignore them when they can, or cynically play them for theatrical effect. The historical parallel to Charles' clemency confirms the point: in June 1804, the not yet crowned Napoleon would pardon the aristocratic Polignac brothers for their participation in royalist conspiracy, at the urging of his brother-in-law Murat

> that such an act of clemency would redound greatly to his honour ... that it would be said the Emperor pardoned the attempt against the life of the First Consul, that this act of mercy would shed more glory over the

commencement of his reign than any security which could accrue from the execution of the prisoners.

(Bourienne 1891 [1829]: Chapter 26)

Sublimation has turned into public relations. More telling is the aftermath, for the Polignac brothers became prominent agents of reaction in the Restoration government, and the younger Armand would, in July 1830, issue the Four Ordinances abrogating the constitution and sending the young men of Paris out to the barricades. Thus, although Napoleonic clemency was no doubt to be preferred to Bourbon tyranny, its outcome was to preserve the forces of reaction for a return. Nietzsche tells us that *Macht verdummt*; Hugo's more precise observation is not that power makes rulers stupid, but that sublimity makes them inattentive.

Conclusion

In our own day, sublimity has followed the Grand Inquisitor's lead into other codes of representation: humans are converted into numbers. As statistics, they are made to bolster a grand narrative of autonomy and/or utility, the kind offered by both the democratic and the totalitarian successors of Emperor Charles. The human cost of the sublime perspective (as the Inquisitor said, the hundred thousand are there to be sacrificed) is well understood.

The problem of attention identified by Hugo is consequently both political and ethical. "Attention must be paid," as Willy Loman's wife declared in a more recent work of theater. The solution is aesthetic: the shaping of form to excite notice and guide feeling. This was exactly the point of Enlightenment theater: to gather the public and focus its collective attention on the social working-out of some perpetual question. As this volume makes clear, the sentimental side of this tradition has had a long afterlife, now in a wide range of genres and media, calling social attention to distant suffering and cultivating a compassionate response. The well-known phenomenon of "compassion fatigue" speaks precisely to the challenges of scale and attention identified by the theater of clemency.

On their different sides of the sublime/beautiful divide, Kant and Lessing made parallel observations and drew identical prescriptions for refreshing attention. Kant acknowledged that sublimity is exhausting and suggested that both art and social life must offer "an unforced alternation between both sorts of sentiment" (Kant 2011 [1764]: 18–19). Lessing proposed, conversely, that dramatists provide intervals of *Bewunderung* as relief from the constant tears of compassion (Fleming 2009: 62) One can imagine comparable prescriptions for political communication and debate, a tacking back and forth between the instrumental and the human scales as remedy for both triviality and tyranny: we can at least be induced to try out both perspectives.

But the scale of Western states, in which the social remove between the everyday life of citizens and the political work of their representatives is so great, makes it hard to imagine positive action that could bridge the gap. Kant and Lessing write inside the tradition of Western aesthetics: they take the dichotomies as given. The aesthetic, holistic approach of theater helps us to see how intractable the dichotomies are. The sublime and the beautiful cannot be reduced to reason and emotion, public and private, large and small, high and low, general and particular, global and local, autonomous and embedded, or any other single dimension: all are involved. In this framework that has shaped our language, our habits, and our institutional design, compassion and effective political action fall on different sides of the gulf. To solve the problem of scale would demand a genuine re-formation of both state and sensibility.

Notes

1 Ned Lebow gave the impetus, Regina Bendix the environment, and Don Brenneis the key for this chapter: thanks to them and to Mervyn Frost for valuable readings. Research was generously supported by the Lichtenberg-Kolleg of the University of Göttingen and the Shelby Cullom Davis Center for Historical Studies at Princeton. Translations are my own unless otherwise noted.

2 The Roman general Lucius Sulla (or Silla) was another frequent protagonist of clemency operas, with examples by both Handel and the young Mozart. Frederick's adaptation was set by the court composer Carl Friedrich Graun as *Silla* for the Berlin opera season in 1753. Manuscript on view at the exhibition "Friedrichs Montezuma. Macht und Sinne in der preußischen Hofoper." Musikinstrumenten-Museum des Staatlichen Instituts für Musikforschung, Preußischer Kulturbesitz, Berlin, January–June 2012.

3 I use the masculine pronoun for the sake of convenience, given that no female monarchs are discussed in this chapter; the period's frameworks associate both sovereignty and sublimity with masculinity.

4 As in ancient Greece (Nussbaum 1986; Lebow 2003), in early modern Europe the trajectories of theater and theory are intertwined.

5 Nagel offers a richly stimulating account of Mozart's place in the clemency tradition, but configures it differently and is primarily interested in the historical succession from aristocratic to bourgeois sensibility; he reads the end of *Tito* as the abdication of the monarch "into mere humanity" (Nagel 1991 [1988]: 9).

6 Nagel does not remark on Servilia's role, but speaks of Pamina in *Die Zauberflöte* as inaugurating a tradition of female victims who, by seizing the initiative and behaving autonomously, become rescuers of their lovers and the general situation: Goethe's Iphigenia and Beethoven's Leonore follow (Nagel 1991 [1988]).

7 Quotations are from the 1805 text.

8 One character consistently and successfully negotiates the claims of domestic feeling, the public good, and sovereign prerogative, but it is Elisabeth, barred from power by gender. Surrounded by unreceptive men, she is unable even to set an example from below like Servilia.

References

Beccaria, Cesare. 1983 (1775). *An Essay on Crimes and Punishments*, ed. Adolph Caso. Boston: Branden.

Berry, Mark. 2007. "Power and Patronage in Mozart's *La Clemenza di Tito* and *Die Zauberflöte*," in *Cultures of Power in Europe During the Long Eighteenth Century*, eds Hamish Scott and Brendan Simms. Cambridge: Cambridge University Press.

Bourienne, Louis Antoine Fauvelet de. 1891 (1829). *Memoirs of Napoleon Bonaparte*, complete, revised edition, tr. R.W. Phipps. New York: Charles Scribner's Sons.

Brooks, Peter. 1984 (1976). *The Melodramatic Imagination: Balzac, Henry James, Melodrama, and the Mode of Excess*. Columbia: Columbia University Press.

De Médécis, François. 2002. "Chanter pour se faire entendre: Le duo d'influence dans les opéras de Mozart," *Acta Musicologica* 74: 35–54.

Feldman, Martha. 2007. *Opera and Sovereignty: Transforming Myths in Eighteenth-Century Italy*. Chicago: University of Chicago Press.

Fiskesjö, Magnus. 2003. *The Thanksgiving Turkey Pardon, the Death of Teddy's Bear, and the Sovereign Exception of Guantánamo*. Chicago: Prickly Paradigm Press.

Fleming, Paul. 2009. *Exemplarity and Mediocrity: The Art of the Average from Bourgeois Tragedy to Realism*. Stanford: Stanford University Press.

Frevert, Ute. 2012. *Gefühlspolitik. Friedrich II als Herr über die Herzen?* Göttingen: Wallstein.

Kant, Immanuel. 2011 (1764). *Observations on the Feeling of the Beautiful and Sublime and Other Writings*. Cambridge: Cambridge University Press.

Konstan, David. 2005. "Clemency as a Virtue," *Classical Philology* 100: 337–46.

Laforgue, Pierre. 2009. "Politique d'Hernani, ou libéralisme, romantisme et révolution en 1830," in *Hugo sous les feux de la rampe. Relire Hernani et Ruy Blas*, eds Arnaud Laster and Bertrand Marchal. Paris: Presses universitaires de Paris.

Laurent, Franck. 2009. "Où est le pouvoir? Sur la dimension politique du rapport scène/ hors scène dans Hernani et Ruy Blas," in *Hugo sous les feux de la rampe. Relire Hernani et Ruy Blas*, eds Arnaud Laster and Bertrand Marchal. Paris: Presses universitaires de Paris.

Lebow, Richard Ned. 2003. *The Tragic Vision of Politics*. Cambridge: Cambridge University Press.

Ledda, Sylvain. 2008. *Hernani et Ruy Blas: de flamme ou de sang*. Toulouse: Presses universitaires du Mirail.

Lessing, Gotthold Ephraim. 2010 (1767). *Minna von Barnhelm. Hamburgische Dramaturgie. Werke 1767–1769*, ed. Klaus Bohnen. Berlin: Deutscher Klassiker Verlag.

Luedtke, David M. 1999. "Frederick the Great and the Celebrated Case of the Millers Arnold (1770–1779): A Reappraisal," *Central European History* 32: 379–408.

Moore, Kathleen. 1991. "The Pardoning Power in Democracies: An Unfinished Revolution," in *Revolution and Enlightenment in Europe*, ed. Timothy O'Hagan. Aberdeen: Aberdeen University Press.

Nagel, Ivan. 1991 (1988). *Autonomy and Mercy: Reflections on Mozart's Operas*, tr. Marion Faber and Ivan Nagel. Cambridge, MA: Harvard University Press.

Nussbaum, Martha. 1986. *The Fragility of Goodness: Luck and Ethics in Greek Tragedy and Philosophy*. Cambridge: Cambridge University Press.

Oschmann, Susanne. 1991. "Gedankenspiele: der Opernheld Friedrich II," in *Opernheld und Opernheldin im 18. Jahrhundert: Aspekte der Librettoforschung*, ed. Klaus Hortschansky. Hamburg: K. D. Wagner.

Reddy, William M. 2000. "Sentimentalism and Its Erasure: The Role of Emotions in the Era of the French Revolution," *Journal of Modern History* 72: 109–52.

Sarat, Austin. 2005. *Mercy on Trial: What It Means to Stop an Execution*. Princeton, NJ: Princeton University Press.

Schütz, Alfred. 1951. "Making Music Together," *Social Research* 18: 76–95.

Senici, Emanuele. 1995. "'Adapted to the Modern Stage': La clemenza di Tito in London," *Cambridge Opera Journal* 7: 1–22.

14

SYMPATHY AND ANTIPATHY IN THE EXTRA-MORAL SENSE

Michael Ure

This chapter addresses the challenges that Adam Smith's theory of moral sentiments implies for a democratic politics of compassion. Smith conceives sympathy as a mechanism that enables individuals to understand and assess the whole spectrum of others' sentiments, including sorrow, resentment, and joy. His basic sense of sympathy prefigures contemporary evolutionary biologists' identification of our species' highly evolved capacity to mirror sentiments (Iacoboni 2009; Decety 2009; De Waal 2006). Many philosophical analyses of Smith's concept of sympathy focus on how he links this embodied, reflex capacity to the imagination and thence to the making of moral judgements. One of the central questions in this context is how Smith thinks we translate our involuntary, physiological response to others' emotional expression into cognitive appraisals, causal explanations and targeted helping. The key epistemological issue is how these physiological reflexes contribute to the genesis of 'objective' or 'impartial' judgements of the propriety of others' sentiments. These accounts focus on Smith's analysis of the role of sympathy in constituting impartial judgements.

In this chapter I bracket these epistemological issues in order to focus on Smith's account of our *motivation* to sympathise. Frans De Waal maintains that our species' hard-wired capacity to be in tune with others' goals and feelings 'primes us to take these goals and feelings into account' (De Waal 2006: 176). He argues that these mimetic reflexes can form the basis of sympathetic understanding, compassion and co-operative political practices. Here I focus on Smith's analysis of what we might call the *extra-moral* motives he believes shape our ability and desire to put ourselves in others' shoes. These extra-moral motives, as we shall see, are crucial to understanding the scope of compassion and its potential contribution to social equality and political solidarity. As we shall see, Smith's analysis shows how we are motivated to use our capacity for empathy and sympathy for 'extra-moral' ends. He argues that vanity can motivate us to have sympathy for those who exercise or enjoy 'sovereignty' and antipathy for those who lack self-command. On his analysis, vanity motivates us to go along with the sentiments of those whose sovereignty derives from their self-command or their elevated social status. According to Smith, the flipside of our sympathy for sovereign heroes is contempt for those who 'lack' self-command or are socially invisible. When sympathy serves the 'extra-moral' end of vanity it creates undemocratic, unjust partialities. On the one hand, vanity motivates us *first* to enter into all the sentiments of the great and *then* to appraise their grief and resentment as significant and worthy of our compassion; and on the other, it motivates us to limit or avoid our exposure to the sentiments of the vulnerable and if we do suffer from their emotional contagion to appraise their grief and resentment as insignificant. In such cases the mimetic reflexes that enable us to share others' sentiments do not form the basis of compassionate and just political practices, but of social and political division. In Smith's judgement our sympathies are refracted through our hierarchical disposition, or '(o)ur obsequiousness', as he calls it (Smith 2002 [1790]: 63). *Whether* we enter into and *how* we appraise others' sentiments is often shaped by this obsequiousness. We will first examine Smith's analysis of the partiality of sympathy before identifying and assessing his proposed solutions to the way vanity skews this capacity in favour of sovereign heroes.

If we examine Smith's analysis we can see that despite his providential view of sympathy as a natural propensity designed for the purpose of harmonising society, he also shows sympathy as a neutral mechanism that we put to a range of different uses, many of which work against this political end. Smith conceives social and political harmony in terms of collective sentimental concordance: in order to live together harmoniously citizens need to share similar emotional responses to the same circumstances. Ideally then when we see others experience joy, grief or resentment our sympathy will enable us to experience the same type of sentiment. Smith adds the important caveat, of course, that our judgement of propriety ought to regulate our capacity for shared joy and suffering.

However, while Smith tends to see our natural capacities as providentially designed to help us achieve this concord, he also acknowledges that these same capacities can go awry and fail to achieve their 'purpose'. Smith acknowledges that whether or not sympathy achieves its final purpose of harmonising, society is partly contingent upon how we shape this capacity. *The Theory of Moral Sentiments* is not just a description and analysis of how sympathy works; nor is it simply a normative defence of sympathy. It is also a guidebook of how to cultivate sympathy in order to construct a certain kind of 'sentimental' citizen and community. Smith shows that sympathy is a mechanism through which we can mirror and understand others' sentiment, but understanding others is not sufficient to guarantee that we will *care* about their suffering. Sympathising with others' suffering does not necessarily entail compassion understood in the ethical and political sense of caring about their suffering or attempting to address its causes. Sympathy alone does not necessarily motivate commitment to democratic values of equal respect and concern. Indeed Smith's analysis suggests that the mechanism of sympathy is only *precariously* tied to the democratic political hope that compassion can be evenly distributed according to principles of seriousness or desert. He shows how sympathy is an instrument that can and does serve a number of 'extra-moral' ends that have inegalitarian, undemocratic outcomes. The challenge Smith confronts is whether and how we can transform sympathy and the sympathetic imagination into an instrument of justice.

In order to see why Smith believes the connection between sympathy and the moral concern we call 'compassion' is precarious, we need to understand his account of our species' 'vanity' or what we might call our need for sympathetic attunement. Vanity, as he defines it:

> ... is founded on the belief of our being the object of attention and approbation. The rich man glories in his riches because he feels that they naturally draw upon him the attentions of the world, and that mankind are disposed to go along with him in all those agreeable emotions ... At the thought of this, his heart seems to swell and dilate itself within him, and he is fonder of his wealth, upon this account, than for all the other advantages is procures him. The poor man, on the contrary, is ashamed of his poverty. He feels that it either places him out of the sight of mankind, or, that if they take any notice of him, they have, however, scarce an fellow-feeling with the misery and distress which he suffers.
>
> (Smith 2002 [1790]: 62)

In Smith's lexicon, vanity is the desire for maximal sympathy. For Smith the emotional attunement that 'sympathy' enables has become one of our most highly valued ends. What we value above all else, he suggests, is for others to sympathise (or 'go along with') all of our sentiments. We are prepared for any amount of toil and anxiety in order to render ourselves the object of the observation and fellow-feeling of everybody about us (Smith 2002 [1790]: 62). Put in counter-factual terms, his claim is that if wealth or status did not bring with it others' sympathetic attunement to our feelings we would not pursue them. According to Smith, we value mutual sympathy regardless of whether or not we derive any material advantages from it. 'To be observed, to be attended, to be taken notice of with sympathy', he writes, ' ... are all the advantages we can propose to derive from [bettering our condition]. It is the vanity, not the ease, or the pleasure, which interests us' (Smith 2002 [1790]: 61). Smith observes that it is especially the painful emotions of grief and resentment, the latter often caused by political injustice, which 'require the healing consolation of sympathy' (Smith 2002 [1790]: 19). Smith suggests that the flipside of our vanity is our fear of social oblivion and contempt. He believes our deepest fear is that others will lack sympathy or have antipathy for our grief and resentment. 'The cruelest insult that ... can be offered to the unfortunate', he notes, 'is to make light of their calamities ... not to wear a serious countenance when [our companions] tells us of their afflictions, is real and gross inhumanity' (Smith 2002 [1790]: 19). We fear social invisibility, he claims, more than death itself. After the death sentence, Smith observes the punishment we most fear is solitary confinement (see also De Waal 2006: 5). Indeed, he goes so far as to suggest that to be held in contempt by others is the worst of all evils:

> Human virtue is superior to pain, to poverty, to danger, and to death; nor does it even require the utmost efforts to despise them. But to have their misery exposed to insult and derision, to be led in triumph, to be set up for the hand of scorn to point at, is a situation in which its constancy is much more apt to fail. Compared with the contempt of mankind, all other external evils are easily supported.
>
> (Smith 2002 [1790]: 72)

Our well-being or flourishing is more dependent on receiving recognition or sympathy than on anything else. We can endure, if not conquer, the emotional distress of pain, poverty, danger and even the prospect of death, but we cannot endure others' indifference, or worse still their contempt. According to Smith, the challenge of despising pain, poverty, even death pales in comparison with the challenge of freeing ourselves from our dependence on sympathy or social esteem. We fear social death – i.e. becoming an object of scorn or contempt – more than death itself. On Smith's view, therefore, we are extremely vulnerable to contempt, shame and humiliation. It is almost unbearable or intolerable for us when others deride or mock our sentiments, especially our grief and resentment. 'The theatre of sympathy in *Theory of Moral Sentiment*', as Marshall puts it, 'is based on the simultaneous necessity of spectators and fear of spectators. The ultimate threat in the world that Smith represents is the prospect of the spectators who would deny sympathy' (Marshall 1986: 191). For Smith, then, our emotional flourishing requires others to share our sentiments. Sympathy is therefore our most valued social currency. To borrow Smith's own musical metaphor, we want our passions to 'beat in time' with others' and vice versa. Smith's musical analogy is apt since it captures the way in which playing or listening to music together creates an emotional or mood convergence – and the pleasure of such musical experience lies precisely in this emotional synchronicity.

Yet, as Smith goes on to show, our need for sympathetic attunement is not easily satisfied. We can distinguish in his analysis at least two kinds of obstacles to our desire for others' attention and attunement. First, Smith believes that the sentiments others experience through their sympathetic imagination vary significantly in intensity, and even in kind, from our original feeling. Smith proposes that the persons principally concerned – i.e. the person suffering grief or resentment – can resolve this problem through adopting a neo-Stoic political therapy that enables them to rise above their misfortunes and make themselves objects of sublime admiration and contemplation. If they aim to secure active, political compassion, he suggests, then they must elicit this sympathy by giving others grounds to admire their Stoic heroism. Smith implies we can overcome the limits of sympathetic attunement through neo-Stoic work on the self. Second, Smith suggests that when we give sympathy, our vanity makes us distribute it unevenly and unjustly. Our manner of trying to satisfy this vanity, he suggests, can engender unjust patterns of sympathy and antipathy. As we shall see, Smith again reverts to a Stoic perspective to try to correct this partial sympathy that derives from our vanity. Ironically, however, in trying to resolve the problem of partial sympathy Smith only succeeds in banishing it as a moral compass. Let us consider in more detail how Smith conceives these obstacles to sympathetic attunement and how he proposes to overcome them.

In the first place, as we have observed, Smith suggests that the scope and degree of our sympathy is limited by virtue of the fact that it turns on how, through the imagination, we compare ourselves and our circumstances with those we observe. He conceives sympathy's limit by way of analogy: we can only experience others' sentiments in the manner that a spectator experiences those of a stage performer. We temporarily change places with stage performers in our imagination and by that means experience 'analogous' or 'reflected passions'. If, like spectators, we can only experience analogous sentiments, then those whose suffering we witness cannot expect to receive the kind of sympathetic attunement they crave:

> That imaginary change of situation upon which sympathy is founded is but momentary. The thought of their own safety, the thought that they themselves are not really sufferers, continually intrudes upon them; and though it does not hinder them from conceiving a passion somewhat analogous to what is felt by the sufferer, hinders them from conceiving anything that approaches the same degree of violence.
>
> (Smith 2002 [1790]: 27)

Smith alludes here to Lucretius' famous image of the spectator of a shipwreck who conceives the sentiments of those suffering this terrible fate, but also derives joy from the knowledge of his own safety (Lucretius 1966: 60). Lucretius identifies the profound pleasure we derive from seeing others in peril when we know that we are safe from the storm. Or as Rousseau glosses Lucretius' Epicurean observation: 'Pity is sweet because, when we put ourselves in the place of the one who suffers, we are aware, nevertheless of the pleasures of not suffering like him' (Rousseau 1974 [1762]): 182). Lucretius uses the spectator as an allegory of Epicurean tranquillity. Like all the Hellenistic philosophies, Epicurean philosophy promises to give us the greatest joy of all: 'to stand aloof in a quiet citadel, stoutly fortified by the teaching of the wise, and to gaze down from that elevation on others wandering aimlessly in search for the way of life ...' (Lucretius 1966: 60). Epicureans are spectators of the shipwreck that is ordinary human life. Smith baulks at Lucretius' acknowledgement of the pleasure that these spectators derive from comparing the misfortune they witness with their own safety, but he does recognise that they cannot experience the sentiments they observe in a sustained way or with anything like the violence of those suffering misfortune. Given what we might call this Epicurean limit on sympathy, therefore, we cannot expect that others will sympathise with us to the extent that we ardently desire.

Smith believes that when we are, in his terms, the 'person principally concerned' – the shipwrecked, so to speak – we recognise that even in the best possible cases the sympathy others have for us does not enable them to experience the same kind of sentiment or with the same degree of intensity. We recognise that because they only experience sorrow or resentment, for example, through an imaginary and temporary change of places, this lowers their shared sentiment in degree and varies it in kind. Our friends may suffer distress when we mourn, but the limits of sympathy mean that they cannot suffer the same sting of loss. They change places only temporarily with us and they know that even as they do so they are safe from the same troubles.

> (W)hen we condole with our friends in their afflictions, how little do we feel in comparison of what they feel ... how far are our languid emotions of our hearts from keeping time to the transports of theirs? ... We may even inwardly reproach ourselves with our own want of sensibility, and perhaps, on that account, work ourselves up into an artificial sympathy, which, however, when it is raised, is always the slightest and most transitory imaginable; and generally, as soon as we have left the room, vanishes, and is gone forever.
>
> (Smith 2002 [1790]: 57–8).

Indeed, the admixture of pleasure others derive from comparing our troubles with their own security prevents them from sharing the same kind of sentiment. When we suffer we know that others, even our friends, are to some extent Epicurean spectators of the shipwreck. Compassion, Smith explains:

> ... can never be exactly the same with the original sorrow; because the secret consciousness that the change of situation, from which the sympathetic imagination arises, is but imaginary, not only lowers it in degree, but, in some measure, varies it in kind.
>
> (Smith 2002 [1790]: 27)

Yet the 'person principally concerned', Smith stresses, 'passionately desires a more complete sympathy ... To see the emotions of their hearts, in every respect, beat time to his own, in the violent and disagreeable passions, constitutes his sole consolation' (Smith 2002 [1790]: 27).

The challenge Smith confronts is how we might secure the sympathetic attunement we desire despite the limits Epicureanism places on this mechanism. Smith argues we can resolve the first problem by learning how to lower the pitch of our sentiments to that which spectators can go along with. Here Smith assigns responsibility for resolving this sentimental discord to the person principally concerned – the victim of misfortune or injustice. In this way Smith concedes ground to Epicureanism's hedonistic psychology. The 'person principally concerned', he suggests, can only hope to obtain others' sympathy 'by lowering his passions to that pitch, in which the spectators are capable of going along with him. He must flatten ... the sharpness of his natural tone, in order to reduce it to harmony and concord with the emotions of those who are about him' (Smith 2002 [1790]: 27). Smith devises the impartial spectator as a neo-Stoic therapy that enables us to adjust our sentiments so that others can sympathise with us to the degree that this is possible, given the limits of this mechanism. By seeing our own circumstances from the standpoint of an impartial spectator, he argues, we can tune our emotions to the lower pitch that is acceptable to our fellows. In order to bring our passion down to the pitch that others can go along with, we should begin by seeing our situation from the perspective of a friend, then of an acquaintance, and finally of an assembly of strangers. We can then treat our misfortunes and injuries as impartially or as indifferently as we treat those of strangers (Smith 2002 [1790]: 28). Smith's neo-Stoic political therapy requires us to join an assembly of strangers and view ourselves through their tranquil, impartial eyes. By seeing ourselves from their standpoint, we too become spectators of the shipwreck – in this case, our own. This view from a distance or above, as he puts it, restores our 'mind to its tranquillity' (Smith 2002 [1790]: 28) and in doing so makes it possible for us to attune ourselves to others.

Smith's impartial spectator is the sociological version of the Stoic's cosmological view from above. Just as the Stoics held that seeing oneself from the cosmic perspective enabled one to harmonise his will with the whole, Smith held that seeing oneself from the impartial spectator's standpoint enables one to harmonise his sentiments with those of the social whole. Smith, as Forman-Barzilai argues, develops this neo-Stoic therapy more for the purposes of social co-ordination than moral perfection (Forman-Barzilai 2011: 12–13; Ure 2013). By means of this sociological view from above, Smith ensures 'propriety' of the sentiments of the person principally concerned: that is, if we adopt the impartial spectator's standpoint on our own sentiments we will only express these sentiments to the degree that others will consider proper in the given circumstances. It enables us to 'reduce the violence of [our] passions to that pitch of moderation, in which the impartial spectator can entirely enter into them' (Smith 2002 [1790]: 31). Smith argues that his neo-Stoic political therapy is necessary for the sake of social harmony – that is, so that citizens have a basic set of shared sentimental responses to all the turns of fortune's wheel. Smith believes this sentimental concord is the basis of civic peace. He identifies neo-Stoicism as a political therapy: the mechanism of the impartial spectator not only enables individuals to moderate their emotions; in doing so it contributes to social harmonisation (see Muller 1995; Forman-Barzilai 2011; Ure 2013; Nussbaum forthcoming).

In fact, Smith maintains that cultivating Stoic insensibility has great utility for the person principally concerned: paradoxically, it ensures that he/she will attract the greatest possible degree of compassionate support. Smith maintains that the greater our Stoic magnanimity and fortitude, the more we maintain our tranquillity and rise above misfortune in the manner Cato famously displayed in executing his fatal resolution, the more we can ensure that spectators will feel compassion for us and act to console us in our misfortune or combat the injustice we suffer. 'We are more apt to weep and shed tears for such as ... *feel nothing for themselves*, than for all those who give way to all the weakness of sorrow' (Smith 2002 [1790]: 59, italics added). Smith's suggestion is that we more readily console and support Stoic heroes because they do not demand of us that we enter into their painful, distressing feelings, but only their cheerfulness and 'triumphant gaiety' in the face of misfortune. We admire those who are capable of adopting the classical maxim '*nihil admirari*'; their composure and insensibility is an object of wonder. We consider their ability to rise above fate sublime. It is this feeling of sublime awe before the Stoic hero that motivates us to feel and act compassionately. On the other hand, Smith maintains that those who give way to sorrow or grief on account of some calamity of their *own*, are met with *contempt* rather than sympathy (Smith 2002 [1790]: 60). Those who weep for themselves if they are reduced to poverty or even if they are led out to public execution become objects of shame and disgust.

> We are disgusted with that clamorous grief, which, without any delicacy, calls upon our compassion with sighs and tears and importunate lamentations. But we reverence that reserved, that silent and majestic sorrow ... that concerted tranquillity, which it requires so great an effort to support.
>
> (Smith 2002 [1790]: 29)

Smith suggests that we can achieve this majestic Stoic fortitude in the face of misfortune, and lower the pitch of our passions to coincide with others' 'insensibility', by learning how to see ourselves from the spectator's impartial, distant perspective and bearing in mind 'the applause and *admiration* which we deserve by the heroic magnanimity of (our) behaviour' (Smith 2002 [1790]: 58, 59). Smith identifies a deeply un-Stoic motive for subscribing to the principle of Stoic indifference: the admiration we will receive for our heroism (Kerhof 1995: 220–1). Smith's supposition is that it is only a veneer of Stoicism that helps us tune our passions to the pitch required to beat in time with others' insensibility to our grief and resentment: we appear to rise above these passions in order to win others' admiration and esteem.

According to Smith, this neo-Stoic therapy can help overcome the first obstacle to sympathy or sentimental correspondence. If sympathy is the mechanism that mediates our social and political relations, then those capable of Stoic heroism, or magnanimity in the face of misfortune, will receive strong compassion and support. Smith's view, then, is that receiving compassion is conditional upon a cultivating a certain kind of Stoic insensibility to our own suffering that makes it possible for others to go along with our sentiments. Only through Stoic cheerfulness can one 'render himself the object of complete sympathy and approbation of the spectators' (Smith 2002 [1790]: 59). On Smith's analysis we need to aspire to become like Socrates and Seneca: we must face misfortune and injustice, even death, with equanimity in order to ensure that our fellows will sympathise with us rather than despise us for weakness. Smith's theory of sympathy adapts itself to the limits set down by Epicurean hedonism: it implies that we are motivated to sympathise with others as long as we can derive pleasure from this exercise. Smith claims that we derive pleasure not from feeling or identifying with others' suffering, or indeed from maliciously delighting in their distress (*Schadenfreude*), but from identifying with their Stoic heroism. In such cases it is the feeling of the sublime that motivates us to act compassionately. Smith believes spectators are motivated to exercise political compassion, or to redress injustice, by victims' ability to heroically overcome their resentment so that when they seek retribution they appear to do so not because they feel in themselves the 'furies' or resentment, but because they wish to protect humanity.

> (W)e admire that noble and generous resentment which governs its pursuit of the greatest injuries, not by the rage which they are apt to excite in the breast of the sufferer, but by the indignation which they naturally call forth in the impartial spectator; which allows no word, no gesture, to escape it beyond what this more equitable sentiment would dictate; which never, even in thought, attempts any greater vengeance, nor desires to inflict greater punishment, than what every indifferent person would rejoice to see executed.
>
> (Smith 2002 [1790]: 30)

We might take Nelson Mandela as an illustration of Smith's point: arguably it was his magnanimity, his ability to rise above 'petty' personal resentment and pursue justice as an objective, impersonal matter of principle, that enabled him to motivate international support for the anti-apartheid movement. Compassion for those who suffer injustice, Smith argues, rises with the degree of their composure and magnanimity and declines as they give way to the furies of resentment. If we suffer political injustice we must, among others things, heroically rise above those feelings that distress and disturb spectators if we want them to 'thoroughly sympathise with our revenge' (Smith 2002 [1790]: 46). Smith's theory of sympathy therefore sets fairly severe limits on the scope of compassion: in order to receive active compassion we must not only suffer undeservedly, we must also appear to suffer heroically.

Let us sum up this first point then: Smith claims that we must exercise a neo-Stoic therapy and heroically discipline our sentiments in order to become the object of solicitude, approbation and compassion. Yet Smith's neo-Stoic 'solution' only reproduces the partiality problem. We can see how this is the case by looking at it both from the perspective of the person principally concerned and the spectator. As we have seen, Smith suggests that the person principally concerned must cultivate at least the appearance of being insensible towards their own grief and resentment in order to win others' compassion. Yet to the extent that they endorse this Stoic insensibility they will also lack any compassion for others; they will expect others to exercise the same indifference to their own suffering and malign them if they fail to rise above their grief and suffering. Smith attempts to sidestep this problem by means of his asymmetry thesis (Nussbaum 2008: 156; Nussbaum forthcoming). On the one hand, as we have seen, Smith suggests that when it comes to their misfortunes and injuries, the persons principally concerned should cultivate what he calls the *noble* virtues; that is to say, like true Stoics they should spurn their own grief and resentment as expressions of weakness and misjudgement. On the one hand, Smith suggests as spectators they need to cultivate what he calls *amiable* virtues; that is to say, they should learn to re-echo all the sentiments of those with whom they converse, who grieve for their calamities, who resent their injuries, and who rejoice at their good fortune. As Smith puts it, we need to have a 'tender sympathy' for all the sentiments of others. We need to be good friends to others, yet strangers to ourselves. As he explains this asymmetry:

> (H)ence it is that to feel much for others and little for ourselves, that to restrain our selfish, and to indulge our benevolent affections, constitutes the perfection of human nature; and can alone produce among mankind that harmony of sentiments and passions in which consists their [i.e. mankind's] whole grace and propriety.
>
> (Smith 2002 [1790]: 30)

Smith's asymmetry thesis, however, does not wash philosophically or psychologically. If the persons principally concerned believe that it is praiseworthy to remain insensible to misfortune and injustice in their own case then they must extend this belief to others. If they believe life's calamities are proper occasions for insensibility when they strike themselves then they must also believe that they are similarly occasions for insensibility when they strike their friends, family and fellow-citizens.[1] Second, if they win praise for their Stoic fortitude then they will be ill-disposed towards those who express grief and resentment about their misfortunes and injustices.

This partiality problem also reappears if we examine Smith's neo-Stoic solution from the vantage point of the spectator. The assumption underpinning Smith's analysis of the conditions of sympathy is that our fellow citizens enter into or go along with our sentiments only if they can derive some pleasure from this exercise. We can see that for Smith, political compassion is motivated by a kind of aesthetic pleasure. If we suffer undeserved injustices we can solicit political compassion by giving our fellow citizens the aesthetic pleasure of the sublime: the awe-inspiring sight of our ability to rise above the storms of fate and misfortune. Politically effective sympathy and compassion is motivated by *admiration* for stoic nobility in the face of injustice; antipathy is motivated by *contempt* for pitiable weakness and distress. According to Smith, judgements of admiration and contempt play a strong part in regulating whether and to what extent spectators have active compassion for those who suffer moral and political injuries. And spectators' admiration and contempt tracks the sufferers' majestic ability to 'rise far above ... vulgar and ordinary' responses to such injuries, not the gravity of the harm they suffer, their culpability or their capacity to seek redress. Even when Smith later argues that sympathy, not utility, calculations motivate spectators to act against the injustices others suffer and that they 'enter into the resentment *even* of the odious person', he stresses that their sympathy for these individuals is dampened if they 'have not been accustomed to correct and regulate their sentiments by general rules' (Smith 2002 [1790]: 106, italics added). According to Smith, one of the irregularities of spectators' sympathy for those who suffer injustice is the way their compassion tracks the latter's character, particularly their ability to rise above the furies of resentment, rather than simply the harm they have endured.

Even if we acknowledge Smith's claim that the motive for the spectators' political compassion is often tied to their admiration for the Stoic heroism of the persons principally concerned, his full analysis of these motives suggest that such admiration is not sufficient to guarantee this outcome. Smith in fact acknowledges that spectators do not necessarily extend their sympathy to the victims of injustice simply because they rise above the furies of resentment. In other words, on his analysis, these victims might exercise the noble virtues and cool down their passions, but whether spectators will 'go along' with their passions is not necessarily determined by how they modulate them. Their Stoicism about their own calamities might be to no avail in terms of motivating political compassion and support.

Smith then conceives a further obstacle that can prevent our capacity to sympathetically imagine others' sentiments from becoming a motive for even-handed political compassion. Smith argues that human vanity engenders what we might call a discriminatory or invidious sympathy (Dupuy 2006). Put simply, he fears that our vanity ensures that we will *sympathise* with heroes and *despise* losers. We have already seen glimmerings of this view in Smith's claim that spectators need to *admire* others if they are to fully and actively sympathise with and act on their behalf. On other hand, he claims that those who clamour for pity disgust spectators (see also Nietzsche 1997 [1881]: 135). However, Smith maintains that spectators distribute their sympathy not only by assessing the Stoic character of the 'person principally concerned', but also in response to his/her exalted social status. The issue revolves around what Smith believes *motivates* sympathy. Smith suggests that if we examine these motivations we discover that the scope and direction of human sympathy is often governed by our incorrigible vanity. Our vanity distributes our sympathies and antipathies. Smith believes that if our vanity regulates the scope and direction of our sympathy we will have *sympathy* with the great and *antipathy* for the small, regardless of any moral considerations of seriousness or culpability.

Smith explains our invidious sympathy as the *indirect* means we use to satisfy our vain need to secure social esteem and ward off the fear of social obscurity. Why does Smith believe we accord the rich and great so much sympathy and compassion? He argues that they embody the highest ideal of the imagination: namely, the ideal of accruing the greatest degree of sympathy, approval and attention. It is easy and enjoyable for the spectators to bring home to themselves the sentiments of the great and rich because they occupy the place they want to occupy. According to Smith, we readily sympathise with great individuals' joys, sorrows and resentments and shun these same sentiments when we observe them in common or wretched individuals, because through this mechanism we satisfy our desire for universal attention and acclaim. Smith claims that it is highly desirable to enter into the shoes of the former because they occupy precisely the place we wish to occupy. By sympathising with the rich and great we bring home to ourselves what it would be like – or what we imagine it would be like – to satisfy our vanity. He observes:

When we consider the condition of the great, in those delusive colours in which the imagination is apt to paint it, it seems to be almost the abstract idea of a perfect and happy state. It is the very state that in all our waking dreams and idle reveries, we had sketched out to ourselves as the final object of all our desires. We feel, therefore, a peculiar sympathy with the satisfaction of those who are in it. We favour *all* their inclinations, and forward *all* their wishes ... Every calamity that befalls them, every injury that is done to them, excites in the breast of the spectator ten times more compassion and resentment than he would have felt, had the same things happened to other men. It is the misfortunes of Kings only which affords us the subjects of tragedy.

(Smith 2002 [1790]: 63, italics added)

Smith conceives the way vanity motivates our sympathy as analogous to the sympathetic identifications of theatre-goers. As he acknowledges spectators of tragedies and romances do not observe impartially, rather they take sides and sympathise with all the passions of their heroes and heroines (Smith 2002 [1790]: 13). Smith assumes that the unlimited or unconditional sympathy spectators seem to lavish on these dramatic heroes is in short supply for the wretched of the earth. This type of spectatorship, as Nussbaum puts it:

... is in league with hierarchies of heroism and birth. We weep for people whose exploits catch our attention, who are brought before us as fascinating. Such people ... will be kings rather than commoners, heroes rather than ordinary foot soldiers. Kings are fascinating and fun, even when they suffer; the ordinary foot soldier's suffering is boring. Could a commoner even be a tragic hero?

(Nussbaum 2008: 165)

However, Smith points out that vanity corrupts our sympathy in a much more serious way: we are not merely bored by ordinary sufferers, rather we are disgusted by and ashamed of them. It is not just that we have much greater sympathy for the exalted than the wretched, but that we esteem the former and despise the latter.

The poor man goes out and comes in unheeded, and when in the midst of a crowd is in the same obscurity as if shut up in his hovel. Those humble cares and painful attentions which occupy those in this situation, afford no amusement to the dissipated and the gay. They turn away their eyes from him, of if the extremity of his distress forces them to look at him, it is only to spurn so disagreeable an object from among them. The fortunate and the proud wonder at the insolence of human wretchedness, that it should dare to present itself before them, and with the loathsome aspect of its misery presume to disturb the serenity of their happiness. The man of rank and distinction, on the contrary, is observed by all the world.

(Smith 2002 [1790]: 62)

On the one hand, he suggests we sympathise with or enter into another's shoes and see the world from his/her vantage point only if their greatness allows us to indirectly satisfy our vanity. On the other hand, he suggests that we reserve our contempt for and refuse to enter into another's shoes and see the world from his/her vantage point if their wretchedness reminds us of our own vulnerability and weakness.

In effect, Smith argues sympathy for the great enables us to indirectly or vicariously satisfy our vanity. Smith claims that we give the great our *complete* sympathy because this is what we would like to have for ourselves: maximal social sympathy or social pre-eminence. Smith argues that our need for this kind of social pre-eminence is such that if we cannot realise it for ourselves we take vicarious pleasure in seeing and giving it to a select few. Indeed, he suggests that we will sympathise with great individuals independently of considerations of reciprocity. We can sustain our sympathy for the great, he claims, even when we have no hope or expectation that they will reciprocate.

> We are eager to assist them in completing their system of happiness that approaches so near to perfection; and we desire to serve them for their own sake, without any other recompense but the vanity or the honour of obliging them. Neither is our deference to their inclinations founded chiefly, or altogether, upon a regard to the utility of such submission, and or the order of society, which is best supported by it.
>
> (Smith 2002 [1790]: 64)

In short, Smith claims that we value the satisfaction of our vanity through sympathy with the great independently of any expectations of personal material rewards, and even if our sympathy and support for them jeopardises the just order of society.

Smith holds then that (1) our sympathy is motivated by the value we accord its object; (2) that we accord a much higher value to the rich and great and (3) we more easily and readily sympathise with the joys, sorrows and resentments of the rich and great while we neglect, shun and despise the suffering and wretchedness of the poor and neglected. As Smith concludes:

> A stranger to human nature, who saw the indifference of men about the misery of their inferiors, and the regret and indignation which they feel for the misfortunes and sufferings of those above them, would be apt to imagine, that pain must be more agonizing, and the convulsions of death more terrible to persons of higher rank, than to those of meaner stations.
>
> (Smith 2002 [1790]: 63)

According to Smith, if this extra-moral need he calls vanity motivates our sympathies and antipathies, we will oscillate between defending political and social hierarchy on the one hand, and resentful, envious social levelling on the other. Smith believes that for the most part our vanity will motivate us to support inegalitarian social and political arrangements. 'Upon this disposition of mankind, to go along with all the passions of the rich and powerful', he proclaims, 'is founded the distinctions of rank, and the order of society' (Smith 2002 [1790]: 63). We defend orders of rank, he argues, because they enable us to take vicarious pleasure in the ideal condition enjoyed by the few and ward off our fears of social oblivion through our contempt for the wretched. Smith acknowledges that our protection of the few can easily slide over into resentment and envy of their privileged condition, and with it the motive for destroying their ideal condition. The common run of men, he acknowledges, will sympathise with the joys, sorrows and resentments of the rich and great as a way of vicariously satisfying their own vanity, unless, that is, they envy them. Smith believes then we have complete sympathy or extreme envy for the rare few who occupy the position that we wish to occupy, though, we should note, he does not explain what motivates us to switch from one to the other. Yet, he holds that this envious levelling is a fleeting aberration from our natural disposition to defer to and respect social and political superiors. Representative forms of government, he maintains, may be the 'doctrine of reason and philosophy, but it is not the doctrine of Nature. Nature would teach us to submit to (natural superiors) for their own sake ...' (Smith 2002 [1790]: 64). 'The strongest motives, the most furious passions, fear, hatred, and resentment are scarce sufficient to balance this natural disposition to respect [superiors]', so that should these passions motivate the bulk of the people to violent opposition:

> ... they easily relapse into their habitual state of deference to those whom they have been accustomed to look upon as their social superiors ... Compassion soon takes the place of resentment, they forget all past provocations, their old principles of loyalty revive, and they run to re-establish the ruined authority of their old masters.
>
> (Smith 2002 [1790]: 64–5)

Both of Smith's political options clearly ride roughshod over the political hope that sympathy can function as a mechanism that engenders stable, even-handed compassion and political respect. Smith implies that if we do not address the problem of vanity, our societies will oscillate between two undemocratic poles. On the one hand, it can generate a hierarchical society characterised by citizens who defer obsequiously towards those few at the pinnacle and hold in contempt as shameful, disgusting objects the many at the bottom. On the other hand, if these citizens are not satisfied with indirectly or vicariously enjoying the spoils of the few, they will seek to satisfy their vanity by enviously destroying or spoiling the (alleged) goods enjoyed by the few. We oscillate then between unconditional sympathy and envy for the successful and persons of rank (Smith 2002 [1790]: 54, 56–7, 62). Greatness is an object of unconditional sympathy or envy. We either satisfy our vanity through deference to the great and contempt for the wretched or through the envious destruction of the former's good fortune. As we have seen, Smith believes that this envious destruction of the great will only take place sporadically and briefly before a natural disposition to respect those of exalted station reasserts itself and the majority retreat to their default position of finding satisfaction and solace in vicariously enjoying the spoils of greatness. We either vicariously enjoy the spoils of good fortune and social status or enviously destroy the lucky few; we never imagine the suffering of the majority and put them on a par with those of the few. Rather when vanity regulates our sympathetic imagination the suffering of the majority is seen as a shameful, disgusting reminder of our own weakness and vulnerability. Our vanity short-circuits our sympathy and aligns it with undemocratic partialities. If we take seriously Smith's view of vanity we should emblazon humanity's shield with the motto 'sympathy for the great, antipathy for the wretched'.

Clearly Smith's view of vanity as the regulator of sympathy requires qualifying his opening programmatic declaration that:

> How selfish soever man may be supposed, there are evidently some principles in his nature, which interest him in the fortune of others, and render their happiness necessary to him, though he derives nothing from it except the pleasure of seeing it.
>
> (Smith 2002 [1790]: 11)

By suggesting later in Book 1 that our sympathy is mediated by our desire for pre-eminence, Smith allows the concept of vanity or self-love to return with a vengeance. How does this qualify his opening claim? First, Smith evidently holds that we derive far more from seeing another's happiness than mere innocent or unmotivated pleasure – the pleasure we derive from it resides in the way it satisfies our vanity. How else might Smith explain the natural aversion towards the suffering of the weak and pathetic that he observes? Sympathy for the rich and great indirectly satisfies the sympathiser's vanity, the wish to be the cynosure of all eyes, and aversion to the passions of the poor and lowly ensures that the spectator does not have to enter into, even in imagination, this most unwanted condition. Second, Smith suggests that we distribute this sympathy unevenly: for the great we have limitless sympathy, for the wretched we reserve our antipathy and contempt. On this view, our vanity ensures that only the happiness of a select few is necessary to us. We are only interested in the fortunes of a select few, and even then not disinterestedly. Smith claims that if our vanity regulates our sympathy we must dampen any hope that it might facilitate universal, impartial or even-handed political compassion. Clearly Smith does not hold much hope that we can distribute our sympathy on the basis of considerations of merit or desert. If it is our vanity we aim to satisfy through sympathy then we will sympathise with the sorrows and resentments of the rich and powerful regardless of the merits of their case. Vanity, not justice, regulates the scope and intensity of our sympathy.

Needless to say, Smith laments this 'distorted' sympathy for the great and powerful as 'the great and most universal cause of the corruption of our morals'. However, while we should acknowledge Smith's moral unease about the limitations human vanity appears to place on the scope of sympathy, we still need to ask whether he gives us any grounds for expecting or hoping that we might cultivate motives for a broader, more impartial distribution of this 'healing consolation'. As we have seen, he claims that through a kind of neo-Stoic therapy, the persons principally concerned can cultivate an insensibility towards their own suffering that agrees with spectators' lack of fellow-feeling, and inspire in the latter admiration for their noble sovereignty. Yet this neo-Stoic therapy backfires: first it ensures that the persons principally concerned are philosophically and psychologically primed to be similarly indifferent to others' sorrow and resentment; and second, even if spectators are impressed by their noble Stoicism, this merely guarantees that they will have sympathy for those who sublimely rise above their misfortune and antipathy for the weak of will. Smith's neo-Stoic therapy merely recreates the problem of partial sympathy. Indeed, Smith's neo-Stoic therapy must be to no avail if spectators use their sympathy as an instrument to satisfy their vanity. If they wish to claim a sense of esteem through the mechanism of sympathy they will go along with all the sentiments of the great and no amount of Stoic fortitude on the part of the wretched will make them fitting objects of their sympathy. In other words, Smith's analysis suggests that if we wish to address the problem of partial, invidious sympathy we need to overcome or dampen human vanity.

Smith identifies at least two ways that individuals can come to despise human vanity, or the need to 'stand in that situation which sets them most in the view of general sympathy and attention' (Smith 2002 [1790]: 69–70). We might call these the view from above and the view from below. On the one hand, he argues we can follow the path of (Stoic) philosophy by rising above the 'ordinary' vanity of human nature and judging that 'externals' such as public esteem are matters of indifference that have no bearing on our virtue or flourishing. For Stoics who stand above the economy of esteem, virtue must be its own reward. Alternatively, we can sink below the common level of human nature into 'sottish indifference' in which we no longer experience ourselves as social creatures participating in the economy of esteem. As Smith explains:

> But rank, distinction, pre-eminence, no man despises, unless he is either raised very much above, or sunk very much below, the ordinary standard of human nature; unless he is so confirmed in wisdom and real philosophy as to be satisfied that ... it is of little consequence though he not be attended to, nor approved of; or so habituated to the idea of his own meanness, so sunk in slothful and sottish indifference, as entirely to have forgot the desire, and almost the very wish for superiority.
>
> (Smith 2002 [1790]: 70)

Smith identifies only one possible solution to the problem of vanity. We can free ourselves from vanity and become entirely indifferent to whether we receive others' sympathy. We can do so either by the path of Stoic philosophy, which rises above all social vulnerability, or by the path of brutalisation, which sinks us beneath the level of social esteem. Smith identifies either divine or animal indifference as the solution to vanity's invidious sympathy.

Both of these alternatives take the radical 'all or nothing' response to the problem of vanity. That is to say, they entail the complete extirpation of the desire for esteem and with it the very possibility of sympathy. They therefore do not illuminate whether or how we might distribute our sympathy evenly, but rather how we might eliminate sympathy from human life. Smith 'solves' the problem of vanity simply by eliminating it altogether and with it the very possibility and significance of sympathy. On the one hand, those who are too 'drunk' to care about their own social standing obviously have no capacity for sympathy. On the other hand, Stoics who have raised themselves above vanity, have no reason to give or receive sympathy because they conceive it as a source of disease and distress that they ought to eliminate for the sake of their own flourishing. Stoics who judge externals such as sympathy or esteem as a matter of indifference will not attempt to enter into others' sentiments, but rather to guide them to eliminate the 'false' judgements that fuel these sentiments: e.g. the judgement that esteem, approval, status and so on matter to human flourishing. In other words, they will not enter into others' perspective in the Smithean sense, but suggest to those bound to their vain need for sympathy that they ought to take the view from above and judge their own fortune and social standing as matters of no account.

Smith's analysis then leads to a political and moral impasse. It does not show us how we can moderate or regulate our vanity – our need for social esteem – so that we can sympathise impartially or evenly. Rather, Smith only canvases solutions that eliminate vanity altogether and with it the very need for sympathy. In the Stoic framework sympathy has no place because it denies all value 'external' goods such as honour and esteem. However, the Stoic solution to this problem comes at the price of indifference to ordinary human life, or 'death within life' as Nussbaum describes it (Nussbaum 2003, reprinted in this volume). In other words, Stoicism supplies no motive for political compassion. If, as Stoics hold, external goods such as approval, esteem, honour, status, wealth and so on are matters of indifference that make no contribution to human flourishing, then they have no grounds for concern about material wretchedness or social invisibility. If ordinary vanity leads us to antipathy towards the weak and vulnerable, then divine Stoicism leads us to indifference towards social suffering and political injustice. It is partly for this reason that in the last edition of *The Theory of Moral Sentiments* Smith ultimately rejected Stoic ethics (see also Griswold 1999: 320; Forman-Barzilai 2011: 19; Nussbaum forthcoming):

> By the perfect apathy which it prescribes to us, by endeavouring not merely to moderate, but to eradicate our all our private, partial and selfish affec-
> tions, by suffering us to feel for whatever can befall ourselves, our friends, our country, not even the sympathetic and reduced passions of the impartial spectator, it endeavours to render us altogether indifferent and unconcerned in the success or miscarriage of every thing which Nature has prescribed for us as the proper business and occupation of our lives.
>
> (Smith 2002 [1790]: 345)

Smith's theory of moral sentiments leaves us with a puzzle for political compassion: how can we chart a course between the Scylla of vain antipathy and Charybdis of Stoic indifference towards suffering and injustice? The failure of Smith's attempt to resolve the problem of partial and invidious sympathy does however indicate where the middle course lies. If our natural capacity for sympathy is to become a moral compass, it must be informed by a perspective that acknowledges rather than despises human vulnerability.

Note

1 I deliberately invert Nussbaum's argument that Smith's asymmetry thesis is conceptually incoherent. Against Smith's asymmetry thesis, she argues that 'If life's calamities are proper occasions for pity when they strike our friends and family they are similarly important when they strike us, and we would be right to ask for and accept pity in such circumstances' (Nussbaum 2008: 156).

References

Decety, J. (ed.) (2009) *The Social Neuroscience of Empathy*. Massachusetts: MIT Press.

De Waal, F. (2006) *Primates and Philosophers: How Morality Evolved*. New Jersey: Princeton University Press.

Dupuy, J.-P. (2008) 'Invidious Sympathy in *The Theory of Moral Sentiments*', *Revue du Mauss* 1:31, 81–112.

Forman-Barzilai, F. (2011) *Adam Smith and the Circles of Sympathy: Cosmopolitanism and Moral Theory*. Cambridge: Cambridge University Press.

Griswold, C. L. (1999) *Adam Smith and the Virtues of Enlightenment*. Cambridge: Cambridge University Press.

Iacoboni, M. (2009) *Mirroring People: The Science of Empathy and How We Connect with Others*. New York: Picador.

Kerhof, B. (1995) 'A Fatal Attraction: Smith's "Theory of Moral Sentiments" and Mandeville's "Fable"', *History of Political Thought* XVI: 2, 219–233.

Lucretius (1966) *The Nature of the Universe* (R. E. Latham Trans.). Harmondsworth: Penguin.

Marshall, D. (1986) *The Figure of Theater: Shaftesbury, Defoe, Adam Smith, and George Eliot*. New York: Columbia University Press.

Muller, J. (1995) *Adam Smith In His Time and Ours*. New Jersey: Princeton University Press.

Nietzsche, F. (1997 [1881]) *Daybreak: Thoughts on the Prejudices of Morality* (R. J. Hollingdale Trans.). Cambridge: Cambridge University Press.

Nussbaum, M. (2003) 'Compassion & Terror' *Daedalus* 132(1): 10–26 [reprinted in this volume].

Nussbaum, M. (2008) 'The "Morality of Pity: Sophocles' *Philoctetes*" in Rita Felski (ed.) *Rethinking Tragedy*. Baltimore: John Hopkins University Press, 148–169.

Nussbaum, M (forthcoming) '"Mutilated and Deformed": Adam Smith on the Material Basis of Human Dignity'.

Rousseau, J.-J. (1974 [1762]) *Émile* (B. Foxley Trans.). London: Dent.

Smith, A. (2002 [1790]) *The Theory of Moral Sentiments*. Cambridge: Cambridge University Press.

Ure, M. (2013) 'Nietzsche's Political Therapy' in Keith Ansell-Pearson (ed.) *Nietzsche and Political Thought*. London: Bloomsbury Press.

Index

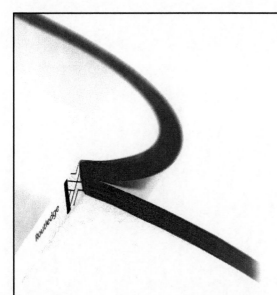